This book from the Centre for Economic Policy Research deals with the implications of the exchange rate regimes and capital flows of the 1990s for government macroeconomic policy-making and EC policy coordination. It has long been recognized that openness is a mixed blessing for many European economies. While it offers the opportunity of international and intertemporal trade, it also imposes additional constraints on the design of stabilization policies. The exact nature of these constraints is not always clear, and there remains much uncertainty about their quantitative importance and their dependence on the exchange rate regime.

Under the fixed exchange rates of the 1950s, economists and policy-makers had a much clearer idea of the nature of the external constraints. The current situation is markedly different and changing rapidly. The commitment to defending the exchange rate is stronger in the 1990s than in the 1970s and 1980s, but at the same time international capital flows are now far greater and freer than in the 1950s and 1960s, with many countries able to borrow almost indefinitely and on good terms on the Eurodollar market in order to finance their balance-of-payments deficits.

This volume, derived from a conference organized jointly by CEPR and the Bank of Greece, deals with these issues in depth and includes both cross-country comparisons and case studies of individual countries.

External constraints on macroeconomic policy: the European experience

Centre for Economic Policy Research

The Centre for Economic Policy Research is a network of over 140 Research Fellows, based primarily in European universities. The Centre coordinates its Fellows' research activities and communicates their results to the public and private sectors. CEPR is an entrepreneur, developing research initiatives with the producers, consumers and sponsors of research. Established in 1983, CEPR is already a European economics research organization with uniquely wide-ranging scope and activities.

CEPR is a registered educational charity. Grants from the Leverhulme Trust, the Esmée Fairbairn Charitable Trust, the Baring Foundation, the Bank of England and Citibank provide institutional finance. The ESRC supports the Centre's dissemination programme and, with the Nuffield Foundation, its programme of research workshops. None of these organizations gives prior review to the Centre's publications nor necessarily endorses the views expressed therein.

The Centre is pluralist and non-partisan, bringing economic research to bear on the analysis of medium- and long-run policy questions. CEPR research may include views on policy, but the Executive Committee of the Centre does not give prior review to its publication, and the Centre takes no institutional policy positions. The opinions expressed in this volume are those of the authors and not those of the Centre for Economic Policy Research.

External constraints on macroeconomic policy: the European experience

Edited by

GEORGE ALOGOSKOUFIS,

LUCAS PAPADEMOS

and

RICHARD PORTES

The right of the
University of Cambridge
to print and sell
all manner of books
was granted by
Henry VIII in 1534.
The University has printed
and published continuously
since 1584.

Cambridge University Press
Cambridge   New York   Port Chester
Melbourne   Sydney

Published by the Press Syndicate of the University of Cambridge
The Pitt Building, Trumpington Street, Cambridge CB2 1RP
40 West 20th Street, New York, NY 10011–4211, USA
10 Stamford Road, Oakleigh, Melbourne 3166, Australia

© Cambridge University Press 1991

First published 1991

Printed in Great Britain by the Redwood Press Ltd, Melksham, Wiltshire

British Library cataloguing in publication data

External constraints on macroeconomic policy.
  1. Europe, economics
  I. Alogoskoufis, George S. II. Papademos, Lucas
  III. Portes, Richard 1941–
  300.94

Library of Congress cataloguing in publication data applied for

ISBN 0 521 40527 0   hardback

Contents

Figures

Tables

Preface

This volume contains a selection from the papers presented in the conference on 'Macroeconomic Policy and the External Constraint: The European Experience', jointly sponsored by the Centre for Economic Policy Research and the Bank of Greece. The conference was part of the CEPR's Research Programme in International Macroeconomics, and was hosted by the Bank of Greece in Athens on 24–26 May 1990. Our thanks are due to the staff of both CEPR and the Bank for their help in organizing the conference, especially Efi Vrontissi and Mary Theodoratou at the Bank and Ann Shearlock at CEPR.

We gratefully acknowledge financial support for the conference from the Ford Foundation, the Alfred P. Sloan Foundation, and the Bank of Greece.

David Guthrie and Sarah Wellburn at CEPR have been responsible for guiding this volume to press. We thank them for having done an admirable job, keeping everybody to the production schedule. We also extend our thanks to John Black of the University of Exeter, whose work as Production Editor has, as always, been invaluable.

George Alogoskoufis
Lucas Papademos
Richard Portes

Conference participants

George Alogoskoufis *Birkbeck College, London, and CEPR*
Michael Artis *University of Manchester and CEPR*
Panagiotis Athanasoglou *Bank of Greece*
Yves Barroux *Banque de France*
Tamim Bayoumi *International Monetary Fund*
Charles Bean *London School of Economics and CEPR*
Sophocles Brissimis *Bank of Greece*
Nicos Christodoulakis *Athens School of Economics and Business Science*
Daniel Cohen *Centre d'Etudes Prospectives d'Economie Mathématique
    Appliquées à la Planification, Paris, and CEPR*
Bernard Connolly *Commission of the European Communities*
David Currie *London Business School and CEPR*
Juan Dolado *Banco de España*
Barry Eichengreen *University of California, Berkeley, and CEPR*
Nicos Floros *University of Athens*
Jacob A. Frenkel *International Monetary Fund*
Nicholas Garganas *Bank of Greece*
Emmanuel Gyparakis *Bank of Greece*
Nicholas Karamouzis *Bank of Greece*
Louka Katseli *University of Athens and CEPR*
Hugo Keuzenkamp *Center for Economic Research, Tilburg*
Maria Konstantopoulou *KEPE and Athens School of Economics*
Anthony Latter *Bank of England*
Paul Levine *London Business School and CEPR*
Leslie Lipschitz *International Monetary Fund*
Vassilios Manessiotis *Bank of Greece*
Christopher Martin *Queen Mary and Westfield College, London*
Andrew Newell *University of Sussex*
Søren Bo Nielsen *Kobenhavn Universitet and CEPR*
Nicholas Paleokrassas *Bank of Greece*

John Papadakis *Institute of Economic and Industrial Research and University of Athens*
Lucas Papademos *Bank of Greece and University of Athens*
Richard Portes *CEPR and Birkbeck College, London*
Fabio Schiantarelli *Boston University*
Jørgen Søndergaard *Economic Council of Denmark*
Haris Stamatopoulos *Bank of Greece*
Yannis Stournaras *Bank of Greece*
Charles Wyplosz *INSEAD and CEPR*
George Zombanakis *Bank of Greece*

1 Introduction

GEORGE ALOGOSKOUFIS, LUCAS
PAPADEMOS, and RICHARD PORTES

It has long been recognized that the openness of a national economy –
high participation in international trade and capital flows – is a mixed
blessing. It offers the opportunity of gains from trade, both international
and intertemporal, but it subjects an economy to additional shocks.
Openness also implies some additional constraints for stabilization
policy. The precise nature of these external constraints is not always clear,
however, and there is considerable uncertainty about their importance
and their dependence on the exchange rate regime.

   The collection of essays in this book represents an attempt to clarify the
nature of external constraints and to examine their importance for macroeconomic policy in Western Europe. West European economies are far
more open to international trade than either the United States or Japan.
In addition, both the interwar and postwar periods exhibit cases in which
macroeconomic policy has clearly been affected by external considerations. The devaluations of the 1930s, the stop-go cycles of the 1950s and
1960s, the policy reversals of the 1970s and early 1980s, and the EMS
experience are all examples of the important role of external factors in
European macroeconomic policy. Finally, as the European Community
countries are now engaged in a process of economic and monetary
unification, this is an opportune time to reexamine their past experience
with macroeconomic policies and the lessons it may have to offer for the
future.

1   The nature of external constraints

Under fixed exchange rates with limited capital mobility, as for example
in the 1950s and 1960s, economists and policy-makers had a relatively
clear idea of the nature of external constraints. A government trying to
expand unilaterally would soon deplete its foreign exchange reserves and
would be forced to adjust through a reversal of the original expansion and

1

possibly with a politically damaging devaluation. The 'stop-go' cycles of the 1950s and 1960s are well documented for many European economies, including Britain and France.

The situation in the 1970s and 1980s differed markedly from this stylized version of external constraints that have to do with foreign exchange reserves in a regime of fixed exchange rates. The commitment to defend the exchange rate was looser in the last two decades. On the other hand, private capital flows have been far more important and free than in the 1950s and 1960s, and the development of the Eurodollar market allowed many countries to borrow much more easily and on good terms to finance balance of payments deficits. Yet, despite these developments, policy-makers in Europe still felt constrained by external considerations, and there were many policy reversals following sharp deteriorations in the balance of payments. Britain and Italy in the 1970s and Germany and France in the early 1980s are among the best-known such examples.

This suggests that there are external constraints in addition to those that operate through foreign exchange reserves in a regime of fixed exchange rates. Even in regimes of floating exchange rates with high capital mobility, the currency depreciation that will accompany any attempt at uni-lateral monetary expansion may overshoot the medium-run equilibrium exchange rate. This will produce a higher rise in inflation than in a closed economy, as rises in import prices affect domestic wage-setting and feed into the prices of domestic goods. Thus, in an open economy with high capital mobility, flexible exchange rates change the trade-off between inflation and unemployment. Governments may therefore be less willing to use monetary policy to counteract shocks that increase unemployment. But this cannot be the whole story, since they could alternatively resort to expansionary fiscal policies, which with no monetary accommodation would cause an exchange rate appreciation. That improves the trade-off between inflation and unemployment relative to a closed economy, although it worsens possible trade-offs between unemployment and the current account. To summarize, under flexible exchange rate regimes and high capital mobility, we have a different, much looser, concept of external constraints. In a relatively open economy, an aggregate demand expansion may create either a worse inflation problem or a worse current account problem, depending on the policy mix, in comparison with a relatively closed economy.

The third concept of the external constraint operates in the longer run: the intertemporal budget constraint. In a world of high capital mobility, macroeconomic policies are eventually constrained by the solvency requirement that the value of external debt should not exceed the present discounted value of future current account surpluses, net of interest payments. This means that, ultimately, real external debt must rise at a rate lower than the real interest rate, or that debt as a proportion of GDP must be rising at a rate lower than the difference between the real interest rate and the growth rate of GDP. A stronger (steady-state) version of this solvency requirement is that the ratio of net foreign debt (or external assets) to GDP must eventually be stabilized. In other words, an economy must ultimately be in a position to service its external debt, without borrowing at a rate different from the growth rate of GDP. This sustainability or solvency requirement is the third concept of the external constraint on macroeconomic policies.

In conclusion, one can distinguish at least three types of external constraint on macroeconomic policy. The first is the traditional liquidity constraint operating in fixed exchange rate regimes with low capital mobility. The second is the different trade-off between unemployment and inflation and unemployment and the current account in relatively open compared to relatively closed economies. This applies under floating exchange rates with high capital mobility. Finally, there is the sustainability or solvency constraint that the value of external debt should not, ultimately, exceed the present discounted value of future current account surpluses, net of interest payments.

2   External constraints in theory and practice

Chapters 2 to 5 deal with the various aspects of external constraints and offer overviews of the European experience in both the interwar and the postwar periods.

In Chapter 2, Michael Artis and Tamim Bayoumi examine the extent of international financial integration and its consequences for the current account. The authors argue that, notwithstanding the closer links among capital markets in recent years and the associated increase in short-term capital mobility, the evidence suggests that overall net flows of national savings and investment are still markedly insular when compared with the predictions of models with full capital mobility or with experience under the gold standard. The principal explanation that they suggest is that the authorities treat the current account balance as an objective of national policy and act to offset fluctuations in the savings–investment balance. Exchange rate risk may also play a role. The authors argue, however, that the closer integration of capital markets should make the current account more of a residual factor in agents' decisions and may reduce its status as a policy objective. Indeed the higher current account imbalances of the 1980s can be seen as a step in this direction. Does this mean that we should abandon the first and second concepts of the external constraint referred to above and be concerned solely with national solvency? Not necessarily, the authors maintain. There is still an important function of current account statistics for the policy authorities, as they indicate the net effect of saving and investment decisions, the policies that affect them, and the net contribution of countries to the world pool of savings.

Chapter 3 by David Currie and Paul Levine is solely concerned with the implications of the national solvency constraint. It deals with a single open economy in which the real interest rate exceeds the steady-state growth rate, and it elucidates the implications for the conduct of fiscal policy of the requirement that both the government (domestically) and the nation (internationally) must be solvent. Solvency is defined by the requirement that the ratios of public and external debt to GDP should remain constant. The paper treats the government as an agent optimizing intertemporally in a neo-Keynesian economy, and it examines the role of reputational issues. The authors analyse both the situation in which the government has an ambitious output (unemployment) target in a deterministic context and the case of stabilization in the face of random shocks. A possible objection to the time-consistent solution is that there may be an incentive to 'defer solvency' by postponing the stabilization of the relevant asset/GDP ratios to some time in the future. The authors argue that such an incentive does not exist if the policy-makers know that solvency must be imposed sometime in the future.

In the type of model presented by Currie and Levine the national (external) solvency constraint is distinct from the government solvency constraint, because in this type of model the private sector is not viewed as choosing its savings in an intertemporally optimal fashion. Thus it is not enough for the government to be solvent, as private consumption behaviour may be such as to make the private sector, and therefore the national economy, insolvent. This is in sharp contrast to intertemporal models of private sector savings (e.g. Blanchard–Yaari–Weil), in which the private sector respects its own solvency constraint. This type of model is analysed for the case of Greece, in Chapter 9, by Alogoskoufis and Christodoulakis. The implications of the two models can be reconciled if the wealth elasticity of private sector savings in the Currie–Levine type of model is high enough. In that case, even though the private sector is not modelled as forward-looking, the high response to its wealth suffices to ensure its solvency.

The next two chapters, by Eichengreen on the 1920s and 1930s and by Alogoskoufis and Martin on the 1970s and 1980s, focus on the shorter-run types of external constraints. They look at the exchange rate regimes and their implications for inflation–unemployment and unemployment–current account trade-offs.

In chapter 4, Barry Eichengreen points out that the new conventional wisdom on the macroeconomics of the 1930s focuses on the external constraint, in particular the propagation of the Great Depression from the United States to Europe in a world of high capital mobility and fixed exchange rates. Only by abandoning the gold standard (fixed exchange rates), and thus relaxing the external constraint, did it prove possible for European economies to recover from the Depression. Eichengreen argues that devaluation was a necessary precondition for recovery because reflation without devaluation required international cooperation, which was not forthcoming mainly because of different views among policy-makers about the operation of the economy. Using a sample of some three dozen countries, the author analyses the effects of devaluation. He finds the policies quite effective, although he also stresses their costs in terms of higher uncertainty about nominal and real exchange rates which appear to have disrupted the smooth operation of the price mechanism. He also contrasts the 1930s, a decade of managed exchange rates, with the period of floating in the 1920s. He finds that, although exchange rate management reduced the variability and unpredictability of short-run nominal and real exchange rates, over longer periods intervention appears to have aggravated real exchange rate uncertainty and interest rate volatility.

Chapter 5, by George Alogoskoufis and Christopher Martin, focuses on external constraints on European unemployment in the 1970s and 1980s. They argue that many of the stylized facts about European unemployment in the 1970s and 1980s and the differences between Europe and the United States can be explained by macroeconomic policies and their interaction. They present a family of models of unemployment in interdependent open economies. These focus on monopolistic competition in the output market and wage-setting by monopoly unions that may operate at different levels of centralization. They argue that their most general model can explain the different unemployment experiences in Europe and the USA, in terms of the more cautious macroeconomic policy stance in the large European economies following both the first and second oil shock. Furthermore, this explanation is consistent with the evolution of other macroeconomic variables such as inflation, real interest rates, and primary-commodity prices. The authors suggest that external constraints, in the form of worse inflation–unemployment and unemployment–current account trade-offs, may have been responsible for the less expansionary macroeconomic policy stance in Europe. The tighter European external constraints are attributed to a higher degree of openness, asymmetries in the international monetary system, and the preferences of European policy-makers for stable exchange rates reflected in EEC institutions, combined with aversion to inflation and current account deficits in Germany.

3   Country studies

In Chapter 6, Daniel Cohen and Charles Wyplosz develop a theme similar to that of Alogoskoufis and Martin. Their focus is on France and Germany in the EMS. Their model emphasizes two channels through which real exchange rates have an impact on policy-making: inflation and the trade account (output). For example, an appreciation lessens inflationary pressure, but at the same time brings about a worsening in the trade account and a reduction in aggregate demand and output. The authors show that for two closely integrated economies like France and Germany, the trade-off depends on the relative size of these two effects, both between the two economies themselves and also *vis-à-vis* the rest of the world. In an empirical investigation, they find some evidence that in Germany and France the trade balance is quite sensitive to the intra-EMS effective exchange rate, but not to the extra-EMS rate. The opposite seems to be the case with inflation. They use these findings to suggest that French and German policy actions have been dominated by the need to avoid disrupting the trade balance (and with it output and employment). Thus both countries seem to have unexploited gains in inflation–output trade-offs, gains which could be reaped through beggar-thy-neighbour policies *vis-à-vis* the rest of the world. Monetary union would remove this inefficiency, the authors argue, and this could be quite desirable if the US dollar were to depreciate further.

In Chapter 7, Charles Bean deals with the external constraint in the United Kingdom. The author first examines the historical record, high-lighting the central role played by foreign asset income in ensuring the strong current account performance during the Victorian and Edwardian eras, and the role of the two world wars in eliminating this foreign asset buffer. While trade performance actually improved in the period after the world wars, this only partly offset the fall in interest income. At the same time, British economic policy-making has apparently been constrained by external considerations. In an empirical investigation, the author does not seem to find a very good matching between periods of external pressure and periods of a strongly rising supply price of foreign borrowing. For most of the sample period the external constraint seems to have been little more than an intertemporal solvency requirement. Bean then assesses the reasons for the sharp deterioration in the British current account in the late 1980s. He argues that financial deregulation and optimistic per-manent income expectations are primarily responsible for the fall in savings. As both these factors are likely to be largely temporary, implying that the current account deficit should be self-correcting, should the government intervene to tackle the current account deficit? Bean stresses that, if the government does have some reason for influencing the national savings rate, it should use fiscal rather than monetary policy, as financial deregulation is a real shock despite its monetary consequences.

The Dutch experience is examined by Hugo Keuzenkamp and Frederick van der Ploeg in Chapter 8. The emphasis is on the relevance of the exchange rate policy of closely pegging to the Deutschmark, tax-smoothing, consumption-smoothing, and the apparent lack of capital mobility. The authors conclude that the latter may be due to legal constraints on foreign investment by pension funds, but more generally is an indication of the low importance of tax and consumption-smoothing in the Netherlands. They view the two external constraints of a rigid guilder–Deutschmark rate and the high association of investment with domestic savings as self-imposed.

George Alogoskoufis and Nicos Christodoulakis in Chapter 9 examine the Greek experience in the 1980s and assess the options for stabilization. Among the countries studied in this volume, Greece seems to be the only one for which the external constraint as a solvency constraint is likely to be binding for macroeconomic policy in the 1990s. Successive governments in the 1980s have pushed up government deficits. The authors present a model of optimal private sector savings and suggest that to the extent that the private sector is forward-looking and can engage in consumption-smoothing, there is no separate external constraint. If the government respects its own intertemporal solvency constraint, then the external debt to GDP ratio will also be stabilized. They examine three options for public and external debt stabilization in Greece: a fall in government expenditure, a rise in taxes, and a rise in steady-state seigniorage. Their estimates of the money–demand function suggest that steady-state seigniorage is maximized at inflation rates of the order of 20% currently prevailing in Greece. Thus a rise in steady-state inflation is likely to result in a reduction in seigniorage revenue and cannot be used to stabilize the external debt to GDP ratio. Of the other two options, stabilization of the public debt to GDP ratio at its current level through a rise in taxation will result in a much higher equilibrium external debt to GDP ratio than a similar stabilization through a reduction in government expenditure. The authors suggest that for the public and external debt to GDP ratios to be stabilized, the primary deficit must be set to zero.

The Spanish experience is examined in Chapter 10 by Juan Dolado and José Viñals. The authors argue that, while the true external constraint of

the economy is a long-run constraint in the absence of distortions and
market imperfections, it nevertheless may be rational for governments to
monitor the short-run evolution of external accounts for the purpose of
avoiding future difficulties. Moreover, whenever such distortions and
imperfections are important, governments may even be justified in setting
specific external targets. They argue that in Spain over the last twenty
years there have been clear and unambiguous examples of major policy
changes following unfavourable developments in the external accounts.
They also present cointegration tests suggesting that the Spanish
economy is at present more than respecting its external solvency constraint. The authors warn against complacency, especially in view of the
elimination of capital controls by 1993, and argue in favour of further
fiscal restraint and supply-side policies. They also present tentative calculations of real exchange rates and output gaps consistent with an equilibrium balance of payments in the longer run.

Søren Bo Nielsen and Jørgen Søndergaard consider the experience of
Denmark in Chapter 11. Denmark has a long history of current account
deficits, and it belongs to the small group of heavily indebted OECD
countries. The authors examine the historical record and a variety of
possible reasons for the rising external indebtedness of Denmark. These
include exogenous and policy shocks as well as structural characteristics
of the Danish economy, such as the exchange rate regime, the tax system,
and capital, product and labour markets. The authors remain eclectic to
the end, refusing to endorse any single explanation. They argue that the
external constraint has been a soft constraint, but that it is likely to
become tighter as a result of further integration in the EEC.

The studies presented in this volume underline the importance of the
three types of external constraints for macroeconomic policy in Europe.
One of the questions that arises is whether these constraints are likely to
become tighter or looser following the process of economic and monetary
integration in the EEC. The constraints relating to inflation–
unemployment and unemployment–current account trade-offs are likely
to be relaxed, if the conclusions of Alogoskoufis–Martin and Cohen–
Wyplosz are correct. On the other hand, Artis–Bayoumi, Keuzenkamp–
van der Ploeg, and a number of other studies in the volume suggest that at
the present stage of financial integration, domestic investment is still highly
correlated with national savings. This implies that the long-run external
constraint is still tighter than just a solvency constraint. To the extent that
there is further financial liberalization in Europe, however, we may see a
relaxation even of longer-run external constraints. In any case, we find it
unlikely that the considerations that now take the form of the external
constraint will disappear completely, even with full economic and

monetary union. For example, the question of solvency of fiscal authorities in the European economies, which under the current arrangements often manifests itself as an external constraint, will still be important after economic and monetary union, although evidently in a different way.

2 Global financial integration and current account imbalances

MICHAEL ARTIS and TAMIM BAYOUMI

1 Introduction

The last decade has witnessed a marked increase in the degree of current account imbalances among the industrial countries. At the same time, it is evident that the capital markets of these same countries have become more closely linked to each other. The coincidence of these two observations sets the agenda for this chapter, which is the extent of global financial integration and its consequences. In particular, in view of the significance traditionally attached to current account balance as a policy objective and the role that current account balance has acquired in the exercise of international economic policy coordination, the chapter enquires whether the new circumstances brought about by capital market integration justify these policy emphases.

The plan for the rest of the chapter is as follows. Section 2 looks at some definitions associated with the balance of payments. Section 3 discusses the determination of the external current account balance under various conditions, and the role of international capital market integration in that process. Section 4 examines some evidence on the question of whether capital markets are highly integrated. In Section 5 the same issue is considered from a different perspective, asking whether consumption-saving choices have been less constrained in the recent period, as they should have been if capital markets have become more efficient. The main conclusions are summarized in Section 6.

2 Definitions

The basic definition of the balance of payments in focus here is, as explained below, that provided by a rearrangement of the national accounts definitions as the residual of savings and investment. To clarify this, recall the following definitions of (i) the current account of the balance of payments and (ii) the gross national product

10

$$CAB \equiv X - M + NPI \tag{1}$$

$$GNP \equiv GDP + NPI \tag{2}$$

where X is the value of exports, M the value of imports and NPI is net property income from overseas.[1] The definition of GDP can be written in the usual way as

$$GDP \equiv C + I + G + X - M \tag{3}$$

Disposable income of the private sector is spent on consumption or saved

$$GNP - T \equiv C + S \tag{4}$$

Substituting (3) into (1) yields an alternative equation for the current account as

$$CAB \equiv GNP - (C + I + G) \tag{5}$$

Substituting (4) into (5) then yields

$$CAB \equiv (S - I) + (T - G) \tag{6}$$

$$CAB \equiv NFAp + NFAg \tag{6a}$$

or　　$$CAB \equiv (S + T - G) - I \tag{7}$$

In (6, 6a) the current account appears as identically equal to the sum of the net acquisition of financial assets by the private and government sectors (the CAB itself may be defined as the negative of the overseas sector's net acquisition of financial assets). In (7) the current account is written as the difference between overall national saving–private savings plus government saving, $T - G$ – and investment.[2]

3　Analysis of the balance of payments

Table 2.1 summarizes the trends in current account balances of the major industrial countries. As can be seen from the ratio of the absolute sum of these balances to GNP/GDP, the external imbalances are, in the 1980s, some three to four times the levels reached in the late 1960s and early 1970s. This increase is predominantly due to the large surpluses run by Germany and Japan, and the large deficits appearing in the US accounts in the 1980s. (Current account imbalance among the industrial countries outside the seven largest countries has also increased between the 1970s and 1980s, but only by about 20%.) The basic evidence would thus appear to suggest that the growing integration of the world's capital markets may have facilitated the emergence of the US deficit and its counterparts in Germany and Japan. In less accommodating circumstances, some adjustment might have been required at a relatively early stage.

Table 2.1. *Major industrial countries: current account balances, 1965–88* *(in percent of GDP/GNP)*

	Canada	United States	Japan	France	Federal Republic of Germany	Italy	United Kingdom	Weighted average absolute value
1965	− 1.9	0.8	1.0	− 0.6	− 1.1	3.4	− 0.2	0.9
1966	− 1.7	0.4	1.2	− 1.1	0.3	3.0	0.3	0.7
1967	− 0.7	0.3	− 0.2	− 1.0	2.3	2.1	− 0.7	0.7
1968	− 0.1	0.1	0.7	− 0.7	2.5	3.1	− 0.6	0.6
1969	− 1.2	0.0	1.2	− 1.1	1.5	2.5	1.0	0.6
1970	1.2	0.2	1.0	0.0	0.7	0.8	1.6	0.5
1971	0.4	− 0.1	2.5	0.4	0.4	1.7	1.9	0.7
1972	− 0.3	− 0.5	2.2	1.1	0.5	1.5	0.3	0.7
1973	0.2	0.5	0.0	0.6	1.5	− 1.6	− 1.3	0.7
1974	− 0.9	0.1	− 1.0	− 1.4	2.8	− 4.4	− 3.8	1.2
1975	− 2.7	1.1	− 0.1	0.8	1.0	− 0.3	− 1.4	1.0
1976	− 2.1	0.2	0.7	− 1.0	0.8	− 1.3	− 0.8	0.6
1977	− 2.0	− 0.7	1.6	− 0.1	0.8	1.0	− 0.1	0.9
1978	− 2.0	− 0.7	1.7	1.5	1.4	2.1	0.6	1.2
1979	− 1.8	0.0	− 0.9	0.9	− 0.7	1.5	− 0.3	0.5
1980	− 0.4	0.1	− 1.0	− 0.6	− 1.7	− 2.2	1.4	0.7
1981	− 1.7	0.3	0.4	− 0.8	− 0.5	− 2.3	2.7	0.7
1982	0.8	− 0.2	0.6	− 2.2	0.8	− 1.5	1.7	0.7
1983	0.8	− 1.3	1.8	− 0.9	0.8	0.4	1.3	1.2
1984	0.6	− 2.8	2.8	− 0.1	1.6	− 0.6	0.6	2.1
1985	− 0.4	− 2.8	3.7	− 0.1	2.6	− 0.9	0.9	2.4
1986	− 2.1	− 3.1	4.3	0.4	4.4	0.4	0.0	2.9
1987	− 1.7	− 3.2	3.6	− 0.5	4.0	− 0.2	− 0.7	2.7
1988	− 1.7	− 2.6	2.8	− 0.4	4.0	− 0.6	− 3.2	2.5

Source: International Monetary Fund, *World Economic Outlook*, October 1989.

As already described, the current account of the balance of payments is definitionally equivalent to the difference between a nation's overall saving rate and its rate of investment. It can also be stated as the difference between exports and imports, adjusted for factor income flows and transfers. These two ways of writing the balance of payments identity have given rise to different theoretical approaches, which should be regarded as offering complementary rather than competing explanations.

The approach which proceeds from the identity of the current account balance with the difference between exports and imports is the well-known 'elasticities' approach; this is based on assumptions about the supply and demand conditions in the markets for exports and imports, the dependence on relative prices being summarized in the relevant elasticities. The focus on elasticities connects the analysis directly to the exchange rate in that changes in the latter, through their impact on relative prices will, *ceteris paribus*, lead to consequential adjustments in the supply and demand for imports and exports. (The caveat *'ceteris paribus'* indicates that a *complete* account of the effects of an exchange rate change requires a broader analysis of its origin.)

The complementary 'absorption' approach identifies the current account as the difference between national saving and investment (Alexander, 1952). Viewed in this way it is clear that the current account improves or deteriorates as the excess of saving over investment rises or falls. Or, since saving is the difference between income and consumption (including government consumption), the current account improves or deteriorates as 'absorption' (consumption plus investment) falls or rises relative to output.

A more modern elaboration of balance of payments theory in the context of integrated capital markets (Sachs, 1981; Frenkel and Razin, 1987) applies modern intertemporal consumption and saving theory for the behaviour of the individual to the economy as a whole. The economy is assumed to be able to freely lend to, or borrow from, other economies. The paradigm for individual consumer behaviour is that of 'consumption-smoothing'. In the absence of liquidity constraints, consumers smooth their consumption path relative to their lumpy income stream.[3]

This forward-looking behaviour has important implications. *Ceteris paribus*, a rising income trajectory will lead to contemporaneous current account deficits that eventually would be followed by surpluses. Temporary shocks will have different effects from permanent shifts. A temporary decline in income will be covered by an increase in the deficit (decrease in the surplus) to support consumption, while a permanent decline in income necessitates a complete readjustment of consumption. The opening up of new investment opportunities that outperform existing returns can be shown to lead to an increase in the deficit (decrease in the surplus) on current account that is somewhat larger than the investment itself (the excess reflects the expected superior returns).

A complication is introduced into the analysis to the extent that government policy may also influence the outcome. Failing full 'Ricardian equivalence' when consumers 'see through' the government's financial policies, fiscal policy will affect the current account, which by definition is the residual of total investment and saving, both private and public. Nevertheless, the general thrust of the argument remains unimpaired.

3.1   *The role of financial integration*

The basic property of a financially integrated area is that there should be no regionally differentiated barriers to the free flow of capital within it. In consequence, arbitrage will drive the risk-adjusted nominal rate of return into uniformity across the area as a whole. Most political unions are normally also currency unions so there is no exchange risk. Following this definition, what has been identified as a movement in the direction of greater integration at the international level is (i) the widespread dismantling of exchange controls and related impediments to the flow of capital between nations, and (ii) the consequent arbitraging of rates of return of assets in different currencies of denomination in different locations. This process began in the mid 1970s with liberalization in Germany, the United States, and Canada among the large countries, but gathered pace at the end of the decade when additional measures of liberalization were undertaken, notably by Japan and the United Kingdom. Since that time, further liberalization has occurred, notably in Europe, where Italy, France, and the other EC member countries have eliminated exchange controls.[4]

Since the hallmark of financial integration is the arbitraged uniform risk-adjusted rate of return, its correlate at the level of the global economy is interest parity adjusted for expected exchange rate depreciation. One

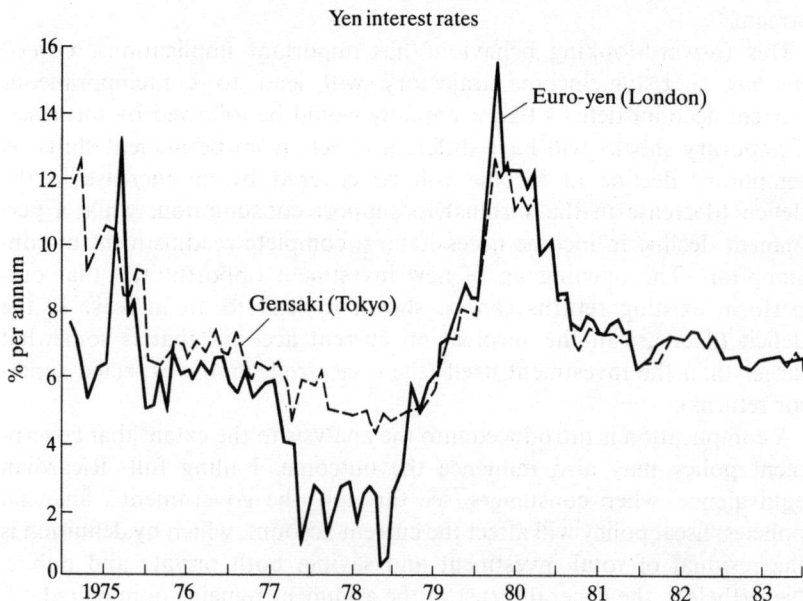

Yen interest rates

Interest arbitrage: 3-month funds
(UK: averages for week ending Wednesday)
(Plus (+) differential in favour of dollar assets)

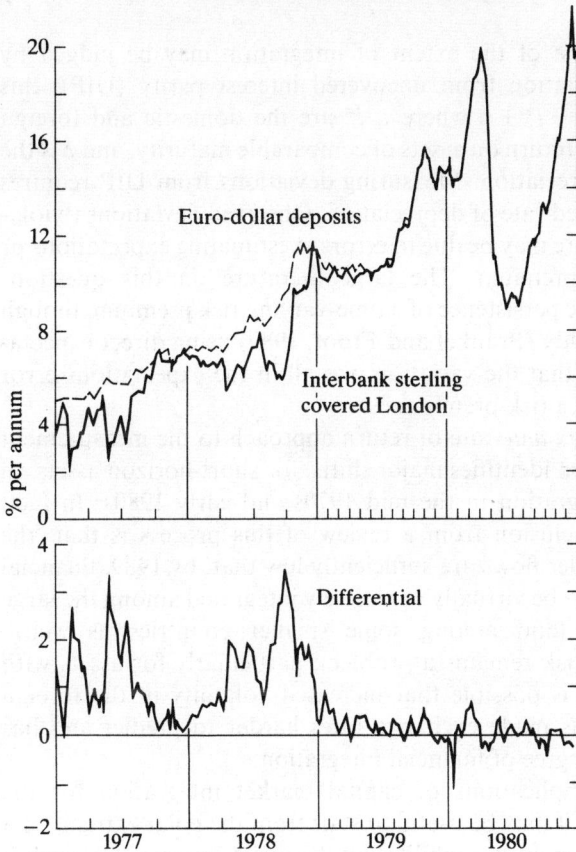

Figure 2.1   Financial liberalization in Japan and the UK: the impact on the offshore–onshore differential, 1975–83. *Source:* Frankel (1989), based on *Economic Report of the President,* 1984.

measurable concept is that of parity between onshore rates of return in different locations after allowing for the cost of cover in the forward market – i.e., covered interest parity (CIP).[5] What the removal of exchange controls does is to remove barriers to arbitrage between offshore and onshore assets in a currency, and to enable arbitrage – by removing the 'country premium' – to bind the onshore rates of return in assets of different currencies located in the corresponding countries of currency issue. The dramatic effect on the onshore–offshore differential of removing exchange controls is illustrated for the cases of Japan and the United Kingdom (both of which removed controls in 1979) in Figure 2.1.[6] The removal of controls implies that these differentials are essentially arbitraged to zero.

A more rigorous test of the extent of integration may be judged by estimates of the deviation from uncovered interest parity (UIP); this deviation is simply $i - i^* + \delta$ where i, i^* are the domestic and foreign risk-adjusted rates of return on assets of comparable maturity, and δ is the expected rate of depreciation. Measuring deviations from UIP requires estimating the expected rate of depreciation. Observed deviations ('violations' of UIP) therefore may be due to errors in estimating expectations or may reflect a risk premium. The large literature on this question[7] generally identifies the persistence of a time-varying risk premium, though one related recent study (Frankel and Froot, 1989) using direct expectations data suggested that the variation was all in the expectations error rather than reflecting a risk premium.[8]

To summarize, the *ex ante* rate of return approach to the measurement of financial integration identifies major shifts, for short-horizon assets, in the direction of integration in the mid 1970s and early 1980s. In fact, Frankel's (1989) conclusion from a review of this process is that 'the barriers to cross-border flows are sufficiently low that, by 1989, financial markets can be said to be virtually completely integrated among the large industrial countries (and among some smaller countries as well)'. However, exchange risk remains a problem; particularly for assets with longer maturities. It is possible that increased volatility in the foreign exchange markets has made exchange rates harder to predict and has thereby limited the degree of financial integration.

To illustrate the implications of capital market integration for the balance of payments, it may be useful to start from the polar extreme of a world of complete capital immobility, or 'financial autarky'. In such a world the current account would be required to clear continuously (up to the limit allowed by the availability of official foreign exchange reserves). Given the right conditions for stability, a freely flexible exchange rate could be expected to perform this task with the saving–investment balance cleared domestically by the rate of interest. If the level of output were not fixed, then the task of clearing the external and internal balance could be shared by the level of income. There would be no reason for the rate of interest in different countries to be connected. In such a model there is a binding liquidity constraint on the size of current account deficits, and the 'sustainability' question is correspondingly easy to answer: no deficit or surplus is sustainable.

Now consider an intermediate regime of relatively, but not completely, immobile capital. It may be appropriate to think of this in stock rather than flow terms; as a country's stock of borrowing rises, so does the cost of borrowing, ultimately very steeply. A liquidity constraint is still binding but sustainability takes on a more interesting connotation. To answer the sustainability question would require computing whether a country's present and likely future policies will push its accumulated net foreign debt into the constrained region. Deficits that are matched by investments in profitable projects will be rated differently from deficits which correspond to excess consumption because the former may promise a reversal of the cumulative deficit. It is convenient to characterize this intermediate regime as one in which the liquidity constraint, though less tight, is likely to bind prior to a solvency constraint.

In the event, finally, of a fully integrated capital market (in the sense of a market without exchange risk), a borrower – private or public sector agent – needs to meet a solvency constraint, but there is no binding liquidity constraint prior to this. Governments, of course, have greater liberty to meet their solvency constraints than private sector agents; they have taxing powers, for example. Sustainability now becomes a question of solvency; and there will usually be a variety of policy and current account trajectories which are sustainable in the sense of obeying this constraint, and the concept loses, inevitably, some of its apparent precision. This taxonomy illustrates how the significance of the concept of sustainability is diminished as the relevance of liquidity constraints decreases and ultimately converges towards that, simply, of solvency.

3.2   The role of the exchange rate

It is important to consider the relationship between the current account balance and the exchange rate. The fixed point here must be the insight of the elasticities approach, which remains valid. Estimated trade equations universally attribute an important role to exchange rates in determining imports and exports, along with other factors.

In this regard, there are two propositions which at first sight might appear contradictory: one is that a current account deficit presages a devaluation, the other that current account deficits are associated with appreciating exchange rates. Both propositions are correct in certain circumstances. For example, when capital mobility is low, the current account deficit is limited; therefore, a prospective rise in the deficit, given the level of other factors, must induce a corrective devaluation. On the other hand, when capital mobility is high and an economy takes advantage of the fact to run a persistent current account deficit, the exchange rate must assume a value, which in conjunction with other determinants,

satisfies the elasticities conditions governing the balance. In these circumstances, other things equal, a deficit requires an appreciation to emerge.

Under the Bretton Woods regime, in which capital mobility was restricted, the 'fixed but adjustable' exchange rate had to be at the level required
(the 'fundamental equilibrium level'), along with the setting of demand
management policy, to clear the current account (up to the limit given by
any long-term net capital inflow). Thus the connection between the
current account and the exchange rate was relatively direct. In the liberalized system prevailing today, this link has essentially disappeared.

3.3   Policy towards the current account

The discussion above raises the question of whether a country should
conduct policy on the basis of targets for its current account. Traditionally, there is little doubt that for most countries the balance of
payments on current account has been a principal objective of (or constraint upon) economic policy. It is easy to see why this came to be so in a
regime of limited capital mobility – like the Bretton Woods regime. In
such a regime an incipient current account deficit requires exchange rate
devaluation or deflation. In the Bretton Woods system, however,
devaluation became invested with negative connotations, and in practice
the exchange rate was used only sparingly. Accordingly, current account
balance, at least up to the limits indicated by the inflow or outflow of
long-term capital (as in the notion of the 'basic balance'), became a target
for generalized economic management, so that an incipient deficit
(surplus) prompted deflation (relaxation).

Under conditions of a low degree of capital mobility, the current
account is likely to continue to be a target of policy even if the exchange
rate regime is formally transformed from a fixed-but-adjustable to a
flexible system. Despite the corresponding reduction in the political
sensitivity that attaches to exchange rate change, governments are still
unlikely to accept the consequences of exchange rate adjustment with
indifference and so will continue to treat the current account in some
version as a legitimate target for, or constraint upon, economic policy.
The question of whether there are rationales for current account targets
when capital markets are highly integrated is discussed below.

The starting point for this discussion is the insight that when capital
markets are highly integrated the current account is simply a residual of
decisions taken by agents within a framework of constrained optimization. Cooper (1981) makes the point in this way: 'In the context of
overall saving-investment analysis countries should not take any particular view of their current account positions at all. Some will draw

savings form the rest of the world, others will invest in the rest of the world. Nothing is wrong with this, it is as it should be.'[9] So, while the degree of capital mobility and the adoption of the current account as a target or constraint governing generalized fiscal or monetary policy are conceptually separate items, in practice it seems that the two are likely to go together.

Even in a world of highly integrated capital markets, however, there may be reasons for the government to target the current account. One set of arguments focuses on the inverse of the current account, the capital account, and identifies the possibility of a departure of social from private benefit in decisions about net foreign investments. Private decisions to invest at home or overseas will be taken on the basis of expected after-tax returns; from the point of view of the social benefit of the potential capital exporting country, however, the relevant comparison is between the foreign after-tax rate of return and the domestic *pre-tax* rate of return since the domestic tax proceeds are retained at home. This suggests that a measure of retraint over capital outflow might be an appropriate response. In a similar vein, where the private investor will compare expected rates of return adjusted for the probability of losses due to fraud or confiscation, the government of the potential capital exporter could argue that this does not fully take account of the social interest. If confiscation or fraud occurs at home, the losses of one domestic private investor become the gains of another – whereas, if the loss occurs over-seas, it is an overseas resident (or government) who benefits. These considerations also could justify an interest in limiting capital outflow. By contrast, concern about the influence of foreign capital on the domestic economy may motivate restrictions on capital inflows. Explicit restric-tions reduce the mobility of capital and will tend to elevate the current account as a policy goal; even in the absence of such restrictions – and their progressive dismantling is a feature of post-war history – it can be argued (e.g., Summers, 1988) that the state of the current account (which is after all just the *inverse* of the capital account) will not be a matter of indifference to governments.

It is also possible to think of policy motivations which, though not aimed at the current account *per se*, nevertheless have predictable implications for it. In practice, the degree of imbalance on current account, even if not itself an explicit target, will therefore be limited in some way. For example, current account deficits may be a symptom of inflationary pressure, representing a vent for excess demand: this, after all, is the interpretation customarily associated with the 'absorption approach'. To the extent this is true, it would not be surprising to find that the conduct of counter-inflationary policy could look rather like a policy of targeting the current account. But it is very far from the case that the reduction of inflation and the reduction of current account deficits are synonymous; in fact, the policy combination of lax fiscal policy and tight monetary policy, which promises the reduction of inflation through the appreciation of the exchange rate, has the opposite implication for the current account. Indeed, it is interesting to note that the targeting of national wealth has been advocated recently by writers in the Keynesian tradition (Weale *et al.*, 1989) precisely on the grounds that it is necessary to correct for a bias towards the tight money–lax fiscal policy solution to the full employment–inflation problem. For given value of capital investment, such a target would again imply, residually, a current account target. In contrast to this, policies designed to secure the 'over'-devaluation of a currency with a view to promoting the growth of tradables production may result in current account surpluses and thus look like a latter-day mercantilism, postulating a trade surplus as a policy goal.[10]

4   Saving–investment correlations

The *ex ante* rate of return approach to the measurement of financial integration described above may be contrasted with the *ex post* approach of examining whether flows of saving and investment have exhibited behaviour indicative of integration. Such an alternative test, based upon the behaviour of saving and investment between countries, was proposed by Feldstein and Horioka (1980). They argued that in a world characterized by high capital mobility there is no *a priori* reason to expect saving and investment to be correlated across countries. Savers in different countries face the same interest rate; hence the relative level of saving in one country compared with another is determined by structural factors in the different economies. Similarly, investors also face the same interest rate, so investment decisions simply depend upon relative investment opportunities. Assuming that structural factors affecting saving and investment are not correlated, domestic savings and investment rates will also be uncorrelated. If, on the other hand, capital mobility is restricted then domestic investors will face a wedge between the cost of domestic and foreign saving, and hence domestic saving and investment will be correlated. Indeed, in the extreme case of zero capital mobility, saving and investment would be perfectly correlated.

In order to test this hypothesis, Feldstein and Horioka ran the following cross-section regression

$$(I/Y)_i = \alpha + \beta(S/Y)_i + \epsilon_i \qquad (8)$$

where I represents domestic investment, S national saving, Y output, subscript i represents different countries, and ϵ is an error term. They

Table 2.2. *Results from regressions of investment on national savings*

Sample period	1960–86	1960–73	1974–86	1980–6
Gross saving and investment	0.79 (0.09)	0.91 (0.07)	0.67 (0.15)	0.61 (0.13)
Net saving and investment	0.87 (0.11)	0.89 (0.08)	0.88 (0.15)	0.79 (0.14)

Notes: The table reports estimates of the coefficient β in equation (8). Standard errors are indicated in parentheses.
Source: Feldstein and Bacchetta (1989).

interpreted the coefficient β as measuring the proportion of domestic saving that is invested domestically. These regressions revealed that saving and investment rates were highly correlated, in terms both of levels and medium-term changes over time. The estimated coefficients were generally significantly different from zero, but not from one, using both ordinary least squares and instrumental variable techniques, and showed no signs of declining over time. Subsequent work has confirmed that these coefficients are large and significantly different from zero, although recent data indicate that the coefficients may have fallen somewhat in the 1980s.[11]

The results from regressions using equation (8) on data for twenty-three industrial countries over various time periods are presented in Table 2.2. The regressions show large and significant coefficients; for the full 1960–86 period the estimated coefficient using gross saving and investment is 0.79.[12] There is also some evidence that the coefficient has been falling over time. The coefficient estimate for the period 1960–73 is 0.91, and insignificantly different from unity; for the 1974–86 period the estimated coefficient falls to 0.67, and for the period 1980–6 it falls further to 0.61.[13] When net saving and investment data are used, however, the coefficient shows almost no decline over time.

In addition to these cross-section results, various authors have found a close correlation between saving and investment over time. Bayoumi (1990), for example, reports the results from running the following equation on annual time series data for ten industrial countries

$$\Delta(I/Y)_t = \alpha + \beta\Delta(S/Y)_t + \epsilon_t \qquad (9)$$

This equation is found to yield a positive correlation between saving and investment in all cases except Norway. Moreover, the estimated coefficient is insignificantly different from unity and significantly different from zero for seven of the ten countries.[14]

Three broad sets of explanations for these high correlations have emerged:

Low international capital mobility. Despite other evidence, international capital mobility may be low, owing to factors such as information constraints, lack of enforceability of contracts, exchange rate risk, and, in earlier periods, exchange controls. This is the original interpretation proposed by Feldstein and Horioka (1980), reaffirmed in Feldstein and Bacchetta (1989).

Private sector behaviour. Several authors have built models in which there is perfect capital mobility, but saving and investment are correlated because of factors such as productivity shocks, population growth, or low integration of international goods markets. In this interpretation saving and investment are correlated because they both react to some common conditions (Tesar, 1988).

Government targeting of the current account. Governments may use fiscal and monetary policy to target the current account (Summers, 1988).

These explanations have substantially different policy implications. Low international capital mobility implies that policies to promote domestic saving should also raise domestic investment. In contrast, if the correlations reflect private sector behaviour in a world of high capital mobility, policy-induced increases in domestic saving will tend to flow abroad unless accommodated by measures to promote investment. Finally, the possibility that governments have been targeting the current account raises the question of the optimality of such a policy, as discussed above.

In order to differentiate among these hypotheses, it is necessary to go beyond the simple regressions outlined in Table 2.2. One avenue of investigation involves calculating the behaviour implied by theoretical models. Obstfeld (1986) found that the correlations implied by a simple model of saving–investment behaviour were of the same order of magnitude as the observed ones; Frankel (1989) and Tesar (1988) report similar results for somewhat different theoretical models. Although these results show that the correlations can be explained by private sector behaviour, they do not demonstrate that they *are* caused by such behaviour.[15] Furthermore, these models are usually directed at the time series behaviour of saving and investment, and hence are less useful for explaining the cross-section correlations.

A second line of inquiry has involved disaggregating total saving and investment. Feldstein and Horioka examine data for several sectors and conclude that there is little evidence of different sectoral behaviour. Summers (1988) regresses the private sector saving investment balance on the government deficit, and finds a strong negative correlation, a result which he attributes to government targeting of the current account. Roubini (1988) proposes a model where government policies to smooth taxation produce time series correlations between total saving and investment, and presents regressions supporting this model. However, in both these cases the results also appear compatible with the hypothesis of low international capital mobility.[16] Bayoumi (1990) looks at the correlation between private sector saving and investment, and finds lower correlations for private sector data than for total data. He argues that this is evidence against explanations based on private sector behaviour. He also finds that the time series correlations between saving and investment are reduced when fixed investment is substituted for total investment.

Studies have also been made of saving and investment correlations for alternative data sets. Murphy (1984) reports the results of running saving–investment regressions using data for the top 150 US corporations. He finds high correlations and argues this shows evidence that the observed correlations are caused by private sector behaviour. Another approach has been to process data derived from regimes which are known to exemplify a high degree of capital market integration. In this spirit, Bayoumi (1990) run saving–investment regressions on international data from the classical gold standard period (1880–1913), while Bayoumi and Rose (1989) use postwar data on regional saving and investment for the British Isles: in neither case do the correlations reveal any significant relationship between saving and investment.[17] These results stand in striking contrast to the results for the postwar period; the graphical evidence, illustrated in Figures 2.2 and 2.3, is quite convincing on this point. Figure 2.2 shows the relationship between saving and investment (gross definition) for the eleven most developed countries from 1960–87, while Figure 2.3 shows saving–investment relationships estimated by Bayoumi (1990) for the gold standard period. The strong correlation which is obvious in Figure 2.2 (the value of 'β' is 0.917, with a standard error of just over 0.1) all but disappears when the gold standard data are used. Similarly, the behaviour of the UK current accounts over time (shown in Figure 7.1 of Bean, 1991, in this volume) shows a large change between the gold standard and postwar periods. Thus the evidence from alternative regimes appears to argue strongly against the private sector behaviour hypothesis, since one would not expect different behaviour across regimes.

At the same time, however, this evidence does not help distinguish between the government policy and low mobility hypothesis. Unlike the currency union of the United Kingdom and the stable exchange rate of the gold standard period, today's capital markets have to cope with

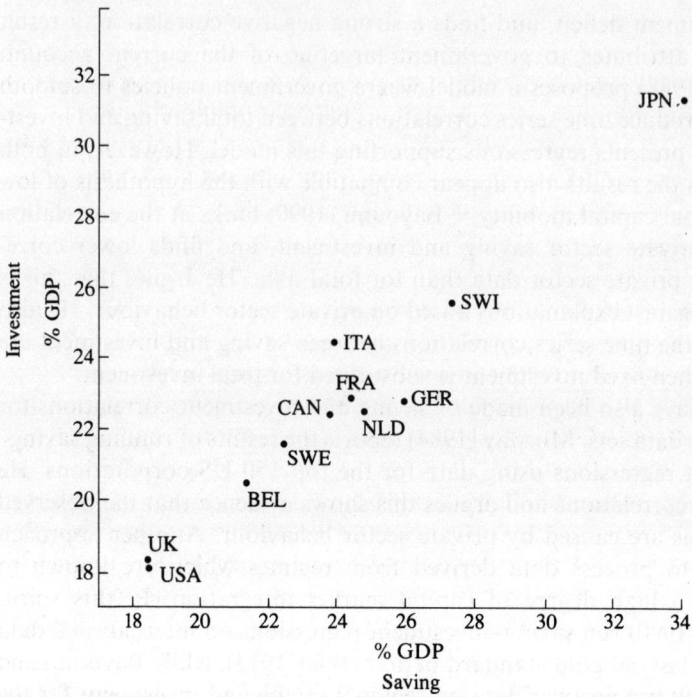

Figure 2.2   Saving–investment imbalance in G11 countries, 1960–87 (as % of GDP/GNP)

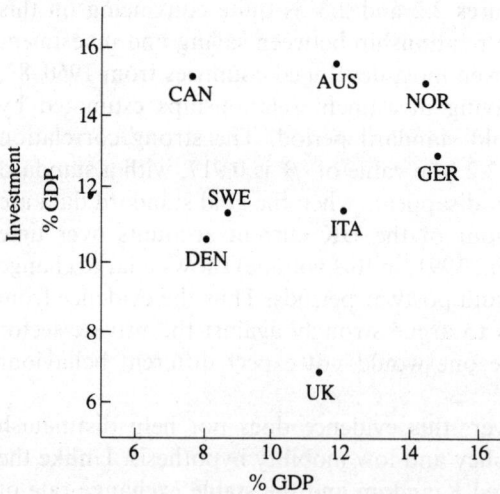

Figure 2.3   Saving–investment imbalances during the classical gold standard, 1880–1913 (% of GDP/GNP)

exchange risk; and whereas it can be assumed that government intervention in the gold standard period or between the regions of the United Kingdom was minimal or zero, no such confidence can be expressed about the absence of current account targeting in the postwar period. A direct approach to this last question is possible, however.

A third approach is to estimate government reaction functions to establish whether the current account has been a major policy objective and, if so, whether there is any evidence of change in this regard. Generally, policy reaction functions are estimated as reduced-form equations with the government policy variable as the dependent variable, and lagged values of policy targets as the independent variables. Black (1983), in a wide-ranging study of monetary policy in the major industrial countries, concludes that external variables (which in his case do not include the current account) are relatively unimportant for the United States, but generally have greater weight for other major countries. Joyce (1986), in a summary of the reaction function literature, comes to similar conclusions about monetary policy; she also surveys the rather smaller literature on fiscal reaction functions and concludes that the evidence of systematic fiscal policy 'is weaker' than for monetary policy.

The appendix reports some new work on government reaction functions. Reasonably stable monetary policy reaction functions are identified for several countries; these functions suggest that the current account was a policy target in the 1970s, and that its importance declined in the 1980s. Interestingly, these results appear as strong for the United States as for other countries. While attempts to estimate stable fiscal policy reaction functions based on lagged variables were not successful, this work did identify a strong negative contemporaneous correlation between the saving–investment balance of the government and private sectors. These results indicate that the two balances almost completely offset each other in the 1970s, although the correlations have fallen somewhat in the 1980s. If this reflects a policy response, it must be admitted that the degree of policy success is rather surprising; the correlation is of course not incompatible with the alternative hypothesis of low capital mobility.

5   Consumption paths and financial integration

The fundamental advantage of closer financial integration between countries is that it allows countries to choose paths for consumption and investment which are independent of each other (subject to a long-run budget constraint). In a situation of financial autarky, consumption and investment are constrained to add up to the product of the economy, and therefore cannot be considered to be independently determined. On the other hand, if international financial markets are open, then the sum of consumption and investment can diverge from national product since foreign saving can be used to bridge such gaps. This section looks at evidence as to whether national consumption paths have become more 'optimal' over time, as international financial markets have become increasingly integrated.

Modern work on consumption usually starts from the Euler equations implied by maximizing behaviour. These models assume that the consumer can borrow and lend freely at a given real interest rate. When these assumptions are combined with other more technical ones, the intertemporal path of consumption can be characterized by the following relationship

$$U'(C_t) = \beta E_t\{(1 + r_t) U'(C_{t+1})\} \tag{10}$$

where C_t is the level of consumption in period t, $U(.)$ is the utility function of the consumer, β is the consumer's discount factor, r_t is the real interest rate faced by the consumer and E_t is the expectations operator conditional on information known at time t.

This equation states that the marginal utility of consumption today is equal to the expected marginal utility tomorrow, adjusted by the real interest rate and discount factor. Combined with the assumption of rational expectations, this model predicts that the current change in consumption should not depend upon any lagged information, except the first lag of the real interest rate. The intuition behind this result is that consumption simply depends upon permanent income and the real interest rate. In any given period, the estimate of permanent income includes all information up to that point, hence no other information should be pertinent to the decision. This characteristic can be used to test whether consumption paths deviate significantly from the 'optimal' path implied by (10).[18]

The international implications of equation (10) have been explored by Obstfeld (1987). He noted that, in a world of perfect capital mobility, consumers have access to both home and foreign capital markets. As a result, while home consumers have access to a real return of $(1 + i_t)(P_t/P_{t+1})$, the foreign consumer has access to a real return of $(1 + i_t)(P^*_t X_t/P^*_{t+1} X_{t+1})$, where asterisks represent foreign variables and X_t is the current exchange rate measured in home currency. Using a particular functional form for the utility functions, and equating the terms in interest rates for home and foreign consumers, produces the following equation

$$E_t\{(C_t/C_{t+1})^\alpha (P_t/P_{t+1}) - (C^*_t/C^*_{t+1})^{\alpha*} (P^*_t X_t/P^*_{t+1} X_{t+1})\} = 0 \tag{11}$$

A similar expression can be derived using the foreign interest rate.

Obstfeld estimated equation (11) using data for the United States, Japan and the Federal Republic of Germany. He rejected the model for the period up to the break-up of the Bretton Woods system, but not for the period afterwards. While these results are suggestive of an improvement in the path of consumption, considerable caution should be exercised. The reason for this is the inclusion of a term in the change in the exchange rate in equation (11). The floating rate period has been characterized by considerable volatility in exchange rates. This adds noise to the realizations of the term within the expectation, making it more difficult to reject the hypothesis.

This framework was also used by Bayoumi and Koujianou (1989), using data for six countries from the floating exchange rate period, to examine two hypotheses: whether the model holds for the entire period, and whether it holds better for the (more deregulated) 1980s than for the 1970s. Their results indicate that for the entire time period the model can be rejected. There is, however, some evidence that the path of consumption has become 'more optimal' as a result of international financial market deregulation in the 1980s.

6   Conclusions

The interpretation of the evidence presented above is not entirely without ambiguity. Certain facts are, however, clear. First, considerable liberalization has continued from earlier decades through the 1980s, which has resulted in a closer integration of world capital markets. For low-risk, short-horizon instruments, at least, capital is now very highly mobile. Second, there has been a marked increase in current account imbalances in the 1980s compared with earlier decades. Third, however, the evidence shows that overall net flows of saving and investment are still markedly insular compared with the paradigms offered by fully integrated capital markets and the evidence from the gold standard period. The research reported in this paper suggests that the principal explanation for this is probably that policy has been conducted in such a way as to offset to a large extent the fluctuations in private sector saving–investment balances, reducing countries' net involvement in the world capital market. Another part of the explanation probably has to do with exchange risk. Exchange risk raises the cost of forward cover and may exert a strong deterrent force for those maturities for which forward facilities are non-existent.

If it is accepted as a basic finding that there has been a genuine increase in the integration of the world's capital markets, a movement more likely to be continued than reversed, the next question to be addressed concerns the implications of this trend for policy. Current account imbalances have long been a leading target of economic policy and are an indicator which is closely monitored. Clearly, any movement towards more integrated capital markets makes the current account more of a residual factor in agents' decisions, and inevitably weakens its role as a policy objective. Indeed, it is possible to view both events in the 1980s and the policy reaction results in this paper as already confirming this.

Appendix   Policy reaction functions

This appendix reports the results obtained from policy reaction functions estimated across a number of different countries. The main focus is to examine the degree to which government policy has reacted to the current account, in order to investigate the hypothesis of Summers (1988), among others, that the observed cross-country correlations between saving and investment are due to government policy. Since there has been a fall in the observed correlation between the 1970s and the 1980s, this work investigates whether there has been a fall in the importance of the current account as a policy target over the last twenty years.

Monetary and fiscal policy reaction functions are estimated directly, using reduced form equations with a policy instrument as the dependent variable and (lagged) targets as the independent variables. While there are other, more structural, methods of estimating reactions functions (Pissarides, 1972), the reduced form approach has been widely used in the literature (Joyce, 1986). Since they have rather different problems and complications, the monetary and fiscal reaction functions will be discussed separately.

1   Monetary reaction functions

The monetary reaction functions are based on estimated equations of the following form

$$\Delta(i_t) = \alpha_1 + \alpha_2(i)\,\Delta(y_{t-i}) + \alpha_3(i)\,\Delta(p_{t-i}) + \alpha_4(i)(CA/Y)_{t-i} \quad \text{(A1)}$$
$$? \qquad + \qquad\qquad + \qquad\qquad -$$

where i is an interest rate, y is the logarithm of real output, p is the logarithm of the price level, (CA/Y) is the ratio of the current account surplus to output and Δ is the first difference operator. This equation states that the authorities raise or lower interest rates depending upon the recent behaviour of three target variables, namely growth of output, inflation, and the size of the current account. The expected signs on these targets are given below the coefficients. Growth and inflation represent the basic internal targets of monetary policy, while the current account variable represents the external target.

Before estimating an equation such as (A1) above, there are several issues that should be discussed. The first is the possible endogeneity of the policy variable; if the chosen interest rate is not fully under the control of the authorities, the estimated coefficients may in fact represent endogenous behaviour rather than policy decisions. To avoid this problem the interest rates chosen were the official discount rates. These rates are fully under the control of the authorities, and are generally adjusted in discrete steps such as half a point.

A second issue involves the treatment of expectations. The authorities react to expected future changes in the economy, not those which have occurred; hence, ideally, rather than using lagged values of the targets, it would be preferable to use expected future values. Unfortunately, it is not the actual outcomes of the targets which should be used, but the outcome in the absence of any policy intervention. Since changes in the policy variable affects the future outcome of the targets, it would be necessary to specify a model of the effects of targets upon the economy before the correct expected values could be derived, and any results for the reaction function would involve a joint test of the rest of the model. To avoid these problems, lagged targets were used in the regressions. This procedure is justified if future expected outcomes are based upon past behaviour.[19]

Finally, there is an econometric issue which should be considered. As was noted above, the dependent variable in these regressions moves in discrete steps, while standard regression analysis assumes that the dependent variable is continuous. If it is assumed that there exists an underlying continuous reaction function, but that the actual outcomes are then rounded to the nearest (say) half a percentage point, the rounding introduces a new source of error into the regression. As a result, while the estimated coefficients are unbiased, standard errors are overestimated. The reported results have been adjusted to take this into account.

Table 2A.1 reports monetary policy reaction functions for four countries: the United States, Japan, the Federal Republic of Germany, and Italy.[20] If government policy is a major cause of the observed correlations between saving and investment, the fall in these correlations between the 1970s and the 1980s should show up in terms of a decline in the importance of the current account as a policy target. Table 2A.1 reports the results of regressions designed to investigate this hypothesis. In addition to the targets, these regressions include dummy variables that represent the values of the targets in the 1980s. The coefficients on the target variables represent the importance of these targets in the 1970s, while the coefficients on the associated dummy variable show the change in the value of the targets between the 1970s and the 1980s. (The coefficient on the targets for the 1980s can be calculated from the sum of the coefficient

Table 2A.1. *Regression of change in interest rates on targets in the 1970s and 1980s*[1]

	United States	Japan	Federal Republic of Germany	Italy
Growth	21.9 (9.4)	0.0 (10.0)	2.7 (8.5)	6.3 (5.6)
$DUM \times$ growth	27.1 (13.9)	18.4 (15.8)	− 1.5 (12.1)	− 10.8 (8.7)
Inflation	39.5 (10.5)	6.0 (6.7)	21.7 (14.4)	23.4 (12.4)
$DUM \times$ inflation	− 17.9 (9.0)	− 2.1 (13.0)	− 13.2 (14.7)	− 10.7 (11.1)
CA/Y	− 26.5 (14.6)	− 11.4 (8.7)	− 12.6 (7.8)	− 12.9 (8.8)
$DUM \times CA/Y$	30.7 (16.3)	1.5 (9.8)	9.0 (8.9)	6.5 (16.4)
DW	2.16	1.17	1.24	2.19
R^2	0.42	0.13	0.09	0.18
Se	0.59	0.63	0.56	1.19

Notes: [1] The estimation period is 1973: 3–1988: 2.
Adjusted standard errors are indicated in parentheses. DUM equals 0 in the 1970s and 1 in the 1980s.

on the target and its associated dummy variable.) In order to simplify the presentation only current values of the targets are included in the regressions; results which included lagged values are broadly similar.

The results are encouraging. The most striking results pertain to the current account variable; all the coefficients relating to the current account in the 1970s have the expected sign and have t-ratios well above unity. Furthermore, all the regressions show a fall in the size of the current account coefficient between the 1970s and the 1980s.[21] This fall reduces the coefficient to near zero for the United States and the Federal Republic of Germany, and halves the coefficient for Italy while leaving it relatively unchanged in the case of Japan. Turning to the domestic targets, in the 1970s inflation has a larger and more significant coefficient than growth in all the regressions, and is significant at conventional levels in three of the four.[22] The results for the 1980s show less uniformity, with growth becoming more important than inflation in the United States and Japan, but not in the Federal Republic of Germany or Italy. These results appear to confirm that the current account was a significant policy target for monetary policy in the 1970s, but that its importance diminished somewhat in the 1980s. This behaviour appears to correspond to a reduction in the correlation between saving and investment among

OECD countries. Since the major effect of monetary policy is probably on private sector saving and investment, rather than on the government balance, these data do not provide support for the hypothesis of Summers (1988) that it is fiscal policy which has been used to target the current account, rather it appears that governments have sought to influence private sector behaviour in response to current account imbalances.

2   Fiscal reaction functions

In theory, fiscal reaction functions can be estimated in exactly the same manner as monetary functions. However, in practice several factors make estimation more difficult. The first, and most important, has to do with the exogeneity of policy. Fiscal systems are extremely complex, and the policy instruments which are under the direct control of the government, such as tax rates or allowance provisions, are numerous. Summary measures of policy, such as the deficit or average tax rate, are not entirely under the control of the government given that they are likely to be affected by growth and other factors.[23] The empirical work used the budget deficit as the basic definition of policy, but allows for some endogenous effects. (This work could be extended to other summary statistics, such as average tax rates.)

A second issue concerns the time scale over which fiscal policy is planned. While some adjustments often take place during the year, most fiscal policy changes are announced in the budget. Hence, while monetary policy can be analysed on a quarterly or monthly basis, fiscal policy is probably best approached using annual data. This reduces the number of data points available, and lowers the precision of the estimates.

Two reaction functions were estimated for twelve industrial countries. The first regressed the ratio of the budget deficit[24] to GDP (the policy variable) against its own lagged value and lagged values of the three targets, growth, inflation, and the current account; in the second, contemporaneous values for growth and inflation were included as proxies for possible endogeneity effects. The expected signs for the targets are the same as in the monetary regressions; growth and inflation should be associated with rises in the government surplus (reductions in the deficit) in order to stabilize demand, while changes in the current account should be negatively correlated with the government surplus if the current account is a target.

The results from estimating these equations, both over the full period and differentiating between the 1970s and the 1980s (not reported for the sake of brevity) were universally unsatisfactory. The coefficients were rarely significant, and those on inflation were often incorrectly signed.[25]

Table 2A.2. *Regressions of private sector and government saving–investment imbalances*[1]

Private$(S - I)/Y = \alpha + \beta$Government$(S - I)/Y + e_t$

$e_t = \rho e_{t-1} + \epsilon_t$

	β	ρ	R^2
United States	− 1.07 (0.13)	0.91 (0.09)	0.84
Japan	− 1.05 (0.28)	0.77 (0.16)	0.52
Germany, Fed. Rep. of	− 0.83 (0.21)	0.68 (0.23)	0.47
France	− 0.98 (0.21)	0.03 (0.29)	0.62
United Kingdom	0.43 (0.52)	0.69 (0.18)	0.05
Canada	− 0.99 (0.15)	0.29 (0.27)	0.77
Belgium	− 0.93 (0.24)	0.85 (0.12)	0.59
Finland	− 1.00 (0.32)	0.33 (0.25)	0.44
Norway	0.11 (0.47)	0.65 (0.20)	0.01
Sweden	− 0.66 (0.16)	0.35 (0.26)	0.57
Austria	− 0.56 (0.11)	− 0.29 (0.28)	0.65
Australia	− 0.80 (0.37)	0.70 (0.17)	0.29

Notes: [1] The estimation period is 1972–86.
Standard errors are indicated in parentheses.

3   The contemporaneous saving–investment correlation

The results from estimating policy reaction functions are mixed. Monetary policy appears to have reacted to the current account, but there is little evidence that fiscal policy did. This section explores the existence of a contemporaneous correlation between the government and private saving–investment imbalances.

The following regressions were estimated using a first-order autocorrelation adjustment

$$Priv\{(S - I)/Y\} = \alpha + \beta Govt\{(S - I)Y\} \qquad (A2)$$

where *Priv* means private sector, *Govt* is general government, and S, I and Y represent nominal saving, investment, and GDP respectively. The coefficient β can be regarded as the degree to which changes in the government balance affect changes in private sector balance; a coefficient of − 1 indicates that changes are fully offset. It should be emphasized, however, that the direction of causation is not clear.

The results from these regressions are presented in Table 2A.2. In eight of the twelve regressions the estimate of β is insignificantly different from − 1, with estimated values ranging from − 0.8 to − 1.1. Of the other four regressions, two have sizeable negative estimates of β, while the two

Table 2A.3. *Differences in saving–investment correlations in the 1970s and 1980s*[1]

$\text{Priv}(S - I)/Y = \alpha + \beta \text{Govt}(S - I)/Y + \gamma\{DUM^*\text{Govt}(S - I)/Y\} + e_t$
$\qquad e_t = \rho e_{t-1} + \epsilon_t$

	β	γ	ρ	R^2
United States	− 1.17 (0.18)	0.28 (0.26)	0.83 (0.14)	0.83
Japan	− 1.10 (0.29)	0.31 (0.37)	0.78 (0.17)	0.55
Germany, Fed. Rep. of	0.88 (0.24)	0.69 (0.63)	0.53 (0.29)	0.51
France	− 1.68 (0.34)	0.87 (0.48)	0.40 (0.31)	0.72
United Kingdom	0.59 (0.50)	− 0.92 (0.44)	0.47 (0.24)	0.30
Canada	− 0.43 (0.18)	− 0.62 (0.18)	− 0.01 (0.35)	0.92
Belgium	− 1.17 (0.36)	0.20 (0.24)	0.87 (0.11)	0.61
Finland	− 1.03 (0.32)	0.54 (0.89)	0.31 (0.27)	0.47
Norway	− 0.24 (0.94)	0.39 (0.43)	0.62 (0.23)	0.03
Sweden	− 0.84 (0.28)	0.40 (0.46)	0.41 (0.25)	0.56
Austria	− 0.53 (0.13)	− 0.21 (0.42)	− 0.33 (0.29)	0.67
Australia	− 0.54 (0.45)	− 0.63 (0.58)	− 0.63 (0.20)	0.35

Notes: [1] The estimation period is 1972–86.
Standard errors are indicated in parentheses. *DUM* is a variable equal to 0 for the 1970s and 1 for the 1980s.

regressions with positive estimates of β, for the United Kingdom and Norway, also have the highest standard errors.[26]

To test how robust these findings are two further sets of regressions were estimated. Contemporaneous values of growth and inflation were included to test whether the correlations were caused by automatic stabilizers; the results were similar to the initial regressions. Finally, the possibility that these correlations reflect the treatment of all nominal interest payments as income in the national accounts was also examined. In times of inflation this artificially boosts the income, and hence saving, of net creditors, such as the private sector, while lowering the income and saving of net debtors, such as the government. A crude adjustment for this can be made by increasing government saving by the product of net outstanding government debt and inflation and reducing saving by the private sector by an equal amount. These calculations were made for the six major industrial countries in the sample, starting in 1977; the resulting regressions were similar to those without the inflation adjustment.

There is also evidence that the importance of these correlations has fallen over time. Table 2A.3 reports the results when a dummy variable representing the change in the coefficient β in the 1980s is included in the regressions. The results support the thesis that the coefficient has fallen between the 1970s and the 1980s. Although rarely significant at conventional levels, the results show a fall in the implied correlation over the 1980s in eight of the 12 equations.[27] This fall in the observed correlations parallels the observed decline in the correlation of national saving and investment rates.

Overall, there is powerful evidence of a negative correlation between the saving and investment balances of the private and government sectors. The causes of this correlation suggests two explanations, not necessarily exclusive. The first is that international capital mobility is low, although it has risen somewhat over time; hence any imbalance between saving and investment in one area of the economy requires an offsetting imbalance in another sector due to crowding out. An alternative explanation is that the government targets the current account. Fiscal policy adjustments could be made during the year, producing the contemporaneous correlation, or monetary policy could be directed to the current account, causing movements in both the private and government balances.

NOTES

The authors would like to thank Flemming Larsen for suggesting the topic and Jim Boughton, Jeff Frankel, Graham Hacche, Lars Svensson, and other participants at an IMF seminar for useful suggestions and comments. The present paper is similar to one published under a similar title ('Saving, Investment, Financial Integration and the Balance of Payments') in *Staff Studies for the World Economic Outlook* 1990, with amendments suggested by further helpful discussions at the Conference on External Constraints and Macroeconomic Policy: the European Experience held in Athens during May 1990. None of those acknowledged or our respective institutions have any responsibility for the views expressed which are our own.

1 For convenience of exposition transfers are omitted.
2 These definitions follow convention in assuming that all of G is a 'consumption good'. In effect, of course, governments typically perform a large amount of investment and this should be recognized in empirical analysis of the problem (as in the work reported on below – see Section 4).
3 As saving is simply the addition to wealth, another way to think about this process is as an adjustment towards a desired wealth/income position (which itself may be an evolving target). This in turn indicates that current account surpluses (and deficits) are not unbounded; verification of the nature of these processes over long periods is an important objective for future research though one that is somewhat hampered by lack of data availability.
4 Frankel (1989) provided a comprehensive review of the process of liberalization and computes various associated measures of financial integration.
5 Offshore CIP (i.e., covered parity of returns in Euromarkets) does not imply that arbitrage can operate freely across national boundaries: since the same

institutions set both the forward rate for a currency and the Euro-interest rate in that currency by reference to CIP (Johnston 1979), observed deviations from offshore CIP are invariably due to no more than the employment of imprecise (perhaps averaged or inexactly date-matched) data.

6 We are grateful to Jeffrey Frankel for permission to reproduce this diagram.

7 A representative recent paper is Hodrick and Srivastava (1986).

8 Note however that there is no incentive to arbitrage *real* rates of return. Real return equalization is predicted only where expected depreciation is (correctly) given by relative expected inflation, i.e., where PPP governs the determination of exchange rates.

9 The fact that markets react to current account announcements does not necessarily indicate that capital mobility is low. If markets look to governments as a source of information and governments act as if financial constraints require current account balance, then the market will continue to react to deviations from balance since they imply changes in policy stance, and governments will feel justified in continuing to target the current account.

10 This case was elaborated by Schmitt (1979); the subsequent findings of Krugman and others in regard to the nature of international trade underline the relevance of this model (see Vines and Stevenson, 1991).

11 Both gross and net saving and investment have been used in the literature. The data are generally averaged over several years in order to avoid bias caused by the correlation of saving and investment over the business cycle.

12 Similar regressions for developing countries also show a significant correlation over time, although the coefficients are somewhat lower than that for industrial countries (Dooley *et al.*, 1987).

13 These estimates use ordinary least squares. Typically researchers have found instrumental variables results to be similar to OLS.

14 Frankel (1989) reports that for similar regressions using US data, the inclusion of the period 1984–7 significantly reduces the estimated correlations.

15 Feldstein and Bacchetta (1989) argue that Obstfeld's model cannot explain the correlations when 'realistic' parameter values are used.

16 Feldstein and Bacchetta (1989) disaggregate the data in the Summers study further and argue that they support the hypothesis that capital mobility is low.

17 Issues of data reliability suggest that cross-section correlations are more reliable for the gold standard period than correlations performed on the time series. However, it should be noted that Obstfeld (1986), using a different data source to Bayoumi's, reports quite a high coefficient for a gold standard time series equation for the United Kingdom.

18 This model has been tested extensively on data for the United States. The overall conclusion is that the model works reasonably well as a first approximation, but that a significant proportion of consumption emanates from households that are liquidity-constrained. These households consume out of current, rather than permanent, income. Tests for other countries have tended to reject the model more readily than for the United States (Hall, 1988).

19 For example, if a variable is projected using a first-order autoregressive process, the first lag will contain all the information needed to project its future values.

20 Full data sets were not available for other countries. The interest rates are end-quarter data, while the other variables are quarterly averages. For each country the change in the interest rate was regressed on the current value and

first lag of growth, inflation, and the current account ratio. Since the interest rate data are end-period, the use of current-period data on targets is justified, although it does assume a short lag between changes in targets and changes in instruments.

21 Using a simple sign test, the probability of four coefficients all turning up negative is 6.25%, close to conventional significance levels.

22 However, these results are not robust to the inclusion of lags.

23 Concepts such as the full employment deficit, which aim to take out these endogenous factors, depend upon the model used; furthermore, using such concepts in a reaction function assumes that governments disregard endogenous effects when choosing their fiscal stance.

24 General government data were used because central government data were only available for a few countries.

25 More details on these regressions are given in Artis and Bayoumi (1990).

26 These results are not simply a product of Ricardian effects. Using similar data, Bayoumi (1990) finds a negative correlation between government and private saving, but the effect is not as powerful as the one documented here.

27 Using a simple one-tailed sign test this result is significant at the 10% level, but not at the 5% level.

REFERENCES

Alexander, A. (1952), 'The Effects of Devaluation on the Trade Balance', *IMF Staff Papers* **2**, 1–18.

Artis, M. and T. Bayoumi (1990), 'Saving, Investment, Financial Integration, and the Balance of Payments', *Staff Studies for the World Economic Outlook 1990*, International Monetary Fund, Washington.

Bayoumi, T. (1990), 'Saving–Investment Correlations: Immobile Capital, Government Policy or Endogenous Behavior?', *IMF Staff Papers* **37**, 360–87.

Bayoumi, T. and P. Koujianou (1989), 'The Effects of Financial Deregulation on Consumption', Working Paper 89/66, International Monetary Fund, Washington.

Bayoumi, T. and A. Rose (1989), 'Domestic Saving and Intra-National Capital Flows', unpublished, International Monetary Fund.

Bean, C. (1991), 'The External Constraint in the UK', this volume.

Black, S. (1983), 'The Use of Monetary Policy for Internal and External Balance in Ten Industrial Countries', in J. Frenkel (ed.), *Exchange Rates and International Economics*, Chicago: University of Chicago Press.

Cooper, R.N. (1981), 'Comment on Sachs', *Brookings Papers on Economic Activity* **3**, 269–73.

Dooley, M., J. Frankel and D. Mathieson (1987), 'International Capital Mobility: What Do the Saving–Investment Correlations Tell Us?', *IMF Staff Papers* **31**, 503–30.

Feldstein, M. and P. Bacchetta (1989), 'National Saving and International Investment', National Bureau of Economic Research, Working Paper No. 3164.

Feldstein, M. and C. Horioka (1980), 'Domestic Saving and International Capital Flows', *Economic Journal* **90**, 314–29.

Frankel, J. (1989), 'Quantifying International Capital Mobility in the 1980s', in Doug Bernheim and John Shoven (eds.), *Saving*, Chicago: University of Chicago Press.

Frankel, J. and K. Froot (1989), 'Chartists, Fundamentalists, and the Demand for Dollars', in A. Courakis and M. Taylor (eds.), *Policy Issues for Interdependent Economies*, London: Macmillan.

Frenkel, Jacob A. and Assaf Razin (1987), *Fiscal Policies and the World Economy*, Cambridge, MA: MIT Press.

Froot, Kenneth and Jeffrey Frankel (1989), 'Forward Discount Bias: is it an Exchange Risk Premium?', *Quarterly Journal of Economics* **104**, 139–61.

Hall, R. (1988), 'Intertemporal Substitution in Consumption', *Journal of Political Economy* **96**, 339–57.

Hodrick, R.J. and S. Srivastava (1986), 'The Covariation of Risk Premiums and Expected Future Exchange Rates', *Journal of International Money and Finance* **5**, 587–613.

Johnston, B. (1979), 'Some Aspects of the Determination of Euro-currency Interest Rates', *Bank of England Quarterly Bulletin* **19**, 35–46.

Joyce, J. (1986), 'On the Specification and Estimation of Macro-Economic Policy Functions', *Quarterly Journal of Business and Economics* **25**, 16–37.

Murphy, R. (1984), 'Capital Mobility and the Relationship Between Saving and Investment Rates in OECD Countries', *Journal of International Money and Finance* **3**, 327–42.

Obstfeld, M. (1986), 'Capital Mobility in the World Economy: Theory and Measurement', *Carnegie Rochester Series on Public Policy* **24**, 55–104.

 (1987), 'How Mobile is Capital? Some New Tests', National Bureau of Economic Research, Working Paper No. 2075.

Pissarides, C. (1972), 'A Model of British Macro-Economic Policy, 1955–1969', *Manchester School of Economic and Social Studies* **3**, 245–60.

Roubini, N. (1988), 'Current Account and Budget Deficits in an Intertemporal Model of Consumption and Taxation Smoothing. A Solution to the "Feldstein–Horioka Puzzle"?', National Bureau of Economic Research, Working Paper No. 2773.

Sachs, J. (1981), 'The Current Account and Macroeconomic Adjustment in the 1970s', *Brookings Papers in Economic Activity* **1**, 201–86.

Schmitt, H. (1979), 'Mercantilism: A Modern Argument', *Manchester School of Economic and Social Studies* **47**, 39–111.

Summers, L. (1988), 'Tax Policy and International Competitiveness', in J. Frenkel (ed.), *Aspect of Fiscal Policies*, Chicago: Chicago University Press.

Tesar, L. (1988), 'Savings, Investment and International Capital Flows', University of Rochester, Working Paper No. 154.

Vines, D. and A. Stevenson (eds.) (1991), *Information, Strategy and Public Policy*, Oxford: Blackwell.

Weale, Martin, Andrew Blake, Nicos Christodoulakis, James Meade and David Vines (1989), *Macroeconomic Policy, Inflation, Wealth and the Exchange Rate*, London: Unwin Hyman.

Discussion

CHARLES WYPLOSZ

This chapter offers an interesting overview of the literature, both theoretical and empirical, on international capital mobility. It is indeed a good idea to put in perspective the country case studies which follow by linking the external constraint to the degree of capital mobility.

The authors make two useful observations. First, they remind us that, in the presence of full capital mobility, there is no external constraint, there is just a solvency constraint. Then, when (if) the public and private sectors look after their solvency – or are made to look after it by their debtors – the current account is irrelevant. With limited capital mobility, there may occur liquidity constraints and the current account becomes a public good, the focal point of a borrowing externality.

Second, Artis and Bayoumi note that the degree of capital mobility can be assessed from two angles. A direct approach asks whether asset returns are equalized internationally *ex ante*. An indirect approach seeks to find out if borrowing/lending activities are constrained. The problem, as we know, is that the direct approach requires that we estimate expected exchange rate changes (and possibly expected inflation rates) and that we account for currency-specific risk premia. Years of active and increasingly sophisticated empirical research have not turned up any fully convincing evidence. My own reading is that time-varying risk premia exist, but are relatively small in comparison to expectational errors.[1] In the end, evidence supports a high degree of capital mobility among countries which do not use explicit restrictions.

Because the authors apparently do not trust these results, they focus here on the indirect approach, dominated by the Feldstein–Horioka puzzle. This indirect approach rests on the premise that, under full capital mobility, the correlation, both over time and among countries, between saving and investment should be zero. As we know, the evidence is that this correlation is empirically close to unity. However, Frankel (1988) shows that two steps are required to go from the hypothesis of full capital mobility to the assumption that investment and savings are not correlated. First, it must be that full capital mobility implies *ex-ante* equalization of real interest rates. This is only true if goods markets are perfectly integrated so that PPP holds. We know that PPP does not hold in practice, except maybe in the very long run. Second, assuming that real interest rates are equal, we need zero correlation between savings and innovations in investment. If savings and investment are, for example, affected by cyclical conditions, we do not expect to find a zero correlation between savings and investment. As a result, the indirect approach tests several hypotheses (full capital mobility, perfect goods markets integration, and no correlation between savings and innovations in investment), and is thus very indirect indeed.

Artis and Bayoumi ask why the correlation between saving and investment is almost always near unity but has declined over the 1980s. They explore three possible explanations. The first one is that capital mobility has increased. The second one, which they call private sector behaviour, relies upon a non-zero correlation between savings and innovations in investment. The last explanation focuses on a variant of the second one, the possibility that governments target the current account and thus tend to systematically offset private sector imbalances. They conclude in favour of the last explanation.

The problem – and they come close to acknowledging it – with both the observation that the correlation between saving and investment has declined over the 1980s, and their conclusion, is that they rest heavily on the massive twin (budget and current account) deficits of the US since 1981. They feel reassured by their large data set which relies on quarterly data. Table 2.1, however, shows clearly that over the whole period 1965–90 we really have one observation: the US deficits of the 1980s. High frequency data do not add any degrees of freedom when we have *one* very low frequency observation.

While they may be right and governments may be unduly concerned with current accounts, I do not think that the conclusion is warranted yet. It rests primarily on the elimination on the two other hypotheses: that capital is immobile and that private behaviour does not lead to response of savings to investment innovations. I already noted that the direct approach is supportive of the first hypothesis. This leaves us with the second hypothesis. Artis and Bayoumi rule it out by looking at estimates of Euler equations and being unconvinced by what they see. Yet, a simple thought experiment might be illuminating.

Imagine Robinson Crusoe on his island. True, as long as he is alone, saving must equal investment. If he can borrow or lend, investment may be, say, higher than saving. This would occur if Robinson Crusoe found that the (marginal) expected return on investment in his island exceeded the (marginal) cost of borrowing. In steady state, both should be equal so that investment is equal to saving, even though Robinson Crusoe carefully computes his Euler condition. If the real world is not too far away from steady state, perfect capital mobility takes the form of portfolio diversification and equality between investment and net savings in each country.

This observation suggests that, maybe, in the 1960s most countries were close to their steady state paths – or felt that way – and the necessary global equality between saving and investment occurred at the country level. To be sure, there were asymmetric shocks and countries away from steady state because of their initial conditions (many LDCs) but these shocks and countries did not weigh much financially. Interestingly, Artis and Bayoumi find almost no correlation between saving and investment from 1880 to 1913, at the time when the industrial revolution was still spreading and the US growing fast. Nor should we be surprised that in the post-oil shocks period significant deviations from steady state occurred. (I guess that the entry of Eastern Europe to the club of capitalist countries will also help break down the Feldstein–Horioka result.)

Finally, Artis and Bayoumi choose to interpret the strong negative correlation between public and private net savings as providing support to their preferred hypothesis, namely that governments act to smooth out current account imbalances which automatically leads to the near equality between total savings and investment. In doing so, they overlook an alternative interpretation. The Ricardian equivalence asserts that it is the private sector which offsets public actions. While I would not wish to assert that the Ricardian equivalence is a good starting point, I find their dismissal of this hypothesis a bit rushed.

In conclusion, this chapter provides a good background for the book. The authors have carefully summarized the literature and add their own evidence to what has already been accumulated by many others. I have much sympathy for their two substantive conclusions: that capital is highly mobile internationally, and that governments' concern with their current accounts are the key explanation of the Feldstein–Horioka puzzle. Too bad that these conclusions do not flow more directly from their data.

NOTE

1 This result is most clearly established by Frankel and Froot (1987).

REFERENCES

Frankel, J. (1988), 'Quantifying International Capital Mobility in the 1980s', mimeo.
Frankel, J. and K. Froot (1987), Using Survey Data to Test Standard Propositions regarding Exchange Rate Expectations', *American Economic Review* 77, 133–53.

3 The solvency constraint and fiscal policy in an open economy

DAVID CURRIE and PAUL LEVINE

1 Introduction

A feature of the early open economy models from Mundell–Fleming through to Dornbusch is the neglect of current account dynamics. In Dornbusch (1976) a fiscal expansion causes an immediate appreciation of the exchange rate to a new long-run equilibrium. If in this policy scenario the current account was in balance before the fiscal shock, then the new equilibrium will be associated with a current account deficit; if the fiscal shock is permanent, so too is the current account deficit.

In a growing economy in which the growth rate is greater than the real interest rate incurred by the nation's liabilities, the debt-to-income ratio is prevented from escalating upwards if the fiscal-monetary mix is such that the trade balance-to-income ratio is stabilized. Overall stability (or, in Dornbusch-type models, saddlepath stability) is then sufficient to achieve a stable debt-to-income ratio. In this rather special case policy studies which ignore current account dynamics are valid (Buiter and Miller, 1982; Levine and Currie, 1985, for example).

This paper is concerned with the open economy in which the real interest rate exceeds the growth rate in the long run. It examines fiscal policy in the form of the government's intertemporal choice of spending and borrowing, keeping tax rates fixed. The primary objective of the chapter is to highlight the importance of the consistent modelling of the intertemporal budget or solvency constraints, for both the government and the nation, in the analysis of policy options.

The government budget *identity* and the nation's balance of payments *identity* are transformed into intertemporal *constraints* by solvency conditions, which we take to be stable liability or asset-to-income ratios. Those solvency conditions require of a debtor government or nation to generate primary surpluses sometime in the future. The importance of these constraints on fiscal and monetary policy is, of course, well known

41

and has been highlighted by some notable studies including Sargent and Wallace (1981) and a series of papers in Buiter (1990).

Much of this literature assumes that the government acts in a rather mechanical way, engaging in arbitrary changes to fiscal and monetary policy. In this chapter we assume that the fiscal authority is an intertemporal optimizing agent. Within such a framework reputational issues may be examined, especially in the way they relate to the budget solvency constraint facing the policy-maker. A further important distinction is drawn between the average (deterministic) path of the economy which is determined by the government's ambitious output target and the stabilization of the economy about that path in the face of random shocks.

The plan of the chapter is as follows. Section 2 sets out the government budget and balance of payments identities and transforms them into solvency constraints. Section 3 describes a fairly conventional 'textbook' macromodel of an open economy with capital accumulation and with uncovered interest rate parity and rational expectations assumed in the foreign exchange market. Section 4 examines national solvency in the simplest case of fiscal inactivism and no capital accumulation.

Section 5 considers optimal fiscal policy under the assumption that the policy-maker can credibly precommit herself to the resulting optimal rule. Section 6 addresses the case where the policy-maker lacks a reputation for precommitment and is consequently constrained to a fiscal rule which is time-consistent. The particular problems associated with time-consistency and the government solvency constraint are examined in this section. Section 7 concludes the chapter.

2   The public sector and national budget constraints

Assume that the asset portfolios of the private sector consist of domestic government bonds, private sector traded bonds, domestic money, and domestic equity. There is no currency substitution nor holdings of overseas equity but domestic and foreign bonds are perfect substitutes. All bonds are denominated in the currency of the home country and earn the same nominal rate of interest, i_t.

The government issues real debt D_t denominated in its own currency and held only by domestic residents. Then the government budget identity is

$$\Delta M_t + \Delta(P_t D_t) = P_t(G_t - T_t) + i_t P_t D_t \tag{1}$$

where G_t is real government spending on goods and services, T_t is total real taxation, net of transfers, i_t is the nominal short-term interest rate and M_t is base money. The national budget identity is

$$\Delta(P_t F_t) = P_t T B_t + i_t P_t F_t \tag{2}$$

where TB_t is the real trade balance and F_t are the private sector real claims on the rest of the world.

It is convenient to work in terms of asset-to-GDP ratios; $d_t = D_t/Y_t$, $m_t = M_t/P_t Y_t$, $f_t = F_t/Y_t$. Then (1) becomes

$$m_{t+1} + d_{t+1} = \frac{1}{(1 + \pi_t)(1 + n_t)} ((1 + i_t)d_t + g_t - t_t + m_t) \qquad (3)$$

where $g_t = G_t/Y_t$, and $t_t = T_t/Y_t$, $\pi_t = (P_{t+1} - P_t)/P_t$ is inflation during period t and $n_t = (Y_{t+1} - Y_t)/Y_t$ is GDP growth.

We now linearize about a steady state in which government debt is paid off and where steady-state values of π_t and n_t, $\bar\pi$ and $\bar n$ say, are small. Then ignoring second-order terms in $\bar\pi$ and $\bar n$, (3) becomes

$$d_{t+1} = (1 + \bar g)d_t + pd_t - [\Delta m_t + (\bar\pi + \bar n)m_t] \qquad (4)$$

where $\bar g = \bar\imath - \bar\pi - \bar n$ is the long-run real interest rate minus the growth rate and $pd_t = (1 - \bar\pi - \bar n)(g_t - t_t)$ is the primary deficit of the government adjusted for the fact that it is expressed as a proportion of nominal GDP. All variables in (4) are now expressed in deviation form about their long-run values.

Similarly we linearize (2) about a long run in which no foreign debt is incurred and $\bar\pi$ and $\bar n$ are small. Then

$$f_{t+1} = (1 + \bar g)f_t + tb_t \qquad (5)$$

where $tb_t = (1 - \bar\pi - \bar n)TB_t/Y_t$ is the trade balance as a proportion of GDP adjusted in the same way as for the government primary deficit. All variables in (5) are expressed in deviation form about long-run values.

The subsequent analysis turns on the sign of $\bar g$. If GDP growth in the long run exceeds the real interest rate then $\bar g < 0$ and *any* stable path for the public sector deficit minus seigniorage taxes is consistent with a stable government debt-to-GDP ratio. Similarly any stable path for the trade balance as a proportion of GDP is consistent with a stable overseas asset-to-GDP ratio. If, on the other hand, $\bar g > 0$ we can solve (4) forward in time to give

$$d_t = - \sum_{i=0}^{\infty} \frac{pd_{t+i} - [\Delta m_{t+i} + (\bar\pi + \bar n)m_{t+i}]}{(1 + \bar g)^{i+1}} \qquad (6)$$

provided $\lim_{i \to \infty} \dfrac{d_{t+i}}{(1 + \bar g)^i} = 0$. Similarly for (5) we have

$$f_t = - \sum_{i=0}^{\infty} \frac{tb_{t+i}}{(1 + \bar g)^{i+1}} \qquad (7)$$

Table 3.1. *Comparisons of real interest rates for the G7 and individual growth rates, 1970–78*

	Ex post real interest rate $i - \pi$ % average for G7	Annual GDP growth rates %						
		US	FRG	Japan	UK	France	Italy	Canada
1970	2.2	− 0.3	5.0	10.8	2.2	5.7	5.3	2.6
1971	0.6	2.8	3.0	4.4	2.0	4.8	1.6	5.8
1972	0.7	5.0	4.2	8.5	3.0	4.4	3.2	5.7
1973	1.2	5.2	4.7	7.9	7.4	5.4	7.0	7.7
1974	− 1.9	− 0.5	0.2	− 1.4	− 1.9	3.1	4.1	4.4
1975	− 3.4	− 1.3	− 1.4	2.7	− 0.9	− 0.3	− 3.6	2.6
1976	− 0.8	4.9	5.6	4.8	2.8	4.2	5.9	6.2
1977	− 1.5	4.7	2.7	5.3	2.3	3.2	1.9	3.6
1978	0.6	5.3	3.3	5.2	3.7	3.4	2.7	4.6
1979	0.6	2.5	4.0	5.3	2.7	3.2	4.9	3.9
1980	0.6	− 0.2	1.5	4.3	− 2.3	1.6	3.9	1.5
1981	2.3	1.9	0.0	3.7	− 1.2	1.2	1.1	3.7
1982	4.9	− 2.5	− 1.0	3.1	1.8	2.5	0.2	− 3.2
1983	4.9	3.6	1.9	3.2	3.7	0.7	1.1	3.2
1984	5.4	6.8	3.3	5.1	2.2	1.3	3.2	6.3
1985	4.8	3.4	1.9	4.9	3.5	1.7	2.9	4.6
1986	5.1	2.8	2.3	2.4	3.2	2.1	2.9	3.2
1987	4.0	3.4	1.8	4.3	4.3	2.3	3.1	4.0

Source: OECD *Economic Outlook*.

provided $\lim_{i \to \infty} \dfrac{f_{t+i}}{(1 + \bar{g})^i} = 0.$

Equation (6) expresses the intertemporal budget or 'solvency' constraint facing the government when $\bar{g} > 0$. It says that the current government debt as a proportion of GDP must be equal to the present value of future government surpluses (including seigniorage), also expressed as a proportion of GDP, discounted at a rate $\bar{g}$. A government in debt with $d_t > 0$ must sometime in the future run primary surpluses. This contrasts with the situation of $\bar{g} < 0$ where a government in debt only needs to stabilize its borrowing-to-GDP ratio to achieve a stable debt-to-GDP ratio and need never run surpluses.

Similarly (7) expresses the budget of solvency constraint facing the nation for $\bar{g} > 0$. The current net external debt as a proportion of GDP must be equal to the present value of future primary surpluses (also as a proportion of GDP) discounted at a rate $\bar{g}$. A debtor country with $f_t < 0$

must sometime in the future run primary trade surpluses. If $\bar{g} < 0$ a debtor country only needs to stabilize its trade balance GDP ratio to achieve a stable debt-to-GDP ratio.

The solvency conditions (6) and (7) follow from the asset accumulation identities (4) and (5) provided that the asset-to-GDP ratios eventually grow at a rate slower than $\bar{g}$. Certainly if these ratios d_t and f_t are *stable* then solvency is ensured. In what follows we shall associate solvency with this stronger stability condition.

Both theory and empirical evidence seems to suggest that $\bar{g} > 0$. The Ramsey problem of the optimal intertemporal choice of savings and consumption leads to the 'modified golden rule' that $\bar{g}$, the real interest rate minus the growth rate, should equal the rate of time preference of consumers (see Blanchard and Fischer, 1989, Chapter 2, for example). Regarding empirical data, Table 3.1 compares annual individual GDP growth rates for the G7 countries with global real *ex post* short-term interest rates. The underlined growth rates indicate where growth rates dip below real interest rates. What is apparent is that the 1970s decade was one in which $g_t < 0$ whereas in the 1980s $g_t > 0$.

3   The model

The analysis and simulations are conducted using a single open economy model. Expectations are assumed to be rational only in the foreign exchange market. Thus consumption, investment, and wage setting are not forward-looking in character. Consumption is affected by wealth which includes capital stock. Nominal wages are perfectly indexed to the consumer price index. The government and national solvency constraints discussed in the previous section are fully incorporated into the model.

The details of the model are as follows:

Demand

$$Y_{dt} = C(Y_{dt}, R_t, A_t) + I(R_t) + X(Q_t, Y_t^*) - Q_t M(Q_t, Y_{dt}) + G_t \quad (8)$$

where $C_1, C_3, X_1, X_2, M_2 > 0$; $C_2, I^1, M_1 < 0$, Y_d is aggregate demand, C is consumption, R is the expected real interest rate, A is private sector wealth, I is investment, X denotes exports, Y^* is foreign demand, M denotes imports, Q is competitiveness, and G is government spending. Tax rates are held fixed. All variables are in real terms. An assumption implied by (8) is that imports consist only of consumption goods; that is capital accumulation takes the form of accumulation of domestic output only.

Supply

$$Y_{st} = F(K_t, L_t) = L_t g(K_t/L_t) \qquad (9)$$

$$L_t = f(W_t/P_{dt}, \bar{K}), f^1 < 0 \qquad (10)$$

$$W_t/P_t = \text{constant} \qquad (11)$$

$$P_t = P_{dt}^\theta (P_t^* E_t)^{1-\theta} \qquad (12)$$

where Y_s is aggregate supply, θ is a constant, K is capital stock, L is employment, P_d is the price level of domestically produced goods, W is the nominal wage, P is the consumer price index, P^* is the price of imported goods, and E is the nominal exchange rate. Cost-competitiveness is given by $Q = P^* E/P$.

Equation (9) is a neo-classical production function, (10) is the labour demand curve for a profit-maximizing firm, where capital and labour demand decisions are made in a recursive fashion, the latter being made with capital stock assumed to be along its long-term trend $\bar{K}$. Equation (11) says that nominal wages are perfectly indexed to the consumer price index which is given by a geometrically weighted average of the domestic price level and the price of imported goods in domestic currency, equation (12).

Output market equilibrium

$$Y_{st} = Y_{dt} \qquad (13)$$

Asset accumulation

Private sector wealth is given by

$$A_t = K_t + M_t + F_t + D_t \qquad (14)$$

where capital accumulation is given by

$$\Delta K_t = K_{t+1} - K_t = I_t - \delta K_t \qquad (15)$$

where δ is the rate of depreciation of the capital stock. The government solvency constraint and the national solvency constraint of Section 2 complete the asset accumulation side of the model.

Exchange rate

The dynamics of competitiveness is given by the familiar UIP condition

$$(Q^e_{t+1,t} - Q_t)/Q_t = R_t - R^*_t \tag{16}$$

where R^*_t is the foreign expected real interest rate and $(Q^e_{t+1,t})$ denotes rational expectations of Q_{t+1} formed at time t.

Linearization

The linearized model takes the form

$$y_{dt} = -\alpha_1 r_t + \alpha_2 a_t + \alpha_3(tb_t + g_t) \tag{17}$$

$$tb_t = \beta_1 q_t - \beta_2 y_t + \beta_3 y^*_t \tag{18}$$

$$y_{st} = \alpha \bar{k}_t + (1 - \alpha) l_t + as_t \tag{19}$$

where $\bar{k}_t = \xi k_t + y_t$

$$l_t = -\eta(w_t - p_{dt}) \tag{20}$$

$$w_t - p_t = 0 \tag{21}$$

$$p_t = p_{dt} + \frac{(1 - \theta)}{\theta} q_t \tag{22}$$

$$q_t = p^*_t + e_t - p_t \tag{23}$$

$$y_{st} = y_{dt} \tag{24}$$

$$a_t = k_t + m_t + f_t + d_t \tag{25}$$

$$k_{t+1} = (1 - \bar{n} - \delta)k_t - \mu_1 r_t - \mu_2 y_t \tag{26}$$

$$f_{t+1} = (1 + \bar{g})f_t + tb_t \tag{27}$$

$$d_{t+1} = (1 + \bar{g})d_t + pd_t - st_t \tag{28a}$$

where

$$pd_t = (1 - \bar{\imath} - \bar{\pi})(g_t - \tau y_t) \tag{28b}$$

$$st_t = \Delta m_t + (\bar{\pi} + \bar{n})m_t \tag{28c}$$

$$q^e_{t+1,t} - q_t = r_t - r^*_t \tag{29}$$

where $y_t = \log Y/\bar{Y} \simeq (Y - \bar{Y})/\bar{Y}$ with q_t, y^*_t, l_t, w_t, p_{dt}, p_t, e_t defined similarly; $a_t = A_t/Y_t - \bar{A}/\bar{Y}$, tb_t, g_t, k_t, m_t, f_t, d_t defined similarly; $r = R - \bar{R}, r^* = R^* - \bar{R}^*$. Bars denote long-run equilibria. $TB = X - QM$ denotes the trade balance and as_t is an aggregate supply shock. The parameters can be expressed in terms of structural parameters of the original model, details of which are given in the Appendix.

4 National solvency without stabilization policy

We now pose the following question: is this partially rational model consistent with national solvency in the absence of fiscal or monetary policy intervention? To keep the analysis tractable we ignore capital formation putting $k_t = 0$. Fiscal and monetary policy instruments are held fixed at their long-run values. Thus $g_t = \tau_t = d_t = \Delta M_t = 0$ and ignoring the contribution of money holdings in wealth we may approximate $a_t = f_t$. With those assumptions the model becomes

$$y_{dt} = -\alpha_1 r_t + \alpha_2 f_t + \alpha_3(\beta_1 q_t - \beta_2 y_{dt} + \beta_3 y_t^*) \tag{30}$$

$$y_{st} = -[(1-\alpha)\eta(1-\theta)/\theta]q_t + as_t \tag{31}$$

$$y_{dt} = y_{st} \tag{32}$$

$$f_{t+1} = (1+\bar{g})f_t + \beta_1 q_t - \beta_2 y_{dt} + \beta_3 y_t^* \tag{33}$$

$$q_{t+1,t}^e - q_t = r_t - r_t^* \tag{34}$$

Solving (30) for y_{dt} we have

$$y_{dt} = -\alpha_4 r_t + \alpha_5 f_t + \alpha_6 q_t + \alpha_7 y_t^* \tag{35}$$

where $\alpha_4 = (1+\alpha_3\beta_2)^{-1}\alpha_1$, $\alpha_5 = (1+\alpha_3\beta_2)^{-1}\alpha_2$, $\alpha_6 = (1+\alpha_3\beta_2)^{-1}\alpha_3\beta_1$ and $\alpha_7 = (1+\alpha_3\beta_2)^{-1}\alpha_3\beta_3$. Using the equilibrium relationship (32) we may eliminate r_t from (30) and (31) to give

$$\begin{aligned} r_t &= \alpha_4^{-1}(\alpha_5 f_t + (\alpha_6 + \alpha_8)q_t + \alpha_7 y_t^* - as_t) \\ &= \gamma_1 f_t + \gamma_2 q_t + \gamma_3 y_t^* - \gamma_4 as_t \end{aligned} \tag{36}$$

where $\alpha_8 = (1-\alpha)\eta(1-\theta)/\theta$.

Hence (33) and (34) become

$$f_{t+1} = (1+\bar{g})f_t + (\beta_1 + \beta_2\alpha_8)q_t - \beta_2 as_t + \beta_3 y_t^* \tag{37}$$

$$q_{t+1,t}^e = \gamma_1 f_t + (1+\gamma_2)q_t + \gamma_3 y_t^* - \gamma_4 as_t - r_t^* \tag{38}$$

which may be expressed in state–space form as

$$\begin{bmatrix} f_{t+1} \\ q_{t+1,t}^e \end{bmatrix} = \begin{bmatrix} 1+\bar{g} & \beta_1 + \beta_2\alpha_8 \\ \gamma_1 & 1+\gamma_2 \end{bmatrix} \begin{bmatrix} f_t \\ q_t \end{bmatrix}$$

$$+ \begin{bmatrix} -\beta_2 & \beta_3 & 0 \\ -\gamma_4 & \gamma_3 & -1 \end{bmatrix} \begin{bmatrix} as_t \\ y_t^* \\ r_t^* \end{bmatrix} \tag{39}$$

The system given by (39) has one predetermined state variable f_t and one non-predetermined 'jump' variable q_t. It is saddlepath stable if the transition matrix has one eigenvalue within the unit circle and one outside the unit circle.

The characteristic equation is

$$\psi(\lambda) = (1 + \bar{g} - \lambda)(1 + \gamma_2 - \lambda) - (\beta_1 + \beta_2 \alpha_8)\gamma_1$$
$$= \lambda^2 - (2 + \bar{g} + \gamma_2)\lambda + (1 + \bar{g})(1 + \gamma_2) - (\beta_1 + \beta_2 \alpha_8)\gamma_1 \quad (40)$$

It can be shown that (40) has one root inside and one root outside the unit circle if and only if $\psi(1)\psi(-1) < 0$. This gives the necessary and sufficient condition for saddlepath stability as

$$\bar{g}\gamma_2 < (\beta_1 + \beta_2 \alpha_8)\gamma_1 < 4 + 2(\bar{g} + \gamma_2) + \bar{g}\gamma_2 \quad (41)$$

or in terms of the original parameters of the model

$$\bar{g}(\alpha_6 + \alpha_8) < (\beta_1 + \beta_2 \alpha_8)\alpha_5 < \alpha_4(4 + 2(\bar{g} + \alpha_4^{-1}(\alpha_6 + \alpha_8))) \quad (42)$$

We can understand condition (41) (or equivalently (42)) by suppressing exogenous shocks and solving the exchange rate equation (38) forward in time (assuming saddlepath stability) to give

$$q_t = -\frac{\gamma_1}{(1 + \gamma_2)}\left(f_t + \frac{1}{(1 + \gamma_2)}f^e_{t+1,t} + \frac{1}{(1 + \gamma_2)^2}f^e_{t+2,t} + \cdots\right)$$

Thus the real exchange rate depreciates strongly in response to a drop in foreign assets (q_t rises) if $\gamma_1 = \alpha_4^{-1}\alpha_5$ is high and/or $\gamma_2 = \alpha_4^{-1}(\alpha_6 + \alpha_8)$ is low. The wealth effect in consumption is captured by the parameter α_5. A drop in foreign assets reduces demand and the expected real interest rate falls provided the real exchange rate effects on output ($\alpha_6 + \alpha_8$ in (36)) are not excessively strong. The real exchange rate then depreciates, output (seen from the supply side) falls and the trade balance moves strongly into surplus, as required by the national solvency condition, if the responses of tb_t to a depreciation of the real exchange rate and to a drop in output (captured by parameters β_1 and β_2 respectively) are sufficiently strong. This explains the first part of the inequality in (42). If the wealth effect is not excessive the second part of the inequality is easily satisfied and we do not consider it further. Finally if $\bar{g} < 0$ or in other words if the real interest rate is less or equal to the growth rate in the long run, then any wealth effect will ensure saddlepath stability.

The phase diagrams for the three cases $\bar{g} > 0$, saddlepath stability; $\bar{g} > 0$, saddlepath instability, and $\bar{g} < 0$, saddlepath stability are shown in Figure 3.1. Suppressing exogenous shocks, partial equilibrium for assets, $\Delta f_t = 0$, gives $f_t = -\bar{g}^{-1}(\beta_1 + \beta_2 \alpha_8)q_t$ and the exchange rate, $\Delta q_t = 0$, gives $f_t = -\gamma_1^{-1}\gamma_2 q_t$. Saddlepath stability then depends on the relative slopes

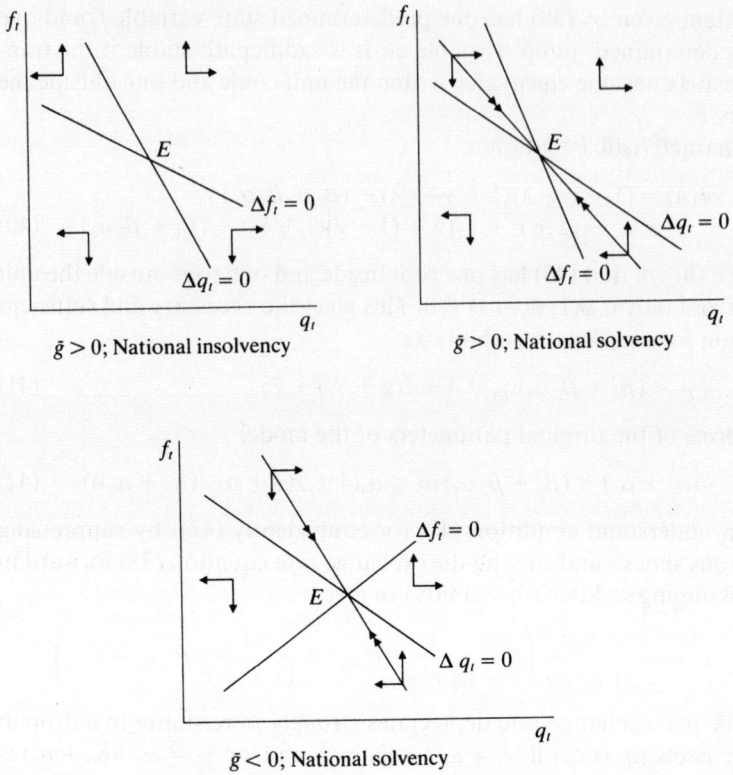

Figure 3.1   The saddlepath condition

of these two partial equilibrium relationships. As Figure 3.1 shows for $\bar{g} > 0$, if

$$\bar{g}^{-1}(\beta_1 + \beta_2 \alpha_8) > \gamma_1^{-1} \gamma_2 \tag{43}$$

or if $\bar{g} < 0$ then a saddlepath solution exists. If the inequality is not satisfied then the model is unstable. Clearly (43) is equivalent to the first part of the inequality in (41).

Finally, how stringent is the saddlepath condition (41)? For plausible parameter values, given in the Appendix (41) reduces to

$$1.80\bar{g} < 1.78\eta_{CA} < 7.6 + 3.8\bar{g} \tag{44}$$

where

$$\eta_{CA} = \frac{\bar{A}}{\bar{C}} \frac{\partial C}{\partial A}$$

is the elasticity of consumption with respect to wealth (evaluated at equilibrium). If $\eta_{CA} < 1$ then the second inequality is easily satisfied. If $\bar{g} < 0.05$ then (44) is satisfied if $\eta_{CA} > 0.051$ which is not a strong wealth effect. For instance in the LBS consumption function (March 1990), $\eta_{CA} = 0.15$ in the long run.

We have shown that if the policy-maker keeps her fiscal instruments fixed at their long-run values where the budget is balanced and the money supply is held fixed, then quite a modest wealth effect in consumption is sufficient to ensure national solvency. It is straightforward to generalize this result to the case where fiscal policy is activist but still ensures a stable government debt-to-income ratio (see the fiscal rules 51a or 51b). In other words government solvency plus a small wealth effect is sufficient to ensure national solvency. This result is analogous to that obtained by Newell and Symons (1990) and Alogoskoufis and Christodoulakis (chapter 9 of the present volume) who in a *forward-looking* context show that the household budget constraint and the government budget together imply the foreign budget constraint. This section has shown that a similar result holds in the case where consumption decisions are *not* forward-looking in character.

5   Fiscal policy with reputation

In this section using the full model, we examine fiscal policy where the government enjoys a reputation for precommitment. First we consider a purely deterministic exercise with the economy at its long-run equilibrium and not subjected to any exogenous shocks. The policy-maker sets a target $\hat{y}$ which denotes a proportional deviation about the original long-run level of output; but the original long-run value for the government spending-to-GDP ratio is at its bliss point. These objectives are captured by a welfare loss function of the form

$$W_0 = \tfrac{1}{2} \sum_{i=0}^{\infty} \lambda^i (a(y_i - \hat{y})^2 + bg_i^2) \tag{45}$$

where W_t denotes the 'cost-to-go' at time t and λ, lying between 0 and 1, is a discount factor.

The optimal policy with reputation may then be found by minimizing W_0 given by (45) subject to the model (17) to (29) with the monetary instrument M_t fixed at its long-run value. Proceeding in this way however will not lead to a stable government debt-to-income ratio d_t; in other words government solvency is not achieved.

There are two ways in which one can now proceed. The first is to recast the optimization problem with a finite time horizon T and impose a constraint at time $t = T$ that the debt-to-income ratio is constant. From (28) (with monetary policy fixed) this implies that

$$d_{T-1} - d_T = \bar{g}d_T + (1 + \bar{\imath} - \bar{\pi})(g_T - \tau y_T) = 0 \qquad (46)$$

The problem is now transformed from a 'free-final-state' optimization exercise to one where the final state is constrained. The problem is

$$\min_{\{g_i\}} \sum_{i=0}^{T} \lambda^i (a(y_i - \hat{y})^2 + bg_i^2) \qquad (47)$$

subject to the model plus the terminal condition (46).

The solution has a highly undesirable characteristic – the optimal instrument path for g_t is crucially dependent upon the selected terminal date T. As $T \to \infty$ the debt-to-income ratio becomes unstable and we arrive at the solution described above with government insolvency.

The second and preferred way of imposing government solvency is to remain within an infinite time horizon framework and add a term in the welfare loss function that penalizes large departures of the debt-to-income ratio from its long-run value. The loss function now becomes

$$W_0 = \tfrac{1}{2} \sum_{i=0}^{\infty} \lambda^i (a(y_i - \hat{y})^2 + bg_i^2 + cd_i^2) \qquad (48)$$

The weight on d_i^2 is chosen to be small but sufficiently large to ensure stability of the debt-to-income ratio. For no discounting ($\lambda = 1$) it is a standard result in control theory that any $c > 0$ will ensure stability. For $\lambda < 1$ (which we assume), c must be sufficiently large, although for λ close to 1 a small value (relative to the other weights in (48), a and b) is sufficient.

The optimization problem now is to minimize (48) subject to the model but evaluate the actual welfare using the original loss function (45). The solution procedure for evaluating the optimal policy with precommitment given a linear rational expectations model is now commonplace in the policy literature (see, for example, Levine, 1988, for a detailed description of both the reputational and non-reputational optimization problems).

The complexity of the model precludes an analytical solution for the optimal policy so we report numerical simulations using the ACES software (Gaines, al-Nowaihi, and Levine, 1989). The parameter values chosen for the model are given in the Appendix. For the welfare loss function we put $\lambda = 0.95$ (giving a 5% rate of time preference per year), $\hat{y} = 5$, $b = 1$, $c = 0.1$, and the weight on output takes a range of values: $a = 1, 5, 10, 15$. The output and government spending trade-off is shown in Table 3.2, and Figure 3.2 gives trajectories for key variables for the case of $a = 5$.

The reputational policy involves a precommitment by the policy-maker to an initial lowering of government spending and consequently the public deficit (both as a proportion of GDP). The debt-to-income ratio

Table 3.2. *Cumulative output and cumulative government spending under optimal policy with reputation*

Weight	Cumulative output $= \sum_{i=0}^{T-1} y_i$				Cumulative government spending $= \sum_{i=0}^{T-1} g_i$			
a	$T=5$	$T=10$	$T=25$	$T=100$	$T=5$	$T=10$	$T=25$	$T=100$
1	0.47	0.78	0.69	− 0.64	0.43	1.00	1.08	− 1.15
5	1.65	2.92	2.83	− 3.18	1.10	3.93	5.00	− 5.53
10	2.01	4.77	1.77	− 6.17	2.97	6.60	9.62	− 10.59
15	2.62	6.23	7.85	− 8.92	2.84	8.74	13.80	− 15.18

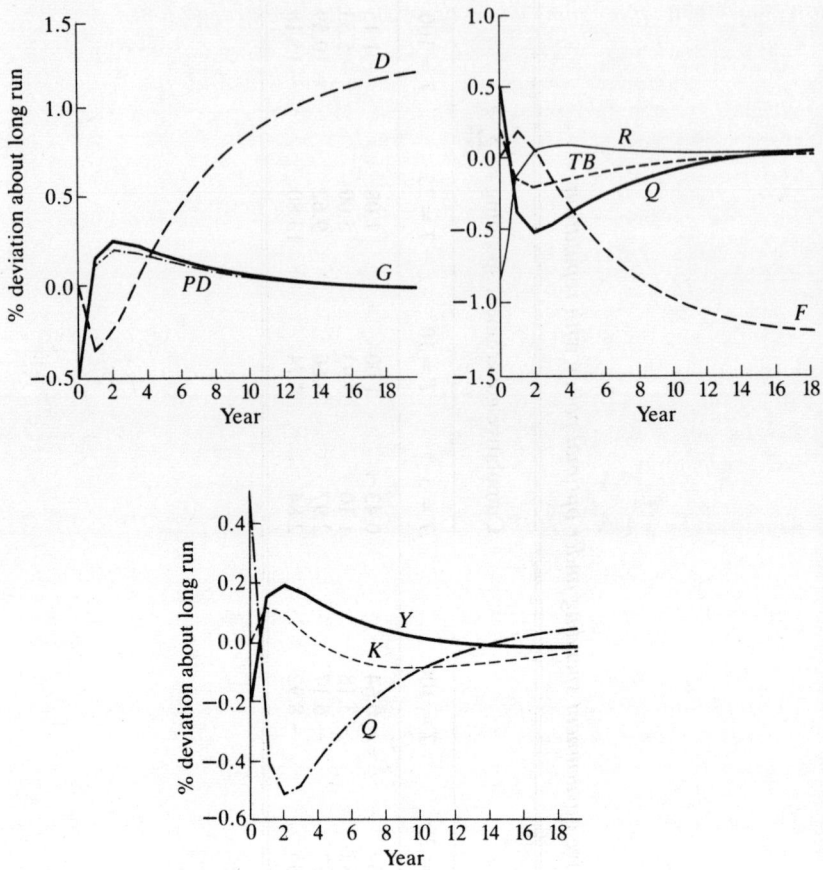

Figure 3.2   Optimal reputational policy

falls and real interest rates also fall initially. Subsequent precommitment is to a raising of the government spending–GDP ratio above its equilibrium which brings about a rise in the real interest rate. The promise of a real interest rate above its equilibrium from about the third year onwards soon causes the real exchange rate to appreciate. The combination of an initially lower real interest rate and an appreciating exchange rate causes the capital stock and output to rise, but the latter after an initial drop (due to an immediate exchange rate depreciation).

From Table 3.2 both cumulative output and government spending rise in the short to medium term but both fall in the very long term. The promise of lower government spending in the long run ensures government

Table 3.3. *Welfare gains under optimal policy with reputation*

Weight	Welfare loss under optimal policy	Welfare loss without fiscal activism	% equivalent output gain
1	248	250	0.02
5	1,207	1,250	0.09
10	2,346	2,500	0.16
15	3,429	3,750	0.22

solvency and the initial fall in real interest rates crowds-in capital accumulation and an increase in output in the medium term. From Table 3.3 for an output target of 5%, the welfare gain (as compared with no intervention) is small and dependent upon the weight attached to output in the welfare criteria.

Stabilization policy

Now consider exogenous shocks to foreign demand, aggregate supply, and the foreign expected real interest rate (y^*, as, and r^* respectively). In principle one could estimate exogenous processes as a system and use the estimated coefficients including the covariance matrix to assess the stabilization gains. In this stylized exercise however we assume shocks to be independent and to follow AR(1) processes

$$y_t^* = \rho_1 y_{t-1}^* + \epsilon_{1t} \tag{49a}$$

$$as_t^* = \rho_2 as_{t-1}^* + \epsilon_{2t} \tag{49b}$$

$$r_t^* = \rho_3 r_{t-1}^* + \epsilon_{3t} \tag{49c}$$

where $\text{var}(\epsilon_{it}) = \sigma_i^2$, $\text{cov}(\epsilon_{it}, \epsilon_{jt}) = 0$, $i \neq j$, and $y_0^* = as_0^* = r_0^* = 0$.

The stochastic welfare loss function is now measured in deviation form about the deterministic equilibrium and is given by $E_0(W_0)$ where

$$W_0 = \tfrac{1}{2} \sum_{i=0}^{\infty} \lambda^i (a y_i^2 + b g_i^2) \tag{50}$$

and where $E_t(W_t)$ denotes the expected welfare loss at time t. Table 3.4 shows the welfare loss under the optimal policy with reputation, starting at equilibrium and following each of the three shocks considered on its own. Parameter values for $E_0(W_0)$ are given by $\lambda = 0.95$, $q = 5$, $b = 1$, $c = 0.1$, and $\sigma_i^2 = 1$.

In order to quantify the stabilization gains a 'no control' benchmark is necessary. With output changing in response to shocks this is no longer as

Table 3.4. *Stabilization welfare gains under optimal policy with reputation*

Disturbance	Welfare loss under optimal policy (1)	Welfare loss with $g_t = 0$ (automatic (stabilizers) (2)	Welfare loss with $psbr = 0$ (3)	% equivalent output gain of (1) cf. with (2)	% equivalent output gain of (1) cf. with (3)
y^*	1.16	2.24	2.82	0.16	0.18
as^*	18.8	35.4	44.8	0.58	0.72
r^*	0.60	1.04	1.32	0.09	0.12

straightforward as for the ambitious output target exercise in Table 3.3. We consider two benchmarks for fiscal policy. The first keeps the government spending to GDP ratio fixed at its long-run value and allows automatic stabilizers to operate. Thus the primary deficit pd_t falls in a boom and rises in a slump. The second benchmark keeps the primary deficit itself fixed at its long-run level. From (28b) this implies that, in effect, fiscal policy follows a rule, $g_t = \tau y_t$ where τ is the difference between the marginal and average rates of tax.

A problem with both these benchmark fiscal stances is that they do not ensure government solvency. This is achieved if we add a small feedback from g_t onto the debt-to-income ratio. (This is analogous to '*ad hoc*' fiscal rules considered by Buiter, 1987.) With these adjustments the two 'no-control' rules become

$$g_t = -\gamma d_t \qquad \text{(automatic stabilizers)} \qquad (51a)$$

$$g_t = \tau y_t - \gamma d_t \qquad (pd_t \simeq 0) \qquad (51b)$$

where $\gamma > \bar{g}$ is sufficient to stabilize the debt-to-income ratio.

From Table 3.4 we observe that the operation of automatic stabilizers brings only small welfare gains compared with targeting the public deficit. Both fiscal regimes are substantially inferior to the optimal policy with precommitment (which in a stochastic environment must be implemented as a feedback rule – see Levine and Currie, 1987). For white-noise disturbances of unit variances the gains from the optimal rule (as compared with the benchmark regime) are greatest for the supply shock; not a surprising result given the supply-side determination of output in both the short term and long term in the model.

Table 3.5. *Cumulative output and cumulative government spending under optimal policy without reputation*

Weight	Cumulative output = $\sum_{i=0}^{T-1} y_i$				Cumulative government spending = $\sum_{i=0}^{T-1} g_i$			
a	$T=5$	$T=10$	$T=25$	$T=100$	$T=5$	$T=10$	$T=25$	$T=100$
1	− 0.95	− 1.01	− 0.57	1.26	− 1.51	− 1.84	− 1.37	2.10
5	− 2.79	− 3.35	− 2.18	4.14	− 4.31	− 5.80	− 4.89	6.93
10	− 3.43	− 4.46	− 3.33	5.63	− 5.18	− 7.48	− 7.10	9.47
15	− 3.44	− 4.71	− 3.92	6.15	− 5.13	− 7.76	− 8.05	10.35

Table 3.6. *Welfare gains under optimal policy without reputation*

Weight	Welfare loss under optimal policy	Welfare loss without fiscal activism	% equivalent output gain
1	253	250	− 0.02
5	1,308	1,250	− 0.11
10	2,658	2,500	− 0.15
15	4,005	3,750	− 0.17

6   Fiscal policy without reputation

We now repeat the policy exercises of the previous section but in the case where the government does not have a reputation for precommitment. Assuming, for the moment, the same welfare loss function which penalizes an escalating debt-to-income ratio the policy-maker minimizes at time t a loss function W_t (or $E_t(W_t)$ for a stochastic setting) such that

$$W_t = U_t + \lambda W_{t+1} \qquad (52)$$

where U_t is the single-period welfare loss and W_{t+1} is evaluated on the assumption that an identical optimization exercise is carried out from time $t + 1$ onwards. The solution to this optimization problem is found by applying Bellman's Principle of Optimality. Unlike the reputational policy it is time-consistent (given the welfare loss function).

The simulation results are shown in Tables 3.5–7 and Figure 3.3. The key difference between the non-reputational, time-consistent policy and the reputational, time-inconsistent policy lies in the paths for the real interest rate and the real exchange rate. The precommitment involved in the

Table 3.7. *Stabilization welfare gains under optimal policy without reputation*

Disturbance	Welfare loss under optimal policy (1)	Welfare loss with $g_t = 0$ (automatic (stabilizers) (2)	Welfare loss with $pd_t = 0$ (3)	% equivalent output gain of (1) cf. with (2)	% equivalent output gain of (1) cf. with (3)
y^*	1.38	2.24	2.82	0.13	0.17
as^*	22.6	35.4	44.8	0.51	0.67
r^*	0.73	1.04	1.32	0.08	0.11

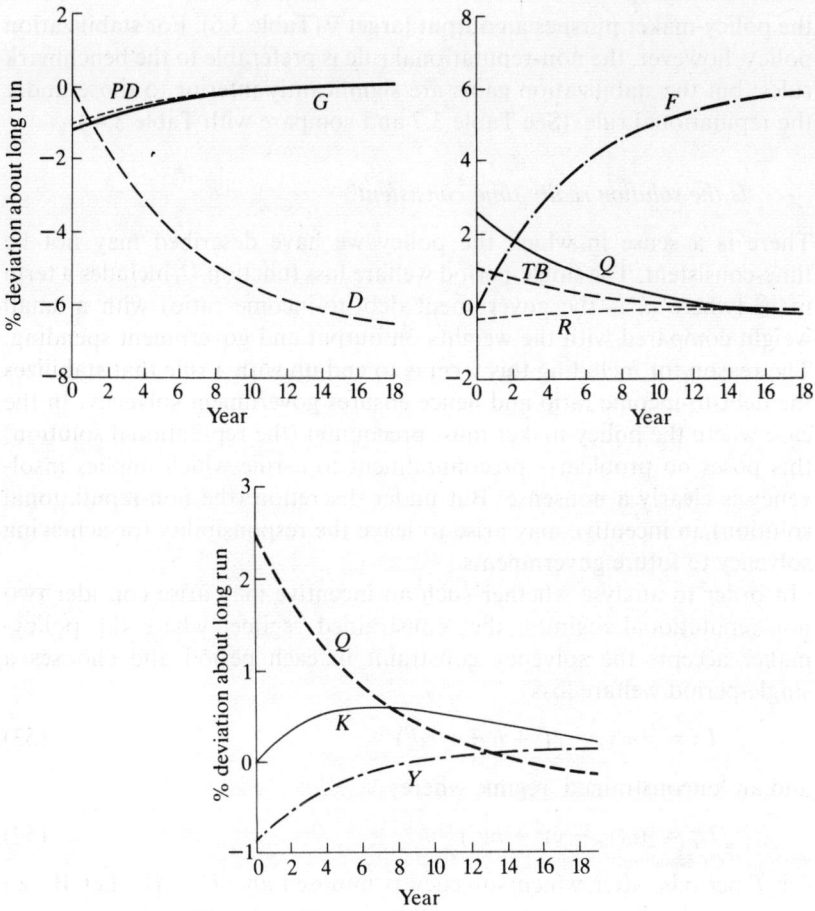

Figure 3.3 Optimal non-reputational policy

reputational policy of lower government spending and real interest rates in the short term, but higher values later is time-inconsistent; there exists an incentive to reoptimize and 'start again'. Ruling out such time-inconsistent behaviour leaves an optimal policy involving a protracted lowering of government spending and a low interest rate. Hence the real exchange rate depreciates. Although capital accumulation is crowded in by lower interest rates, the effect of a lowering of the real exchange rate dominates on the supply side and output experiences a long period of being below its equilibrium before eventually rising above the long-run level. The upshot of these characteristics is that the non-reputational policy is worse than fiscal inactivism for the deterministic exercise where the policy-maker pursues an output target $\hat{y}$ (Table 3.6). For stabilization policy, however, the non-reputational rule is preferable to the benchmark rules; but the stabilization gains are significantly inferior to those under the reputational rule. (See Table 3.7 and compare with Table 3.4.)

Is the solution really time-consistent?

There is a sense in which the policy we have described may not be time-consistent. The single-period welfare loss function U_t includes a term in d_t^2 (where d_t is the government debt-to-income ratio) with a small weight compared with the weights on output and government spending. The reason for including this term is to end up with a rule that stabilizes the debt-to-income ratio and hence ensures government solvency. In the case where the policy-maker must precommit (the reputational solution) this poses no problem – precommitment to a rule which implies insolvency is clearly a nonsense. But under discretion (the non-reputational solution) an incentive may arise to leave the responsibility for achieving solvency to future governments.

In order to analyse whether such an incentive may arise consider two non-reputational regimes; the 'constrained regime' where the policy-maker accepts the solvency constraint in each period and chooses a single-period welfare loss

$$U_t^c = \tfrac{1}{2}(a(y_t - \hat{y})^2 + bg_t^2 + cd_t^2) \tag{53}$$

and an 'unconstrained' regime where

$$U_t^u = \tfrac{1}{2}(a(y_t - \hat{y})^2 + bg_t^2) \tag{54}$$

for T periods, after which solvency is imposed and $U_t = U_t^c$. Let $W_t^c(\mathbf{z}_t)$ and $W_t^u(\mathbf{z}_t)$ be the corresponding welfare losses under the regimes where $\mathbf{z}_t$ is the state vector of predetermined variables (equal to $[k_t, f_t, d_t]$ for our model). Then an incentive to switch regimes does not exist if and only if

$$W_t^c(\mathbf{z}_t) < W_t^u(\mathbf{z}_t) \tag{55}$$

anywhere along the trajectory $\mathbf{z}_t = \mathbf{z}_t^c$ of the constrained regime. Write

$$W_t^c(\mathbf{z}_t) = \sum_{i=0}^{T-1} \lambda^i U_{t+i}^c + \lambda^T W_{t+T}^c(\mathbf{z}_{t+T}^c) \tag{56a}$$

and

$$W_t^u(\mathbf{z}_t) = \sum_{i=0}^{T-1} \lambda^i U_{t+i}^u + \lambda^T W_{t+T}^c(\mathbf{z}_{t+T}^u) \tag{56b}$$

Then (55) is equivalent to

$$\sum_{i=0}^{T-1} \lambda^i (U_{t+i}^c - U_{t+i}^u) < \lambda^T (W_{t+T}^c(\mathbf{z}_{t+T}^u) - W_{t+T}^c(\mathbf{z}_{t+T}^c)) \tag{57}$$

The intuition behind (57) is as follows. The left-hand side represents the discounted single-period gains from abandoning the need to stabilize the debt-to-income ratio for T periods. It represents the *temptation* to leave responsibility for solvency to a future government assuming office after T periods. The right-hand side is the *penalty* which is the discounted difference between the welfare loss under a constraint regime having allowed the debt-to-income ratio to rise (or fall) unchecked for T periods and that having pursued a regime which stabilizes the debt-to-income ratio.

As $T \to \infty$, $W_{t+T}^c(\mathbf{z}_{t+T}^u)$ grows at a rate equal to the unstable eigenvalue under the unconstrained regime, namely $\bar{g}$. Hence, writing $\lambda = 1/(1 + r_g)$ where r_g is the policy-maker's subjective rate of time preference, if $r_g > \bar{g}$ then the penalty approaches zero as T becomes large. Thus if T is sufficiently large and if $r_g > \bar{g}$, then temptation can never be less than the penalty and the constrained regime is not incentive-compatible given the choice of deferring the adjustment towards solvency. But for T sufficiently small $W_{t+T}^c(\mathbf{z}_{t+T}^u)$ may grow at a rate greater than r_g and then (57) is satisfied.

Figure 3.4 shows the rate of growth of $W_T^c(\mathbf{z}_T^u)$ along the unconstrained regime as T, the period for which the debt-to-income ratio is ignored, is increased. This confirms that the cost of adjustment to a solvent regime initially grows, but eventually is dominated by the unstable debt-to-income ratio which asymptotically grows at a rate $\bar{g}$. Thus W_T^c eventually

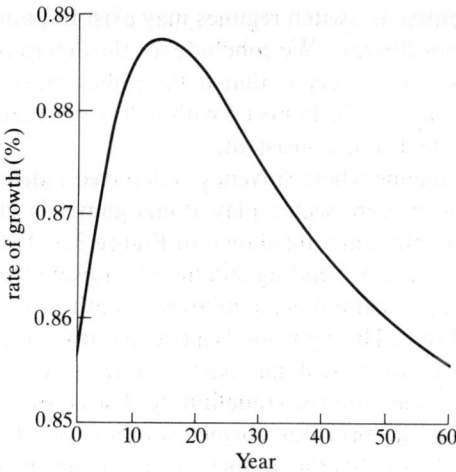

Figure 3.4 The rate of growth of W_T^c

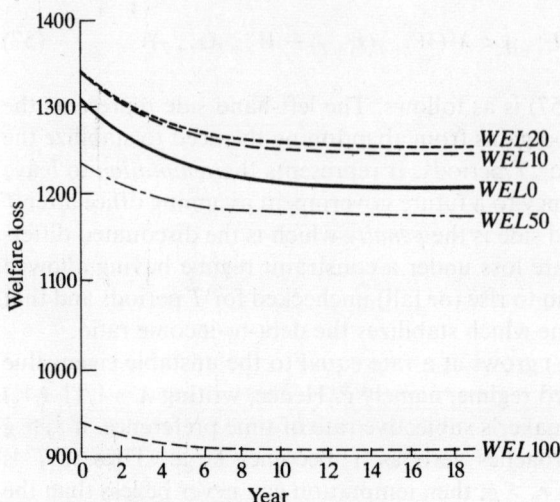

Figure 3.5 The incentive to defer solvency

grows at this rate also. Since we have chosen $r_g > \bar{g}$ ($r_g = 0.05$, $\bar{g} = 0.02$) for the simulations, this implies, from (57), that as T increases, the temptation to defer solvency will dominate the penalty. For T reasonably large however W_T^c grows at a rate greater than $r_g = 5\%$.

In Figure 3.5 the welfare loss along the constrained regime ($WEL0$) is compared with that if a switch to the unconstrained regime is made for 10, 20, 50, and 100 years ($WEL10$, $WEL20$, $WEL50$, $WEL100$ respectively). The graph indicates that an incentive to switch regimes may exist but not if solvency must be restored within 20 years. We conclude for the deterministic problem of pursuing an output target $\hat{y}$, that if the policy-maker knows that the solvency constraint must be imposed within 20 years then the non-reputational policy is in fact time-consistent.

The completely unconstrained regime where solvency is deferred indefinitely and both government and private sector play Ponzi games is of some interest. The trajectories for this case are shown in Figure 3.6. The policy-maker now increases government spending indefinitely, raising the real exchange rate but crowding out capital accumulation – both as the result of a rise in the real interest rate. The net result is a rise in output and a significant welfare gain compared with fiscal inactivism; but the government and the nation's debt-to-income ratio rises indefinitely. The contrast between this bogus solution and the previous correct solutions to the non-reputational optimal policy highlights the importance of incorporating intertemporal budget constraints into macroeconomic models before conducting policy studies.

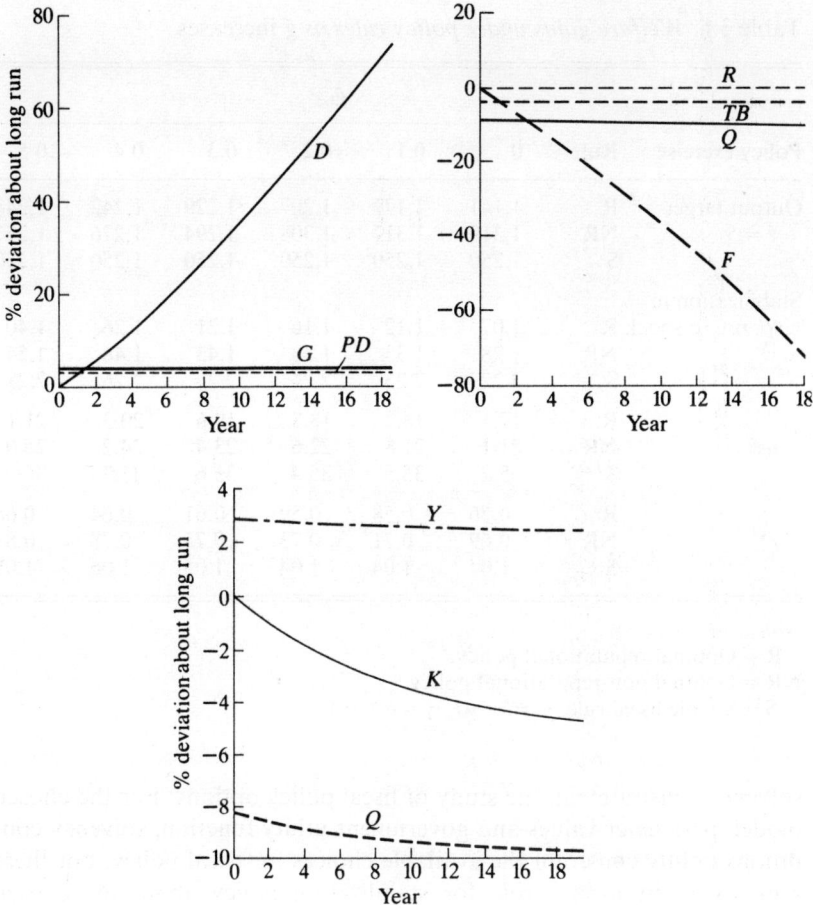

Figure 3.6   Non-reputational policy as a Ponzi game

This point is reinforced by considering what happens as the solvency constraints are gradually relaxed. This occurs as $\bar{g}$ approaches zero and the primary surpluses required to pay off initial liabilities fall. Table 3.8 repeats the previous exercises in the chapter allowing $\bar{g}$ to vary from zero to 0.05. The welfare gains associated with the output target, deterministic component of policy grows significantly; but the stabilization gains, about this deterministic average path, remain of the same order.

7   Conclusions

The chapter has used a simple stylized open economy model to demonstrate the importance of debt dynamics and the government and nation's

Table 3.8. *Welfare gains under policy rules as $\bar{g}$ increases*

Policy exercise	Rule	$\bar{g}$					
		0	0.1	0.2	0.3	0.4	0.5
Output target	R	1,141	1,177	1,207	1,229	1,242	1,248
$\hat{y} = 5$	NR	1,319	1,317	1,308	1,294	1,276	1,257
	S	1,250	1,250	1,250	1,250	1,250	1,250
Stabilization in							
response to shock	R	1.07	1.12	1.16	1.21	1.26	1.40
y^*	NR	1.28	1.33	1.38	1.43	1.48	1.54
	S	2.22	2.23	2.24	2.25	2.26	2.28
	R	17.5	18.2	18.8	19.6	20.3	21.1
as^*	NR	21.1	21.8	22.6	23.4	24.2	25.0
	S	35.2	35.5	35.4	35.6	35.7	35.9
	R	0.56	0.58	0.59	0.61	0.64	0.68
r^*	NR	0.69	0.71	0.73	0.75	0.78	0.83
	S	1.04	1.04	1.04	1.05	1.06	1.08

Notes:
R = Optimal reputational policy.
NR = Optimal non-reputational policy.
S = Simple fiscal rule; $g_t = -\gamma d_t$; $\gamma = \bar{g} + 0.1$.

solvency constraints in the study of fiscal policy options. For the chosen model, parameter values and government utility function, solvency conditions tightly constrain the available choices for fiscal policy, but there remains an important role for stabilization policy about the chosen average, deterministic path. Reputation can significantly improve welfare.

In making comparisons between reputational (time-inconsistent) and non-reputational (time-consistent) policies, the chapter addresses a possible objection to the time-consistent solution that there may exist an incentive to 'defer solvency' in the sense of deferring the achievement of a stable debt-to-income ratio. We show in fact that this incentive does not exist (for our model) provided the policy-maker knows that solvency must be imposed sometime within a given (and in our model, long) time interval.

Interesting extensions of this study would be to re-examine these issues using a more developed model, particularly in respect to the modelling of investment and the real wage. A more drastic alternative would be to treat all agents as forward-looking and rational as in Buiter (1987) and van der Ploeg (1990). The fiscal rules examined in the paper involve policy spillovers in an international context. Thus the chapter leads naturally onto international policy coordination issues. If we consider both fiscal and monetary policy a further coordination issue arises to do with the relationship between the fiscal and monetary authorities. As pointed out by one of the first studies to stress solvency constraints – Sargent and Wallace (1981) – monetary policy conducted by a weak monetary authority, which simply chooses a financing rule given the fiscal deficit, leads to a quite different outcome to that under the discipline of monetary policy leadership. Both these coordination issues have a direct relevance for the conduct of fiscal policy under EMU. (See Currie, Levine, and Pearlman, 1990.)

Appendix   Linearization and calibration

Linearizing (8) about a long-run equilibrium we have

$$y_{dt} = -\alpha_1 r_t + \alpha_2 a_t + \alpha_3(tb_t + g_t) \tag{A1a}$$

where

$$\alpha_3 = 1/(1 - \bar{C}/\bar{Y}(\eta_{CY} + \eta_{CA}) - \bar{G}/\bar{Y}) \tag{A1b}$$

$$\alpha_1 = (\eta_{CR} + \eta_{IR}\bar{I}/\bar{Y})\alpha_3 \tag{A1c}$$

$$\alpha_2 = \eta_{CA}\bar{Y}/\bar{A}\,\alpha_3 \tag{A1d}$$

and $\eta_{CY} = \dfrac{\bar{Y}}{\bar{C}}\dfrac{\partial C}{\partial Y}$ evaluated at equilibrium where bars denote equilibria

values. η_{CA} is defined similarly, $\eta_{CR} = -\dfrac{1}{\bar{C}}\dfrac{\partial C}{\partial R}$ with η_{IR} defined similarly,

$y_{dt} = (Y - \bar{Y})/\bar{Y}$, $r = R - \bar{R}$, $a_t = \dfrac{A}{Y} - \dfrac{\bar{A}}{\bar{Y}}$, $tb = TB/Y - \overline{TB}/\bar{Y} = TB/Y$,

assuming $\overline{TB} = 0$, where $TB = X - QM$ is the trade balance and $g = G/Y - \bar{G}/\bar{Y}$.

Linearizing $TB = X(Q_t, Y_t^*) - Q_t M(Q_t, Y_{dt})$ about a long run with $\overline{TB} = 0$ we have

$$tb_t = \beta_1 q_t - \beta_2 y_t + \beta_3 y_t^* \tag{A2a}$$

where

$$\beta_1 = \bar{X}/\bar{Y}(\eta_{XQ} + \eta_{MQ} - 1) \tag{A2b}$$

$$\beta_2 = \frac{\bar{X}}{\bar{Y}}\,\eta_{MY} \tag{A2c}$$

$$\beta_3 = \bar{X}/\bar{Y}\,\eta_{XY^*} \tag{A2d}$$

where η_{XQ}, η_{MQ}, η_{MY}, and η_{XY^*} are elasticities defined as for η_{CW} and defined to be positive.

Linearizing the supply-side equations

$$y_{st} = \alpha \bar{k}_t + (1 - \alpha) l_t \tag{A3}$$

$$l_t = - \eta(w_t - k_{dt}) \tag{A4}$$

where $\bar{k} = \log K_t \bar{K} \simeq \bar{Y}/\bar{K} k_t + y_t$, $\eta = \dfrac{\bar{W}}{\bar{P}_d \bar{L}} f^1$ is the elasticity of labour demand with respect to the real product wage, and

$$w_t - p_t = 0 \tag{A5}$$

$$p_t = \theta p_{dt} + (1 - \theta)(p_t^* + e_t) \tag{A6}$$

Hence from $q_t = p_t^* + e_t - p_t$ and from (A6) we have that

$$p_t = p_{dt} + (1 - \theta)/\theta q_t \tag{A7}$$

From (15) we have

$$\frac{K_{t+1}}{Y_{t+1}} = \frac{(1 - \delta) K_t + I_t}{Y_t(1 + n_t)} \tag{A8}$$

where $n_t = (Y_{t+1} - Y_t)/Y_t$ is GDP growth. Hence

$$k_{t+1} = (1 - \bar{n} - \delta) k_t + (1 - \bar{n}) i_t \tag{A9}$$

approximately, where $k_t = K_t/Y_t - \bar{K}/\bar{Y}$, $i_t = I_t/Y_t - \bar{I}/\bar{Y}$ and terms in $n_t - \bar{n}$ have been ignored, and

$$i_t = \frac{\bar{I}}{\bar{Y}} (- \eta_{IR} r - y) \tag{A10}$$

Hence combining (A9) and (A10)

$$k_{t+1} = (1 - \bar{n} - \delta) k_t - \mu_1 r - \mu_2 y \tag{A11a}$$

where

$$\mu_1 = (1 - \bar{n}) \frac{\bar{I}}{\bar{Y}} \eta_{IR} \tag{A11b}$$

$$\mu_2 = (1 - \bar{n}) \frac{\bar{I}}{\bar{Y}} \tag{A11c}$$

The long-run values $\bar{K}/\bar{Y}$, $\bar{I}/\bar{Y}$ and $\bar{n}$ are, from (A8), related by

$$\frac{\bar{K}}{\bar{Y}} = \frac{1 - \bar{n}}{\bar{n} + \delta} \frac{\bar{I}}{\bar{Y}} \tag{A11}$$

The public sector borrowing requirement (excluding interest payments) as a proportion of GDP is in deviation form

$$psbr_t = \frac{G_t - T(Y_t)}{Y_t} - \frac{(\bar{G} - \bar{T})}{\bar{Y}}$$

$$\approx g_t - \left[\frac{T'(Y - \bar{Y})}{\bar{Y}} - \frac{\bar{T}}{\bar{Y}^2}(Y - \bar{Y}) \right]$$

$$= g_t - \tau y_t \qquad\qquad (A12)$$

where $\tau = T' - \bar{T}/\bar{Y}$ is the marginal minus the average rate of taxation at equilibrium.

The fundamental parameter values are taken to be $\bar{C}/\bar{Y} = 0.6$, $\bar{I}/\bar{Y} = \bar{G}/\bar{Y} = 0.2$, $\bar{X}/\bar{Y} = \bar{M}/\bar{Y} = 0.3$, $\eta_{CY} = \eta_{XQ} = \eta_{MQ} = \eta_{MY} = \eta_{XY^*} = \eta = 1$, $\eta_{CA} = 0.15$, $\eta_{CR} = 0.10$, $\eta_{IR} = 0.5$; $\alpha = 0.2$, $\theta = 0.7$, $\delta = 0.05$, $\bar{r} = 0.05$, $\bar{n} = 0.03$ and $\tau = 0.2$. (The model is assumed to be annual.) Hence assuming $\bar{F} = \bar{D} = 0$, (A11) gives $\frac{\bar{K}}{\bar{Y}} = \frac{\bar{A}}{\bar{Y}} = 2.425$ and the remaining derived parameters become $\alpha_1 = 1.82$, $\alpha_2 = 0.56$, $\alpha_3 = 9.09$, $\beta_1 = \beta_2 = \beta_3 = 0.3$, $\mu_1 = 0.097$, $\mu_2 = 0.194$ and $\bar{g} = 0.02$.

NOTES

We have benefited from the comments of our discussant, Lucas Papademos and the other participants in the Athens conference. The financial assistance of the ESRC is also acknowledged: this research was carried out under ESRC grant number B01250012. This paper was previously published as Centre for Economic Forecasting Discussion paper No. 09–90.

REFERENCES

Alogoskoufis, G.S. and N. Christodoulakis (1991), 'Fiscal Deficits, Seigniorage and External Debt: the Case of Greece', this volume.

Blanchard, O.J. and S. Fischer (1989), *Lectures on Macroeconomics*, Cambridge, MA: MIT Press.

Buiter, W.H. (1990), *International Macroeconomics*, Oxford: Clarendon Press.

(1987), 'Fiscal Policy in Open, Interdependent Economies', in A. Razin and E. Sadka (eds.), *Economic Policy in Theory and Practice*, New York: St. Martins Press.

Buiter, W.H. and M. Miller (1982), 'Real Exchange Rate Overshooting and the Output Costs of Bringing Down Inflation', *European Economic Review* 18, 85–123.

Currie, D.A., P. Levine, and J. Pearlman (1990), 'European Monetary Union or Hard-EMS?', Centre for Economic Forecasting Discussion Paper No. 05–90, London Business School.

Gaines, J., A. al-Nowaihi, and P. Levine (1988), 'The ACES Package for One Country Rational Expectations Models', Centre for Economic Forecasting, London Business School.

Levine, P. (1988), 'Does Time Inconsistency Matter?', Centre for Economic Policy Research, Discussion Paper No. 227.

Levine, P. and D.A. Currie (1985), 'Optimal Feedback Rules in an Open Economy Macromodel with Rational Expectations', *European Economic Review* **27**, 141–63.

——— (1987), 'The Design of Feedback Rules in Linear Stochastic Rational Expectations Models', *Journal of Economic Dynamics and Control* **11**, 1–28.

Newell, A. and J. Symons (1990), 'The Current Account and Incomes Policy', mimeo.

Sargent, T. and N. Wallace (1981), 'Some Unpleasant Monetarist Arithmetic', *Federal Reserve Bank of Minneapolis Quarterly Review*, 1–17.

van der Ploeg, F. (1990), 'Monetary Disinflation, Fiscal Expansion and the Current Account in an Interdependent World', Centre for Economic Forecasting Discussion Paper No. 366.

Discussion

LUCAS PAPADEMOS

Currie and Levine provide an interesting and stimulating analysis of alternative fiscal policy strategies in an open economy, taking into account the solvency constraints facing a government and a nation when the real rate of interest exceeds the growth rate in the long run. This is the challenging case for policy-makers. It was also the relevant case for policy in the 1980s, as shown by comparisons between real interest rates and growth rates for the G7 countries. When output growth is higher than the real interest rate, a government can stabilize the debt-to-GDP ratio by maintaining a stable path for the public sector primary deficit (net of seigniorage revenue) relative to GDP. Similarly, a debtor nation can stabilize its foreign debt-to-GDP ratio by stabilizing its current account (net of interest payments) as a proportion of GDP. When, on the other hand, the real interest rate exceeds output growth, the stability of both debt-to-GDP ratios requires future surpluses in the government budget and in the trade account, provided that the debt-to-GDP ratios eventually grow more slowly than the difference between the real interest rate and the growth rate.

The authors' analysis of fiscal policy options is based on a stylized macroeconomic model incorporating the two solvency constraints. These constraints are obtained from the government budget constraint and the balance-of-payments identity, respectively, by solving them forward in time for the case when the real rate exceeds output growth. In other respects the model is fairly simple. It incorporates a conventional aggregate demand specification and a neoclassical production function. Employment is demand-determined and labour demand depends on the real product wage and the long-term level of the real capital stock. A key and rather limiting assumption made by the authors is that nominal wages are perfectly indexed to the consumer price level. This assumption of absolute real wage rigidity and the definition of the consumer price index (as a geometric average of the price level of domestically produced and imported goods) imply that, fundamentally, labour demand and thus the supply of output depend only on the real exchange rate (competitiveness), given the stock of capital. The financial structure of the model is also very simple. There is no currency substitution, but domestic and foreign bonds are considered perfect substitutes. It is assumed, however, that government debt, denominated in domestic currency, is held by domestic residents only. Presumably, the perfect substitutability of domestic and foreign bonds reflects only the preferences of domestic residents. Perfect substitutability and capital mobility imply the uncovered interest rate parity condition: the expected rate of change in the real exchange rate is equal to the difference between the domestic and foreign expected real interest rates. This parity condition is the only relation in the model affected by expectations which are forward-looking and are formed 'rationally'. Expectations in the product and labour markets are not forward-looking. This asymmetric treatment of expectations is not easily justifiable and it is likely to affect the results crucially, as will be argued below.

In a very short-run context, taking the stocks of assets and the expected values of variables as given, the model boils down to two equations – the equilibrium condition in the goods market and the interest rate parity condition – in two unknowns – the domestic real interest rate and the real exchange rate. Aggregate output and all other endogenous variables are then obtained as functions of the equilibrium values of real interest and exchange rates. The authors' analysis, however, takes place in a long-term context focusing on the role and implications of asset accumulation and of expectations concerning the real exchange rate. I will first provide a summary of the analysis and results and then discuss the generality of the conclusions and their policy implications.

The importance of the intertemporal solvency constraints for the formulation and implementation of fiscal policy is examined under different assumptions concerning the behaviour, both actual and perceived, of the fiscal authority. Three cases are considered: (1) a passive fiscal authority, (2) an activist welfare-optimizing authority, which formulates policy on the basis of an intertemporal welfare criterion and has the reputation of being able to precommit itself to the resulting optimal rule, and (3) an activist welfare-optimizing authority lacking the credibility for precommitment.

In their analysis of policy inactivism, Currie and Levine assume that fiscal and monetary policy instruments are held fixed at their long-run values and, for the sake of simplicity, ignore the effects of capital accumulation and the contribution of money balances to wealth. Consequently, only the private sector's real net foreign assets change over time, in response to external shocks and to changes in the real interest rate and the real exchange rate. In this case, the model reduces to two first-order difference equations jointly describing the evolution over time of the net foreign asset-to-income ratio, a predetermined state variable, and of the real exchange rate, a non-predetermined variable that may 'jump'. The necessary and sufficient conditions for saddlepath stability are satisfied if the trade balance responds positively enough to a depreciation of the real exchange rate and a fall in output and if the wealth effect on aggregate demand is not too large.

An activist fiscal authority is defined as one which aims at a real output level that differs from its long-run equilibrium value. This policy objective can be formalized as an infinite horizon optimization problem, with the government minimizing a welfare loss function given by the present discounted value of a weighted sum of the squared deviations of output from its target level and of the squared deviations of government spending, as a proportion of GDP, from its own long-run level. The government minimizes the deviations of the policy variable from its long-run level, presumably because it recognizes that the output target is not sustainable. Nevertheless, the optimal policy implied by this criterion, subject to the constraints of the complete model and with the money supply fixed, does not yield a stable government debt-to-income ratio. The authors impose government solvency by modifying the welfare function to include a term which penalizes deviations of the debt-to-income ratio from its long-run value (taken to be zero). The relative weight on this term is chosen to be 'small but sufficiently large' to ensure the stability of the debt-to-income ratio.

The specification of the welfare criterion, though necessary for ensuring the consistency of the optimal policy with government solvency, is rather arbitrary. It purports to capture a government's attempt to achieve a non-sustainable output level without using its policy instrument 'excessively' and deviating 'too much' from a long-run debt–income target. Policy-makers attempt to achieve a compromise between the perceived gains associated with the short-run output target and the undesirable long-term consequences of fiscal activism. The adoption of a myopic fiscal policy (the degree of myopia being determined by the discount factor) is constrained only somewhat by the desire to accept fiscal discipline in the long run, since the deviations of the debt–income ratio are also discounted. In practice, the choice of the relative weights in such a welfare function is not going to be easy. I doubt whether any fiscal authority uses such a criterion to formulate policy, despite its usefulness in determining and evaluating alternative fiscal strategies at a theoretical level.

Currie and Levine have also explored the possibility of formulating the optimization problem over a finite time horizon and subject to a terminal constraint on the value of the debt-to-income ratio. They tend to dismiss this formulation on the grounds that the optimal policy depends on the chosen horizon length. Since the horizon's length is a measure of the policy-makers' myopia, it is not surprising that it affects the optimal policy. It would be of interest to explore for the case when policy is formulated over a finite time horizon (in this case the discount factor could be set equal to one) whether or not there is an *optimal* time horizon which minimizes the welfare loss.

I turn next to a comparison of the optimal fiscal policies obtained under the two alternative assumptions concerning the government's reputation for precommitment to the resulting policy rule. The same infinite horizon welfare criterion, described above, is employed to derive the optimal fiscal policies under both hypotheses. The reported optimal policies are based on numerical simulations for plausible values of the model's parameters. The discrete time intervals involved are taken as years. Optimal paths for the output and government spending variables are first derived on the assumption of no shocks. The expected welfare losses are then calculated when the economy is subject to three types of external shocks, which are assumed to be independent but serially correlated.

The nature of the deterministic optimal policy for a government with a reputation for precommitment is of some interest. It involves an initial *reduction* in government spending, followed by a sharp rise in spending over the next two periods and a very gradual decline from then on, towards the long-run equilibrium value. The initial decline in government spending results in an initial fall of the real interest rate and a fairly large increase in the real exchange rate. But this pattern is reversed after one year. The real interest rate rises and remains relatively high for a long period, whereas the real exchange rate falls sharply for a while and then rises gradually to its long-run equilibrium. The initial reduction in the interest rate and the increase in the real exchange rate (depreciation of the domestic currency) cause a fairly steep rise in output over the next two periods, but following the third period output gradually declines, approaching its long-run equilibrium over a very long period.

A key characteristic of the optimal policy response in this case is the sharp reversals in government spending levels over the first four periods, which cause corresponding cyclical patterns in the behaviour of all other variables. After the first three periods, government spending and all other variables – other than the stocks of government debt and foreign assets – tend towards long-run equilibrium over a period of twenty years. The stocks of the government debt and net foreign assets approach and seem to stabilize at higher and lower levels, respectively, than the long-run equilibrium due to the cumulative effect of government deficits in the previous periods. But later on, about twenty years after the initial change, government debt and foreign assets decline as government spending falls below equilibrium. It is not clear from the reported results how long it takes before the asset-to-income ratios finally reach their long-run equilibrium levels.

By contrast, the deterministic optimal policy response when the government lacks a reputation for precommitment is not characterized by oscillations in the behaviour of the policy instrument and the endogenous variables in the initial periods. In the first period, government spending falls below the equilibrium level and approaches the long-run level from below over a similarly long period of almost twenty years. The initial fall in government spending causes a corresponding drop in the real interest rate and a rise in the real exchange rate, which are then reversed as these variables approach the long-run equilibrium asymptotically. Since government spending and thus the primary deficit are being kept below equilibrium over this whole time, the government debt-to-income ratio falls continuously and the net foreign asset-to-income ratio rises continuously during the first twenty periods following the implementation of the optimal policy. These patterns are the opposite of those observed in the case of a 'reputational' policy. In both cases, however, solvency is imposed very gradually despite the inclusion of the debt-to-income ratio in the welfare function. Apparently, the relative cost associated with deviations in the government debt-to-income ratio was not sufficiently large.

The difference between the optimal fiscal policy of a government with a reputation for precommitment and the optimal policy of a government without such a reputation can be related to the time-inconsistency of the policy with reputation. In that case a future policy decision that forms part of an optimal plan formulated at an initial time period is no longer optimal from the viewpoint of a later date, even if no new relevant information has appeared in the meantime. The fiscal authority therefore has an incentive to reformulate an optimal policy in the subsequent period. The optimal policy of a government without a precommitment reputation is time-consistent, although Currie and Levine provide an interesting argument suggesting that in a certain sense the non-reputational policy may *also* be time-inconsistent, due to the inclusion of the debt-to-income ratio in the welfare function. A government without reputation *and* with such a welfare loss function may have an incentive to leave to future governments the task of achieving solvency. This argument highlights the importance of incorporating intertemporal budget constraints in the models employed in policy studies. It also highlights the important role of the welfare criteria employed in such studies.

The main result obtained from a comparison of alternative fiscal strategies under conditions of uncertainty is that passive fiscal policies, which take the form of a constant government debt-to-GDP ratio or a constant primary deficit – adjusted to allow a given predetermined response of government spending to deviations of the debt-to-income ratio from equilibrium – are considerably inferior to activist optimal policies with or without reputation for precommitment. Moreover, in a stochastic environment the credible (reputational) policy results in significantly higher welfare gains than those from the policy of a government without reputation. Further analysis of stabilization policies under uncertainty is necessary to test the robustness of these appealing results.

The validity of the authors' conclusions on the role and formulation of fiscal policy in an open economy subject to solvency constraints is limited by two factors: (1) the formalization of the government's policy objective as specified in the welfare criterion used and the way solvency is ensured, and (2) the assumptions made concerning the structure of the model and the nature of expectations. As discussed above, the relevance for policy-makers of the specific welfare function employed is doubtful. The way solvency is ensured may be useful for analytical purposes, but it is rather *ad hoc* and not very effective.

The model's structure also limits the generality of the conclusions. The hypothesis of absolute real wage rigidity does not allow examination of the implications of a more complete specification of the determinants of aggregate supply, including the effects of inflationary expectations and of some form of nominal wage–price rigidity. Such an extension would also imply that money is not neutral, as it is in this model, thus bringing into centre stage the interactions between fiscal and monetary policies. The hypothesis that foreign residents do not hold domestic debt is also limiting and not realistic for many countries. Relaxation of this hypothesis would make the two solvency constraints interdependent. The hypothesis that expectations are 'rational' only in the foreign exchange market is also questionable. Of course, it could be argued that participants in the foreign exchange markets are different from those in the product and labour markets and that they are better informed and more forward-looking. On the other hand, expectations in the foreign exchange markets are not only those of foreign exchange dealers, but indirectly reflect the expectations of participants in other markets. Allowing all agents in the economy to have forward-looking expectations is an important extension, especially since the real values of government debt and net foreign assets – and thus real wealth and consumption – will be affected by the expected present value of future surpluses in the government budget and the trade account. Finally, the difference between the real interest rate and the growth of output, which plays a crucial role in the asset accumulation process and is assumed to be fixed at the long-run equilibrium level, could be allowed to be determined endogenously and be influenced in general by the fiscal and monetary policy mix.

Despite the limitations of the analysis implied by the structure of the model and other assumptions, the study by Currie and Levine is an important contribution to the theory of economic policy. Extensions of their analysis would enhance its usefulness for the practice of economic policy.

4 Relaxing the external constraint: Europe in the 1930s

BARRY EICHENGREEN

1 Introduction

The new conventional wisdom on the macroeconomics of the 1930s focuses on the external constraint. The fixed exchange rates and high capital mobility characteristic of the gold standard, it is argued, tied other countries to the United States when its economy succumbed to the Great Depression. Deflation in the US produced deflation in Europe so long as fixed exchange rates linked commodity prices and interest rates internationally. Balance-of-payments pressures inhibited the unilateral adoption of reflationary monetary and fiscal initiatives so long as countries remained committed to fixed rates. Only when they abandoned the gold standard, relaxing the external constraint, was it possible to initiate recovery from the Depression.

This new view has become remarkably widespread. Choudhri and Kochin (1981) were among the first to observe that countries like Spain that never adopted the gold standard were best able to insulate themselves from the deflationary shock emanating from the United States. Eichengreen and Sachs (1985) described the channels through which departing from gold enabled other countries to free themselves from the grip of depression. Eichengreen (1990a) and Temin (1989) emphasized the greater capacity of countries with depreciated currencies to adopt reflationary monetary and fiscal initiatives. Eichengreen (1990a) and Bernanke and James (1990) stressed the superior ability of countries with flexible exchange rates to ward off banking panics and financial crises.[1]

This view is a departure from an older literature in which the Depression was regarded as a US affair and the collapse of the international gold standard was portrayed as an unmitigated evil.[2] In a sense it is a sign of the times: growing awareness of economic interdependence in the 1980s has redirected attention to the importance of economic interdependence in the 1930s. To an extent it reflects the growing popularity of comparative

Table 4.1. *Percent change in industrial production, 1929–36*
(in percentage points)

	1929–32	1929–33	1929–34	1929–35	1929–36
Gold bloc	− 28.2	− 22.6	− 21.8	− 20.6	− 13.9
Exchange control	− 35.7	− 31.7	− 21.2	− 10.3	− 2.3
Sterling	− 8.8	− 2.5	8.9	18.1	27.8
Other depreciators	− 17.5	− 1.6	3.3	14.1	27.1

Notes: Complete country list appears in footnote 3 to the text. Yugoslavia and Bulgaria are omitted from the averages for exchange control countries, as is Australia from the sterling area, due to missing data. Figures shown are arithmetic averages of country data.
Source: See Appendix 4C.

and international history. In part it reflects the powerful message conveyed by simple evidence. Table 4.1 displays rates of change of industrial production starting in 1929 for countries pursuing different international monetary strategies.[3] The five countries which adhered to the gold standard until 1936 (1935 for Belgium) suffered a devastating decline in industrial production and showed few signs of recovery until the end of the period. In contrast, the members of the sterling area, which went off the gold standard in 1931, began recovering strongly by 1933. Other countries that depreciated their currencies suffered a more devastating depression initially than that endured by the sterling area, but by 1936 their recovery was every bit as impressive. The experience of countries that relaxed the external constraint through exchange control lay between these extremes. Table 4.1 suggests that the importance of exchange rate policy was even more general than suggested by previous authors who focused on subsets of these countries.[4]

Notwithstanding the extent of consensus, the recent literature has left important issues unresolved. Why, for example, were countries unable to agree to coordinate their reflationary initiatives internationally, rendering devaluation necessary for recovery? How quickly did economies respond to devaluation, and how persistent was the stimulus it provided? Finally, did countries pay a price for delinking themselves from the gold standard in the form of disruptions to asset and commodity markets?

These are the questions addressed in the remainder of this chapter. Section 2 sketches the background to the period and asks why currency devaluation was a necessary precondition for recovery. The argument is that reflation without devaluation required international cooperation, but that different views of the operation of the economy posed an insurmountable obstacle to collaboration. Section 3 analyses the effects of devaluation in a sample of some three dozen countries. Two innovations are to provide new evidence on the time profile of the response and to control for changes in global economic conditions. The evidence suggests that the economics of devaluation and recovery in the 1930s were more complex than suggested in previous accounts. Explanations for these complexities are offered. Finally, Section 4 examines the implications of the change in exchange rate regime for the behaviour of asset and commodity markets.

2   Why was devaluation a necessary precondition for recovery?

Virtually the entire world was on some form of gold standard when the Great Depression struck. Exceptions, in addition to Spain (which maintained a floating exchange rate throughout), included Japan (which only restored gold convertibility in 1930), Peru, Portugal, and Yugoslavia (which restored convertibility only in 1931), China (which maintained a silver standard throughout the period), and Honduras (which switched from silver to gold in 1931). Forty-five nations were on the gold standard in 1929.

The three defining characteristics of a gold standard are a fixed domestic currency price of gold, freedom to import and export gold, and rules linking monetary liabilities of the central bank or government to its gold reserves. It is easy to see why these arrangements rendered small countries vulnerable to external shocks. The traditional ways of analysing the problem are in terms of shocks to the current and capital accounts and, alternatively, in terms of the monetary approach to the balance of payments. Consider the first alternative. Imagine that countries of Central and Eastern Europe suffer a loss of access to capital imports from the United States, as in 1928. In the absence of other adjustments, this leads to a deterioration in their balance of payments. Any excess of commodity imports plus debt service payments over commodity exports must be financed by exporting gold. The decline in gold reserves produces a decline in the money supply and deflationary pressure on the domestic economy. Imagine next that these same countries suffer a decline in the US demand for their exports, as in 1929. This compounds the deterioration in their balance of payments, leading to further gold losses, additional monetary contraction, and yet more deflationary pressure.

The alternative approach is consistent with the above but complements it by shifting the focus to the source of the shocks. Posit a negative monetary shock in the United States, as in 1928–9.[5] US monetary supply falls relative to demand, causing interest rates to rise. The US balance of payments moves into surplus, as gold is imported to provide backing for additional monetary liabilities that begin to eliminate the excess demand for real balances. Foreign countries experience the disturbance as a decline in capital imports and a deterioration in their payments position. The US price level falls, placing downward pressure on prices abroad. As the shock ramifies through the economy and activity declines, so does the US demand for imports, imparting an additional disturbance to the rest of the world.

This account of the international transmission of the Great Depression is precisely accurate only if countries adhere faithfully to the gold standard. In fact, none of the three defining characteristics of the gold standard were strictly observed. There was a little exchange rate flexibility built into the system. In countries suffering a loss of reserves, the exchange rate was allowed to decline to the gold export point – equivalently, the domestic-currency price of gold was allowed to rise above its official parity. The price of sterling, for example, could slip from its official parity of $4.866 to less than $4.855 before it became profitable, given costs of shipping, insurance, and finance, to engage in gold market arbitrage. This provided a little insulation.

More importantly, central banks and governments rationed gold and foreign exchange to importers and others who demanded it for domestic currency and took other steps to limit gold exports. Moggridge (1972) describes the devices used by the Bank of England to discourage gold exports. More extreme examples were Australia and Brazil. In Australia, the trading banks, which administered the gold standard, formed a cartel to ration foreign exchange to importers. By December 1929 the exchange rate had fallen $2\frac{1}{2}$% below par. In 1930 private citizens were compelled to turn over all gold in their possession. Rationing was intensified, and the Australian pound slipped 6% below par. All the while, Australia remained officially on gold. In Brazil, the authorities similarly placed a variety of obstacles in the way of convertibility. The milreis fell to less than 93% of its official parity in January 1930, despite the country's official adherence to the gold standard.

Thus, both countries, despite official adherence to gold, were able to depreciate their exchange rates surreptitiously and to limit the contraction of their money supplies. The more restrictive the policy of rationing became, however, the higher was the black market price of foreign exchange, and the greater was the incentive for banks to violate their cartel agreement. Eventually rationing broke down, forcing the authorities to officially suspend convertibility.

Finally, countries possessing excess reserves could avoid having to choose between covert depreciation of the currency and overt contraction of the money supply. Central banks sought to maintain an extra margin of gold and foreign exchange reserves, on the order of 7 to 10%, above the 33 to 40% ratio of reserves to monetary liabilities required by statute.[6] They could lose this amount of gold without being forced to contract their domestic liabilities. This provided some insulation when their payments positions deteriorated.

Countries could employ several expedients, then, to moderate the impact of the external shock on their domestic economies. Still, so long as they continued to adhere to the gold standard, they had only limited room to maneuver.

Following the destabilizing impulse came its propagation. However devastating the disturbance, one would think that the self-equilibrating tendencies of the market eventually should have come into play. Domestic prices should have fallen along with US prices to limit the deterioration in international competitiveness and loss of export sales. Domestic costs should have fallen along with domestic prices to limit any rise in real wages and unemployment. Thus, the failure of prices and costs to adjust after four or more years of depression is 'somewhat troubling', as Bernanke and James (1990, p. 19) put it. They continue: 'Given 1) the severity of the unemployment that was experienced during that time, 2) the relative absence of long-term contracts and the weakness of unions, and 3) the presumption that the general public was aware that prices and hence the cost of living were falling, it is hard to understand how nominal wages could have been so unresponsive.'

Part of the explanation lies in the stickiness of other nominal variables. Mortgages were fixed in nominal terms and ran years to maturity. Rents were fixed in nominal terms and ran for extended periods. Bonds, corporate as well as government, paid coupons that were fixed in nominal terms. Civil servants, even when officially non-unionized, delegated spokesmen and lobbied effectively against cuts in money wages. Each of the affected groups – landlords, bondholders, and workers – would have accepted a reduction in their nominal incomes had they been assured that others were prepared to do the same. Absent such an assurance, a coordination problem resulted.

A clear illustration of the operation of these forces is France in 1935. The country had already endured four years of deflation. Yet the decline in prices and costs remained inadequate to restore internal and external balance. Since 1929 wholesale prices in France, adjusted for the exchange rate, had risen by 14% against the US and by 18% against the UK and Sweden, countries which had limited the need for nominal adjustment by devaluing their currencies and expanding their money supplies.[7] Continuing economic difficulties led to the formation of a coalition government headed by Pierre Laval. To head off an incipient financial crisis, the new government was granted plenary powers. It issued more than 500 decrees designed to reduce government expenditure by 10%. To remove resistance to wage cuts, the government unilaterally reduced all rents and mortgages by 10%. Interest payments on government bonds were reduced by decree. Other proclamations allowed debtors to break contracts that had been signed prior to the deflation. These measures, as is evident from their nature, were designed to attack the sources of nominal inertia described above.

Revealingly, however, public sector employees frustrated the government's efforts. Laval sought to apply the 10% to the salaries of government employees. Civil servants resisted demands that they be first to accept salary cuts, with only the promise that private sector salaries would follow. Their opposition forced Laval to draw back. Civil service salaries were reduced by only 3 to 5%. Other parties asked to accept 10% cuts in income intensified their opposition accordingly. Macroeconomic adjustment remained incomplete.

Thus, inertia built into the wage–price mechanism was one source of the persistent monetary non-neutrality. Another was the breakdown of financial intermediation, the mechanism emphasized by Bernanke (1983) for the United States. Deflation eroded the value of the collateral debtors had offered in return for bank loans. Commercial bankruptcies cut the income banks received on their portfolios. The decline in the prices of low grade bonds led to capital losses on investments. Eventually the deterioration in bank balance sheets undermined confidence in the financial system. It took only some additional bad news to provoke a run on the banks. Depositors scrambled to withdraw their balances, and fractional reserve banking systems were unable to satisfy their demands. The banks had to be reorganized by government or close their doors. Firms' access to external funds, and hence fixed investment, as well as households' access to consumer credit, and hence the demand for consumer durables, continued to be disrupted even after the banking panic reached its peak. Eichengreen (1990a) argued that the breakdown of financial intermediation, as emphasized by Bernanke (1983) in the US context, operated also in a variety of other countries. Bernanke and James (1990) argued the same, providing an exhaustive list of thirty-three banking panics between 1931 and 1936.

Given these sources of persistence, policy initiatives were necessary to escape from depressed conditions. Yet adherence to the gold standard severely constrained the authorities' efforts to undertake reflationary action. Open market purchases designed to inject high-powered money into circulation led to a loss of gold. For small countries, increasing domestic credit led to a matching loss of international reserves so long as prices were linked to world levels by commodity market arbitrage and interest rates were pegged to world levels by fixed exchange rates and capital mobility. This was the painful lesson learned by central banks between 1929 and 1931. Large countries had the capacity to expand without threatening gold convertibility insofar as their reflationary iniatiatives affected global conditions. But in practice, even the large countries with the most ample gold reserves, the United States and France, had little freedom of action.

The US case is illustrative. In the spring of 1932, bowing to Congressional pressure, the Federal Reserve initiated a program of open market purchases. Under the direction of the Open Market Committee, the twelve reserve banks purchased more than $1 billion of securities. This led to an alarming decline in the Fed's gold reserves. Between March and June, the monetary gold stock of the United States fell by 11%. Fearing for convertibility, the Fed abandoned the bond buying program as soon as Congress adjourned.

In France, the Flandin government that took office towards the end of 1934 initiated a liberal credit policy and resisted balancing the budget. To avoid driving up the long-term interest rates upon which industrial borrowing depended, government borrowing was shifted to the short end of the market. The Bank of France discounted Treasury bills. Predictably, these policies ran up against the external constraint. Import volumes rose by 12% between January and March of 1935. Starting in May, individuals queued up at the Bank of France to convert banknotes into gold. The Bank's reserves fell by 2% in May and by 11% in June. Flandin demanded powers of decree to raise taxes and cut public spending, measures clearly inconsistent with his reflationary program. Plenary powers were denied, and the government fell. Its successor suspended the reflationary program. The same sequence of events repeated itself in the winter of 1936.

The obvious way to relax the external constraint was by abandoning the gold standard. Suspending convertibility allowed central banks to expand the money supply, even if doing so entailed currency depreciation. Table 4.2 shows the very different evolution of money supplies in countries on and off gold.[8] In gold standard countries, money supplies were still 14% below 1929 levels six years later. Only with their devaluation in 1936 did these countries succeed finally in offsetting the monetary shock. In contrast, the money supplies of sterling area countries had recovered nearly to 1929 levels by 1932, and exceeded those levels thereafter. The experience elsewhere varied. The money supplies of countries outside the sterling area that depreciated their currencies declined even faster than

Table 4.2. *Percent change in M1, 1929–36*
(in percentage points)

	1929–32	1929–33	1929–34	1929–35	1929–36
Gold bloc					
with Switzerland	− 5.8	− 10.1	− 11.7[a]	N/A	N/A
without Switzerland	− 6.1	− 10.3	− 11.1[a]	− 14.1	− 6.9
Exchange control	− 21.3	− 23.8	− 23.7	− 20.8	− 19.0[b]
Sterling	− 2.4	0.7	2.8	6.7	11.7
Other depreciators[c]	− 21.7	− 17.1	− 9.8	− 4.4	9.7

Notes: [a] Missing in Belgium in 1934.
   [b] Missing Italy in 1936.
   [c] Missing Costa Rica, Guatemala, and Nicaragua throughout.
Source: See Appendix 4C.

those of the gold bloc before 1933, because of, among other factors, massive monetary contraction in the United States, but rebounded even more quickly than those of the sterling area thereafter. In exchange control countries, where memory of hyperinflation lingered, few steps were taken in the early years of the depression to offset the decline in money supplies. Still, the suspension of convertibility prevented a further decline in money supplies subsequently like that experienced by the gold bloc.

In contrast, there was little obvious pattern to fiscal balances across currency areas. In part this reflected the absence of conscious manipulation of fiscal instruments. In the sterling area, budget deficits averaged 1% of government expenditure between 1929 and 1936; elsewhere they averaged 8% whether countries were on or off gold. On a constant employment basis, the fiscal policies of the gold bloc countries were by far the most contractionary. There the fiscal authorities were forced repeatedly to cut public expenditure and raise taxes in order to compress domestic spending, limit imports, and defend convertibility (see Table 4.3).

Just as policy-makers were inhibited by the gold standard constraints from pursuing reflationary monetary and fiscal measures, they were prevented from intervening to contain banking panics. Fears that they would be unable to convert deposits into currency led investors to withdraw their balances from the banking system. The standard policy response was for the central bank to lend freely at a punitive rate. Unfortunately, lending freely threatened gold convertibility. Among the individuals withdrawing their balances were those attaching a positive

Table 4.3. *Government budget balance as a share of expenditure, 1929–36*
(in percentage points)

	1929–32	1929–33	1929–34	1929–35	1929–36
Gold bloc	− 3.2	− 5.9	− 7.6	− 7.6	− 7.8
Exchange control	− 6.8	− 6.0	− 7.6	− 8.3	− 7.8
Sterling	− 3.0	− 3.8	− 2.6	− 2.1	− 0.8
Other depreciators	− 10.8	− 9.6	− 9.8	− 9.3	− 7.9

Notes: Negative numbers denote deficits. Each cell is the unweighted average
(across countries in the bloc) of unweighted averages (across the time period for
each column) for each country. Data for Germany are missing for 1936; hence that
country is omitted from the final column.
Source: See Appendix 4C.

probability to devaluation. As foreign depositors repatriated their funds
and domestic residents purchased foreign exchange, the central bank
suffered a loss of gold reserves. Supplying additional liquidity threatened
to violate gold cover restrictions. Some central banks could suspend those
restrictions temporarily or pay a tax to the government if the reserve ratio
fell below the statutory minimum. But either action undermined confidence in convertibility and accelerated the drain of international
reserves. Raising the central bank discount rate to 8 or 10% was no help.
An annualized interest differential of, say, 5% was scarcely sufficient to
attract capital inflows when domestic depositors could avoid a capital loss
of 20% or more in the event of devaluation.[9] If anything, a punitive
discount rate was taken as a signal that the situation threatened to escape
control.

  This limit on the capacity of gold standard countries to intervene in
support of their banking systems has been emphasized by Eichengreen
(1990a), Temin (1989), and Bernanke and James (1990). The problem was
even more profound than commonly suggested, however. Previous
accounts argue that the reserve constraint limited the lender-of-last-resort
activities in which gold standard countries could engage. Their central
banks could discount bills on behalf of the banking system or engage in
expansionary open market operations only until their free reserves were
exhausted. In fact, adherence to the gold standard rendered even feasible
lender-of-last-resort activities counterproductive. By injecting liquidity
into the banking system, the central bank signalled that it attached a
higher priority to domestic financial stability than to gold convertibility.
As its gold cover ratio declined, the implicit probability of devaluation
rose. Domestic depositors had an incentive to get their money out of the

country to avoid capital losses on domestic assets in the event of devaluation. The additional liquidity injected into the banking system leaked back out, if anything at an accelerating pace.

Thus, the association of banking panics with the gold standard reflected more than limited ability to engage in lender-of-last-resort activities; it reflected the perverse effects of lender-of-last-resort intervention by countries on gold. An obvious solution to this problem was to suspend convertibility, allow the exchange rate to depreciate, impose exchange controls if necessary, and inject into the banking system however much liquidity was required for domestic financial stability. It is no coincidence, therefore, that those bank failures that occurred after countries went off gold were generally contained before they had a chance to spread.

The alternative to unilateral depreciation was internationally coordinated reflation. Had countries coordinated their reflationary initiatives, they could have countered the downward spiral of economic activity and stabilized their financial systems without endangering gold convertibility. Monetary reflation at home would have stimulated domestic demand. Monetary reflation abroad would have limited the deterioration in the balance of payments.[10] Lender-of-last-resort activities financed by loans of reserves from other central banks would have cut the link between bank failures and convertibility crises and prevented the injection of reserves from leaking back out of the banking system.

The advantages of coordinated action were appreciated. 'His Majesty's Government . . . are convinced that well coordinated action between the leading Central Banks is likely to have more effect in improving world conditions than isolated efforts by particular countries,' read a 1933 memorandum from the British Embassy to the US State Department.[11] The very rationale for the 1933 World Economic Conference was to negotiate an internationally coordinated response to the global depression. Yet coordinated action proved impossible to achieve. One reason is that policy-makers in different countries subscribed to different models of the economy.[12] This is the hypothesis advanced in a different context by Frankel (1988). But I move beyond Frankel's hypothesis by endogenizing policy-makers' choice of model, and suggesting that it derived from the different historical experiences of the nations involved.

In Britain, the case for monetary reflation was widely acknowledged. Keynes had provided a fully articulated model of the channels through which monetary expansion operated on the economy in his private evidence to the Macmillan Committee and in his *Treatise on Money*, published in 1930. British experts, both within and outside of government, urged monetary expansion on the Bank of France and the Federal Reserve, the two central banks that were absorbing gold at a rapid rate.

The Bank of England repeatedly warned the Bank of France that the latter's failure to initiate reflationary policies was limiting the former's freedom of action.[13]

Britain's appreciation of the merits of monetary reflation derived from the historical experience of the preceding decade. Discretionary monetary policy undertaken by the Bank of England had not given rise to runaway inflation. On the contrary, the deflation associated with the return to gold and the high interest rates required subsequently to maintain the sterling parity were blamed for the unemployment and slow growth suffered by the British economy since 1925. The effects of monetary restriction were clear to see, rendering the advantages of monetary reflation compelling.

In France, in contrast, monetary reflation was viewed as undesirable. There the Depression was seen as a product of excessive credit creation on the part of central banks that had failed to abide by the rules of the gold standard.[14] In this view, productive capacity worldwide had expanded more rapidly than the supply of monetary gold. Since the demand for money rose with the level of economic activity, lower prices were necessary to provide a matching increase in the supply of real money balances. Under the gold standard, a smooth deflation like that of 1873–93 was the normal response. But in the 1920s central banks had used discretionary policy to block the downward adjustment of prices. They had recklessly pyramided domestic credit on foreign exchange reserves. Liberal supplies of credit had fuelled speculation, raising asset prices to unsustainable heights and setting the stage for their collapse in the autumn of 1929. With this shock, central banks rushed to liquidate their exchange reserves, and prices fell abruptly to more realistic levels. This sudden deflation was far from smooth: it produced bankruptcies among debtors, discouraged investment, and disrupted economic activity, provoking the Depression through which the world was suffering.

In this view, the Great Depression was an inevitable consequence of unrealistic policies pursued by central banks in preceding years. To now prevent deflation from running its course threatened to provoke another era of speculative excess and, ultimately, another depression. It was better to allow excess liquidity to be purged and prices to fall to sustainable levels. Only when adjustment had run its course would investors be confident that an era of sound finance was at hand. Only then could recovery commence.

The origins of this view can be traced, once again, to the experience of the preceding decade. In France, discretionary monetary policy before 1927 had given rise to an explosive inflationary spiral. Monetary reflation was associated in the public mind not with prosperity but with financial and political chaos. Stabilization in 1926 had been followed not by monetary stringency and slow growth but by capital inflows and prosperity. It was this experience that led French policy-makers to formulate their favoured view of the economy.

The US model lay somewhere between these extremes. Federal Reserve officials tended to share the French perspective. They blamed excessive credit creation for the excesses of the Wall Street boom and for the Crash that inaugurated the Depression. Only by purging excessive liquidity from the financial system, they argued, could a sound basis for sustained growth be laid. This 'liquidationist view' continued to guide Federal Reserve policy through much of the period. Outside the Fed, pressure for reflationary policy mounted as the Depression persisted. By 1932 Congressional pressure, particularly from the representatives of agricultural and silver-mining states, had become intense. In 1933 the reflationists' arguments were taken on board by the new president, Franklin Delano Roosevelt.

These three very different models of the economy posed an insuperable obstacle to international economic cooperation. The first model led British officials to attach priority to an international commitment to monetary reflation, and to regard an agreement to stabilize exchange rates as contingent upon that commitment. The second model led French officials to attach priority to exchange rate stabilization and to regard proposals for monetary reflation with suspicion. The United States gravitated over time from the first position to the second. These very different views of the operation of the economy prevented effective international cooperation, rendering currency depreciation a necessary precondition for reflation.

3   The response to devaluation

Choudri and Kochin (1981), Eichengreen and Sachs (1985), and Bernanke and James (1990) all have argued that countries that devalued their currencies recovered more quickly from the Great Depression than countries that remained on gold. In this section I re-examine the question, sketching the time profile of the response to devaluation and controlling more precisely for changes in global conditions.

I take a sample of thirty-seven countries, all those for which data could be obtained. Some variables are not available for some countries, which explains the variation across tables in the number of observations.[15] Following Donovon (1981) and Kamin (1988), I centre the annual observations for each country on the year of devaluation. Year T, which denotes the central observation, is 1931 for Britain, for example, 1933 for the United States. I analyse the variables of interest from three years prior to devaluation to three years after. Since data are not available for 1939, the seven-year window precludes consideration of devaluations taking place in 1936.[16]

The first panels of Tables 4.4–4.11 show two measures (mean and median) of the average rate of change of the indicator variable concerned, the number of countries in which the variable rises and falls, the t-test of the null hypothesis that the change in the variable is zero, and the binomial-sign test of the probability that the indicator in question is equally likely to rise and fall. (The t-static is the more powerful test but is valid only under the assumption that the indicator variables are normally distributed.)

Table 4.4 summarizes the behaviour of industrial production. The first line shows that industrial output was growing at an average annual rate of 3.0% three years prior to devaluation. Two years prior to devaluation, however, output fell by an average of 5.4%. It continued downward at approximately the same rate in the year preceding the abandonment of gold. In the year of devaluation, output rose in half of the countries concerned. After a year passed, industrial production was growing rapidly in nearly every country, at an average annual rate of nearly 10%. Recovery spread and accelerated the second post-devaluation year before slowing somewhat in the third.

Table 4.5 analyses the behaviour of wholesale prices. In the vast majority of countries, prices fell rapidly in all three years preceding devaluation. The cumulative fall was on the order of 20%. With devaluation, deflation halted immediately in nearly half of the countries. The situation remained basically the same in the first post-devaluation year: prices continued to fall in half of the countries, although where they rose they did so at an accelerating pace. By the second post-devaluation year, reflation was quite general. The rise in prices slowed by the third post-devaluation year, as if the nominal effects of devaluation had worked their way through the economy.

Table 4.6 shows the behaviour of the volume of exports. These contracted on average by a total of 17% in the two years preceding devaluation. They stabilized in the year devaluation took place and recovered their lost ground in the three subsequent years. Table 4.7 indicates that the time profile of nominal exports is essentially the same as that of export volumes, although their pre-devaluation decline is even greater.

Table 4.8 documents a somewhat different picture on the import side. Import volumes not only declined in the two pre-devaluation years but continued to fall in the year of devaluaton. Only in the second and third post-devaluation year is there evidence of their recovery. Table 4.9

Table 4.4. *Changes in industrial production*

	Year relative to devaluation						
	$T-3$	$T-2$	$T-1$	T	$T+1$	$T+2$	$T+3$
Devaluing countries							
Summary statistics (%)							
Mean	2.96	− 5.41	− 4.87	1.41	8.86	11.44	6.68
Median	2.25	− 5.20	− 5.70	1.00	6.25	12.38	9.70
Changes from previous period							
Number ↑	15	8	7	12	19	21	19
Number ↓	7	14	16	11	4	2	4
Probability that H_0 true (%)	6.7	14.3	4.6	50	0	0	0
t-statistic	1.542	− 2.496	− 2.086	0.4657	3.475	5.437	4.236
Total sample							
Summary statistics (%)							
Mean	2.48	− 5.56	− 5.51	0.08	8.31	10.15	6.20
Median	1.89	− 5.20	− 6.80	− 1.00	5.88	11.43	8.61
Changes from previous period							
Number ↑	17	8	7	12	23	24	23
Number ↓	9	18	20	15	4	3	4
Probability that H_0 true (%)	8.5	3.9	1	34.9	0	0	0
t-statistic	− 0.6703	− 0.1831	− 0.7444	− 1.212	− 0.5995	− 1.655	− 0.8141

Table 4.5. *Changes in the wholesale price index*

	Year relative to devaluation						
	$T-3$	$T-2$	$T-1$	T	$T+1$	$T+2$	$T+3$
Devaluing countries							
Summary statistics (%)							
Mean	-3.64	-9.29	-5.98	1.22	3.10	4.49	1.73
Median	-2.72	-9.40	-9.19	-2.13	-0.24	3.10	2.27
Changes from previous period							
Number ↑	8	6	4	12	13	22	21
Number ↓	19	22	24	16	15	6	7
Probability that H_0 true (%)	2.5	0	0	30	43	0	1
t-statistic	-2.676	-6.401	-2.470	0.4248	1.379	2.224	1.021
Total sample							
Summary statistics (%)							
Mean	-3.88	-9.39	-6.66	-0.27	2.08	3.73	1.52
Median	-3.94	-9.95	-11.01	-2.60	-1.08	1.83	1.81
Changes from previous period							
Number ↑	8	6	4	12	13	23	23
Number ↓	23	26	28	20	19	9	9
Probability that H_0 true (%)	0	0	0	10.5	19	1	1
t-statistic	-0.5309	-0.1998	-0.8395	-1.547	-1.353	-1.116	-0.3761

Table 4.6. *Changes in export volume*

	Year relative to devaluation						
	$T-3$	$T-2$	$T-1$	T	$T+1$	$T+2$	$T+3$
Devaluing countries							
Summary statistics (%)							
Mean	3.36	−5.48	−11.71	−1.59	16.08	4.48	3.81
Median	0.00	−4.36	−12.10	−6.40	9.70	3.80	3.50
Changes from previous period							
Number ↑	12	9	5	11	20	16	16
Number ↓	12	16	20	14	5	9	9
Probability that H_0 true (%)	50	11.4	0	34.5	0	11.4	11.4
t-statistic	0.7229	−1.155	−2.739	−0.2545	2.769	1.454	1.463
Total sample							
Summary statistics (%)							
Mean	3.01	−5.47	−11.43	−2.96	14.12	4.53	3.39
Median	−0.38	−7.17	−8.22	−12.30	6.60	5.06	1.90
Changes from previous period							
Number ↑	13	10	5	11	21	19	17
Number ↓	14	18	23	17	7	9	11
Probability that H_0 true (%)	50	12.7	0	16.5	1	4.5	16.5
t-statistic	−0.2410	0.0098	0.2060	−0.6907	−1.069	0.0471	−0.5088

Table 4.7. *Changes in nominal exports*

	Year relative to devaluation						
	$T-3$	$T-2$	$T-1$	T	$T+1$	$T+2$	$T+3$
Devaluing countries							
Summary statistics (%)							
Mean	−4.88	−15.95	−19.34	−5.66	12.16	13.28	8.10
Median	0.70	−15.40	−18.18	−7.69	7.09	7.64	8.05
Changes from previous period							
Number ↑	16	3	4	15	24	26	24
Number ↓	15	29	28	17	8	6	8
Probability that H_0 true (%)	50	0	0	42	0	0	0
t-statistic	−1.345	−6.110	−6.450	−1.262	2.209	3.268	2.708
Total sample							
Summary statistics (%)							
Mean	−5.07	−16.64	−20.14	−6.39	10.51	12.78	8.14
Median	−0.90	−15.96	−21.87	−10.14	5.82	3.32	6.78
Changes from previous period							
Number ↑	16	3	4	15	24	27	26
Number ↓	18	32	31	20	11	8	9
Probability that H_0 true (%)	42.2	0	0	24.9	1.9	0	0
t-statistic	−0.1885	−0.0415	−0.5544	−1.301	−1.165	−1.103	−0.7392

Table 4.8. Changes in import volume

	Year relative to devaluation						
	$T-3$	$T-2$	$T-1$	T	$T+1$	$T+2$	$T+3$
Devaluing countries							
Summary statistics (%)							
Mean	3.26	−12.67	−10.69	−14.08	0.57	11.71	7.35
Median	4.95	−7.97	−8.13	−14.92	1.55	10.70	6.22
Changes from previous period							
Number ↑	16	8	8	4	13	19	20
Number ↓	7	16	16	20	11	5	4
Probability that H_0 true (%)	4.6	7.5	7.5	0	41.9	0	0
t-statistic	0.8608	−3.457	−2.918	−3.604	0.2026	3.911	3.417
Total sample							
Summary statistics (%)							
Mean	3.27	−12.08	−10.73	−14.21	0.83	10.47	6.52
Median	3.03	−4.40	−6.90	−13.97	1.55	9.43	5.29
Changes from previous period							
Number ↑	18	9	8	4	14	20	21
Number ↓	8	18	19	23	13	7	6
Probability that H_0 true (%)	3.9	6	2.5	0	50	1	0
t-statistic	0.0004	0.4929	−0.0329	−0.1028	0.2833	−1.273	−1.183

Table 4.9. Changes in nominal imports

	Year relative to devaluation						
	$T-3$	$T-2$	$T-1$	T	$T+1$	$T+2$	$T+3$
Devaluing countries							
Summary statistics (%)							
Mean	−8.86	−19.30	−22.32	−7.39	9.77	21.08	8.31
Median	−3.96	−19.86	−19.13	−13.12	3.88	19.17	8.15
Changes from previous period							
Number ↑	15	3	6	14	16	29	23
Number ↓	16	29	26	18	16	3	9
Probability that H_0 true (%)	50	0	0	30	50	0	1
t-statistic	−2.833	−5.939	−6.509	−1.588	1.825	4.714	2.748
Total sample							
Summary statistics (%)							
Mean	−8.75	−18.69	−21.81	−8.75	7.05	19.52	7.99
Median	−5.46	−17.26	−19.97	−14.95	−3.80	19.06	7.29
Changes from previous period							
Number ↑	15	3	6	14	16	30	25
Number ↓	19	32	29	21	19	5	10
Probability that H_0 true (%)	29.4	0	0	15.4	36.7	0	1
t-statistic	0.1225	0.0883	−0.2920	−0.8984	−0.9375	−0.2257	−0.3372

suggests that the relatively large rise in import prices already became apparent in the first post-devaluation year.

Table 4.10 shows the behaviour of international reserves. Reserves declined precipitously in the three years preceding devaluation. There is little evidence that they began to recover contemporaneously with devaluation. In the first post-devaluation year, they continued to decline in fully half the countries, although in a few cases there were relatively large gains. In the second post-devaluation year, the recovery of reserves became quite general, though its magnitude remained small. Only in the third post-devaluation year did most countries gain significant quantities of reserves.

This analysis of the aftermath of devaluation paints a picture of rapidly accelerating growth, rapidly rising exports, gradually recovering imports, and a delayed reflux of international reserves. But it is limited to devaluing countries. A more stringent test is to compare devaluing countries with a control group of nations that faced the same global economic conditions but did not depreciate their currencies during this period. This tests the hypothesis that devaluation was followed by recovery not because of any salutary effects of the change in exchange rates but because abandonment of the gold standard happened to coincide with the length of the Great Depression.

A simple example can illustrate the construction of figures for the control group. Imagine that the analysis is limited to three countries: Britain, the United States, and France (the last of which did not devalue between 1930 and 1935 and hence is a member of the control group). T is 1931 for Britain and 1933 for the United States. I control for global economic conditions by comparing British and French performance in 1931 and American and French performance in 1933. The indicator variables for France for year T are calculated as unweighted averages of the figures for 1931 and 1933. Year $T - 1$ figures for France are averages for French figures for 1930 and 1932; for year $T - 2$ they are averages for 1929 and 1931. Generalizing to the case of more countries is straightforward.

This more stringent test yields weaker results. Devaluing countries grow more quickly than countries in the control group in years T through $T + 2$, but only in years T and $T + 2$ does the difference begin to approach statistical significance at standard confidence intervals. (A negative sign on the second t-statistic in a column indicates a lower value for countries in the control group than for devaluing countries.) Only two years after devaluation is wholesale price inflation significantly more rapid in devaluing countries than in the control group. The recovery of exports is more rapid in devaluing countries than in the control group only in years

Table 4.10. *Changes in reserves*
(*between ends of respective years*)

	Year relative to devaluation						
	$T-3$	$T-2$	$T-1$	T	$T+1$	$T+2$	$T+3$
Devaluing countries							
Summary statistics (%)							
Mean	-7.61	-7.90	-19.75	0.32	2.66	0.25	18.58
Median	-6.28	-3.80	-19.30	-0.46	-0.15	2.60	15.20
Changes from previous period							
Number ↑	6	9	4	11	12	17	21
Number ↓	18	16	22	15	14	9	4
Probability that H_0 true (%)	1	11.4	0	28	42	9	0
t-statistic	-2.696	-1.871	-4.173	0.0744	0.4318	0.0527	3.888
Total sample							
Summary statistics (%)							
Mean	-7.20	-6.94	-17.18	-0.18	1.36	-0.24	15.60
Median	-6.28	-3.72	-18.20	-0.58	-4.27	0.57	13.34
Changes from previous period							
Number ↑	7	11	6	12	12	17	21
Number ↓	19	17	23	17	17	12	7
Probability that H_0 true (%)	9	15.6	0	22.8	22.8	22.8	1
t-statistic	0.5316	0.7033	1.702	-0.3695	-0.6821	-0.3345	-1.976

T, $T + 1$, and $T + 3$. While import volumes fall in the year of devaluation and rise thereafter, there is little discernible difference in the behaviour of devaluing countries and the control group.

Why is there such weak evidence of a differential response between devaluing countries and the control group? Part of the reason is likely to be that the control group is small. (It comprises only four countries: France, the Netherlands, Switzerland, and Poland.) Part of the explanation may also lie in the monetary policies of devaluing countries. Table 4.11 shows rates of growth of M1 over the devaluation periods. It is evident that devaluing countries hesitated to adopt reflationary monetary policies in the immediate aftermath of devaluation. Even when they subsequently turned to reflation, the monetary stimulus remained tentative.

What accounts for this hesitancy to reflate? To a remarkable extent, policy-makers' actions were conditioned by memories of the last episode when the gold standard had been in abeyance. Suspension had been marked by inflation, social turmoil, and political instability. Only when domestic interest groups had agreed to compromise over the distribution of incomes and the burden of taxation and had sealed their compact by reimposing the gold standard had this chaos been vanquished. Now that the gold standard was gone, it was regarded as all the more important for politicians to affirm their commitment to budgetary orthodoxy and for central banks to demonstrate their opposition to inflation. Only as it became clear that inconvertibility was not a threat to price stability did policy-makers begin to take on a more active role.

More than a year of experience was required to convince officials that inconvertibility did not pose an inflationary threat. Gradually they moved from accommodating the credit demands of industry and enterprise to a policy of price stabilization, and then to a policy of reflation. But the transformation was slow. As one observer wrote of Sweden, which abandoned gold in 1931: 'The Board of Directors of the Riksbank apparently formulated their policies during the first part of 1932 much as though Sweden had not abandoned gold.'[17] The gold standard may have disintegrated in 1931, but its ethos continued to influence the formulation of policy even where it no longer prevailed.

4   Implications for the performance of financial and commodity markets

The preceding suggests that exchange rate flexibility, by relaxing the external constraint, facilitated the pursuit of policies that sped recovery from the Great Depression. This should not be viewed, however, as a

Table 4.11. *Changes in M1*
(*between ends of respective years*)

| | \multicolumn{7}{c}{Year relative to devaluation} |
	$T-3$	$T-2$	$T-1$	T	$T+1$	$T+2$	$T+3$
Devaluing countries							
Summary statistics (%)							
Mean	0.45	-4.01	-4.24	3.64	5.31	3.74	6.03
Median	1.84	-1.48	-3.30	1.51	2.96	4.06	5.46
Changes from previous period							
Number ↑	14	11	5	17	18	22	23
Number ↓	12	16	22	10	9	5	3
Probability that H_0 true (%)	42	22	0	12.3	6	0	0
t-statistic	0.2833	-1.792	-1.380	1.547	2.795	3.754	4.256
Total sample							
Summary statistics (%)							
Mean	0.74	-3.53	-4.22	2.74	4.51	3.31	5.98
Median	2.31	-0.89	-2.94	0.49	2.15	2.21	4.91
Changes from previous period							
Number ↑	16	13	6	17	19	23	24
Number ↓	13	17	24	13	11	7	3
Probability that H_0 true (%)	35.4	29	0	29	10.3	0	0
t-statistic	0.5790	0.7043	0.0296	-1.244	-1.376	-1.388	-0.1806

blanket endorsement of floating exchange rates. The advantages of flexibility were predicated on the impossibility of international policy coordination. Moreover, exchange rate variability may have had other costs, in the form of the uncertainties and the relative price variability to which they gave rise.

In Eichengreen (1989) I analysed the behaviour of real and nominal exchange rates under the three interwar international monetary regimes: the free float of 1922–6, the fixed rates of 1927–31, and the managed float of 1932–6. I found that the variability of real as well as nominal exchange rates declined with the move from free floating to managed floating and from there to fixed rates. It did not follow, however, that policies which rendered real and nominal exchange rates less variable also rendered them proportionately more predictable.

That analysis was based on the behaviour of bilateral exchange rates against sterling and on naive forecasting equations. Here I extend the analysis to the behaviour of effective exchange rates. I consider also the behaviour of other variables, notably interest rates and prices, across the three exchange rate regimes. And I estimate a variety of more sophisticated forecasting equations.

The data for this analysis are taken, in the main, from Einzig (1937) and League of Nations publications. Einzig provided weekly data on spot exchange rates; to render these compatible with the wholesale price and money supply data drawn from Einzig and from League of Nations *Monthly Bulletin* monthly averages were taken. Additional exchange rate data were taken from this same League of Nations source. I interpolated along weighed averages of annual data for foreign trade to construct effective exchange rates.[18] The three periods I consider are January 1922 through August 1926 (free floating), January 1927 through August 1931 (fixed exchange rates), and January 1932 through August 1936 (managed floating). The transition periods between regimes are omitted. The division into periods inevitably has an element of arbitrariness. The rationale for this particular periodization is discussed in Eichengreen (1989).

Table 4.12 displays percentage changes in nominal effective exchange rates under the three regimes. There are pronounced differences across periods. To a large extent, the extreme behaviour of nominal rates in 1922–6 is due, however, to the exceptional variability of the German mark. (Given the use of trade weights that include Germany, this affects each effective rate.) Leaving Germany out of the calculation entirely, as in the bottom panel of the table, changes the picture. (Except where explicitly noted to the contrary, any comparisons across periods cited in the text omit Germany for 1922–6.) The bottom panel suggests that effective nominal rates were about twice as variable under free floating as

Table 4.12. *Standard deviations of change in spot rates: monthly effective (trade-weighted) nominal exchange rates in logs*
$(\log EER_t - \log EER_{t-1}) \times 100$

	Period 1 1922.01–1923.06 1924.01–1926.07	Period 2 1927.01–1931.07	Period 3 1932.01–1935.10 1936.01–1936.07
Belgium	28.82	0.81	4.08
Germany[a]	29.35	0.75	1.41
Netherlands	32.31	0.30	0.99
Italy	31.31	2.17	1.77
USA	32.80	0.67	3.25
France	29.26	0.55	1.39
Switzerland	31.68	0.74	0.88
Sweden	32.34	0.38	3.87
Norway	32.64	0.78	3.94
Denmark	31.46	0.40	4.28
Finland	33.17	1.00	4.28
UK	32.43	1.44	1.98
mean	31.47	0.83	2.68

	Without Germany		
	1922.01–1926.07	1927.01–1931.07	1932.01–1935.10 1936.01–1936.07
Belgium	3.71	0.55	3.87
Netherlands	5.44	0.41	1.16
Italy	4.97	1.89	1.71
USA	4.68	0.68	2.35
France	3.15	1.05	1.65
Switzerland	4.44	1.40	0.56
Sweden	3.46	0.73	2.05
Norway	4.63	1.14	2.15
Denmark	3.77	0.37	2.34
Finland	5.85	0.71	3.14
UK	4.08	0.30	1.65
mean	4.38	0.84	2.06

Note: [a] 1923.01 and onwards only.
Source: See text.

Table 4.13. *Monthly percentage change in wholesale prices*
(mean and standard deviation in per cent)

	Number of observations	mean	S.D.	kurtosis	skewness
1922.01–1926.08					
USA	55	1.55	1.22	7.65	− 4.54
France	55	1.72	4.02	1.07	− 0.13
Belgium	55	1.60	4.37	1.53	0.61
Netherlands	55	− 0.27	1.80	0.37	− 0.05
Italy	55	0.41	1.95	0.09	− 0.00
Switzerland	55	− 0.28	1.55	1.49	0.52
UK	55	− 0.17	1.18	− 0.75	− 0.02
Group w/o Ger.	385	0.65	2.30	N/A	N/A
Ger. 1/22–6/23	18	63.75	70.26	2.81	1.63
Ger. 2/24–8/26	30	− 0.05	1.90	1.23	− 0.09
Group w/Ger.	433	3.23	5.10	N/A	N/A
1927.01–1931.08					
USA	55	− 0.52	0.10	− 0.80	− 0.14
France	55	− 0.60	1.34	− 0.86	0.08
Belgium	55	− 0.60	1.10	− 0.57	− 0.28
Netherlands	55	− 0.77	1.51	− 0.80	− 0.08
Italy	55	− 1.08	1.39	1.16	− 1.01
Switzerland	55	− 0.54	0.94	0.34	0.18
Germany	55	− 0.38	0.94	0.01	− 0.02
UK	55	− 0.66	1.01	− 0.47	0.09
Group	440	− 0.64	1.15	N/A	N/A
1932.01–1936.08					
USA	55	0.36	1.53	2.13	1.00
France	55	− 0.07	1.64	− 0.01	0.51
Belgium	55	0.10	2.29	25.25	4.52
Netherlands	55	− 0.22	1.46	− 0.32	0.04
Italy	55	0.04	1.29	− 0.45	0.27
Switzerland	55	− 0.15	0.99	− 0.92	− 0.25
Germany	55	0.08	0.67	0.61	− 0.31
UK	55	0.12	1.04	− 0.33	0.11
Group	440	0.03	1.36	N/A	N/A

Note: Wholesale price data are from Einzig (1937). Statistics are constructed using procedures describes in the text.
Source: See text.

under managed floating, and $2\frac{1}{2}$ times as variable under managed floating as in the gold standard period.

Table 4.13 compares the behaviour of prices. As measured by the standard deviation of monthly inflation rates, prices were 50% more

Table 4.14. *Standard deviations of monthly change in real effective exchange rates (trade-weighted)*
(log REER$_t$ − log REER$_{t-1}$) × 100

	Period 1 1922.01–1923.06 1924.01–1926.07	Period 2 1927.01–1931.07	Period 3 1932.01–1935.10 1936.01–1936.07
Belgium	7.84	1.25	2.71
Germany	4.68	0.75	2.41
Netherlands	5.09	1.33	1.72
Italy	5.75	1.70	2.02
USA	4.67	1.18	2.83
France	7.51	1.49	2.09
Switzerland	4.27	1.16	1.27
Sweden	4.77	0.75	3.86
Norway	4.76	1.14	4.11
Denmark	4.86	1.12	3.97
Finland	4.45	1.35	4.18
UK	3.24	1.44	1.97
mean	5.28	1.23	2.78

	Without Germany and Finland		
	1922.01–1926.07	1927.01–1931.07	1932.01–1935.10 1936.01–1936.07
Belgium	2.30	0.96	2.50
Netherlands	2.99	1.41	1.82
Italy	2.73	1.55	1.63
USA	2.88	1.16	1.95
France	2.47	1.28	1.55
Switzerland	2.78	1.33	1.42
Sweden	9.15	0.83	1.93
Norway	3.02	1.38	2.12
Denmark	2.04	1.06	1.99
UK	1.71	0.77	1.82
mean	2.48	1.17	1.87

Note: Because WPI data for Finland begin only in 1923, in the top panel Period 1 omits 1922.
Source: See text.

Table 4.15. *Percentage change in short-term interest rates*
(mean and standard deviation in per cent per annum)

	Number of observations	mean	S.D.	kurtosis	skewness
1922.01–1926.08					
USA	55	0.03	7.92	4.71	− 1.02
France	55	0.45	5.05	1.74	0.64
Belgium	55	0.62	3.97	12.64	2.90
Netherlands	55	0.55	17.52	1.11	0.81
Italy	55	0.48	3.05	2.68	0.57
Switzerland	55	0.72	14.98	4.98	1.91
UK	55	1.17	13.48	12.59	2.65
Group w/o Ger.	385	0.58	9.42	N/A	N/A
Ger. 1/22–6/23	18	34.31	92.61	7.36	2.77
Ger. 2/24–8/26	30	− 5.73	12.43	4.04	0.48
Group w/Ger.	433	1.54	13.12	N/A	N/A
1927.01–1931.08					
USA	55	− 2.05	8.18	1.65	− 1.24
France	55	− 1.37	11.15	6.92	1.68
Belgium	55	− 0.67	6.39	3.62	0.04
Netherlands	55	− 0.85	11.09	1.68	0.49
Italy	55	− 0.76	4.63	2.93	− 0.51
Switzerland	55	− 0.52	8.49	7.94	2.03
Germany	55	2.35	11.33	4.22	1.96
UK	55	1.08	16.88	20.18	3.77
Group	440	− 0.35	9.77	N/A	N/A
1932.01–1936.08					
USA	55	4.29	63.16	34.57	5.51
France	55	3.66	26.30	6.34	2.04
Belgium	55	− 1.24	5.38	2.18	− 0.54
Netherlands	55	14.73	93.79	22.23	4.40
Italy	55	− 0.72	6.66	4.46	1.46
Switzerland	55	0.68	5.88	15.82	3.38
Germany	55	− 1.49	4.43	7.86	− 1.31
UK	55	− 1.43	24.85	2.82	1.27
Group	440	2.31	28.81	N/A	N/A

Source: Interest rate data are from Einzig (1937).

variable under free floating than under managed floating, and 20% more variable under managed floating than under fixed rates. Though the pattern is the same as in Table 4.12, differentials in the variability of inflation across periods were small compared with differentials in the variability of nominal exchange rates. This presumably reflects the failure

Table 4.16. *Exchange rate predictability (standard deviations of residuals from exchange rate forecasts): effective nominal exchange rates (monthly data, in logs × 100)*

	Period 1 1922.01–1923.06 1924.01–1926.07	Period 2 1927.01–1931.07	Period 3 1932.01–1935.10 1936.01–1936.07
Denmark	25.53	0.34	4.02
Germany	26.40	0.87	4.21
Norway	26.49	0.71	3.85
Sweden	26.17	0.38	3.74
Switzerland	25.87	0.66	0.87
USA	26.31	0.67	3.23
France	23.94	0.51	1.28
Netherlands	26.05	0.29	0.96
Belgium	23.70	0.79	4.08
Italy	25.07	1.81	1.75
Germany[a]	21.11	0.75	1.40
UK	26.35	1.43	1.91
mean	25.25	0.77	2.61

	Without Germany		
	1922.01–1926.07	1927.01–1931.07	1932.01–1935.10 1936.01–1936.07
Denmark	3.68	0.31	2.28
Finland	5.76	0.70	3.08
Norway	4.52	1.13	2.12
Sweden	3.45	0.72	2.00
Switzerland	4.43	1.33	0.55
USA	4.68	0.67	2.33
France	3.13	0.90	1.64
Netherlands	5.44	0.41	1.13
Belgium	3.60	0.54	3.84
Italy	4.85	1.52	1.47
UK	3.95	0.28	1.59
mean	4.32	0.77	2.01

Note: [a] 1923.01–1923.06 and 1924.01–07 only.
Source: See text.

Table 4.17. Exchange rate predictability; standard deviations for various lag structures of residuals from effective exchange rate forecasts (in per cent)

lags	Period 1				Period 2				Period 3			
	−3	−3, −4	−6	−6, −7	−3	−3, −4	−6	−6, −7	−3	−3, −4	−6	−6, −7
Nominal												
Netherlands	9.82	—	12.61	—	0.97	0.73	1.67	1.19	2.18	—	2.92	—
Belgium	6.89	—	8.15	—	1.34	0.68	1.74	1.05	7.08	—	10.13	—
France	6.32	—	7.98	—	1.89	1.16	1.96	1.43	3.57	3.22	5.47	5.12
Italy	8.45	—	10.34	—	1.47	—	1.01	—	5.28	4.62	10.31	8.69
Sweden	5.85	—	7.09	—	1.83	1.09	2.41	1.56	4.27	3.97	6.77	6.32
UK	6.72	6.15	7.45	—	0.52	—	0.85	0.77	3.25	3.12	5.44	5.00
Finland	9.53	—	12.13	—	1.93	1.18	3.00	1.99	6.41	5.75	7.66	7.50
US	8.05	—	9.27	—	1.61	1.35	2.07	1.57	5.26	4.62	8.78	5.06
Denmark	7.90	7.62	13.96	13.19	0.67	0.53	1.02	0.80	4.19	3.60	6.22	
Germany[a]	5.04	4.69	6.03	5.38	1.84	1.47	2.41	1.76	2.57		3.34	
Norway	7.74	—	11.13	—	3.08	2.07	4.99	3.80	4.56	4.04	7.11	6.25
Switzerland	7.43	6.89	7.12	—	3.38	2.04	4.51	3.00	0.97	—	1.39	—
mean	7.48	—	9.44	—	1.71	—	2.30	—	4.13	—	6.30	—
Real (without Finland and Germany)												
Netherlands	4.10	—	4.64	—	2.41	—	3.26	2.97	3.41	—	4.95	—
Belgium	3.23	—	3.38	3.18	1.46	—	1.35	—	4.64	—	6.39	—
France	3.12	—	3.13	—	2.41	2.34	3.09	2.85	2.90	—	3.93	—
Italy	4.16	—	4.82	—	2.77	—	1.73	—	3.90	—	5.23	4.57

Table 4.17 (cont.)

Sweden	2.98	—	3.40	—	1.77	—	2.73	1.65	2.47	3.90	—	5.69	—
UK	2.39	—	2.68	—	1.22	—	1.67	—	—	3.50	3.45	5.67	5.17
Finland[b]	3.54	—	4.69	—	2.53	—	3.84	—	—	4.59	4.28	5.65	—
US	4.16	—	4.14	—	2.37	—	2.71	—	—	3.58	—	5.24	4.89
Denmark	3.34	2.37	4.01	3.77	1.54	1.50	1.68	—	—	3.94	3.43	5.80	5.00
Germany[a]	2.84	—	3.22	2.98	1.70	1.60	2.57	—	4.30	3.88	3.63	6.17	5.80
Norway	4.86	—	6.94	—	3.14	—	4.77	2.76	—	4.42	4.16	6.60	6.16
Switzerland	4.40	—	4.41	—	3.08	—	4.01	2.61	—	2.42	—	3.03	—
mean	3.59	—	4.12	—	2.20	—	2.78	—	—	3.75	—	5.36	—

Notes: Blanks indicate that regressions to create extra lags that were not statistically significant at standard confidence levels.
[a] 1924.01–1926.08 only.
[b] 1923.01–1926.08 only.

of prices to respond proportionately to month-to-month exchange-rate movements.

Table 4.14 displays the implications for the behaviour of real effective rates. Real rates were roughly 33% more variable under free floating than under managed floating, and 66% more variable under managed floating than during the gold standard period. It appears, then, that increased nominal exchange rate variability in the floating periods translated into an increase in the variability of relative prices, although the increase was not proportionate.

A common criticism of policies to stabilize exchange rates is that they simply shift the impact of disturbances on to other variables. The evidence in Table 4.13 on wholesale price inflation provided little support for this view. Table 4.15, which considers the variability of interest rates, is more supportive of the hypothesis. The absolute value of the monthly change in the interest rate was larger in the fixed rate period than under free floating for every country but Germany, Switzerland, and Britain. The standard deviation was larger under fixed rates for these three countries and the Netherlands but not for the others. The United Kingdom has an unusually variable nominal interest rate in the gold standard period; this may reflect persistent fears about the capacity of the UK to continue to stabilize its exchange rate. The results for 1932–6 confirm that interest rates were highly variable in countries that attempted to stabilize their exchange rates but whose capacity to do so was seriously tested by the market. The large standard deviations for the United States are dominated by outliers for March and April of 1933, months preceding and contemporaneous with devaluation. The large standard deviations for the Netherlands reflect repeated speculative attacks on a currency still pegged to gold.

Exchange rate variability is not the same thing as exchange rate uncertainty. Yet Table 4.16 shows that the variability of exchange rates is a good proxy for their predictability, as measured by a naive exchange rate forecast. The log effective nominal rate is regressed on its own lagged value, and the standard deviations of the forecast errors are computed. The forecasting equations have little predictive power, reflecting the well-known random walk character of exchange rate movements. Hence reductions in nominal exchange rate volatility imply commensurate reductions in exchange rate uncertainty. These results suggest that nominal effective rates were twice as difficult to predict under free floating as under managed floating, and $2\frac{1}{2}$ to 3 times as difficult to predict under managed floating as in the gold standard period.

Similar conclusions emerge when we consider predictability at longer horizons. Table 4.17 regresses the effective nominal rate on itself lagged

Table 4.18. *Standard deviations of residuals of log exchange rate forecasts using effective nominal rates*[a]
(in per cent)

	Period 1 1922.01–1926.08		Period 2 1927.01–1931.08		Period 3 1932.01–1936.08		
	A	B	A	B	A	B	C
Finland	5.51[d]	5.09[d]	0.36	0.32	2.65	2.22	2.23
Denmark	3.40	3.18	0.24	0.19	2.04	1.91	1.91
Sweden	3.42	3.14	0.40	0.37	1.76	1.57	1.61
Norway	4.59	4.24	0.70	0.54	1.63	1.59	1.57
Netherlands	5.38	4.57	0.27	0.23	1.07	1.02	N/A
Switzerland	4.14	3.88	0.44	0.25	0.50	0.45	N/A
France	2.79	2.54	0.35	0.34	1.45	1.39	1.37
Italy	4.80	4.37	0.70	0.61	1.13[c]	0.81[c]	N/A
UK	3.80	3.47	0.20	0.19	1.47	1.41	1.31
USA[b]	4.44[b]	4.34[b]	0.43	0.41	1.78	1.11	N/A
Belgium	3.42	3.02	0.26	0.25	3.78	3.16	N/A
Germany	N/A	N/A	N/A	N/A	N/A	N/A	N/A
mean w/o Germany	4.15	3.80	0.39	0.34	1.75	1.51	—

Notes:
[a] Effective exchange rates do not include Germany.
[b] 1922.02 to 1926.08 only.
[c] 1932.01 to 1935.11 only.
[d] 1923.01 to 1926.08 only.

A: $\log s_T = \alpha + \beta_1 \log s_{T-1} + \beta_2 \log s_{T-2} + \beta_3 \log s_{T-3} + \epsilon_T$

B: $\log s_T = \alpha + \beta_1 \log s_{T-1} + \beta_2 \log s_{T-2} + \beta_3 \log s_{T-3}$
$+ \beta_4 \log M_{T-1} + \beta_5 \log M_{T-2} + \beta_6 \log M_{T-3}$
$+ \beta_7 \log WPI_{T-1} + \beta_8 \log WPI_{T-2} + \beta_9 \log WPI_{T-3} + \epsilon_T$

C Same as B except M1 is used instead of currency in circulation. Data for deposits available only starting in 1932.
Source: See text.

three and six months.[19] Nominal effective rates three months ahead are about twice as difficult to predict under free floating as under managed floating, $2\frac{1}{2}$ times as difficult to predict under managed floating as under the gold standard. Six months ahead, the comparison between managed floating and the gold standard period is unchanged; the difference between the periods of free and managed floating is, however, somewhat attenuated.

A limitation of these results is that they fail to employ information on

108   **Barry Eichengreen**

Table 4.19. *Significance of alternative information sets in exchange rate forecasting equations*
(F-statistics)

	Period 1 A vs B	Period 2 A vs B	Period 3 A vs B	A vs C
Finland	0.88[a]	2.02	2.97*	2.97*
Denmark	1.03	5.01*	1.00	1.04
Sweden	1.36	1.23	1.82	1.38
Norway	1.22	4.62	0.43	0.55
Netherlands	2.73*	2.55*	0.71	N/A
Switzerland	0.96	15.57*	1.67	N/A
France	2.09	0.21	0.65	0.83
Italy	1.47	2.19	5.28*[c]	N/A
UK	1.41	1.00	0.54*	N/A
USA	3.13[b]	0.61	11.23*	N/A
Belgium	2.04	0.18	3.09*	N/A

Notes:
[a] $F_{6,31}$
[b] $F_{6,42}$
[c] $F_{6,33}$
H_0 is that all the lags of WPI and M jointly equal 0.
$F_{6,43}$ unless otherwise noted.
$F_{6,43}$: 5% = 2.32
$F_{6,31}$: 5% = 2.41
* = significant at 5% level
Source: Based on Table 4.18.

other variables useful for predicting exchange rate movements. Tables 4.18 and 4.19 therefore compare forecast errors derived from equations regressing the nominal effective rate on three own lags with forecasts derived from equations to which three lags of money supplies and wholesale prices are added. More information obviously improves the forecasts. Table 4.19 shows, however, that the improvement is statistically significant only in a minority of cases. Plausibly enough, the additional information has the greatest tendency to make a significant difference in the period of managed floating, when sporadic intervention by the monetary authorities took place.

Tables 4.19 and 4.20 show the results of comparable exercises using the real effective rate. When the real rate lagged one month is the only information included in the forecasting equation, real exchange rate variability and real exchange rate predictability point to virtually identical

Table 4.20. *Exchange rate predictability*
(Standard deviations of residuals from exchange rate forecasts, monthly
real exchange rates, trade-weighted, in logs × 100)

	Period 1 1923.01–1923.06 1924.01–1926.07	Period 2 1927.01–1931.07	Period 3 1932.01–1934.10 1936.01–1936.07
Denmark	4.89	1.09	3.82
Finland	4.43	1.27	4.12
Norway	4.75	1.11	4.04
Sweden	4.77	0.74	3.77
Switzerland	4.24	1.05	1.25
USA	4.87	1.18	2.82
France	6.77	1.44	2.08
Netherlands	5.04	1.32	1.71
Belgium	7.07	1.25	2.71
Italy	5.48	1.70	1.93
Germany	4.68	0.73	2.39
UK	4.68	1.52	2.17
mean	5.11	1.29	2.73

Without Germany and Finland		
1922.01–1926.07	1927.01–1931.07	1932.01–1935.10 1936.01–1936.07
Denmark 2.16	1.04	1.96
Norway 3.00	1.37	2.08
Sweden 1.90	0.82	1.89
Switzerland 2.70	1.33	1.41
USA 2.78	1.16	1.92
France 2.27	1.26	1.49
Netherlands 2.84	1.39	1.79
Belgium 2.23	0.93	2.50
Italy 2.60	1.53	1.62
UK 1.80	0.76	1.78
mean 2.43	1.16	1.85

Source: see text.

conclusions. Real exchange rate uncertainty, measured by the standard deviation of forecast errors, was 33% greater under free floating than under managed floating, and 66% greater under managed floating than in the fixed rate period. The implication, then, is that allowing exchange rates to vary, as in the 1930s, conferred significant costs in terms of increased uncertainty regarding the short-term behaviour of relative prices.

This conclusion is modified when real exchange rate forecasts are constructed for longer horizons. At three and six month intervals, there remains evidence of greater real exchange rate uncertainty under floating than under fixed rates. Yet real rates three and six months out actually appear to have been more difficult to predict under managed floating in the 1930s than under free floating in the 1920s. One suspects that this may reflect the nature of underlying real disturbances as much as the effects of the exchange rate regime, however. Future research may be able to separate out these effects.

5   Conclusions

This paper has documented the effects of exchange rates and the external constraints in the interwar years. In the absence of international policy coordination, exchange rate depreciation has been shown to have been a necessary precondition for the adoption of policies promoting recovery from the Great Depression. Those policies were shown to have been highly effective. At the same time, currency depreciation was not without costs. Depreciation both increased the variability of nominal exchange rates and rendered them increasingly difficult to predict. Increased variability and uncertainty about nominal exchange rates carried over to short-term changes in real rates as well. Thus, exchange rate variability appears to have introduced additional noise into the operation of the price mechanism.

From the vantage point of Europe in the 1990s, these results point to an obvious dilemma. Fixed exchange rates have advantages in terms of greater stability and predictability of relative prices. This has been one of the traditional arguments in favour of the European Monetary System. Exchange rates that are systematically stabilized, as in the second half of the 1920s, have similar advantages over exchange rates that are stabilized through sporadic intervention and are subject to periodic realignment, as in the 1930s. This has been one of the arguments for moving from the European Monetary System to a European central bank. The other side of the coin, so dramatically illustrated by the experience of the 1930s, is that fixed rates tighten the external constraint. Eurocrats may argue that nominal exchange rates have lost their ability to affect real variables, even in the short run, or that all significant obstacles to effective policy coordination in Europe have been removed. But the outside observer would feel more confident seeing systematic evidence on both questions before irrevocable policy decisions are made.

Appendix 4A: Devaluing countries, by year of devaluation, and members of the control group

1929	*1931*	*1932*	*1934*
Argentina	Mexico	Colombia	Czechoslovakia
	Canada	Costa Rica	Italy
	United Kingdom	Ecuador	
1930	Denmark	Nicaragua	*1935*
	Norway	Chile	
Australia	Sweden	Greece	Belgium
Brazil	Finland	Yugoslavia	
New Zealand	El Salvador	Paraguay	
Venezuela	Japan	Uruguay	*Control Group*
	Ireland		
	Austria	*1933*	Poland
	Germany		France
	Hungary	United States	Netherlands
	Bulgaria	Guatemala	Switzerland

Countries excluded from each table due to missing data

Industrial Production: Australia, Venezuela, Ireland, Ecuador, Yugoslavia, Czechoslovakia, Bulgaria, Uruguay, Paraguay, and Argentina (1926/27–1927/28 only).

M1: Austria, Costa Rica, Nicaragua, Paraguay, Guatemala, and Czechoslovakia (1937/38), Switzerland, Argentina (1926/27), France and the Netherlands (1937/39 only).

Volume of Exports: Ecuador, Nicaragua, Yugoslavia, Guatemala, Czechoslovakia, Paraguay, Italy, Switzerland and Argentina (1926/27).

Volume of Imports: Same as Volume of Exports, except Uruguay is also excluded

Nominal Imports and *Nominal Exports*: Switzerland and Argentina (1926/27).

WPI: Costa Rica, Nicaragua, Guatemala, and Paraguay.

Reserves: Paraguay, Mexico, Costa Rica, Greece. Nicaragua, Brazil, Switzerland, Bulgaria (1927/8 only), Denmark (1936/7 only), Chile (1930/1), New Zealand (1928/9), and Argentina (1926/7).

Appendix 4B   Construction of effective exchange rates

From the League of Nations *International Trade Statistics* volumes, I gathered annual data on bilateral imports and exports among the following countries: Belgium, Denmark, Finland, France, Germany, Italy, Netherlands, Norway, Sweden, Switzerland, the United Kingdom, and the United States. Trade weights, for each country, w_{ij}, were constructed as

$$w_{ij} = \frac{x_{ij} + m_{ij}}{x_i + m_i}$$

where x_{ij} and m_{ij} are the value, in the currency of country i, of the exports and imports of country i with country j; and x_i and m_i are the sums of the x_{ij} and m_{ij} (summing across all eleven trading partners considered in this study).

When considering a subset of the twelve country sample, I do not alter the trade weights, w_{ij}.

These trade weights are annual, whereas the exchange rate data are monthly. I interpolate to develop monthly weights. For example, the January 1931 trade weight for each country equals 50% of the 1931 and 50% of the 1932 annual trade weights. Effective nominal and real exchange rates are then constructed as

$$EER_{i,t} = \sum_{j=1}^{11} w_{ij} S_{ij}$$

S_{ij} = spot exchange rate in units of currency of country j per unit of country i's currency

t = time, monthly

and

$$REER_{i,t} = \sum_{j=1}^{11} w_{ij} S_{ij} \frac{P_i}{P_j}$$

where P_i = price level of country i
P_j = price level of country j

Appendix 4C   Macroeconomic data for Tables 4.4–4.11

Exports and imports. Special trade, which excludes gold and silver bullion and specie. Current values, in local currency, are from League of Nations publications on trade when available, and supplemented with Mitchell (1981).

Volume of exports and imports. These data are special trade whenever possible. However, in several cases, volume figures were reported for general trade only. Source is the League of Nations publications on trade, supplemented with Thorp (1984) for Latin America where League of

Nations data were not available. The League of Nations publications report volume figures for 1927 to 1935 only. For 1936 to 1938, I used nominal exports (imports) divided by League export (import) price indices.

Wholesale Price Indices (WPI). European figures are from the League of Nations *Statistical Yearbooks.* For Latin America, Mitchell and Thorp were also used. The base year is 1929. For some Latin American countries for which consistent wholesale price indices were not available, consumer price indices were used instead. For El Salvador and Ecuador, national government publications were used. Butlin (1962) was used for Australia.

Industrial Production. Data for Belgium, Ireland, Poland, and New Zealand are from Mitchell (1981, 1983). For Central and South America, except Chile, Thorp (1984) was used. The League of Nations *Statistical Yearbooks* provided data for all other countries.

Money Supply. Derived from the League of Nations *Memorandum on Currency and Finance.* M1 is the sum of coins and currency in circulation and demand (sight) deposits.

Reserves. Foreign reserves are the sum of gold and foreign exchange held as reserves by each country's monetary authority in local currency at current exchange rates. These are reported as separate items in the League of Nations *Statistical Yearbooks* and *Memorandum on Currency and Banking.* Gold reserves are reported at constant parity.

Sources and documents cited in Appendix 4C

Anuario Estadistico de El Salvador (various years), San Salvador: Direccion General de Estadistica y Censos.

Anuario Estadistico de Nicaragua (various years), Managua: Instituto Nacional de Estadisticas y Censos.

Anuario Estadistico de Uruguay (1938), Uruguay: Direccion de Estadistica y Censos.

Butlin, N.G. (1962), *Australian Domestic Product, Investment and Foreign Borrowing, 1861–1938/39,* Cambridge University Press.

Ecuador en Cifras, 1938 à 1942 (1944), Quito: Direccion General de Estadistica.

Estadisticas Historicas de Mexico (1985), Mexico, D.F.: Instituto Nacional de Estadistica, Geografia e Informatica.

League of Nations (various years), *International Trade Statistics,* Geneva: League of Nations.

 (various years), *Memorandum on Currency and Banking,* Geneva: League of Nations.

114   **Barry Eichengreen**

(various years), *Monthly Bulletin of Statistics*, Geneva: League of Nations.

(various years), *Statistical Yearbook*, Geneva: League of Nations.

Mitchell, B.R. (1981), *European Historical Statistics*, London: Macmillan.

(1983), *International Historical Statistics: The Americas and Australasia*, London: Macmillan.

Thorp, Rosemary (ed.) (1984), *Latin America in the 1930s: The Role of the Periphery in World Crisis*, London: Macmillan.

Urquhart, M.C. (1965), *Historical Statistics of Canada*, Cambridge University Press.

NOTES

Financial support was provided by the National Science Foundation, the German Marshall Fund of the United States, and a CEPR summer research grant. The Institute of Business and Economic Research of the University of California at Berkeley provided logistical assistance, Carolyn Werley sterling research assistance, and Steve Kamin valuable advice. Margo Sercarz and Kazumi Uda painstakingly typed the tables. I am grateful to all of the above.

 1 A partial list of other authors who subscribe to this view would include Temin and Wigmore (1988), Broadberry (1989), and most of the contributors to Gregory and Butlin (1988).

 2 Friedman and Schwartz (1963) and Temin (1976) are, of course, the two classic analyses of the Depression which focus mainly on the United States. The negative view of exchange rate changes in the 1930s derives largely from the influential account of Kindleberger (1973).

 3 The countries included in Tables 5.1–5.3 (except as noted) are Belgium, France, the Netherlands, Poland, and Switzerland (members of the gold bloc), Austria, Bulgaria, Czechoslovakia, Germany, Hungary, Italy, and Yugoslavia (countries under exchange control), Australia, Denmark, Finland, New Zealand, Norway, Sweden, and the United Kingdom (members of the sterling area), and Brazil, Colombia, Chile, Mexico, Costa Rica, Guatemala, Nicaragua, El Salvador, and the United States (other countries with depreciated currencies).

 4 Choudri and Kochin (1981) considered Spain and half a dozen smaller European countries that remained on gold for various periods of time. Eichengreen and Sachs (1985) concentrated on ten European countries. Temin (1989) limited his attention to the US, the UK, France, and Germany. Bernanke and James (1990) consider a sample of twenty-two countries and come closest to making this same point.

 5 There is a growing consensus that a monetary shock in the US provides at least part of the explanation for the onset of the Depression. See Hamilton (1987, 1988) and Bernanke and James (1990).

 6 Eichengreen (1990b), p. 249.

 7 League of Nations (1935), p. 221.

 8 The label M1 is used loosely. For each country, the figures represent currency plus deposits of commercial banks, as tabulated by the League of Nations in its *Monetary Reviews*.

9 Twenty per cent was the typical rate of depreciation of exchange rates in the month following devaluation. This implies an annualized rate of return on the order of 790%, meaning that even a small probability of devaluation in the next month rendered a single digit interest differential ineffectual.
10 This argument is spelled out at length in Eichengreen (1985).
11 US Department of State (1933), I, p. 466.
12 There is a large literature concerned with other determinants of economic policy decisions in the 1930s. For example, Gourevitch (1984) considers interest group politics, while Weir and Skocpol (1984) examine the role played by the structure of state bureaucracies. It is certain that factors such as these also affected the scope for international policy coordination. Space limitations permit me to develop here only what I regard as the most novel aspect of the argument, namely the importance of competing conceptual frameworks. For a more extended analysis of one notable attempt to arrange a coordinated response to the Depression, namely the 1933 World Economic Conference, which attempts to incorporate roles for state structures and interest group politics, see Eichengreen and Uzan (1990).
13 A recent discussion of Keynes's Macmillan Committee evidence and its impact is provided by Clarke (1989). A representative sampling of British opinion on Bank of France and Federal Reserve policy may be found in Royal Institute of International Affairs (1931). Correspondence between the Bank of England and the Bank of France is described in Eichengreen (1986).
14 A cogent statement of the prevailing French view is Rist (1933).
15 Appendix A lists the countries in the sample, the subsets included in the various tables, and the sources of data.
16 Since exchange control similarly allowed countries to relax the external constraint, countries utilizing the instrument are treated as having left the gold standard in the year that controls were imposed.
17 Lester (1939), p. 241.
18 Trade data are taken from the League of Nations' *International Trade Statistics* volumes. Appendix B contains a brief description of the methodology used to construct the effective rates.
19 Additional lags were also added. For example, in the column labelled '− 3, − 4' the exchange rate was regressed on its value lagged both three and four months. The standard deviations of the residuals are reported only for those cases where the additional lag was statistically significant.

REFERENCES

Bernanke, Ben (1983), 'Nonmonetary Effects of the Financial Crisis in the Propagation of the Great Depression', *American Economic Review* 73, 257–76.
Bernanke, Ben and Harold James (1990), 'The Gold Standard, Deflation, and Financial Crisis in the Great Depression: An International Comparison', presented to the NBER Conference on Financial Crisis, March 22–4.
Broadberry, Stephen N. (1989), 'Monetary Interdependence and Deflation in Britain and the United States Between the Wars', in Marcus Miller, Barry Eichengreen, and Richard Portes (eds.), *Blueprints for Exchange Rate Management*, New York: Academic Press, pp. 47–70.
Choudri, E. and Levis Kochin (1981), 'The Exchange Rate and the International

Transmission of Business Cycle Disturbances', *Journal of Money, Credit and Banking* **12**, 565–74.

Clarke, Peter (1989), *The Making of the Keynesian Revolution*, Oxford: Clarendon Press.

Donovon, Donal J. (1981), 'Real Responses Associated with Exchange Rate Action in Selected Upper Credit Tranche Stabilization Programs', *IMF Staff Papers* **28**, 698–727.

Eichengreen, Barry (1985), 'International Policy Coordination in Historical Perspective: A View from the Interwar Years', in Willem Buiter and Richard Marston (eds.), *International Economic Policy Coordination*, Cambridge University Press, pp. 139–78.

(1986), 'The Bank of France and the Sterilization of Gold, 1926–1932', *Explorations in Economic History* **23**, 56–84.

(1989), 'The Comparative Performance of Fixed and Flexible Exchange Rate Regimes: Interwar Evidence', NBER Working Paper no. 3097 (September), forthcoming in P. Villipillai (ed.), *Recent Developments in Business Cycle Analysis*, London: Macmillan.

(1990a), 'International Monetary Instability Between the Wars: Structural Flaws or Misguided Policies?', in Yoshio Suzuki, Junichi Miyake, and Mitsuaki Okabe (eds.), *The Evolution of the International Monetary System*, Tokyo: University of Tokyo Press, pp. 71–116.

(1990b), *Elusive Stability: Essays in the History of International Finance, 1919–1939*, Cambridge University Press.

Eichengreen, Barry and Jeffrey Sachs (1985), 'Exchange Rates and Economic Recovery in the 1930s', *Journal of Economic History* **65**, 925–46.

Eichengreen, Barry and Marc Uzan (1990), 'The 1933 World Economic Conference as an Instance of Failed International Cooperation', unpublished, University of California at Berkeley.

Einzig, Paul (1937), *The Theory of Forward Exchange*, London: Macmillan.

Frankel, Jeffrey A. (1988), 'Obstacles to International Economic Policy Coordination', *Princeton Studies in International Finance* no. 64, Princeton: Princeton University Press.

Friedman, Milton and Anna J. Schwartz (1963), *A Monetary History of the United States, 1867–1960*, Princeton: Princeton University Press.

Gourevitch, Peter (1984), 'Breaking with Orthodoxy: The Politics of Economic Policy Responses to the Depression of the 1930s', *International Organization* **38**, 95–129.

Gregory, R.G. and N.G. Butlin (1988), *Recovery from the Depression: Australia and the World Economy in the 1930s*, Cambridge University Press.

Hamilton, James (1987), 'Monetary Factors in the Great Depression', *Journal of Monetary Economics* **19**, 145–69.

(1988), 'The Role of the International Gold Standard in Propagating the Great Depression', *Contemporary Policy Issues* **6**, 67–89.

Kindleberger, Charles (1973), *The World in Depression, 1929–1939*, Berkeley: University of California Press.

Kamin, Steven B. (1988), 'Devaluation, External Balance, and Macroeconomic Performance: A Look at the Numbers', *Princeton Studies in International Finance* no. 62 (August).

Keynes, John Maynard (1930), *A Treatise on Money*, London: Macmillan.

League of Nations (1935), *Economic Survey 1934/35*, Geneva: League of Nations.

(various years), *Monthly Bulletin of Statistics*, Geneva: League of Nations.
(various years), *Monetary Review*, Geneva: League of Nations.
(various years), *Balances of Payments*, Geneva: League of Nations.
Lester, Richard (1939), *Monetary Experiments*, Princeton: Princeton University Press.
Moggridge, Donald (1972), *British Monetary Policy, 1924–1931*. Cambridge University Press.
Rist, Charles (1933), 'Caractère et origine de la crise de 1929', in *Essais sur quelques problèmes économiques et monétaires*, Paris: Recueil Sirey, pp. 325–43.
Royal Institute of International Affairs (1931), *The International Gold Problem*, Oxford University Press.
Temin, Peter (1976), *Did Monetary Forces Cause the Great Depression?*, New York: Norton.
(1989), *Lessons from the Great Depression*, Cambridge, MA: MIT Press.
Temin, Peter and Barrie Wigmore (1988), 'The End of One Big Deflation, 1933', MIT Economics Working Paper no. 503 (October).
United States Department of State (1933), *Foreign Relations of the United States* Washington, D.C.: GPO.
Weir, Margaret and Theda Skocpol (1985), 'State Structures and the Possibilities for "Keynesian" Responses to the Great Depression in Sweden, Britain and the United States', in Peter Evans *et al.* (eds.), *Bringing the State Back In*, New York: Cambridge University Press, pp. 107–63.

Discussion

LOUKA T. KATSELI

Let me start by saying that I found this to be an interesting, thought-provoking, and informative chapter. The author at first demonstrates why, under the gold standard, a negative monetary shock in the US spread through to other countries. As the US money supply fell and interest rates rose, foreign countries experienced an outflow of gold, a deterioration in their balance-of-payments position, a restriction in their money supply, and deflationary pressures in their economy. This was exacerbated by a negative aggregate demand shock as the US demand for imports declined. It was propagated further by nominal wage stickiness in many countries that caused real wages to increase as prices started falling. On the financial side, an additional source of monetary non-neutrality was the breakdown of financial intermediation as deflation eroded the value of the collateral debtors had offered, and the balance sheet position of the banks deteriorated.

Thus, the analysis presented by Eichengreen is a nice application of the standard Mundell–Fleming model to the open economy. The policy implications are also clear: in a world of fixed exchange rates or, for that matter, under the gold standard, monetary reflation by any single country proved to be ineffective as it was translated into reserve losses. The only way to relax the external constraint was to abandon the gold standard and suspend convertibility, allowing central banks to expand their money supply.

The alternative to unilateral depreciation would have been an internationally coordinated reflation. This would have allowed countries to avoid the deflationary spiral and stabilize their financial systems without endangering gold convertibility. Why didn't they pursue such a policy option? This is the central question that the author poses. The answer he gives is still, in my view, tentative and ought to be investigated further. Following J. Frankel's view, he argues that major countries at the time had different models of the economy in mind derived from different historical experiences. Whereas Britain, according to the author, attached priority to coordinated monetary reflation, France and less so the United States attached high priority to exchange rate stabilization as the depression was perceived to be a product of excessive credit creation on the part of the central banks in the preceding years.

Even though these explanations might be valid it would be interesting to investigate why they were held. More specifically, the analysis and evaluation of historical experiences in any single country is usually strongly influenced by the political cycle in that country, the party and the government in place, the relative power of the central bank *vis-à-vis* other parts of the government, the relative power of specific interests in the economy, or the pattern of interdependence between countries; in other words, by internal and international politics and institutional factors. The need for such an analysis becomes evident, for example, when the author notes that by 1932 Congressional pressure in the US, led by representatives of agricultural and silver-mining states, had become so intense that it eventually prompted the election of Franklin Roosevelt. What was the political configuration at that time in Britain or France? Furthermore was 'the noted absence of conscious manipulation of fiscal instruments' noted by the author in his analysis of European policy, completely divorced from the political process: Why was this trend reversed in the US under Roosevelt?

In summary, the chapter adopts what I would call a rather agnostic state-centric view of the political process which is inconsistent with the author's interest in endogenizing the prevalence of different perceptions across countries by trying to explain why countries were unable to coordinate their reflationary initiatives internationally.

Besides institutional factors and the political process itself, it would have been important to analyse the role of differences in structural characteristics such as the pattern of inertia built into the wage–price mechanism in influencing the choice of policy options across countries.

This brings us to an interesting comparison between the interwar experience as presented by Eichengreen with that of Europe in the early 1980s. At that time, even though fixed rates were abandoned for a long time, a US shock that raised interest rates produced a severe deflationary shock as the leading European countries preferred to pursue 'coupling' as opposed to 'decoupling' policies, i.e., preferred to match the interest rate increases and to curtail demand as opposed to letting the exchange rate adjust sufficiently and/or to coordinate reflationist policies. This was justified at the time on supply-rigidity grounds, the famous 'Eurosclerosis' thesis, even though the empirical evidence was rather mixed (see papers by Gordon, 1987; Bruno, 1985, *et al.*). In a recent paper (Katseli, 1989), it was shown that politics had as much to do with it as economics.

This brings me to a more general point bearing on Eichengreen's conclusions. There is no doubt that fixed exchange rates tighten the external constraint. But experience so far has shown that, even under flexible or managed rates, there is substantial room for maneuvering in tightening or loosening the external constraints based on the differences of policymakers that are dictated by economic, political, or institutional factors and by their relative power to translate preferences into concrete policy. In other words, even if 'historical evidence' is produced to support a position that 'all significant obstacles to effective policy coordination in Europe have been now removed', this evidence would be still subject to a particular set of historical and poiltical circumstances, that are easily reversible and thus unpredictable.

REFERENCES

Bruno, M. (1985), 'Aggregate supply and demand factors in OECD unemployment: an update', NBER Working Paper No 1969, September.

Gordon, R. (1987), 'Wage Gaps vs. Output Gaps: Is there a Common Story for all of Europe', NBER Working Paper No. 2454, December.

Katseli, L. (1989), 'The Political Economy of Macroeconomic Policy in Europe' in P. Guerrieri and P.C. Padoan (eds.), *The Political Economy of European Integration*, Harvester Wheatsheaf.

5 External constraints on European unemployment

GEORGE S. ALOGOSKOUFIS and
CHRISTOPHER MARTIN

The persistently high rate of unemployment has probably been Western Europe's most important economic problem of the 1970s and the 1980s. Average unemployment rose relentlessly between the early seventies and the mid eighties. It only turned downwards in 1986. From a peak of 10.6% of the labour force in 1985, unemployment in OECD Europe is estimated to have fallen to 9.0% in 1989, and the OECD predicts that it will be stabilized at 8.9% in 1990 and 1991. The US unemployment rate, which has historically been higher than in Europe, was only 5.2% in 1989, and the projections of the OECD put it at 5.4% in 1990 and 5.5% in 1991. Japan's unemployment rate was 2.3% in 1989, and is predicted to remain constant. Thus, the relative performance of Europe is not expected to improve much during the early part of the 1990s.

In the light of these developments, it is perhaps an appropriate time to stand back and take stock of what we have learned about European unemployment during the long years for which it was rising, and also try to detect whether the recent reversal of this trend has anything to teach us about the nature of the European unemployment problem. In particular, one would like to examine whether there are there any lessons to be learned concerning the demand as opposed to the supply explanations of the European unemployment problem, and the implications of alternative hypotheses about unemployment persistence in Europe.[1]

There is a large body of research that seems to suggest significant structural differences between, on the one hand Europe and the United States, and on the other hand the EEC, the EFTA countries, and Japan. The evidence seems to suggest that the main difference between the EEC and the EFTA countries and Japan is in the steady-state responsiveness of real wages to unemployment. With regard to the comparison between Europe and the United States there are suggestions of important differences in the speed of labour market adjustment to permanent and transitory disturbances. Most of the cross-country econometric studies that have been undertaken to examine the problem of European unemployment, point to one or other source of sluggish adjustment in the labour market, especially for the economies of the European Economic Community (EEC).

The econometric studies that have estimated the response of real wages to unemployment (Grubb et al., 1982, 1983; Bruno and Sachs, 1985; Newell and Symons, 1985; Bean et al., 1986; Alogoskoufis and Manning, 1988b) suggest that this is smaller in the EEC countries than in the EFTA countries and Japan. In addition, Sachs (1979) and Branson and Rotemberg (1980) suggest that Europe is characterized by real wage rigidity (full indexation). Finally, Bruno and Sachs (1985), Grubb, et al. (1982, 1983), Newell and Symons (1987), and Alogoskoufis and Manning (1988b) among others suggest that the speed of adjustment of real wages seems to be slower in Europe than in the United States. Proponents of insider–outsider models in the labour market (Lindbeck and Snower, 1987, 1989; Blanchard and Summers, 1986) suggest that those who lose their jobs get disenfranchised from the labour market much more quickly in Europe than in the United States. Blanchard and Summers (1986) present some evidence on that, although aspects of this evidence are disputed in Alogoskoufis and Manning (1988a, b). In addition, there are those who emphasize the higher costs of employment adjustment in Europe relative to the United States (see Metcalf, 1987; Emerson, 1988). The macroeconomic evidence in cross-country studies (Newell and Symons, 1985; Bean et al., 1986; Alogoskoufis and Manning, 1988a; OECD, 1989) suggest that labour demand may indeed be somewhat more sluggish in Europe than in the United States.

What seems to be often disregarded in this literature is the possibility that a large part of the differences in the behaviour of unemployment may be due to macroeconomic policies and their interaction. The labour market differences have been overemphasized in the academic debate, and, with the exception of the papers of the CEPS Macroeconomic Policy Group, the possibility that the major difference between Europe and the United States may have been in the responsiveness of macroeconomic policy to a rise in unemployment, and to macroeconomic interdependence, has not been entertained very seriously. In this chapter we argue that macroeconomic policies are by themselves an adequate explanation of EEC–US differences in unemployment experience in the 1970s and the 1980s. However, we go somewhat deeper and ask whether the more cautious macroeconomic policy stance in Europe is a manifestation of a more severe external constraint than in the United States.

In Section 1 we present four stylized facts about the European unemployment experience since the early 1970s. It is argued that what needs to be generally accounted for is the following set of characteristics: first, the significant rise in average unemployment in both Europe and the United States in the mid 1970s and the early 1980s. Second, the much smaller rise in unemployment in the EFTA countries and Japan. Third, the rapid fall of unemployment in the United States after both 1975 and 1982, compared to a continuous rise in Europe until 1986, and finally, the simultaneous fall of European and US unemployment between 1986 and 1989.

In Section 2 of the chapter, we present a prototype static model of equilibrium unemployment in open economies, and examine the extent to which it can account for the four stylized facts reported above. Equilibrium unemployment in this model is the rate at which wage setting by workers is consistent with price setting by firms, given that demand is equal to domestic output in the product market. The equilibrium rate depends on both supply side and demand factors. This model can explain the rise in OECD unemployment in the 1970s and early 1980s, in terms of the productivity slowdown and the supply shocks that hit the OECD economies, and the rise in marginal tax rates in Europe. The differential experience of the EFTA countries and Japan can be attributed to the higher responsiveness of real wages to unemployment in these countries, compared to both the rest of Europe and the United States. Theories that stress centralization in wage setting (or corporatism) seem to explain the major differences between the EFTA countries on the one hand, and the rest of Europe on the other. However, they fail to adequately explain the differences between Europe and Japan, as well as the experience of Switzerland. Other institutional factors have been proposed for these countries. This equilibrium model also seems able to explain the fall of US unemployment after 1982, in terms of the US fiscal expansion. However, it has problems in accounting for the other two stylized facts, namely the fall in US unemployment after 1975, as opposed to the persistence of unemployment in Europe, and the reasons for the simultaneous fall of unemployment in both Europe and the US after 1986.

In Section 3 we introduce a model that allows for imports of commodities from LDCs. With this modification one can explain the simultaneous rise or fall in OECD unemployment following contractionary or expansionary fiscal policies. A fiscal expansion in the OECD causes a reduction in the relative price of commodities, which allows a fall in OECD unemployment because it affects the wedge between consumer and producer prices. However, such a model cannot explain the events of the 1970s, when demand expansions in the OECD resulted in increases of the relative price of commodities.

In Section 4 we use a model of sluggish price adjustment which allows for the role of monetary policy and price and unemployment dynamics. A monetary expansion in the OECD is shown to result in a reduction in OECD unemployment, a temporary increase in real commodity prices and an inflationary adjustment path with falling relative commodity prices and rising unemployment. On the other hand, a fiscal expansion has more permanent effects on unemployment, and results in a fall of relative commodity prices in both the short and the medium run. In fact, the short-run fall in commodity prices overshoots the medium-run fall. With regard to effects within the OECD, it is shown that a monetary expansion in the United States results in a transitory but persistent real dollar depreciation and a persistent fall in unemployment in the USA relative to Europe. Thus, this model can explain the events of 1976–8, and in addition provides a richer explanation of the other phenomena that the equilibrium models could in principle account for. A fiscal expansion in the United States results in a persistent real appreciation of the US dollar *vis-à-vis* European currencies, and a persistent fall of relative US unemployment. Thus, the model can easily account for the events of the 1980s, when a fiscal expansion in the US exported unemployment and inflation to Europe in the first half of the decade, and a joint expansion in the second half of the decade reduced unemployment everywhere, and simply caused a deterioration in the terms of trade of LDCs.

In conclusion, this eclectic model with price sluggishness can give a satisfactory account of the relative unemployment performance of Europe and the US without resorting to assumptions about differences in labour or product market structure. The differences between the US and Europe that it highlights are related to the timing of aggregate demand expansions and contractions, and the macroeconomic policy mix employed. This is in sharp contrast to the mainly structural explanations of US–European differences in the persistence of unemployment.

Having provided a reasonably full account of the difference in unemployment experience between Europe and the United States, in Section 5 we turn to the question of whether the contractionary macroeconomic policies followed in the EEC after both oil shocks can be attributed to actual or perceived external constraints. After a brief discussion of the nature of external constraints, we turn to an examination of the historical record for the four largest European economies. The record suggests that external constraints do seem to have conditioned macroeconomic policies, and therefore European unemployment. The most important of these constraints seem to have been related to the reaction of foreign exchange markets. Following European attempts to use expansionary monetary and fiscal policy, exchange markets put pressure on the currency in question. European authorities could either use their (limited)

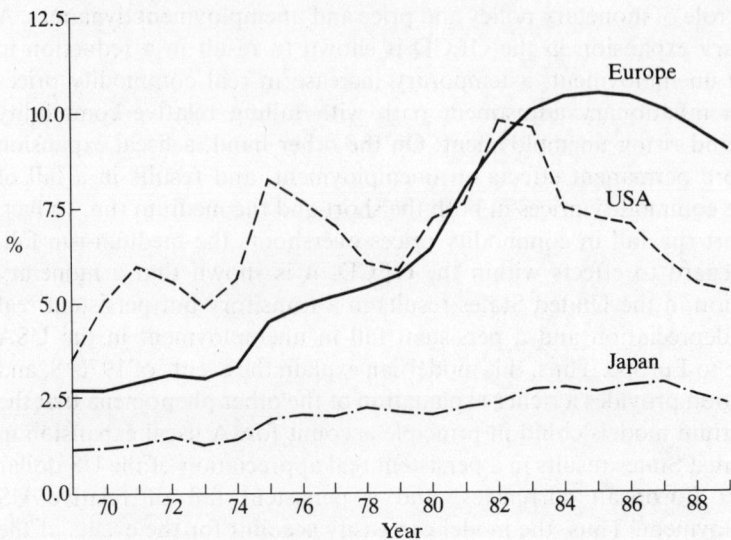

Figure 5.1   Unemployment rates in Europe, the USA, and Japan, 1969–89. *Source:* OECD *Economic Outlook*, June 1990.

reserves to support the exchange rate, or allow the currency to depreciate, or change macroeconomic policies. The first option would soon exhaust their resesrves, while the second would exacerbate the problem of domestic inflation. Thus, the only remaining option was a policy reversal that caused European unemployment to persist. Part of the external constraint on European economies other than the Federal Republic of Germany, stems from the uncompromising aversion to inflation and current account deficits of the German authorities, especially the Bundesbank. While the United States has been prepared to tolerate either higher inflation (1970s) or persistent current account deficits (1980s), the Federal Republic would not tolerate either for any length of time. Given the prominent position of the Bundesbank in monetary arrangements in the EEC, this has also conditioned macroeconomic policy in the rest of the EEC.

1   Stylized facts about European unemployment

The first set of facts about the recent behaviour of aggregate unemployment rates can be gleaned from Figure 5.1. This depicts the average unemployment rates in Europe, Japan, and the United States. One can see that, whereas the unemployment rate in the USA rose more than the average European unemployment rate in 1974–5, by 1978 it had fallen

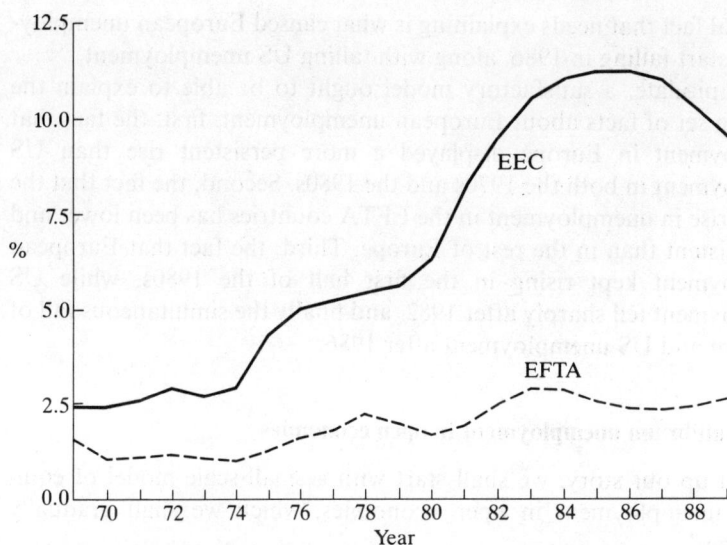

Figure 5.2   Unemployment rates in the EEC and EFTA, 1969–89. *Source:* OECD *Economic Outlook*, June 1990.

back to the European level. After 1979, unemployment rates in Europe and the USA began a parallel rise which lasted until 1982. Following that year, the unemployment rate in the USA started falling, while European unemployment continued rising until 1985. The first year that saw a reversal in this trend was 1986. In 1988, the unemployment rate in Europe stood at 9.6%, compared with only 5.5% in the USA, and 2.5% in Japan. The Japanese unemployment rate remained very low throughout this period. It rose from 1.3% in 1973 to about 2.2% by 1978, and then kept rising with minor fluctuations. However, it stayed between 2% and 3%.

Whereas average European unemployment rose from about 2.7% in 1969 to a peak of 10.6% in 1985, unemployment rates in the EFTA countries (Austria, Finland, Iceland, Norway, Switzerland, and Sweden) stayed remarkably low (Figure 5.2). There was a rise in their average level after 1974, but this was much lower than in the EEC countries for example. There was a peak of 2.2% in 1978, from 0.9% in 1974, then the average unemployment rate fell to 1.7% in 1980, rose again in the early 1980s to peak at 2.9% in 1983. It has since followed a downward trend which was interrupted in 1988 when the EFTA unemployment rate rose slightly. A satisfactory model of unemployment ought to be able to explain the differences between these countries and the rest of Europe.

The final fact that needs explaining is what caused European unemployment to start falling in 1986, along with falling US unemployment.

To recapitulate, a satisfactory model ought to be able to explain the following set of facts about European unemployment: first, the fact that unemployment in Europe displayed a more persistent rise than US unemployment in both the 1970s and the 1980s. Second, the fact that the average rise in unemployment in the EFTA countries has been lower and less persistent than in the rest of Europe. Third, the fact that European unemployment kept rising in the first half of the 1980s, while US unemployment fell sharply after 1982, and finally the simultaneous fall of European and US unemployment after 1986.

2   Equilibrium unemployment in open economies

To build up our story, we shall start with a small-scale model of equilibrium unemployment in open economies, which we shall gradually generalize.[2]

2.1   Price setting, wage setting and aggregate demand

Consider an economy consisting of a large number of firms which interact as predicted by models of monopolistic competition. Technology is linear in employment in the short run, so that, in logarithm, the output of firm i is given by

$$y_i = l_i - \lambda_i \tag{1}$$

where y denotes output, l is employment, and λ the labour requirements coefficient. All variables are in logarithms, and i is an index denoting individual firms, $i = 1, 2, \ldots, I$. The labour requirements coefficient can be thought to depend on the technology embodied in the installed capital stock, and on exogenous shocks to total factor productivity.[3]

Firms face an isoelastic demand curve for their product, of the following type

$$y_i = d - \eta(p_i - p) + v_i \tag{2}$$

where d denotes the log of aggregate (average) demand for domestic goods, η is the elasticity of demand, v_i is a firm-specific demand shock, p_i is the price of the product, and p the aggregate price level. The latter is defined as

$$p = \frac{1}{I} \sum_{i=1}^{I} p_i \tag{3}$$

In the context of this model of monopolistic competition, the optimal price for the firm is a markup on unit labour costs. It is given by[4]

$$p_i = w_i + \lambda_i + \mu \qquad (4)$$

where w is the nominal wage cost (including payroll taxes), and μ is the markup, which is defined as $\eta/(\eta - 1)$.

Wage setting takes place at the level of units indexed by j, which are collections of firms. These can be thought of as single firms, subsets of industries or subsets of regions. The number of units in the economy at which wages are determined is equal to J. Wages are set unilaterally by unions, but once wages are set, firms determine prices. Firms also determine employment, through the demand for output curve. Unions, in their wage-setting decisions, are assumed to understand the dependence of prices on wages and the dependence of demand and employment on relative prices.

I assume that the objective of the wage setters can be represented by the following quadratic loss function

$$\tfrac{1}{2}[w_j - p_c - \tau - \omega_j]^2 + \frac{\theta}{2}[l_j - n_j]^2 \qquad (5)$$

where ω and n represent exogenous target levels of real wages and employment respectively. τ is the tax wedge between take home pay and wage costs, and l the level of employment. θ is the marginal cost of deviations from the employment target relative to the marginal cost of deviations from the wage target. This will be treated as a parameter reflecting the preferences of wage setters (see Alogoskoufis and Manning, 1988b). j denotes the unit (industry, region, etc.) at which wages are being set.[5]

p_c is the log of the consumer price index, net of indirect taxes. It is defined as

$$p_c = \delta p + (1 - \delta)(e + p_f) \qquad (6)$$

where δ is the share of domestically produced goods in the consumption basket, e is the log of the nominal exchange rate (units of domestic currency per unit of foreign currency), and p_f is the log of foreign prices in foreign currency.

The real exchange rate is defined as

$$c = e + p_f - p \qquad (7)$$

Aggregate demand is assumed to depend on the stance of fiscal policy, the real interest rate, the real exchange rate, and foreign demand. In what follows we shall assume the following functional form,

$$d = g - \beta r + \gamma(1 - \delta)c + \epsilon y_f + v \qquad (8)$$

where g is an index of the fiscal impact on aggregate demand, r is the real interest rate, y_f is foreign output, and v is a demand shock. β, γ, δ, and ϵ are positive and fixed parameters. δ is less than one, and measures the share of domestically produced goods in consumption. Thus, $(1 - \delta)$ is a measure of the degree of openness.

When we equate to zero the first derivative of (5) with respect to the wage, taking into account the price equations of the form of (4) and (5), and the employment and demand equations (1), (2), and (8), we end up with the following wage equation

$$(w_j - p_c) = \omega_j + \tau - \phi(n_j - l_j) \qquad (9)$$

where $\phi = \theta \dfrac{\eta(J - 1) + \gamma(1 - \delta)}{J - \delta}$.

The inverse of J can be seen as the degree of centralization in wage setting. The larger the number of units at which wages are determined in an economy with a given number of firms, the lower is the degree of centralization.

Aggregating across units, the aggregate real wage is determined by

$$(w - p_c) = \omega + \tau - \phi(n - l) \cong \omega + \tau - \phi u \qquad (10)$$

where $u \cong n - l$ is the aggregate unemployment rate, as n is assumed to be equal to the log of the labour force. One can see, by using the definition of ϕ, that the responsiveness of real wages to unemployment depends negatively on J, or positively on the degree of centralization in wage setting. It also depends positively on the elasticity of product (and therefore labour) demand with respect to the relative price of the individual firm or industry, and the preferences for employment versus real wages θ, a parameter whose exact meaning was explained above. In addition, other things equal, it depends negatively on the share of imports in total consumption, and positively on γ.

2.2 Equilibrium unemployment and the real exchange rate

The solution of the model is conceptually simple. The first step is to find the conditions under which wage and price setting are consistent, since in that case there will be no pressure for changes in either wages or prices. If the product market is also in equilibrium in the sense that aggregate demand is equal to aggregate output, the economy is in general (internal) equilibrium. This equilibrium will determine a rate of unemployment and a real exchange rate, as functions of the exogenous demand and supply factors.[6]

To derive the equilibrium first aggregate the price equation (4). Then substitute it in the wage equation (10), noting that $p_c = p + (1 - \delta)c$. Solving for unemployment we get

$$u = \frac{1}{\phi}(\mu + \omega + \tau + \lambda) + \frac{1 - \delta}{\phi}c \qquad (11)$$

Equation (11) suggests that consistency between price and wage setting is satisfied along an upward sloping locus in unemployment–real exchange rate space. It can be seen as the equivalent of a labour market equilibrium condition. Equation (11) suggests that, in equilibrium, workers will only accept the lower purchasing power of their wages that is implied by a real exchange rate depreciation (higher c), if this is accompanied by higher unemployment that will mitigate their wage demands. Note that (11) does not suffice to determine equilibrium unemployment, as the real exchange rate is an endogenous variable.

If one uses the aggregate demand curve to derive labour demand, and subtracts the labour demand curve from the labour force n, one gets the following relation between unemployment and competitiveness that satisfies product market equilibrium

$$u = -(g - \beta r + \epsilon y_f + v + \lambda - n) - \gamma(1 - \delta)c \qquad (12)$$

Product market equilibrium, in the sense that demand is equal to output in the goods market, is satisfied along a downward sloping locus in unemployment–real exchange rate space. A real exchange rate depreciation causes an increase in the demand for domestic goods, and therefore an increase in domestic employment and a fall in unemployment.

General equilibrium is a vector $\{u^*, c^*\}$ that satisfies both (11) and (12). Equilibrium unemployment is given by

$$u^* = \frac{1}{1 + \phi\gamma}\{\gamma(\mu + \omega + \tau + \lambda) - (g - \beta r + \epsilon y_f + v + \lambda - n)\} \qquad (13)$$

The corresponding expression for the real exchange rate is

$$c^* = -\frac{1}{(1 + \phi\gamma)(1 - \delta)}\{(\mu + \omega + \tau + \lambda) \\ + \phi(g - \beta r + \epsilon y_f + v + \lambda - n)\} \qquad (14)$$

Equations (13) and (14) can be used to examine the dependence of equilibrium unemployment and the real exchange rate on the various parameters and exogenous factors. It is straightforward to see that a higher market power of domestic firms (as reflected in the markup μ), higher wage targets of unions relative to productivity ($\omega + \lambda$), and a higher tax wedge between labour cost and real take home pay (τ), all result in higher equilibrium unemployment. On the other hand, a more contractionary fiscal stance (lower g), a lower level of activity in the rest of the world (lower y_f), and higher world real interest rates (r), also result in higher equilibrium unemployment.

It is important to note that the equilibrium rate of unemployment depends negatively on ϕ, the responsiveness of real wages to unemployment in the wage equation. A higher responsiveness of real wages to unemployment, either because workers value employment more, or because higher centralization in wage setting internalizes the aggregate demand externalities, will cause real wages to be lower (hence competitiveness higher) per percentage point of unemployment. This will result in higher competitiveness and domestic aggregate demand, and therefore lower unemployment in equilibrium.

In conclusion, in an open economy, even when prices and wages jump instantaneously to bring about equilibrium, changes in aggregate demand will affect the equilibrium level of unemployment. The channel is the real exchange rate. A demand expansion will be accompanied by lower unemployment. This lower unemployment will only be an equilibrium to the extent that the purchasing power of wages is higher, since, with lower unemployment, wage setters demand higher take home pay. An appreciation of the real exchange rate can achieve that, as it changes the wedge between consumer and producer prices. For given product wages $w - p$, and the tax wedge τ, the purchasing power of nominal wages $w - p_c$ goes up, which satisfies the demands of workers. The adjustment process to this new equilibrium is simple to describe. The increased demand and higher employment cause an increase in nominal wages through the wage equation, which in turn is translated into an increase of domestic producer prices. The higher domestic prices relative to foreign prices bring about the real exchange rate appreciation.

2.3   Explaining European and OECD unemployment in the 1970s and 1980s

How would this model explain the stylized facts about European unemployment emphasized in Section 1?

With regard to the average rise in OECD unemployment in the 1970s and early 1980s, one approach is to stress that the productivity slowdown (rise in λ) caused an increase in the difference between the wage targets of wage setters ω and productivity $-\lambda$. The productivity slowdown and the 'wage gaps' that it created is the main explanation given in Bruno and Sachs (1985), and Grubb *et al.* (1982, 1983). Additionally, various authors have pointed to the rise in the tax wedge between labour costs and real take home pay (see Bean *et al.*, 1986, for example). Through (13), both would increase equilibrium unemployment.

How would this model explain the smaller rise of unemployment in Japan and the Nordic countries, assuming that the productivity slowdown was the same across the OECD? It would have to rely on differences in the responsiveness of real wages to unemployment ϕ, i.e. on a higher ϕ for Japan and the Nordic countries. This seems to to be the case in most of the international studies on wage setting (Grubb *et al.*, 1983; Bruno and Sachs, 1985; Newell and Symons, 1985; Bean *et al.*, 1986; Gordon, 1987; Alogoskoufis and Manning, 1988b; and others). However, many of these studies have gone deeper than that and asked about the determinants of ϕ. As can be seen from the discussion of equation (9), ϕ depends positively on the degree of centralization in wage setting, the elasticity of demand in the product market, and preferences of wage setters for employment over wages. Bruno and Sachs (1985), Bean *et al.* (1986), and Alogoskoufis and Manning (1988b) can be interpreted as suggesting that centralization in wage setting (or corporatism) can explain the differences within Europe. Japan is more of a puzzle. Short of statistical explanations (Wadhwani, 1987), the remaining explanations are based on the elasticity of product demand and preferences over employment (a large θ), as reflected in Japanese wage setting institutions. This latter explanation was the one favoured by Alogoskoufis and Manning (1988b). The elasticity of product demand explanation was put forward by Calmfors and Driffill (1988), to derive the 'hump shape' hypothesis on the determination of ϕ. According to this explanation, with less centralized wage setting, workers face a higher elasticity of demand for the product whose price they implicitly determine through their wage-setting behaviour. This is because there will be more substitutes for the product produced by smaller bargaining units (say firms rather than industries). Thus, as centralization increases, there are two countervailing forces operating on the responsiveness of real wages to unemployment. The internalization of the aggregate demand externality points towards a higher ϕ, but the smaller labour demand elasticity points towards a lower one. Thus, the relation between ϕ and the degree of centralization in wage setting is a humped one. After some point it will become negative.

The equilibrium model in this section seems to be giving a relatively convincing account of the rise in OECD unemployment, and the differences in the magnitude of this average rise across country blocks. It can also explain the different behaviour of European and US unemployment in the early 1980s. This would have to rely on demand factors, chiefly differences in the fiscal stance. This type of explanation has been put forward by a number of studies emanating from the Centre for Economic Policy Studies (see for example Blanchard *et al.*, 1986). In fact, demand factors seem to be crucial in accounting for the European experience of the early 1980s. Bean *et al.* (1986), using a model allowing for both demand and supply factors, found that supply factors accounted for only 2 of the 4.3 percentage points of the rise in average European unemployment between 1956–66 and 1980–3.

However, although this model can explain the European experience in the early 1980s, it has more trouble accounting for the higher persistence of European unemployment in the aftermath of the first oil shock in the 1970s, as well as for the recent simultaneous fall in US and European unemployment.

Let us first concentrate on the more recent episode. Consider two countries, say E(urope) and U(SA) which have exactly the same parameters.

The supply side consistency conditions for the two countries are given by equations similar to (11)

$$u_E = \frac{1}{\phi}(\mu + \omega + \tau + \lambda) + \frac{1-\delta}{\phi}c \tag{11a}$$

$$u_U = \frac{1}{\phi}(\mu + \omega + \tau + \lambda) - \frac{1-\delta}{\phi}c \tag{11b}$$

where c denotes European competitiveness, i.e., it is given by

$$c \equiv e + p_U - p_E \tag{10'}$$

where e is the European nominal exchange rates, i.e., units of 'ecu' per dollar.

The product market equilibrium conditions expressed in terms of unemployment rates are given by

$$u_E = -g_E + \beta r_E + \epsilon u_U - \gamma(1-\delta)c - [v + (1-\epsilon)(\lambda - n)] \tag{12a}$$

$$u_U = -g_U + \beta r_U + \epsilon u_E + \gamma(1-\delta)c - [v + (1-\epsilon)(\lambda - n)] \tag{12b}$$

Assuming that Europe and the US are equal size, their average equilibrium unemployment rate will be given by averaging (11a) and (11b). This yields

$$u^* = \frac{1}{\phi}(\mu + \omega + \tau + \lambda) \tag{15}$$

where the lack of a subscript denotes the average of the two variables, i.e., we define average unemployment as $u = 0.5(u_E + u_U)$.

As can be seen from (15), average OECD unemployment depends only on supply-side factors in this model. Thus, this model would not be able to explain the simultaneous rise or fall of US and European unemployment on the basis of an aggregate contraction or expansion of demand. One may thus have to consider a more complicated model. A fiscal expansion in this model would only increase OECD real interest rates, to choke off the excess demand, as aggregate output (and unemployment) are fixed from the supply side. This model treats the OECD as a closed economy, and, with instantaneous adjustment in wages and prices, aggregate demand cannot affect output and employment.

To see the effects on real interest rates, we can take the average of the product market equilibrium conditions (12a) and (12b), which yields

$$u = -\frac{1}{1 - \epsilon}[g - \beta r - v] + n - \lambda \qquad (16)$$

Equating the right hand sides of (15) and (16), and solving for the real interest rate we get

$$r = \frac{1}{\beta}\left[g + \frac{1 - \epsilon}{\phi}(\mu + \omega + \tau + \lambda) + v - (1 - \epsilon)(n - \lambda)\right] \qquad (17)$$

As can be seen from (17), a fiscal expansion in the OECD area increases real interest rates, which in turn completely crowd out the effects on OECD unemployment. This full crowding out of fiscal policy is a familiar property of closed economy *IS–LM* type macromodels with flexible wages and prices. It occurs here because the real exchange rate, which is the channel of transmission of fiscal policy effects in an open economy, washes out when we aggregate to derive the OECD variables.

To allow aggregate demand to affect the behaviour of OECD unemployment one either has to treat the OECD as an open economy, or to allow for wage–price sluggishness. We shall examine these two options in turn.

3   An equilibrium model with commodity prices

Consider two open economies producing manufactures. Technology, demand, and market structure are as in the economy discussed in the previous section. The only exception is that in each economy a proportion $1 - \zeta$ of imports is devoted to consuming primary commodities imported from the rest of the world (the LDCs). Thus, the real exchange rate for each of the two economies is defined as

$$e + \zeta p_U + (1 - \zeta)p_L - p_E = c + (1 - \zeta)q_U \qquad (18a)$$

$$\zeta(p_E - e) + (1 - \zeta)p_L - p_U = -c + (1 - \zeta)q_E \qquad (18b)$$

where p_L is the price of commodities expressed in dollars. c is the real exchange rate of manufactures for Europe, i.e., $c = e + p_U - p_E \cdot q_E$ and q_U are the relative prices of commodities for Europe and the USA respectively.

Appropriately modifying the aggregate demand and aggregate supply consistency conditions (13) and (14) for the single economy, we get the following model for Europe and the United States.

$$u_E = \frac{1}{\phi}(\mu + \omega + \tau + \lambda) + \frac{1 - \delta}{\phi}[c + (1 - \zeta)q_U] \qquad (19a)$$

$$u_U = \frac{1}{\phi}(\mu + \omega + \tau + \lambda) - \frac{1 - \delta}{\phi}[c - (1 - \zeta)q_E] \qquad (19b)$$

$$u_E = -g_E + \beta r_E + \epsilon u_U - \gamma(1 - \delta)[c + (1 - \zeta)q_U] \\ - [v + (1 - \epsilon)(\lambda - n)] \qquad (20a)$$

$$u_U = -g_U + \beta r_U + \epsilon u_E + \gamma(1 - \delta)[c - (1 - \zeta)q_E] \\ - [v + (1 - \epsilon)(\lambda - n)] \qquad (20b)$$

where (19a) and (19b) describe the conditions for consistency between price and wage setting (labour market equilibrium) in Europe and the USA respectively, and (20a) and (20b) describe the conditions for consistency between savings and investment (product market equilibrium).

Aggregating the supply side equilibrium conditions and solving for equilibrium 'OECD' unemployment we get[7]

$$u = \frac{1}{\phi}[\mu + \omega + \tau + \lambda + (1 - \delta)(1 - \zeta)q] \qquad (21)$$

Unlike in equation (17), 'OECD' unemployment depends on factors that might be influenced by aggregate demand in the OECD, like the relative price of commodities q. To see this let us first aggregate the output market equilibrium conditions (20a) and (20b). Then we get

$$u = \frac{1}{1 - \epsilon}[-g + \beta r - \gamma(1 - \zeta)q - v - (1 - \epsilon)(\lambda - n)] \qquad (22)$$

To determine equilibrium OECD unemployment, relative commodity prices and real interest rates, one has to provide some model for the commodity-producing countries. Assume that the supply of commodities in the LDCs is a positive function of their relative price, and that their demand is a negative function of their relative price, OECD real interest rates, and the level of activity in the OECD. These can be written as

$$y_L^s = y_0^s + \xi q \tag{23a}$$

$$y_L^d = y_0^d - \chi_1 q - \chi_2 r - \chi_3(u - n + \lambda) \tag{23b}$$

where y_0^s, y_0^d are constants, ξ is the elasticity of commodity supply, χ_1 the price elasticity of commodity demand, χ_2 the real interest rate semi-elasticity of commodity demand, and χ_3 the elasticity of commodity demand with respect to output in the OECD countries. L denotes the South (LDCs).[8]

Product market equilibrium in the South determines equilibrium commodity prices as

$$q = q_0 - \theta r - \psi(u - n + \lambda) \tag{24}$$

where $q_0 = (y_0^d - y_0^s)/(\xi + \chi_1)$, $\theta = \chi_2/(\xi + \chi_1)$, $\psi = \chi_3/(\xi + \chi_1)$.

Equations (21), (22), and (24) can be used to determine equilibrium OECD unemployment u, equilibrium world real interest rates and the equilibrium relative price of commodities q.

The equilibrium is depicted in Figure 5.3. A fiscal expansion in the OECD causes a fall in the relative price of commodities, which increases the wedge between consumer and producer prices. Thus, since consumption wages increase and real labour costs remain constant, the lower unemployment is an equilibrium. Obviously, the commodity producers (the LDCs) take the brunt of the adjustment, as there is a fall in their terms of trade, a reduction in their living standards, and a fall in their output and employment.

Thus, this model, in contrast to equilibrium models that treat the OECD

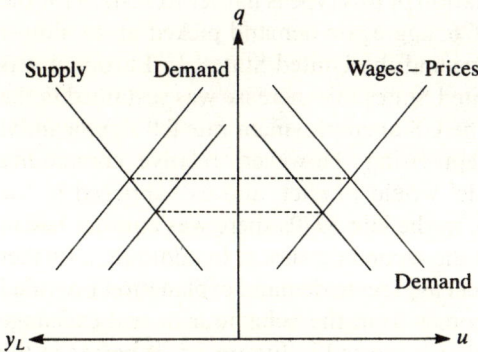

Figure 5.3 North–South equilibrium

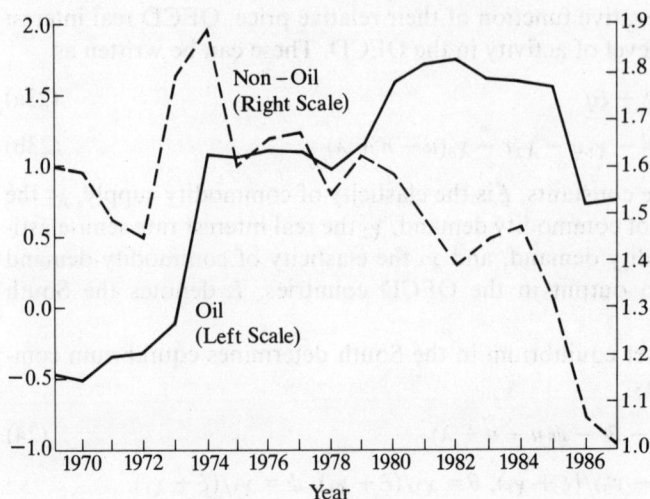

Figure 5.4   The relative price of oil and non-oil commodities, 1969–87. *Source:* **OECD** *Economic Outlook*, **June 1990.**

as a closed economy, could possibly explain the recent simultaneous fall in European and US unemployment on the basis of a fiscal expansion of demand in the OECD area. Since it encompasses the ones in the previous section, it can also account for all the facts the previous models accounted for, namely the rise in average unemployment in response to the productivity slowdown and increases in the tax wedge, differences between EFTA countries and the rest of Europe, and the different experience of Europe and the United States in the early 1980s. The additional fact that it explains is the simultaneous fall in European and US unemployment after 1986, on the basis of a simultaneous fiscal expansion of demand.

An aggregate demand explanation of this type is harder to sustain for the experience of the 1970s. In 1976, aggregate demand picked up to almost the same extent in both Europe and the United States. In Europe it was not sustained, while in the United States this increase was sustained in the two subsequent years. While the US unemployment rate fell significantly, unemployment in Europe kept rising. However, relative commodity prices did not fall as the model would predict, and as happened in the 1980s (see Figure 5.4). In fact, in the late 1970s there was another rise in relative commodity prices and the second oil shock. In addition, a further piece of evidence against the real aggregate demand explanation provided by the model in this section comes from the behaviour of real exchange rates. The real value of the dollar is plotted in Figure 5.5. Whereas in the 1980s the behaviour of the US dollar is consistent with the aggregate

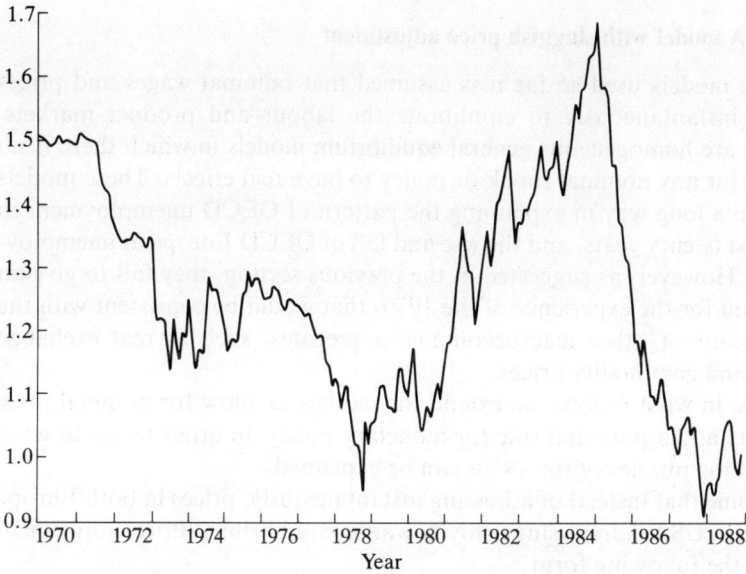

Figure 5.5   The real value of the US dollar, 1969–89 (based on wholesale price indices)

demand explanation, in the 1970s it is not. For example, in the early 1980s the real exchange rate of the dollar shot up following the large demand expansion in the United States, and it fell when this demand expansion stalled, and the European expansion accelerated. This is what one would have predicted on the basis of equation (14), or its generalization to allow for commodity prices. However, in the 1976–8 period the opposite happened. In the face of a much faster US expansion in demand in 1977 and 1978, the real value of the dollar fell, something that contradicts what would have been expected on the basis of (14).

To recapitulate, the experience of the 1980s can be explained on the basis of a real general equilibrium model of the type presented in this section. Openness allows domestic fiscal expansions to produce a real exchange rate appreciation or/and a reduction in the relative price of commodities, which widens the wedge between real labour costs of domestic producers and real take home pay of workers and brings about a fall in the domestic unemployment rate. Such a story cannot be sustained as an explanation of the 1970s, when the real exchange rate of the dollar depreciated instead of appreciating in the wake of the relative US expansion of demand in 1977 and 1978.

We thus turn to another complication, the role of nominal price rigidity.

4   A model with sluggish price adjustment

In the models used so far it is assumed that nominal wages and prices
jump instantaneously to equilibrate the labour and product markets.
These are homogeneous general equilibrium models in which there is no
scope for any nominal shock or policy to have real effects. These models
can go a long way in explaining the pattern of OECD unemployment in
the last twenty years, and the rise and fall of OECD European unemployment. However, as suggested in the previous section, they fail to give an
account for the experience of the 1970s that would be consistent with the
behaviour of other macroeconomic aggregates, such as real exchange
rates and commodity prices.

Thus, in what follows we extend the models to allow for nominal price
rigidity and a potential role for monetary policy, in order to see to what
extent the puzzles of the 1970s can be explained.

Assume that instead of adjusting instantaneously, prices in both Europe
and the USA adjust sluggishly towards equilibrium. Price adjustment
takes the following form

$$\dot{p}_E = - \rho(p_E - p_E^*) = \rho[c + (1 - \zeta)q_U - c^* - (1 - \zeta)q_U^*] \qquad (25a)$$

$$\dot{p}_U = - \rho(p_U - p_U^*) = \rho[- c + (1 - \zeta)q_E + c^* - (1 - \zeta)q_E^*] \quad (25b)$$

where p^* is the equilibrium price level, and a (super) dot denotes a time
derivative. Prices in each instant adjust to close a fraction ρ of the
difference between the actual and equilibrium price. After adding and
subtracting foreign prices, the price adjustment rule can be written in
terms of deviations of the current real exchange rate from its equilibrium
value.

With sluggish price adjustment there is a potential role for monetary
policy. I shall assume permanent income versions of money demand
functions for both Europe and the United States. These can be written as

$$(m - p)_E = - u_E^* + (n - \lambda) - \alpha i_E \qquad (26a)$$

$$(m - p)_U = - u_U^* + (n - \lambda) - \alpha i_U \qquad (26b)$$

where permanent income y^* has been substituted out in terms of equilibrium unemployment, the labour requirements coefficient, and the
labour force. α is the interest rate semi-elasticity of money demand and i is
the nominal interest rate.

We shall assume that European and US bonds are perfect substitutes.
For simplicity, and since the model of this section is a short-run model, we
ignore the behaviour of commodity producers, and instead look at the
behaviour of commodity speculators in the OECD commodity markets.

We assume that commodity stocks and nominal bonds are also perfect substitutes for speculators. These assumptions allow us to write down the following asset market arbitrage conditions

$$i_E = i_U + \dot{e} \qquad (27)$$

$$i_U = \dot{p}_L + k \qquad (28)$$

where k is the non-financial (convenience) return on holding commodities net of storage costs. This is assumed to be an exogenous parameter. Equation (27) is the uncovered interest parity condition for European and American bonds, and (28) is a similar condition for commodities.[9]

Since commodities are in fixed supply in the short run, their price in commodity exchanges can jump to equilibrate the commodity markets.

To look at the implications of price sluggishness for macroeconomic adjustment we shall employ the Aoki (1981) method of diagonalizing the dynamic system formed by (25a), (25b), (26a), (26b), (27), and (28). Thus, we shall first look at a model of aggregates (the OECD), and then at a model of differences (between Europe and the United States). Then, the dynamics of each economy can be inferred by noting that Europe is the difference between the aggregate and the differenced model, and that the United States is the sum of the two.

4.1   The aggregate OECD model

Adding (25b) to (25a) and (26b) to (26a) and dividing by 2, we get the following model for the OECD

$$\dot{p} = \rho(1 - \zeta)(q - q^*) = \rho(1 - \zeta)(p_L - p - q^*) \qquad (29)$$

$$m - p = (n - \lambda) - u^* - \alpha(\dot{p}_L + k) \qquad (30')$$

Solving (30') for $\dot{p}_L$ we get

$$\dot{p}_L = -k - \frac{1}{\alpha}[m - p - n + \lambda + u^*] \qquad (30)$$

Equations (29) and (30) form a pair of autonomous differential equations which can easily be solved. We shall employ a phase diagram in Figure 5.6. It can be seen that there is an equilibrium which is saddlepath stable. In Figures 5.7 and 5.8 we consider two policy experiments.

The first (Figure 5.7) is a monetary expansion in the OECD. The monetary expansion shifts the $\dot{p}_L = 0$ locus upwards, and in the new equilibrium both OECD and commodity prices rise in the same proportion. However, because of the stickiness of OECD prices, commodity prices initially overshoot their equilibrium increase, and thus there is a rise in their relative price. The rise in the relative price of commodities reduces

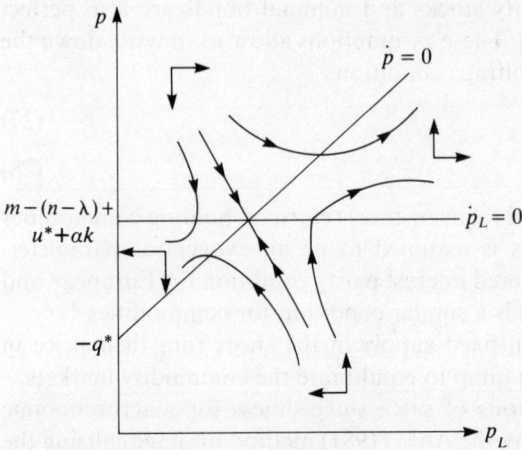

Figure 5.6   Stability of North–South equilibrium

OECD unemployment along the demand curve, both because of the terms of trade effect (commodities are more expensive) and the lower real interest rate (falling relative price of commodities). However, as OECD prices rise, unemployment and the real interest rate return to their previous level. One can thus see that with sluggish price adjustment one could explain the behaviour of OECD unemployment after 1976 in terms of an expansionary monetary policy. The behaviour of OECD unemployment is consistent with the behaviour of OECD inflation, real interest rates and commodity prices in the late 1970s.

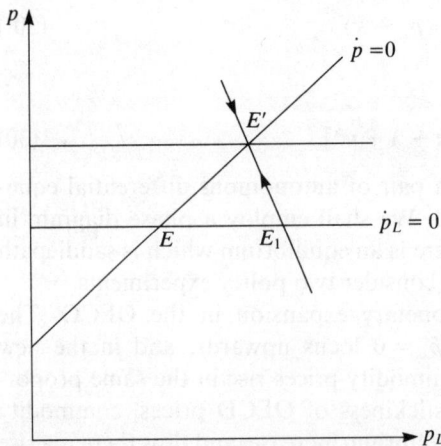

Figure 5.7   An OECD monetary expansion

p

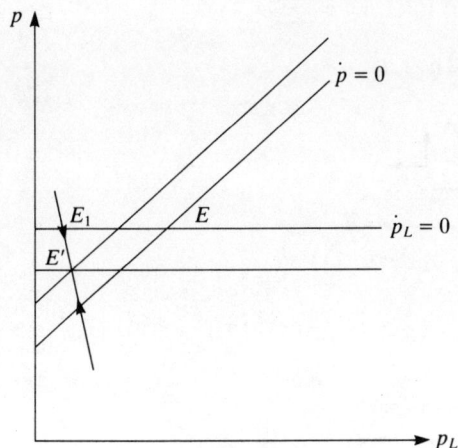

$\dot{p} = 0$

E_1 E $\dot{p}_L = 0$

E'

p_L

Figure 5.8   An OECD fiscal expansion

In Figure 5.8 we examine a fiscal expansion in the OECD area. Unlike the case of the monetary expansion, a fiscal expansion has more permanent real effects. In equilibrium it causes the relative price of commodities to fall. The impact effect is an overshooting of the nominal and real fall in commodity prices, and an undershooting of the fall in OECD unemployment. Along the adjustment path nominal commodity prices are rising and the prices of manufactures are falling. Therefore, the relative price of commodities is rising and unemployment is falling along the aggregate demand curve. Both the nominal and real interest rates in the OECD rise following the fiscal expansion.[10]

4.2   Europe relative to the United States

We can now turn to the relative model, to examine what happens to Europe relative to the United States if the monetary and fiscal expansions originate in the USA.

Subtracting the price equation (25b) from the price equation (25a), and using a bar to denote variables that are the difference between Europe and the United States, we get the following expression for the inflation differential between Europe and the USA

$$\dot{\bar{p}} = -\rho[(1 + \zeta)(e + \bar{p}) - (1 + \zeta)c^*] \tag{31}$$

where we have made use of the fact that $q_E - q_U = c = e + \bar{p}$.

Subtracting the money demand function (26b) from the money demand

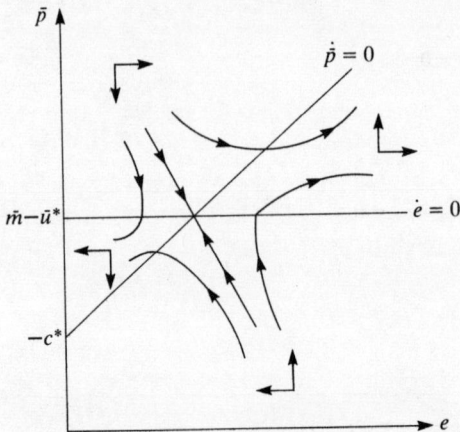

Figure 5.9   US–European equilibrium

function (26a), and using the arbitrage condition (27), we get the following expression for relative money demands

$$\bar{m} - \bar{p} = -\bar{u}^* - \alpha \dot{e} \qquad (32')$$

Solving equation $(32')$ for the expected rate of change of the exchange rate of Europe we get

$$\dot{e} = -\frac{1}{\alpha}(\bar{m} - \bar{p} + \bar{u}^*) \qquad (32)$$

As in the case of the system in (29) and (30), (31) and (32) form a pair of autonomous first-order differential equations in the relative price levels and the exchange rate of Europe and the United States. The phase diagram (Figure 5.9) confirms that the system is saddlepath stable, with the nominal exchange rate being the jump variable. In Figures 5.10 and 5.11 we examine the implications of a monetary and a fiscal expansion in the United States.

The US monetary expansion (Figure 5.10) shifts the $\dot{e} = 0$ locus downwards, as the relative money supply of Europe falls. The dollar depreciates (e falls) immediately, and along the new saddlepath the relative price of European goods is falling, and the dollar rises. This of course is because of the overshooting that takes place. Note that this is simply a variant of the Dornbusch (1976) model. See also Buiter and Miller (1981). The real appreciation that Europe suffers causes its relative unemployment to rise and its relative inflation to fall. Gradually the two economies return to the initial relative unemployment rates and real

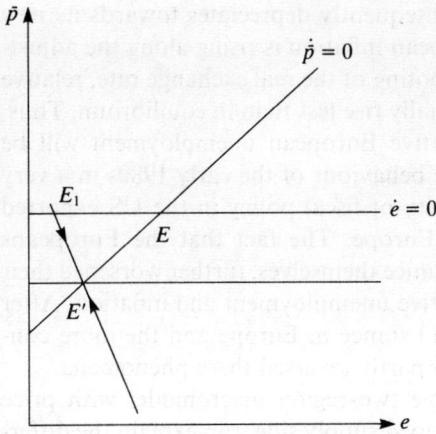

Figure 5.10 A US monetary expansion

exchange rate, although the relative US price level rises permanently, and the dollar takes a lower equilibrium nominal value. It appears that this version of the model could easily explain the 1976–8 experience, which was characterized by a fall in US unemployment relative to Europe, a dollar depreciation, and a fall in relative European inflation.

A US fiscal expansion is examined in Figure 5.11. This shifts both curves, because it changes the equilibrium real exchange rate and relative unemployment rates. The dollar overshoots its nominal and real

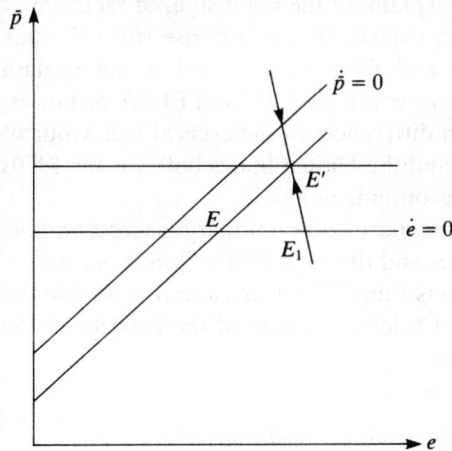

Figure 5.11 A US fiscal expansion

equilibrium appreciation, and subsequently depreciates towards its new equilibrium value. Relative European inflation is rising along the adjustment path. Because of the overshooting of the real exchange rate, relative European unemployment will initially rise less than in equilibrium. Thus, during the adjustment path, relative European unemployment will be rising. The model can explain the behaviour of the early 1980s in a very satisfactory way. The relative laxity of fiscal policy in the US exported unemployment and inflation to Europe. The fact that the Europeans opted for a contractionary fiscal stance themselves, further worsened their position with respect to both relative unemployment and inflation. After 1986, the more expansionary fiscal stance in Europe and the more contractionary fiscal stance in the US partly reversed these phenomena.

In conclusion, a relatively simple two-region macromodel with price sluggishness and a carefully developed supply side, can explain the differences in the behaviour of unemployment between Europe and the US solely in terms of the fiscal and monetary policy mix. There is very little prima facie incentive to look for differences in the structure of product and labour markets.

The deeper question, however, is why the Europeans did not follow the US in its expansion after 1982, and allowed unemployment to remain high. Is it possible that this was because of a perceived external constraint? In the next section we turn to an examination of the recent historical record.

5   European unemployment and the external constraint

We now have a model that can explain all the main stylized facts about European unemployment. It can explain its average rise since the late 1960s in terms of both supply and fiscal shocks, and it can explain differences in the rise of unemployment in the EEC and EFTA countries. More importantly, it can explain differences in the cyclical behaviour of unemployment between Europe and the United States both for the 1970s and the 1980s in terms of macroeconomic policy.

What has been the reason for the more contractionary macroeconomic policy in Europe in both the 1970s and the early 1980s? Was it because of an actual or perceived external constraint? This is the question we address in this section. We first turn to a brief discussion of the concept of the external constraint we shall utilize.

5.1   The different meanings of the external constraint

One can in principle adopt at least two definitions of the external constraint. The first is to interpret the term broadly and define as an external constraint the fact that open economies are subject to important influences emanating from the rest of the world. The second definition is much narrower. It reflects the fact that an open economy that unilaterally conducts a more expansionary macroeconomic policy than the rest of the world, may experience current account deficits. It will then need to either use its foreign exchange reserves or borrow from abroad to finance them. In a world of low capital mobility and fixed exchange rates, such as the Bretton Woods system of the 1950s and 1960s, the reserve losses associated with sustained current account deficits may have constituted an important financing constraint that led to a policy reversal. In a world of high capital mobility, there is the possibility of borrowing from abroad. However, to the extent that the external debt accumulation process is deemed unsustainable by the financial markets, there may be financing difficulties and capital flight. The expanding economy may then be forced to consider adjustment rather than financing. Short-run adjustment is usually attempted through nominal exchange rate depreciations, which in a world of price stickiness results in at least temporary real exchange rate depreciations. More durable adjustment may require a reversal of the original expansion.

In what follows we shall adopt the narrower definition of the external constraint, and ask whether it applies to European unemployment in the 1970s and 1980s.

5.2   The persistence of European unemployment in the 1970s

The different macroeconomic policies adopted in Europe and the USA seem to be able to explain the main differences in the cyclical behaviour of unemployment in the aftermath of the first oil shock. Both the US and Europe eased fiscal policy early in 1975. By the time of the first summit of Rambouillet in November 1985 'it was clear that the recovery had really started' (Putnam and Bayne, 1987, p. 37). However, while the US continued with its expansionary macroeconomic policy, macroeconomic policy in Europe was soon tightened. Putnam and Bayne in their account of the second summit in Puerto Rico report that, 'President Ford . . . proposed that countries with large surpluses should allow their external balance to deteriorate as was happening to the United States. But the other two surplus countries – Germany and Japan – did not respond' (p. 43). The other European summit countries were already experiencing a sharp deterioration of their current account, as a result of expansionary measures in 1975 or earlier. France had experienced a sharp deterioration of its current account, which swang from a surplus of 0.8% of GDP in 1975 to a deficit of 1% of GDP in 1976, and so did Italy, whose current account deficit widened from 0.3% of GDP in 1975 to 1.3% in 1976. The

Table 5.1. *Macroeconomic developments in the USA and Europe, 1971–9*

	1971	1972	1973	1974	1975	1976	1977	1978	1979
GDP growth (%)									
United States	2.8	5.0	5.2	− 0.5	− 1.3	4.9	4.7	5.3	2.5
Europe 4	2.9	3.8	5.9	1.7	− 1.3	4.9	2.9	3.5	4.0
OECD Europe	3.3	4.2	5.8	2.4	− 0.9	4.5	2.7	3.0	3.6
Consumer price inflation (%)									
United States	4.3	3.3	6.2	11.1	9.1	5.7	6.5	7.6	11.3
Europe 4	6.2	6.1	8.2	13.0	13.4	10.7	10.3	7.3	9.7
OECD Europe	6.5	6.4	8.6	13.2	13.2	10.9	11.3	9.0	10.5
Unemployment rate (%)									
United States	6.0	5.6	4.9	5.6	8.3	7.7	7.0	6.1	5.8
Europe 4	2.8	3.1	2.8	3.0	4.4	4.9	5.2	5.2	5.2
OECD Europe	2.9	3.1	3.0	3.3	4.5	4.9	5.2	5.4	5.7
Current account (% of GNP/GDP)									
United States	− 0.1	− 0.5	0.5	0.1	1.1	0.2	− 0.7	− 0.7	0.0
Europe 4	0.9	0.5	0.2	− 0.9	0.3	− 0.3	0.4	1.4	0.2
OECD Europe	0.6	0.7	0.4	− 1.1	− 0.3	− 0.9	− 0.4	0.8	− 0.3

Source: OECD Economic Outlook (December 1989).

UK had been running current account deficits of more than 1% of GDP since 1972, and was later in 1976 to seek a massive IMF loan and adopt a stabilization programme. The next year 1977 saw Jimmy Carter take over at the White House. The US adopted a more expansionary monetary and fiscal policy, and urged the Germans and Japanese to follow suit. Both resisted the pressure until the Bonn Summit of 1978. In Table 5.1 we present data for GDP growth, unemployment, inflation, and the current account for the US and Europe, from 1971 to 1979. The contractionary policies of 1976 to 1978 in the European countries are obvious in output growth, inflation, and unemployment, and in sharp contrast to the expansionary policies followed in the US.

Can we attribute these largely contractionary European policies to external balance considerations? And if so, were these external balance consideration warranted?

It is quite clear that for Germany there was not even a suggestion of an external constraint in that period. The German economy remained comfortably in current account surplus. For the Germans the main fear appears to have been the re-emergence of inflation.[11]

France, Italy, and the United Kingdom all experienced current account deficits in 1976. The question that arises is whether the external deficits were sustainable in the longer run, and thus whether the macroeconomic tightening represented an over-reaction on the part of the authorities. OECD (1988), examining the cases of the UK and Italy in this episode, seems to suggest that the policies that led to the current account deterioration were unsustainable. For the UK it suggests that, 'With hindsight, few would dispute that by early 1975 the situation was unsustainable, and that it was primarily domestic unsustainability of domestic origin' (p. 71). For Italy it suggests that 'There can be little doubt that the economic situation in 1976 was unsustainable both internally and externally' (*ibid* p. 80). On the other hand, Cooper (1987) seems to discount the unsustainability argument, and suggests that the problem in both the United Kingdom and Italy was a confidence crisis. To quote,

> On close examination, it was not the external constraints that forced the change in policy, but discomfiture by domestic policymakers with the consequences of their current line of policy. Both Britain and Italy called the IMF in part to evoke some external discipline over domestic wage settlements. In both cases the main objectives had been outlined by the government before the IMF was engaged. In both cases uncertainty about the government's ability to carry out its announced policies induced capital flight – mainly non-resident capital in Britain, mainly resident capital in Italy. Because of limited reserves, this capital flight compelled a policy reaction that obviously involved the balance of payments. Whether one wants to consider response to doubts about a country's ability to carry out its announced policies an 'external constraint' is a question of semantic taste. (p. 581)

What Cooper seems to suggest is that the very fact that there was doubt about the sustainability of policies triggered a confidence crisis in both cases. This manifested itself in loss of reserves and currency depreciation. Our own 'semantic taste' is to call such a situation an external constraint. In the case of the second half of the 1970s external constraints appear to us to have contributed to the persistence of unemployment in countries such as the United Kingdom and Italy and even France.

We thus conclude that the external constraint appears to have been instrumental in causing at least some of the European countries to abandon expansionary policies to reduce unemployment in the aftermath of the first oil shock. It manifested itself in two ways: one was loss of reserves. This was gradual in the case of France, and precipitous in the case of the UK and Italy who faced confidence crises. The other side of foreign exchange market pressure was currency depreciation which exacerbated the problem of domestic inflation.

5.3   The persistence of European unemployment in the 1980s

We now turn to the second episode, the persistence of high unemployment in Europe in the 1980s, and ask about the significance of the external

Table 5.2. *Macroeconomic developments in the USA and Europe, 1980–9*

	1980	1981	1982	1983	1984	1985	1986	1987	1988
GDP growth (%)									
United States	− 0.2	1.9	− 2.5	3.6	6.8	3.4	2.7	3.7	4.4
Europe 4	1.4	0.3	0.8	1.8	2.5	2.4	2.6	2.6	3.8
OECD Europe	1.7	0.3	0.8	1.7	2.6	2.6	2.6	2.7	3.7
Consumer price inflation (%)									
United States	13.5	10.3	6.1	3.2	4.3	3.5	1.9	3.7	4.1
Europe 4	13.0	11.7	9.9	7.5	6.0	5.4	2.7	2.9	3.2
OECD Europe	14.5	12.2	10.5	8.4	7.5	6.5	4.0	3.8	4.5
Unemployment rate (%)									
United States	7.2	7.6	9.7	9.6	7.5	7.2	7.0	6.2	5.5
Europe 4	5.7	7.4	8.6	9.5	9.9	10.1	10.3	10.1	9.4
OECD Europe	6.5	7.9	9.2	10.1	10.5	10.6	10.5	10.1	9.6
Current account (% of GNP/GDP)									
United States	0.1	0.3	− 0.2	− 1.3	− 2.8	− 2.8	− 3.1	− 3.2	− 2.6
Europe 4	− 0.8	− 0.2	− 0.2	0.4	0.5	0.8	1.6	1.0	0.4
OECD Europe	− 1.4	− 0.6	− 0.6	0.2	0.6	0.8	1.3	0.7	0.3

Source: OECD Economic Outlook (December 1989).

constraint. The main macroeconomic developments in the USA and Europe are summarized in Table 5.2. One can see that the stagflation following the second oil shock was deeper and more persistent in Europe than in the United States.

To assess the significance of the external constraint it is worth concentrating on two episodes, the experience of Germany in the aftermath of the Bonn Summit of 1978, and the aborted attempt of the French to expand in 1981–3.

In the 1978 Bonn summit, the Federal Republic of Germany, partly because of international pressure, partly because of domestic considerations, agreed to play the role of 'locomotive' along with Japan. This was agreed in the context of a wide ranging exercise in economic policy coordination with the rest of the G-7. In fact the stance of monetary policy in Germany had already become more expansionary in 1977. As a result of the fiscal and monetary expansion German unemployment fell from 3.9% in 1977 to 3.3% in 1979 and 1980. Inflation picked up, and the current account swang from a surplus of 1.4% of GDP in 1978 to deficits equal to 0.7% of GDP in 1979 and 1.7% of GDP in 1980. It is difficult to assess the extent to which the inflation and current account developments are due to the macroeconomic expansion *per se* and not the second oil shock, which almost coincided with the period of implementation of the decisions of the Bonn summit. Whatever the cause, these developments caused alarm in Germany (see Cooper, 1987 for an extensive discussion of German reactions). As OECD (1988) puts it, 'when conditions in foreign exchange markets approached crisis level in 1981, there was a clear consensus that a major change of policy priorities was required for internal as well as for external considerations' (p. 52). Finally, monetary and fiscal policy were tightened in late 1981. Unemployment rose precipitously, from 3.3% in 1980, to 8.2% in 1983, where it remained until 1985. The current account improved and consumer price inflation fell from a high of 6.3% in 1981 to 3.3% by 1983, and 2.2% in 1985.

This episode is altogether less dramatic than the UK and Italian experiences of 1976–7. Yet, it has had an overwhelming influence on the attitudes of the public and policy-makers in the Federal Republic, making them unwilling to contemplate the role of locomotive in Europe for the remainder of the 1980s. Thus the perception of an external constraint in Germany during that period probably has a very strong bearing on the problem of European unemployment in the 1980s.

An almost equally important episode for the 1980s is the attempt by France to unilaterally expand and reduce unemployment in 1981–3. This was against the background of macroeconomic policy tightening in both Germany and the United States. This episode is on an equal footing with the UK and Italian experiences of the 1970s, as regards the importance of the external constraint in general, and the significance of sentiment in the foreign exchange markets in particular. In their wide-ranging investigation of this episode Sachs and Wyplosz (1986) suggest that 'the policy measures of 1981 were of moderate magnitude. This stands in contrast with the very strong reactions of the exchange markets' (p. 290). They also suggest that the external constraint in 1981 was tighter than in the cases of the 1970s, as France was committed to the European Monetary System. Given the importance of fixed exchange rates for European trade, the French government decided to change course. Of course, it should also be noted that the attempt to reduce unemployment in 1981–3 failed, perhaps because of the world recession and the parallel increase in the tax wedge between labour cost and take home pay of workers (Sachs and Wyplosz, 1986). Thus, the external constraint may not have been the only reason the policy course was reversed. Had the policy of expanding demand been seen to work in reducing unemployment, the socialists might have persevered for a while longer.

In conclusion, two celebrated manifestations of the external constraint occurred in the early 1980s. The first made the German government change course in 1981, and made it reluctant for the remainder of the decade to follow calls for a leading role in a macroeconomic program of reduction of European unemployment. The German government remained committed to fiscal consolidation and tight money for the remainder of the 1980s. On the other hand, the experience of France in 1981–3 may have convinced many other European governments that it is impossible to go it alone. These manifestations of the external constraint, and the commitment to the EMS, seem to have imparted a deflationary bias to European macroeconomic policy at least until 1986.

The final question we want to address is why European economies seem to be running into actual or perceived external constraints more often than the United States. After all, the fiscal expansion in the United States since 1982 has generated current account deficits which in percentage points of GDP are equal to, if not higher than the highest deficits recorded by any of the large European economies in the 1970s or 1980s. Yet the US has gone on running current account deficits since 1982, deficits that in the last six years averaged almost 3% of GDP per annum.

5.4   Differences between Europe and the United States

There are at least three potential hypotheses about the greater sensitivity of the European economies to current account deficits. The first has to do with differences in the degree of openness between Europe and the USA, that make European economies more vulnerable to demand expansions. The second relates to asymmetries in the international monetary system. Chief among these asymmetries are the greater weight of the US in international asset markets, and the role of the dollar as the main international reserve currency. The third potential hypothesis may be related to the preferences of the policy authorities in Europe for strong current accounts and their perceptions of the associated costs and benefits of demand expansions given the European institutional context. Let us take these hypotheses in turn.

5.4.1 The role of openness

Let us first start with the hypothesis that the European economies are more sensitive to current account deficits because of openness. It is true that the European economies are on average much more open than the United States and Japan. Table 5.3, borrowed from Drèze et al. (1987) confirms that. Even the large European economies are at least two and a half times more open than the United States and Japan. However, because a very large percentage of their trade is intra-EC trade, the EC as an entity is only slightly more open than Japan and the US.

However, the relevant question is not whether the European economies

Table 5.3. *Openness in Europe, the US, and Japan*

	Import share	Net import share
Belgium	76.1	44.2
Denmark	36.7	19.8
W. Germany	28.7	19.8
Spain	20.2	15.7
France	24.9	15.6
Ireland	58.5	40.0
Italy	28.6	18.9
Luxembourg	94.4	
Netherlands	59.4	25.0
Portugal	41.9	25.5
UK	28.2	18.7
Greece	32.5	26.0
EC 10[a]	13.4	
USA	10.1	
Japan	11.4	

Note: [a] EC trade excluding intra-EC trade.
Source: Drèze *et al.* (1987). The data refer to 1985. The net import share excludes the import content of exports.

are more open than the US, but whether a given demand expansion will generate higher current account deficits than a corresponding expansion in the US. Obviously, openness is not the only relevant parameter for answering this question. Much will depend on the interaction between aggregate demand, wage, and price setting (which will affect competitiveness) and import and export price and income elasticities. In Tables 5.4 to 5.9 we report on the results of simulations of demand expansions using an estimated model of the G-5 (USA, Japan, Germany, France, and UK). The model, whose details are reported in the Appendix, has the same structure as the models in the theoretical section, although we abstract from the role of commodity prices and exchange rate dynamics.

From Table 5.4 it is obvious that a simultaneous demand expansion in the G-5 results in a small reduction in unemployment and higher current account deficits for the European economies than in the US. Japan's current account actually improves. With regard to unilateral expansions, a coordinated EC demand expansion results in only slightly higher current account deficits for Europe than a corresponding unilateral expansion in the US. Again, the output and unemployment effects are smaller for Europe, which makes the current account deterioration as a percentage of GDP worse for Europe. Tables 5.7–5.9, which report the

Table 5.4. *Effects of a 3% increase in absorption sustained for 5 years: increase for all G-5 simultaneously*

	Year	US	UK	GE	FR	JA
GDP	1	2.79	2.03	1.56	1.53	3.27
	2	2.67	2.04	1.83	2.13	3.54
	5	2.74	1.84	2.21	3.60	3.57
	10	0.15	− 0.11	0.01	0.80	0.18
Prices	1	9.74	9.07	3.77	2.39	4.14
	2	10.80	13.10	6.66	4.98	7.64
	5	22.30	27.40	19.55	19.03	21.89
	10	36.14	36.66	34.64	43.46	35.62
Unemployment	1	− 1.28	− 0.49	− 0.72	− 0.51	− 0.29
	2	− 1.46	− 1.29	− 1.09	− 0.86	− 0.35
	5	− 1.96	− 1.84	− 1.81	− 1.98	− 0.45
	10	− 0.52	0.10	− 0.36	− 1.40	− 0.17
Real exchange rate	1	− 5.55	− 3.07	2.44	4.18	3.74
	2	− 3.41	− 4.85	1.89	3.95	1.95
	5	− 1.06	− 6.32	2.14	2.59	− 0.14
	10	0.90	0.18	3.59	− 7.80	1.06
Curr. account deficit	1	2.05	3.96	5.56	6.83	− 1.82
	2	3.30	3.87	4.56	4.15	− 5.77
	5	2.27	4.63	3.11	− 3.05	− 3.97
	10	− 1.47	0.43	− 0.01	− 3.47	− 1.19

Note: The numbers are deviations from the base run in percentage points.

effect of unilateral expansions for each of Germany, France, and the UK, confirm these findings.

The simulations reported, which abstract from the reactions of exchange markets, seem to suggest that the trade-offs between unemployment and the current account deficit are noticeably worse for Europe than for the United States. Because of the higher openness in Europe more of the demand expansion spills over abroad, limiting the output and employment effects, and strengthening the current account deterioration as a percentage of GDP. Thus, these results suggest a tighter external constraint for Europe.[12]

5.4.2 Asymmetries in the international monetary system

It has long been recognized that the special role of the dollar in the international monetary system may result in important asymmetries following demand expansions in Europe and in the US. The fact that

Table 5.5. *Effects of a 3% increase in absorption sustained for 5 years: increase for all EEC simultaneously*

	Year	US	UK	GE	FR	JA
GDP	1	0.08	1.99	1.69	1.49	0.08
	2	0.11	1.97	1.78	1.65	0.36
	5	0.14	1.74	1.99	1.86	0.71
	10	0.01	− 0.12	0.09	− 1.05	0.37
Prices	1	1.41	4.20	1.47	1.27	0.40
	2	2.85	7.30	3.28	3.02	1.07
	5	8.32	14.28	10.21	10.86	4.38
	10	12.79	12.94	14.51	17.09	9.90
Unemployment	1	− 0.04	− 0.48	− 0.78	− 0.49	− 0.01
	2	− 0.06	− 1.26	− 1.08	− 0.69	− 0.03
	5	− 0.09	− 1.76	− 1.66	− 1.16	− 0.08
	10	− 0.03	0.13	− 0.34	0.09	− 0.07
Real exchange rate	1	− 0.16	− 3.02	− 0.09	0.17	1.15
	2	− 0.15	− 4.72	− 0.40	− 0.05	2.10
	5	− 0.06	− 6.02	− 1.50	2.22	4.85
	10	0.12	0.27	− 0.34	− 4.24	3.65
Curr. account deficit	1	− 0.84	4.11	4.98	6.84	− 0.56
	2	− 1.12	4.14	4.66	6.09	− 2.46
	5	− 1.42	3.86	3.86	5.12	− 4.78
	10	− 0.08	− 0.32	− 0.32	4.20	− 2.46

international reserves, Euro-currency loans, and issues of Eurobonds and LDC debts are predominantly denominated in dollars, and also the fact that the dollar is the main means of payment and unit of account in the inter-bank market, may differentiate the international effects of current account deficits in the United States from analogous effects of current account deficits in Europe. As Oudiz and Sachs (1984) suggest, it appears that 'the United States can run high budget and current account deficits without a major depreciation of the dollar, while in Europe and Japan, a similar level of budget and external deficits would probably cause a significant depreciation of the currency' (p. 7). These asymmetries may be the reason why the current account deficits in the European cases resulted in a run on the currency and foreign exchange reserves of the expanding economies, and an acceleration of domestic inflation. The opposite happened in the aftermath of the US expansion of 1982–5. In any case, these effects are very difficult to quantify in the context of econometric models, and we can do no more than point to their potential significance for the

Table 5.6. *Effects of a 3% increase in absorption sustained for 5 years: increase for US unilaterally*

	Year	US	UK	GE	FR	JA
GDP	1	2.60	0.02	− 0.11	0.03	0.27
	2	2.46	0.04	0.08	0.35	0.76
	5	2.49	0.07	0.29	0.91	0.69
	10	0.11	0.00	0.04	0.14	0.05
Prices	1	6.70	3.47	1.62	0.80	1.30
	2	4.93	3.04	1.87	1.17	1.77
	5	5.05	4.62	3.75	3.95	4.26
	10	6.60	7.18	6.64	9.56	6.78
Unemployment	1	− 1.20	− 0.01	0.05	− 0.01	− 0.02
	2	− 1.34	− 0.02	− 0.02	− 0.12	− 0.07
	5	− 1.79	− 0.06	− 0.19	− 0.45	− 0.08
	10	− 0.46	− 0.02	− 0.12	− 0.36	− 0.03
Real exchange rate	1	− 5.20	− 0.03	1.80	2.90	3.72
	2	− 3.13	− 0.08	1.05	1.98	2.13
	5	− 0.96	− 0.20	0.76	0.47	0.42
	10	0.75	− 0.06	0.94	− 2.88	0.17
Curr. account deficit	1	3.88	− 0.10	0.41	− 0.11	− 0.81
	2	5.42	− 0.18	− 0.31	− 1.55	− 5.19
	5	5.22	− 0.28	− 1.10	− 4.17	− 4.72
	10	− 1.11	− 0.17	− 0.17	− 0.60	− 0.33

external constraint in Europe. To the extent that the process of European Monetary Unification results in a larger role for the ecu as an international currency, EMU may have the additional benefit of relaxing this type of external constraint (see Alogoskoufis and Portes, 1990).

5.4.3 The preferences of European policy-makers and the institutional context

A third potential explanation for the greater sensitivity of European macroeconomic policy on the current account may have to do with the preferences of European policy-makers for current account surpluses and strong currencies. Such preferences may have been affected by the inter-war experience, and the existence of European Community institutions that make exchange rate variability costly.

In their study of the European Monetary System, Giavazzi and Giovannini (1989) suggest a number of reasons for which the Europeans may be more averse than the Americans to exchange rate fluctuations. They suggest that,

Table 5.7. *Effects of a 3% increase in absorption sustained for 5 years: increase for UK unilaterally*

	Year	US	UK	GE	FR	JA
GDP	1	0.02	1.97	− 0.02	0.00	0.02
	2	0.02	1.95	− 0.01	0.04	0.09
	5	0.03	1.70	0.02	0.25	0.14
	10	0.01	− 0.12	0.02	0.16	0.05
Prices	1	0.53	3.32	0.27	0.12	0.15
	2	0.91	5.26	0.54	0.28	0.33
	5	1.77	7.29	1.36	1.13	0.98
	10	2.13	1.91	2.07	3.16	1.77
Unemployment	1	− 0.01	− 0.47	0.01	0.00	0.00
	2	− 0.01	− 1.25	0.01	− 0.02	− 0.01
	5	− 0.02	− 1.72	− 0.01	− 0.11	− 0.02
	10	− 0.01	0.13	− 0.02	− 0.17	− 0.01
Real exchange rate	1	− 0.03	− 3.00	0.30	0.44	0.44
	2	− 0.03	− 4.67	0.43	0.69	0.68
	5	− 0.01	− 5.89	0.52	0.73	0.94
	10	0.02	0.29	0.26	− 1.13	0.45
Curr. account deficit	1	− 0.18	4.17	0.06	− 0.01	− 0.21
	2	− 0.23	4.24	0.05	− 0.20	− 0.63
	5	− 0.29	5.20	− 0.08	− 1.10	− 0.94
	10	− 0.07	0.49	− 0.06	− 0.70	− 0.35

> Europeans dislike exchange rate fluctuations for three reasons. First, they all live in relatively open countries. Second, many of them hold the floating rates of the 1920s and 1930s responsible for the ensuing collapse of national economies and of the international trading and monetary systems. Third, postwar European institutions – particularly the common agricultural market – depend for their survival on exchange rate stability. (p. 1)

Some of these reasons, especially the last, may partly explain the U-turn in France's macroeconomic policy of 1981–3. To quote from Sachs and Wyplosz (1986):

> The role of external pressure was extremely important, since there is good reason to believe that French commitments to the EMS tipped the balance towards austerity. Unlike the much looser commitment under the European Snake in the 1970s, which France abandoned on two occasions, membership of the EMS has been invested with enormous political importance at the very highest levels of the government. That is why the debate over leaving the EMS was treated as synonymous with the debate over abandoning other spheres of cooperation in Europe, including participation in the Common Market. (p. 294–5)

Table 5.8. *Effects of a 3% increase in absorption sustained for 5 years: increase for Germany unilaterally*

	Year	US	UK	GE	FR	JA
GDP	1	0.04	0.01	1.70	0.03	0.03
	2	0.05	0.02	1.78	0.10	0.16
	5	0.08	0.03	1.97	0.51	0.32
	10	0.04	0.01	0.13	0.76	0.28
Prices	1	0.46	0.46	0.94	0.14	0.13
	2	0.98	1.03	2.06	0.40	0.40
	5	3.23	3.46	6.04	2.25	1.79
	10	6.73	7.01	8.38	8.45	4.88
Unemployment	1	− 0.02	0.00	− 0.78	− 0.01	0.00
	2	− 0.03	− 0.01	− 1.09	− 0.04	− 0.01
	5	− 0.05	− 0.02	− 1.65	− 0.23	− 0.03
	10	− 0.04	− 0.02	− 0.36	− 0.55	− 0.04
Real exchange rate	1	− 0.08	− 0.01	− 0.65	0.42	0.34
	2	− 0.08	− 0.03	− 1.38	0.85	0.71
	5	− 0.05	− 0.08	− 3.41	1.69	1.83
	10	0.02	− 0.05	− 1.53	− 1.48	2.34
Curr. account deficit	1	− 0.40	− 0.04	4.92	− 0.14	− 0.18
	2	− 0.54	− 0.07	4.61	− 0.46	− 1.07
	5	− 0.77	− 0.12	3.85	− 2.32	− 2.13
	10	− 0.36	− 0.05	− 0.47	− 3.42	− 1.90

The above notwithstanding, it is important to recognize that the EMS constraint was binding for European unemployment, only to the extent that Germany was reluctant to contemplate a coordinated expansion in Europe after 1981. Such an expansion was seldom urged on Germany at the highest policital level (e.g., the Seven Power Summits) between 1982 and 1985. For example, in the Versailles summit of 1982, to quote from Putnam and Bayne (1987),

> Macroeconomics was discussed surprisingly little. Mitterrand, the natural advocate of economic stimulus knew privately that within days he would be forced to shift to a restrictive stance. The leaders continued to stress 'prudent monetary policies' and 'greater control of budgetary deficits'. At a time of the highest unemployment in decades, the absence of any call for additional stimulus was a stark reminder of how the political environment had changed in barely four years. (p. 136)

At Williamsburg in 1983,

> all suggestions that they stimulate their economies were sternly rejected by the Americans, British, Germans and Japanese. British Chancellor

Table 5.9. *Effects of a 3% increase in absorption sustained for 5 years: increase for France unilaterally*

	Year	US	UK	GE	FR	JA
GDP	1	0.03	0.01	0.01	1.45	0.02
	2	0.03	0.01	0.02	1.50	0.11
	5	0.04	0.01	− 0.01	1.09	0.25
	10	0.03	− 0.01	− 0.06	− 1.97	0.03
Prices	1	0.41	0.41	0.26	1.00	0.12
	2	0.95	1.00	0.68	2.34	0.35
	5	3.31	3.52	2.80	7.48	1.61
	10	3.90	3.99	4.05	5.46	3.24
Unemployment	1	− 0.01	0.00	0.00	− 0.48	0.00
	2	− 0.02	0.00	− 0.01	− 0.64	− 0.01
	5	− 0.03	− 0.01	0.00	− 0.82	− 0.03
	10	0.01	0.01	0.04	0.81	− 0.02
Real exchange rate	1	− 0.05	− 0.01	0.26	− 0.70	0.33
	2	− 0.04	− 0.02	0.55	− 1.60	0.71
	5	0.01	− 0.04	1.38	− 4.65	2.07
	10	0.09	0.04	0.17	− 1.63	0.86
Curr. account deficit	1	− 0.26	− 0.02	− 0.03	6.95	− 0.16
	2	− 0.34	− 0.04	− 0.05	6.64	− 0.75
	5	− 0.35	− 0.06	0.02	8.06	− 1.69
	10	0.34	0.06	0.22	7.65	− 0.21

> Howe and German Economics Minister Lambsdorff both argued that this approach would simply re-ignite inflation. So firm was the hold of these four conservative governments on the preparations for Williamsburg that proposals for coordinated reflation were not even raised during the sherpa's meetings. (*ibid*, p. 176)

By the time of the second London summit of 1984,

> A broad consensus was emerging that the European economies were less flexible than the American or the Japanese, owing to labour immobility, government regulation, inadequate competition, wage and capital market rigidities and lower profitability – a condition called 'Eurosclerosis' (*ibid*, p. 185)

In contrast, EC-wide coordinated expansions were strongly urged by leading academics. In its first three reports of 1983, 1984, and 1985, the CEPS Macroeconomic Policy Group (see Blanchard *et al.*, 1986) strongly urged coordinated fiscal expansion in the EEC as a means for tackling the unemployment problem without running into external constraints.

To conclude, the celebrated aversion of German policy-makers to even moderate inflation and current account deficits, may well have been the ultimate external constraint on European unemployment.

6   Conclusions

In this chapter we demonstrate that aggregate demand policies and their international interdependence can go a long way towards accounting for the different unemployment experiences of Europe and the United States in the 1970s and the 1980s. The explanations are consistent with the behaviour of other important macroeconomic variables, such as inflation, commodity prices, and nominal and real exchange rates.

We have suggested that the reasons that macroeconomic policies in Europe have been less expansionary than in the United States may have to do with external constraints due to Europe's higher openness, asymmetries in the international monetary system, and European preferences for greater exchange rate stability. The facts do not seem to contradict these hypotheses.

Appendix   Listing of the model for the Group of Five

Reported below is a listing of the G-5 model used for the simulations. The model was estimated with annual data for 1951–86. Sources were the OECD *National Accounts*, the OECD *Labour Force Statistics*, and the IMF *International Financial Statistics*. Estimation was carried out by TSLS. The estimates have been based on the price, wage and employment equations discussed in the text, and conventional import and export demand equations. Allowance was made for lags, through error correction or generalized partial adjustment specifications. To quantify macroeconomic interdependence we used IMF MERM weights. Constants and trends are omitted from the listing. Superscripts u, j, g, f, b symbolize the United States, Japan, Germany, France, and Britain respectively.

1   US model

$$y^u = a^u + 0.10(x^u - c^u - m^u)$$
$$c^u = e^u + p^{*u} - p^u$$
$$w^u = p^u + 0.10c^u + 0.66(w^u_{-1} - p^u_{-1} - 0.10c^u_{-1}) + 0.20(y^u - y^u_{-1})$$
$$p^u = w^u + 0.85(p^u_{-1} - w^u_{-1})$$
$$x^u = 0.22x^u_{-1} + 0.97y^{*u} + 0.85c^u$$
$$m^u = 0.82m^u_{-1} + 1.26y^u - 1.01y^u_{-1} - 0.30c^u$$
$$l^u = 0.85l^u_{-1} + 0.46y^u - 0.31y^u_{-1}$$

2   Japanese model

$$y^j = a^j + 0.15(x^j - c^j - m^j)$$
$$c^j = e^j + p^{*j} - p^j$$
$$w^j = p^j + 0.15c^j + 1.00(w^j_{-1} - p^j_{-1} - 0.15c^j_{-1}) + 0.51y^j$$
$$p^j = 0.65w^j + 0.90p^j_{-1} - 0.55w^j_{-1}$$
$$x^j = 0.25x^j_{-1} + 2.05y^{*j}_1 + 0.21c^j_{-1}$$
$$m^j = 0.93y^j_{-1} - 1.49c^j$$
$$l^j = 0.99l^j_{-1} + 0.09y^j - 0.08y^j_{-1}$$

3   German model

$$y^g = a^g + 0.27(x^g - c^g - m^g)$$
$$c^g = e^g + p^{*g} - p^g$$
$$w^g = p^g + 0.27c^g + 0.79(w^g_{-1} - p^g_{-1} - 0.27c^g_{-1}) + 0.26y^g$$
$$p^g = 0.78w^g + 0.58p^g_{-1} - 0.36w^g_{-1}$$
$$x^g = 0.75x^g_{-1} + 0.58y^{*g} + 0.13c^g$$
$$m^g = 3.13y^g - 0.11c^g$$
$$l^g = 0.71l^g_{-1} + 0.46y^g - 0.17y^g_{-1}$$

4   French model

$$y^f = a^f + 0.23(x^f - c^f - m^f)$$
$$c^f = e^f + p^{*f} - p^f$$
$$w^f = p^f + 0.23c^f + 0.95(w^f_{-1} - p^f_{-1} - 0.23c^f_{-1}) + 0.70y^f$$
$$p^f = 0.54w^f + 0.78p^f_{-1} - 0.32w^f_{-1}$$
$$x^f = 0.98x^f_{-1} + 0.58y^{*f} + 0.55c^f$$
$$m^f = 0.59m^f_{-1} + 4.72y^f - 3.38y^f_{-1} - 0.32c^f$$
$$l^f = 0.85l^f_{-1} + 0.33y^f - 0.18y^f_{-1}$$

5   British model

$$y^b = a^b + 0.25(x^b - c^b - m^b)$$
$$c^b = e^b + p^{*b} - p^b$$
$$w^b = p^b + 0.25c^b + 0.57(w^b_{-1} - p^b_{-1} - 0.25c^b_{-1}) + 0.38y^b$$
$$p^b = w^b + 0.90(p^b_{-1} - w^b_{-1})$$
$$x^b = 0.66x^b_{-1} + 0.14y^{*u} + 0.21c^b$$
$$m^b = 0.56m^b_{-1} + 3.01y^b - 1.44y^b_{-1} - 0.18c^b$$
$$l^b = 0.48l^b_{-1} + 0.24y^b - 0.28y^b_{-1}$$

6   Definitions of foreign variables (weights proportional to MERM)

$$y^{*u} = (0.43y^j + 0.27y^g + 0.20y^f + 0.10y^b)$$
$$p^{*u} = (0.43p^j + 0.27p^g + 0.20p^f + 0.10p^b)$$

$$y^{*j} = (0.67y^u + 0.17y^g + 0.11y^f + 0.05y^b)$$
$$p^{*j} = (0.67p^u + 0.17p^g + 0.11p^f + 0.05p^b)$$
$$y^{*g} = (0.38y^u + 0.23y^j + 0.30y^f + 0.09y^b)$$
$$p^{*g} = (0.38p^u + 0.23p^j + 0.30p^f + 0.09p^b)$$
$$y^{*f} = (0.40y^u + 0.19y^j + 0.34y^g + 0.07y^b)$$
$$p^{*f} = (0.40p^u + 0.19p^j + 0.34p^g + 0.07p^b)$$
$$y^{*b} = (0.40y^u + 0.22y^j + 0.22y^g + 0.16y^f)$$
$$p^{*b} = (0.40p^u + 0.22p^j + 0.22p^g + 0.16p^f)$$

7   Symbols

y = log of GDP at 1980 prices

a = log of absorption at 1980 prices

x = log of exports of goods and services at 1980 prices

m = log of imports of goods and services at 1980 prices

w = log of index of hourly earnings in manufacturing, 1980 = 1

p = log of GDP deflator, 1980 = 1

e = log of effective exchange rate

i = real interest rate

d = foreign debt at constant prices

l = log of total employment

NOTES

We have benefited from the comments of participants in seminars at the Trade Union Institute for Economic Research (FIEF) in Stockholm, Leicester University, the Centre for Labour Economics at the LSE, and the Athens Conference on the External Constraint. We wish to thank the ESRC for financial support through the programme on 'The Macroeconomics of Imperfect Product and Labour Markets' at Birkbeck College. Alogoskoufis would also like to thank the CEPR for financial support through its International Macroeconomics Programme, supported by grants from the Ford and Alfred P. Sloan Foundations, and the Institute for International Economic Studies in Stockholm, where a large part of the first draft of this chapter was put together in September 1989.

1 For an excellent comprehensive survey of research on unemployment see Nickell (1990).

2 The theoretical models in this paper are amended from Alogoskoufis (1990).

3 The assumption of a linear short-run technology is not crucial for what follows. It is adopted mainly for algebraic simplicity and could easily be generalized without important qualitative differences in the results.

4 See for example Dixit and Stiglitz (1977).

5 There is a lot of controversy about the exact nature of the preferences of wage setters. For a survey see Oswald (1986). As we do not wish to employ any particular special assumption, we treat (5) as a quadratic approximation to any arbitrary functional form for the preferences of wage setters.

6 We abstract from external balance considerations until Section 5.

7 For brevity, in what follows we often refer to the sum of Europe and the US as the 'OECD'. Apologies to Japan, Canada, Australia and New Zealand.
8 For a more general discussion of models of North–South interdependence see Currie and Vines (1988).
9 The model employed in this section is a variant of the Frankel (1986) model, which itself is an adaptation of the Dornbusch (1976) exchange rate model to commodity prices. Other 'world' variants of the model can be found in Boughton and Branson (1988) and Moutos and Vines (1988).
10 Beckerman and Jenkinson (1986) have presented evidence that the OECD disinflation of the early 1980s was due to the fall in commodity prices rather than unemployment. Thus, there is some evidence for the mechanism we suggest. Of course, the question of whether inflation fell because of commodity price or unemployment is not very deep in the context of our model, as inflation, unemployment and commodity prices are endogenous, and depend on world macroeconomic policy and other supply and demand factors.
11 The following quotation from Chancellor Schmidt on the eve of the London summit of 1977 supports this: 'I do not believe that the French or the President of the United States will ask us in London to make more inflation. The English might like to see others make a bit more inflation, but I think it would be desirable for the rest of us to help them, as we have been doing up to now, to come down from their inflation rate of 18%' (*Daily Telegraph*, 6 May 1977, quoted in Putnam and Bayne, 1987).
12 In a chapter in this volume, Cohen and Wyplosz (1991) provide a similar argument, and demonstrate how in the presence of a symmetric adverse supply shock, countries in which the trade effects of exchange rate changes dominate the price effects, will undertake insufficient monetary and fiscal policies in the absence of coordination, out of misplaced concern ₁or their bilateral real exchange rate. They conjecture, that if France and Germany had cooperated in the early 1980s, they would have been much better placed to counteract Reaganomics.

REFERENCES

Alogoskoufis, G.S. (1990), 'The Rise and Fall of European Unemployment', mimeo, Birkbeck College, London.
Alogoskoufis, G.S. and A. Manning (1988a), 'Wage Setting and Unemployment Persistence in Europe, Japan and the USA', *European Economic Review* **32**, 698–706.
    (1988b), 'On the Persistence of Unemployment', *Economic Policy* 3 (7), 427–69.
Alogoskoufis, G.S. and R. Portes (1990), 'International Costs and Benefits from EMU', CEPR Discussion Paper No. 424
Aoki, M. (1981), *Dynamic Analysis of Open Economies*, New York: Academic Press.
Bean, C.R., P.R.G. Layard, and S.J. Nickell (1986), 'The Rise in Unemployment: A Multi-country Study', *Economica* **53** (Supplement), S1–S22.
Beckerman, W. and T. Jenkinson (1986), 'What Stopped the Inflation? Unemployment or Commodity Prices', *The Economic Journal* **96**, 39–54.
Blanchard, O.J. and L.H. Summers (1986), 'Hysteresis and the European Unemployment Problem', in S. Fischer (ed.), *NBER Macroeconomic Annual*, Cambridge, MA: MIT Press.

162   **George Alogoskoufis and Christopher Martin**

Blanchard, O.J., R. Dornbusch, and P.R.G. Layard (1986), *Restoring Europe's Prosperity*, Cambridge, MA: MIT Press.

Boughton, J.M. and W.H. Branson (1988), 'Commodity Prices as a Leading Indicator of Inflation', IMF Working Paper No. 88/87.

Branson, W.H. and J.J. Rotemberg (1980), 'International Adjustment with Wage Rigidity', *European Economic Review* **13**, 309–32.

Bruno, M. and J. Sachs (1985), *The Economics of Worldwide Stagflation*, Oxford: Basil Blackwell.

Buiter, W.H. and M. Miller (1981), 'Monetary Policy and International Competitiveness: The Problem of Adjustment', *Oxford Economic Papers* **33** (Supplement), 132–44.

Calmfors, L. and J. Driffill (1988), 'Bargaining Structure, Corporatism and Macroeconomic Performance', *Economic Policy* **3** (6), 14–61.

Cohen, D. and C. Wyplosz (1991), 'France and Germany in the EMS: The Exchange Rate Constraint', this volume.

Cooper, R.N. (1987), 'External Constraints on European Growth', in Lawrence, R.Z., and C.L. Schultze (eds.), *Barriers to European Growth: A Transatlantic View*, Washington D.C.: The Brookings Institute.

Currie, D. and D. Vines (1988), *Macroeconomic Interactions Between North and South*, Cambridge University Press and CEPR.

Dixit, A. and J. Stiglitz (1977), 'Monopolistic Competition and Optimum Product Diversity', *American Economic Review* **67**, 297–308.

Dornbusch, R. (1976), 'Expectations and Exchange Rate Dynamics', *Journal of Political Economy* **84**, 1161–76.

Drèze, J., C. Wyplosz, C. Bean, F. Giavazzi, and H. Giersch (1987), 'The Two-handed Growth Strategy for Europe: Autonomy through Flexible Cooperation', EEC Economic Paper No. 60.

Emerson, M. (1988), 'Regulation or Deregulation of the Labour Market: Policy Regimes for the Recruitment and Dismissal of Employees in the Industrialized Countries', *European Economic Review* **32**, 775–817.

Frankel, J. (1986), 'Expectations and Commodity Price Dynamics: The Overshooting Model', *American Journal of Agricultural Economics* **68**, 344–8.

Giavazzi, F. and A. Giovannini (1989), *Limiting Exchange Rate Flexibility: The European Monetary System*, Cambridge, MA: MIT Press.

Gordon, R.J. (1987), 'Productivity, Wages and Prices Inside and Outside Manufacturing in the USA, Japan and Europe', *European Economic Review* **31**, 685–739.

Grubb, D., R.A. Jackman, and P.R.G. Layard (1982), 'Causes of the Current Stagflation', *Review of Economic Studies* **49**, 707–30.

 (1983), 'Wage Rigidity and Unemployment in the OECD Countries', *European Economic Review* **21**, 11–39.

Lindbeck, A. and D.J. Snower (1986), 'Wage Setting, Unemployment, and Insider Outsider Relations', *American Economic Review*, Papers and Proceedings, **76**, 235–9.

 (1989), *The Insider Outsider Theory of Employment and Unemployment*, Cambridge, MA: MIT Press.

Metcalf, D. (1987), 'Labour Market Flexibility and Jobs – A Survey of Evidence from OECD Countries with Special Reference to Great Britain and Europe', in P.R.G. Layard and L. Calmfors (eds.), *The Fight Against Unemployment*, Cambridge, MA: MIT Press.

Moutos, T. and D. Vines (1988), 'Output, Inflation and Commodity', CEPR Discussion Paper No. 271.

Newell, A. and J.S.V. Symons (1985), 'Wages and Unemployment in the OECD Countries', CLE Discussion Paper No. 219, London School of Economics.

(1987), 'Corporatism, Laissez-Faire and the Rise in Unemployment', *European Economic Review* **31**, 567–614.

Nickell, S.J. (1990), 'Unemployment: A Survey', *Economic Journal* **100**, 391–439.

Organization for Economic Cooperation and Development (1988), *Why Economic Policies Change Course: Eleven Case Studies*, Paris: OECD.

(1989), *Employment Outlook* (July), Paris: OECD.

Oswald, A. (1986), 'The Economic Theory of Trade Unions: An Introductory Survey', in L. Calmfors and H. Horn (eds.), *Trade Unions, Wage Formation and Macroeconomic Activity*, London: Macmillan.

Oudiz, G. and J. Sachs (1984), 'Macroeconomic Policy Coordination among the Industrial Economies', *Brookings Papers on Economic Activity* **1**, 1–64.

Putnam, R.D. and N. Bayne (1987), *Hanging Together: Cooperation and Conflict in the Seven Power Summits*, Cambridge, MA: Harvard University Press.

Sachs, J.D. (1979), 'Wages, Profits and Macroeconomic Adjustment: A Comparative Study', *Brookings Papers on Economic Activity* **2**, 269–332.

Sachs, J.D. and C. Wyplosz (1986), 'The Economic Consequences of President Mitterrand', *Economic Policy* **1** (2), 262–322.

Wadhwani, S. (1987), 'The Macroeconomic Implications of Profit-Sharing: Some Empirical Evidence', *Economic Journal* Conference Papers, **97**, 171–83.

Discussion

CHARLES R. BEAN

The bulk of this rich and varied chapter is concerned with developing a series of increasingly complex models of the international economy designed to help explain the main 'stylized facts' about OECD unemployment over the last two decades. A key claim is that much of the existing literature on European unemployment has 'disregarded . . . the possibility that a large part of the differences in the behaviour of unemployment may be due to macroeconomic policies . . . [and that] labour market differences have been overemphasized'. A great many people (including myself, not to mention one of the authors!) have devoted a large part of the last decade to understanding these labour market differences, so this is a pretty powerful claim. However, I believe the analysis is neither as revolutionary as Algosokoufis and Martin claim, nor as consistent with the evidence as they would think.

A key feature in all the models, except perhaps the last one with nominal rigidities, is the presence of a terms of trade effect on supply. Although the Alogoskoufis–Martin model is one of imperfect competition, this effect will appear in a classical model with perfect competition provided labour supply is not completely inelastic. An improvement in the terms of trade will raise the consumption wage for a given product wage, leading to an expansion in labour supply, a fall in the product wage, and a rise in employment. A fiscal expansion will lead to real exchange rate appreciation and therefore an expansion in activity. In fact this mechanism is already present in Bean, Layard, and Nickell (1986) and the great majority of the other papers in this literature that Alogoskoufis and Martin cite, although it is generally the case that these authors do not decompose the movements in the real exchange rate into that part due to fiscal policy, that part due to the oil price shock, etc. (Note also that claiming that 'changes in aggregate demand will affect the equilibrium level of unemployment' is misleading to the extent that aggregate demand only matters *because* aggregate supply is simultaneously affected. Lucas has argued that we should refer to, e.g., technology, preference, and fiscal shocks rather than shifts in demand or supply, terms which are imprecise and open to misinterpretation; I think the discussion in Alogoskoufis and Martin points to the wisdom of Lucas's words.)

But if this mechanism is present in the earlier literature, how come everybody has failed to spot the significance of these fiscally induced swings in real exchange rates and concentrated instead on exploring labour market differences? Inspector Alogoskoufis and Detective-Sergeant Martin seem to have presented us with an open-and-shut case; it hardly seems worth bothering to go to trial! The problem is that the forensic evidence does not quite fit. If real exchange rate movements *were* the main culprit one would have expected cross-country econometric studies of wage behaviour of the Bean, Layard, and Nickell variety to have clearly signalled their importance; they don't (see, e.g., Table 3 of Bean, Layard, and Nickell). Furthermore, even when these terms of trade effects are included there are wide differences in the response of wages to unemployment and in the dynamic structure, suggesting that labour market institutions are important in determining the magnitude and duration of the response of unemployment to such exogenous shocks. Let me also note that, to explain the contrasting experience of Japan and the Nordic countries on one hand, and the European Community on the other, Alogoskoufis and Martin have themselves to rely on structural differences in the labour market.

In addition, although the model of Bean, Layard, Nickell, and others includes a permanent effect of the terms of trade on equilibrium unemployment, I think there are good reasons for expecting the effect to be at most only transitory. First, in all the theoretical models of the labour market I have been able to write down, the terms of trade enter in the same way as productivity. However, the latter must be neutral with respect to unemployment over the long run because there is no trend in unemployment over the last hundred years or so, only a few wiggles plus the odd periodic jump. Theoretical consistency thus requires only a transitory effect. Second, the empirical work of Newell and Symons (1985) supports this conjecture; if there is a terms of trade effect, differences rather than levels is the preferred specification.

Furthermore, to the extent that terms of trade shift *are* the root cause of the problem, I find it difficult to attribute these all to fiscal shocks. Model II endogenizes commodity prices, a novel extension. However, movements in commodity prices are entirely a reflection of, e.g., movements in fiscal policy. There is no role for autonomous commodity price developments. It seems to be stretching things a bit to classify the two oil price hikes, as well as the fall since 1986, as entirely reactive. The simultaneous fall in US and European unemployment since 1986 surely had something to do with the latter, and perhaps rather less to do with fiscal expansion. (Was there *really* that much of a fiscal expansion in Europe after 1986? I doubt it.)

Finally, to the extent that they are right that real exchange rate movements have been the key factor and that fiscal policies have been the primary driving force behind them, one has also to ask to what extent differences in policy choices are *themselves* a reflection of different underlying structures. Thus my conclusion is that, although misguided fiscal policies may well have been in cahoots with sclerotic labour markets, insider–outsider mechanisms, and the rest of the European Unemployment Gang, the counsel for the prosecution has not really yet provided enough evidence for an indictment; at best the verdict must be 'not proven'.

Let me finish with some remarks about the final section of the chapter which is more directly concerned with the topic of this publication. Alogoskoufis and Martin adopt a 'narrow' view of the external constraint. But even within such a 'narrow' view one can discern two separate strands (which have surfaced repeatedly in this publication). On the one hand there is the issue of solvency and the extent to which countries can borrow on the international capital markets to finance an excess of absorption over income. On the other there is the question of the willingness of the authorities to maintain a given nominal exchange rate through adopting the appropriate monetary policies, with 'incredible' policies leading to speculative attacks. Lack of access to foreign borrowing or a speculative attack can both force a reversal of domestic policies, but a country can certainly experience one without the other. The celebrated reversal of French policies under Mitterrand seems to me to be rather a good example of this. It is not obvious that French access to the international capital markets was heavily circumscribed in 1982–3, but clearly expectations of a second devaluation within the EMS, or even a float of the Franc, meant that maintaining the existing parity was next to impossible with the prevailing policies. Political, as much as economic, considerations dictated that continued membership of the EMS took precedence.

Alogoskoufis and Martin also discuss a number of other instances when they believe the 'external constraint' forced a turnabout in domestic policies. Sometimes I feel the emphasis placed on the external aspects is rather overplayed. For instance the UK experience during 1975–6 seems to me to have had as much to do with internal inflationary pressures as with the deterioration of the current account (the two were, of course, both a manifestation of excess demand in the UK economy). Equally the German tightening of monetary and fiscal policy in 1981 also seem to have been prompted as much by inflationary fears as by concerns over the current account. Identifying the role of the 'external constraint' *per se* requires separating out these two influences, something that is not easy to do since the two generally occur together; an exception of course is the recent American experience.

REFERENCES

Bean, C., R. Layard, and S. Nickell, (1986), 'The Rise in Unemployment: A Multi-Country Study', *Economica* (supplement) 53, S1–22.

Newell, A. and J. Symons (1985), 'Wages and Employment in the OECD Countries', Centre for Labour Economics, Discussion Paper No. 219, London School of Economics.

6 France and Germany in the EMS: the exchange rate constraint

DANIEL COHEN and CHARLES WYPLOSZ

1 Introduction

Over the last ten years, France and Germany have undergone fairly strong stabilization policies. In France, inflation has been gradually brought down from a high of 11.7% to 2.7%, a level below those observed over most of the sixties. The budget deficit, which increased quickly in 1981–2, has been all but eliminated. In Germany, the main effort has concerned the closing down of the budget deficit, by about 3 percentage points of GDP in just four years. During that period, the Bundesbank saw to it that inflation, never very high, would decline further possibly towards the zero mark.[1] These sharp policy actions have been accompanied by fairly large bilateral nominal exchange rate changes between France and Germany.

Yet their bilateral real exchange rate has been remarkably stable, over the stabilization period but also during much of the last two decades. Given that both countries are fairly open to trade, with exports representing 24% and 32% of GDP in France and Germany, respectively, the behaviour of the exchange rate must be of importance to policy-makers. Undoubtedly, the stability of the real exchange rate is a consequence of EMS membership. What is interesting is that France and Germany have *chosen* to operate within the constraints imposed by the EMS. Why they have followed that path and what has been the effect of the external constraint on the conduct of fiscal and monetary policies are the questions that we wish to address.

The effect of EMS membership on policy-making remains a controversial issue. Few doubt that it entails a tightening of the external constraint. How this tightening operates is not fully elucidated however. Giavazzi and Giovannini (1989) are among those who have argued that, *de facto*, the EMS has resulted in Germany charting its own course of action independently of what the other countries were doing, thus imposing its

policy options in return for lending them the credibility of the Bundesbank. This view has been criticized by a number of authors.[2] The arguments are varied but centre on the empirical observation that Germany's
policies have not been immune to influences from its partners. Thus, the
debate revolves around the effects of interdependence, and the channels
through which this interdependence operates.

The issue is not merely of historical interest. By 1993, interdependence will
further increase, and the evolution towards a monetary union seems
inescapable. It is of importance, therefore, to understand whether the
external constraint will further tighten or, put differently, how the
exchange rate discipline will operate and affect policy-making. In this
chapter, we take a step in the direction of dealing with this issue. We do so
by drawing on recent work (Cohen and Wyplosz, 1990) devoted to the
elucidation of the implications of exchange rate changes on the setting of
monetary and fiscal policies. We use the experience of the last period to
pinpoint the main channels of influence. Our framework naturally leads to a
sharp conclusion on the benefits to be drawn from monetary coordination.

We ask what is the optimal policy that a country might want to pursue
under the existing circumstances – which, during our sample period, we
interpret as the oil shock and the stagflation legacy of the seventies – given
the constraints under which it operates. The argument, which is presented
in Section 3, emphasizes two channels through which (real) exchange
rates impact on policy-making: while an appreciation lessens inflationary
pressure, it brings about a worsening in the trade account and a reduction
in output. We show that, for closely integrated economies like those of
France and Germany, the trade-off depends upon the relative size of these
two effects, both amongst the two countries themselves and *vis-à-vis* the
rest of the world.

An assessment of how exchange rates may have affected policies requires
measuring the relative size of both (trade and price) effects. Section 4
presents our estimates. The effects of real exchange rates on the trade
balance and inflation are notoriously difficult to detect, and our results do
not avoid this limitation. However, we do find an indication that, in
Germany and France, the trade balance is quite sensitive to the intra-EMS
effective real exchange rate, not so (actually in a perverse way) for the
extra-EMS rate. The opposite seems to be the case for inflation. Simulation
results from OECD's Interlink model are also presented. This allows us in
Section 5 to interpret policy actions in France and Germany as being dominated by the need to avoid disrupting the trade balance and as a consequence output. Put differently, we conclude that France and Germany
have underexploited the inflation–output trade-off gains which can be
reaped through beggar-thy-neighbour policies of the type underscored

Table 6.1. *Standard deviations of quarterly changes in real effective exchange rates, 1970–89*

	Real effective exchange rate *vis-à-vis*		Trade balance (% GDP)	Share of trade with EC 1988
	EC	Non-EC		
France	1.99	4.63	0.78	61.6
Germany	1.88	4.89	0.85	54.1
Italy	2.20	4.10	1.18	57.1
UK	4.05	4.86	1.24	49.8
USA		3.61	0.44	
Japan		4.30	0.86	

Notes: Trade balances and European effective real exchange rates (logs) computed with nominal exchange rates and CPI from *International Financial Statistics* tape. Weights based on sum of imports and exports. Trade (exports) shares from *European Economy*, November 1989. Sample period: 1970: 1–89: 4, except trade balances for France (70: 1–89: 1), Italy (70: 1–87: 3) and UK (70: 1–87: 3) and UK (70: 1–89: 2). Real effective exchange rates for US and Japan (75: 1–89: 4) from *International Financial Statistics* tape.

by Sachs (1983) and Miller and Salmon (1985). The monetary union would remove this inefficiency, which might be quite desirable in the years to come if the US dollar were to further depreciate, as is likely.

2   Stylized facts

Much of this paper relies on the distinction between two measures of effective real exchange rates: the effective rate *vis-à-vis* other EC countries and the effective rate *vis-à-vis* other advanced countries.[3] We use trade weights (the sum of imports and exports) and as price index the CPI, mainly because GDP/GNP deflators are not available on a quarterly basis for some countries. The two effective real exchange rates for France and Germany are displayed in Figure 6.1, along with comparable data for Italy and the UK.

The variability of effective exchange rate changes *vis-à-vis* non-EC countries is of the same order of magnitude in France, Germany, Italy, and the UK, and within the same range as what is observed for the US and Japanese overall effective real exchange rates. A measure of volatility, the standard deviation of quarterly changes,[4] is shown in Table 6.1. What makes France and Germany stand sharply apart is the very low variability

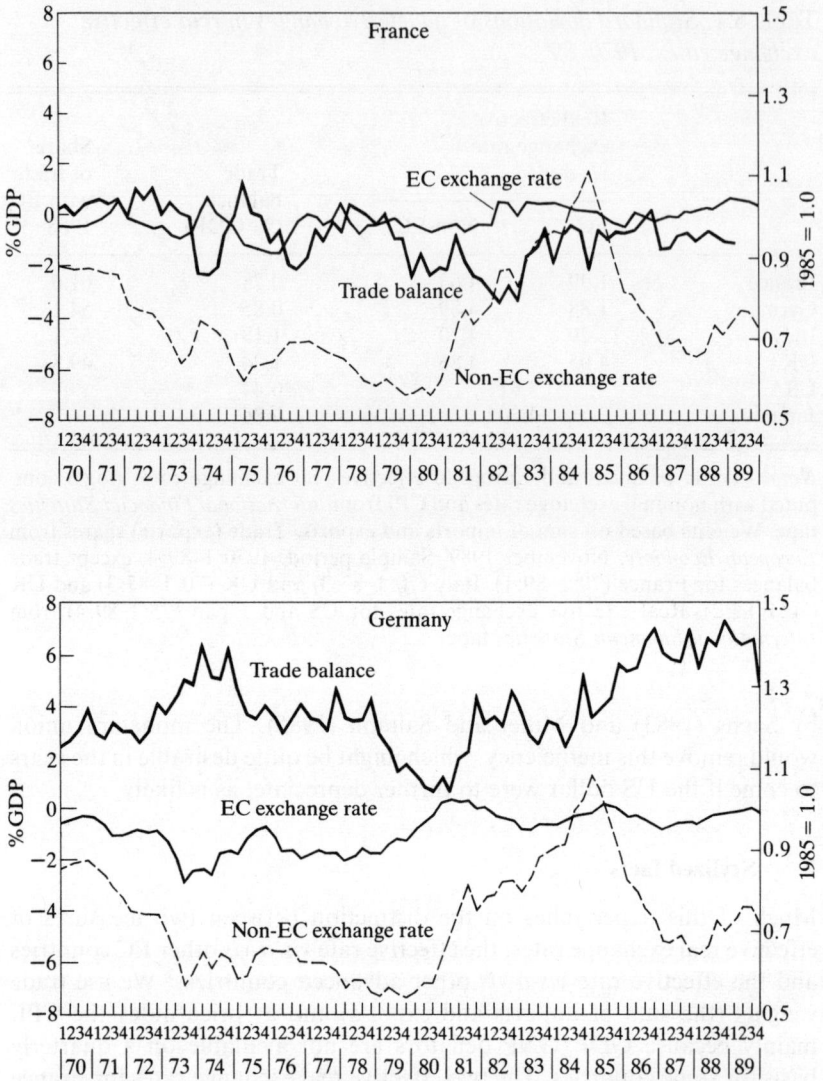

Figure 6.1   Real exchange rates and trade balances, 1960–89. *Note:* Real exchange rates on right-hand scale, as index with 1985 = 1.0. Trade balance on left-hand scale, as % of GDP.

of their EC effective real exchange rates. This is relevant for more than 50% of their external trade. Yet, as both Figure 6.1 and Table 6.1 show, the trade balances of France and Germany, measured as a percentage of the GDP/GNP, are no less volatile than those of the other four countries under consideration. That the stability of EMS–effective real exchange

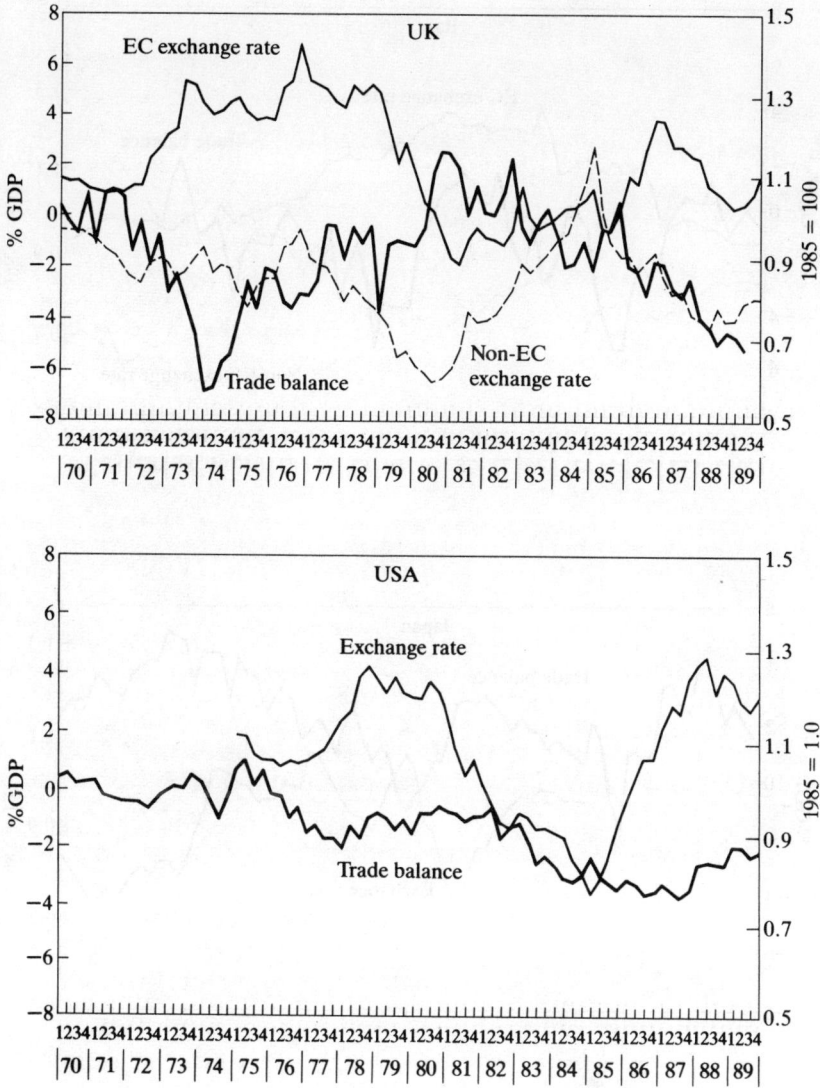

Figure 6.1

rates in France and Germany does not translate into a markedly lower variability of their trade balances suggests a particularly high sensitivity to the exchange rate constraint. Our central objective is to explore and document the implications for France and Germany of this apparent sensitivity to the external constraint.

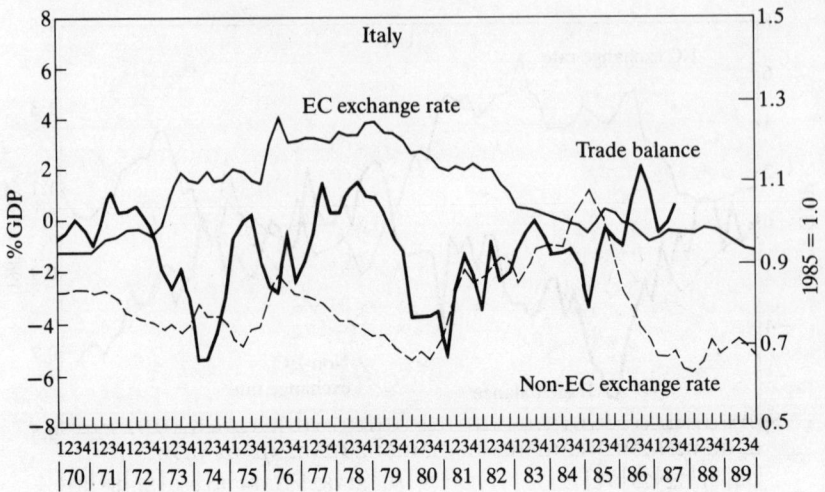

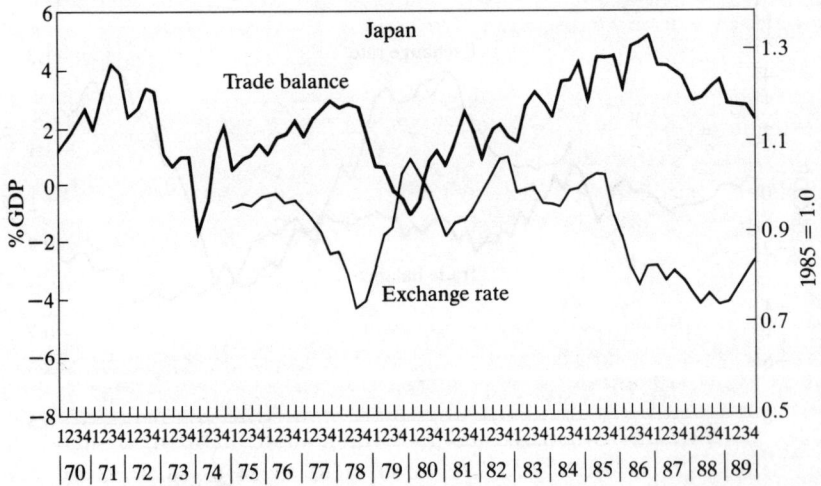

Figure 6.1 (*cont.*)

The inflation-output trade-off is illustrated in Table 6.2. The growth performance of France and Germany is strikingly similar: France simply underwent a somewhat smoother path than Germany (and the UK). Not surprisingly, the key difference concerns inflation. Germany stands apart for its continuously low rate of inflation, yet it seems never to have taken

Table 6.2. *Macroeconomic indicators, 1979–90*

	Inflation rates GDP deflators			Unemployment rate		GDP growth rate	
	Average 81–90	1979	1990	1979	1990	Average 79–90	Std. dev.
France	6.3	10.1	2.7	6.0	9.1	2.2	0.9
Germany	2.7	4.0	2.7	3.3	5.4	2.2	1.6
Italy	10.1	15.9	6.6	7.8	10.6	2.8	1.5
UK	6.1	14.5	5.3	4.7	6.5	2.1	2.0
USA	4.3	8.9	4.5	5.8	5.2	2.6	2.2
Japan	1.5	3.0	2.7	2.1	2.6	4.2	0.9

Source: European Economy, November 1989.

advantage of the much reduced need for disinflation over the eighties to achieve a stronger growth performance. Actually, all four major European countries have experienced similar growth rates despite quite different results in term of disinflation. In contrast, the US has scored great success against inflation, with a superior growth and unemployment performance than in Europe.[5] The relatively unfavourable inflation–growth trade-off in Europe in general, and in Germany particularly, is often interpreted in terms of adverse labour market institutions (see, e.g., Bruno and Sachs, 1985; Calmfors and Driffill, 1988). We wish to explore whether economic policies, more precisely the external constraints shaping policy choices, have not had a role to play too.

Recent work by Sachs (1983) and Miller and Salmon (1985) has emphasized the inflationary consequences of depreciation. A more ancient tradition instead focused on the trade-improving and expansionary effects of depreciation. Both analyses identify the exchange rate as an important externality, likely to impact on policy choices in open economies. Put together, these two channels show that the exchange rate directly affects the output–inflation trade-off which can be expected to shape policy-making. In order to explore this point further, we turn to our theoretical framework.

3   A theoretical interpretation of policy choices

3.1   The model

We briefly present the model developed in Cohen and Wyplosz (1990). We consider a world composed of three countries which we call France,

Germany, and the US. We index with a 1 all variables referring to France and with a 2 all variables referring to Germany. Let us assume that each country produces one (representative) good. The (log of the) price of the good produced by country i is $p_i(t)$. The price of the US goods is constant and normalized to be 1. Each consumer in country i consumes a good produced in country i or a good turned (at a cost) into a product which looks like a country i product. The real exchange rates are defined as

$$z(t) \equiv p_2(t) + e(t) - p_1(t)$$
$$z_1(t) = e_1(t) - p_1(t) \tag{1}$$
$$z_2(t) = e_2(t) - p_2(t)$$

so that $z(t)$ is the Franco–German real exchange rate; $z_i(t)$ the real exchange rate of country i with respect to the rest of the world.

In response to any deviation of $[z(t), z_i(t)]$ from zero, we assume that home or foreign goods are shipped to the least competitive country. The transportation cost includes the cost of turning country i good into country j good. Call $TB_i(t)$ the trade balance which is triggered. We assume a finite response of the following form

$$TB_1(t) = h_1 z_1(t) + hz(t) = Q_1(t) - A_1(t)$$
$$TB_2(t) = h_1 z_2(t) - hz(t) = Q_2(t) - A_2(t) \tag{2}$$

so that $h_i z_i(t)$ represents the trade surplus of country i with the US and $hz(t)$ is the trade surplus of France with Germany. Q and A represent the output level and domestic spending.

We assume that prices in each European country are set through a mark-up above labour cost which depends upon the relative prices $z(t)$ and $z_i(t)$ and upon output. Wage earners set a nominal wage equal to

$$w_i(t) = E_{t-1} p_i(t)$$

Since we shall consider only temporary unexpected disturbances, this implies that $w_i(t) = \bar{\pi}$, where the rate of inflation $\bar{\pi}$ is determined endogenously and rationally, given the authorities' loss function (4), as $\bar{\pi} = (\phi_0 A + \phi_1 Q)/b$. Under these conditions, inflation obeys the following process

$$\pi_1(t) = \bar{\pi} + a_1 z_1(t) + az(t) + bQ_1(t) + \epsilon_1(t)$$
$$\pi_2(t) = \bar{\pi} + a_1 z_2(t) - az(t) + bQ_2(t) + \epsilon_2(t) \tag{3}$$

where $Q_i(t)$ is the real output level in country i. Note from (2) and (3) that France and Germany are identical. $\epsilon_i(t)$, $i = 1, 2$, are two transitory disturbances.

Policy-makers minimize the following loss function:

$$L_i = \tfrac{1}{2} \sum_0^\infty \frac{1}{(1+r)^t} \{\phi_0 [A_i(t) - \bar{A}]^2 + \phi_1 [Q_i(t) - \bar{Q}]^2 + \pi_i(t)^2\} \qquad (4)$$

in which $\pi_i(t)$ is the (current) inflation rate and $A_i(t)$ is domestic absorption. We assume that policy-makers set directly $\pi_i(t)$ – this is monetary policy – and $A_i(t)$ – fiscal policy.

The US financial markets are taken to be large with respect to Europe and set a fixed discount factor $1/(1 + r)$ which is the same as the discount factor of the representative policy-maker in country i. Furthermore, we assume that the US financial markets agree *ex-ante* to grant France and Germany lines of credit to finance transitory flows $TB_i(t)$ at the riskless rate r (and diversify away the risk associated with $\epsilon_i(t)$). With these two assumptions the intertemporal budget constraint faced by country i is simply

$$E_0 \left[\sum_0^\infty \frac{1}{(1+r)^t} TB_i(t) \right] = 0 \qquad (5)$$

in which $TB_i(t) = Q_i(t) - A_i(t)$ is the difference between output and absorption.

3.2   Heuristic interpretation

To highlight the central feature of the model, and the issues that we wish to bring up, we consider here a one-country version of the model. In this case, we drop the distinction between the two exchange rates, so that (2) and (3) reduce to

$$TB = Q - A = hz \qquad (2')$$

$$\pi = \bar{\pi} + az + bQ + \epsilon \qquad (3')$$

The model is illustrated in Figure 6.2: the two schedules depict (2') and (3') for given monetary (i.e., π) and fiscal (i.e., A) policies. In the absence of any policy action, a temporary[6] inflationary shock ($\epsilon > 0$) shifts the inflation schedule down and to the left and equilibrium moves from point A to point B. The shock is absorbed partly through an exchange rate appreciation, partly through a fall in output (see (3')). Given the objective function (4), the optimal policy response calls for spreading the effect of the shock on all three variables π, A and Q. It takes the form of a mix of monetary accommodation – bringing the inflation schedule partly back up – and fiscal expansion – which displaces the trade balance schedule up and to the left. It can be shown that the optimal outcome is at point C: the real exchange rate appreciates relatively to its initial level, which lessens the inflationary effect of the shock. This, in turn, requires a trade deficit,

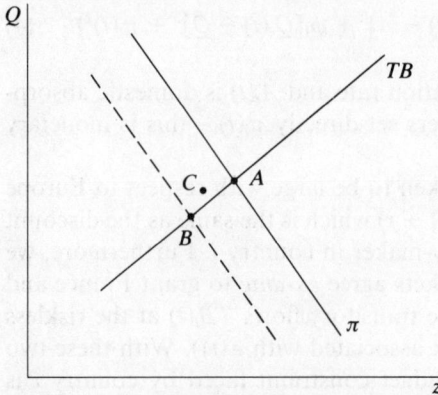

Figure 6.2   Equilibrium outcome

which is obtained as a result of both a fiscal expansion and a fall in output – but less so than in the absence of policy reaction.

Two polar cases illustrate the link between the policy response and the two exchange rate effects. First, we consider the case when the trade balance is very sensitive to the real exchange rate. In the limit case where $h = \infty$ in (2'), the TB schedule is vertical. It is clear that fiscal policy is not used in this case as it has no effect whatsoever: any increase in domestic spending leaks abroad one for one. The policy-maker only adopts a partially accommodating monetary policy, refraining from any attempt at changing the real exchange rate. The other interesting case corresponds to an inflation rate highly sensitive to the real exchange rate. In the limit, $a = \infty$ in (3'), and the inflation schedule is vertical. Monetary policy now becomes fully ineffective. The policy response again eschews any attempt at manipulating the real exchange rate and relies on fiscal policy.

3.3   The Nash solution

When each government sets its optimal policy response to its disturbance $\epsilon_i(t)$, taking for given the other country's own response to its disturbance, we find the familiar Nash outcome. We consider here the case of a symmetric disturbance, $\epsilon_1(t) = \epsilon_2(t) = \epsilon > 0$. The symmetry of the model implies that, at the equilibrium, $z(t) = 0$. It can be shown that the optimal uncoordinated response leads each country to carry a contractionary (i.e., only partially accommodating) monetary policy – the inflation rate increases above its steady state level π by less than the size of the disturbance ϵ – and an expansionary fiscal policy – absorption rises but output falls. The result is a recession, a trade deficit, and an exchange rate appreciation.

Fiscal expansion eases inflationary pressure through the appreciation of the exchange rate, the standard price externality. However, a very large intra-European trade externality (h large) means that intra-European trade prevents any substantial deviation from PPP: as Section 3.2 shows, when h tends towards infinity, the fiscal response tends towards zero, no European country undertakes a fiscal expansion. The failure to internalize the trade externality – and to realize that in equilibrium no change in the intra-European exchange rate is possible – prevents both European countries from recognizing that it is the importance of the trade effect *vis-à-vis* the US, not within Europe, which is relevant. What is desirable, unless h_1 too is very large, is a *joint* fiscal expansion and a real appreciation *vis-à-vis* the dollar.

3.4   Full policy coordination

With full coordination both European countries realize that, given that they are identical and subject to the same shock, they face the same incentives and will act in the same way, leaving their bilateral real exchange rate unchanged. This leaves them free to set optimally their (common) real exchange rate *vis-à-vis* the US. It is the inability to ensure this outcome in the uncoordinated case, and the fear that a change in their bilateral rate may have seriously damaging effects, that prevents them from reaching the globally optimal outcome.

If the trade effect (h) is large,[7] they mostly fear to appreciate *vis-à-vis* each other, and refrain from an active tight money–easy fiscal package which delivers a beneficial appreciation *vis-à-vis* the dollar. This result is reversed when h is small (or a is large). Then, as in Sachs (1983) and Miller and Salmon (1985), each European policy-maker vainly attempts to appreciate its currency against each other to import disinflation. The outcome is an excessively tight money–easy fiscal package. Reversion also occurs when the shocks are asymmetric ($\epsilon_1(t) = -\epsilon_2(t)$). In that case, if h is large, with symmetric shocks both countries underestimate that their own policy reaction will further pull them apart and magnify the change in their bilateral real exchange rate.[8]

3.5   Monetary coordination

Finally, we consider a case of partial coordination: we assume that, while fiscal authorities retain their independence and pursue Nash solutions, monetary policy is fully coordinated. We find that monetary policy is always less restrictive under monetary coordination than with full coordination, irrespective of the relative size of the ratios a/h and a_1/h_1. Indeed the single monetary authority does two things. First, it realizes that the absence of fiscal coordination increases the shadow price of monetary policy, and hence the value of accommodating the supply-side shock with inflation. Second, it recognizes *ex ante* that, given the symmetry of the shocks, the bilateral real exchange rate between France and Germany should not change. Thus the joint authority eliminates any attempt at beggar-thy-neighbour monetary policies.

When relative trade effects dominate ($a/h < a_1/h_1$), the monetary authority recognizes the benefit from an appreciation *vis-à-vis* the US and adopts a more restrictive stance than in the absence of coordination. The fear of disruptive exchange rate changes *within Europe* leads to relatively inactive fiscal policies. In the opposite case ($a/h > a_1/h_1$), in order to expand output, the monetary authority adopts an accommodative stance which results in a joint depreciation *vis-à-vis* the US. Fiscal policy is too expansionary as both countries attempt to appreciate their currencies.

3.6   Policy implications

The results carry important policy implications. If trade effects dominate within Europe, symmetric supply-side shocks are likely to be met with relatively inactive monetary and fiscal policies. This could explain the contrast between the US and Europe in the early 1980s. In contrast, when the shocks are asymmetric, both policies may be used excessively in pulling European countries away from each other. If a monetary union is seen as the case of monetary coordination only, in the future relative fiscal inaction will be mitigated by a more active monetary policy, leaving less room for third countries to play beggar-thy-neighbour. Indeed, it is often asserted that Europe did not react adequately to the dollar swings.[9] The obvious next step is to evaluate empirically the criterion $a/h \gtrless a_1/h_1$. This is the object of the next section.

4   An empirical interpretation

4.1   Methodology

In principle, we would like to measure directly the four key parameters of the model: a, a_1, h, and h_1, which implies estimating equations (2) and (3). In a multi-country world, we need to reinterpret the two real exchange rates z and z_1. In view of the close economic integration within the EC, the natural procedure is to define z as the effective exchange rate of an EC

Table 6.3. *Dickey–Fuller unit root tests*

	Null hypothesis AR(1, 1)	AR(1, 3)
France		
Trade balance	3.34	3.03
Inflation	0.79	0.84
Unemployment rate	1.08	1.06
$\log(y)$	3.72	2.29
$\log(z)$	2.75	2.45
$\log(z_1)$	1.44	2.26
$\log$(rel. com. price)	1.78	3.16
Germany		
Trade balance	2.03	1.79
Inflation	1.00	1.27
Unemployment rate	1.35	1.47
$\log(y)$	1.35	0.53
$\log(z)$	1.56	2.06
$\log(z_1)$	1.47	2.29
$\log$(rel. com. price)	1.54	1.83

Notes: Critical values for the 't-statistics':
AR(1, 1): 3.54 (1%); 2.91 (5%); 2.59 (10%)
AR(1, 3): 3.73 (1%); 3.17 (5%); 2.91 (10%)
Sample periods: 70:1–89:4, except *TB*, $\log(y)$ and $\log$(relative commodity prices)
for France: 70:1–89:1.

country *vis-à-vis* the other EC countries, and z_1 as the effective exchange
rate *vis-à-vis* the rest of the world. The rates z and z_1 for France and
Germany are those shown on Figure 6.1 above.[10]

Then, we need to face the fact that (2) and (3) are best seen as reduced
forms of a more general macroeconomic model. Further, we expect that
these are, in practice, dynamic relationships involving, especially with the
trade balance equation, long lags. There is a well-developed tradition with
the estimation of trade balance and inflation equations. To say the least,
the results are often disappointing and controversial. For example, Rose
and Yellen (1989) seriously question the existence of a statistical link
between the trade balance and the real exchange rate. Similarly, Stiehler
(1987) reports on the evolution of the econometrics of price equations.

In view of these well-known difficulties, we adopt a strategy designed to
stay as close as possible to the statistical properties of the series suggested
by our model. For this purpose, we start by testing the data for stationarity.
The results are shown in Table 6.3. In no case do we reject the

hypothesis that the variables are integrated of order 1.[11] This leads us to adopt the cointegrating approach and deal with the dynamics by way of an error-correction specification.

We face also the standard identification problem as all the variables appearing on both sides of equations (2) and (3) are properly seen as jointly endogenous. Here, it may surface as the possible existence of more than one cointegrating equation. The problem is somewhat alleviated by focusing on the dynamics of real exchange rate effects on the trade balance and inflation. This is so because, in the error-correction approach, the dynamics is captured by the effect of changes in the *lagged* values of the variables of interest.[12]

4.2   Trade balance equations

The theoretical model suggests looking for cointegration between the real trade balance and the two effective exchange rate measures. Growth, as well as theory,[13] suggests including the domestic and foreign real GNPs. We also look at the relative price of materials, i.e., relative to the GDP/GNP deflator. The trade balance is the nominal balance divided by the GDP/GNP deflator. The foreign GDP is proxied by the world index of industrial production. (For all variables, source: *International Financial Statistics.*)

For Germany, all those variables appear to enter significantly in the cointegrating equation but the residual barely passes the stationarity test. For France, only the domestic and foreign GNPs are significant. The cointegrating equations reported in the Appendix and the relevant tests are shown in Table 6.4. Thus, as in Rose and Yellen (1989), we fail to detect clearly a significant long-run link between the trade balance and the real exchange rate.

The error-correction formulation allows us to search freely for lag structures. This is important given the presumption that J-curve effects may be present. Accordingly, we started with a very general specification, initially with four lags of all the variables mentioned above, including the lagged dependent variable, and twelve lags for our two real exchange rate measures.[14] We then eliminated the non-significant entries with a view to achieve parsimony, while retaining four lags for the dependent lagged variable to take care of seasonality. As we are only interested in the relative signs on the two real exchange rates, the precise dynamic structure of the other variables is of no consequence for the interpretation of the results. Table 6.5 presents for France and Germany the two regressions which seemed to match best the two criteria. We only report on the sum of the coefficients on lagged variables. (Note, however, that the

Table 6.4. *Tests for cointegration*

	Dickey–Fuller (1 lag)	Augmented Dickey–Fuller (4 lags)
France		
Trade balance	3.37	3.92
Inflation	2.35	1.69
Germany		
Trade balance	2.85	2.78
Inflation	2.44	1.59
US		
Trade balance	2.60	3.20
Inflation	2.27	1.85

Notes: Sample periods: 70:1–89:1 for TB and 71:–88:1 for inflation; Germany, 70:–89:4 for TB and 71:1 for inflation.
Critical values from Engle and Yoo (1987):
DF Test: 4.45 (1%), 3.95 (5%), 3.59 (10%)
ADF Test: 4.22 (1%), 3.62 (5%), 3.32 (10%)

t-statistics for the sum of coefficients is highly misleading: when successive coefficients change signs and are highly significant, the sum of coefficients is not significant.)

Focusing on the real exchange rate effects, we find that France and Germany broadly follow the same pattern. The EC exchange rate (z) enters significantly, at least at some lags, while the non-EC exchange rate (z_1) enters with the wrong sign at most lags.[15] Furthermore, the absolute value of the sum of the coefficients of the EC exchange rate is much larger than in the case of the non-EC exchange rate. As Rose and Yellen (1989), we do not find any pattern suggestive of a J-curve effect, as the coefficients of various lags often change signs.[16] In contrast to their results, we detect a significant effect of both real exchange rates on the dynamics of the real trade balance. We also find evidence of cointegration of the US trade account with the real effective exchange rate (see Appendix).

4.3 Inflation equations

In line with most recent empirical work on the price–wage mechanism, our model adopts a mark-up formulation for prices – possibly because of monopolistic competition – and a lagged adjustment of wages to expected prices – possibly as a consequence of staggered wage contracts. Accordingly, we wish to relate inflation to past wages, the price of intermediate

Table 6.5. *Trade balance equations*
Dependent variable: real trade balance (TB/P)

France	$\hat{e}_{t-1}$	$\sum \dfrac{TB}{P}_{t-i}$	$\sum z_{t-i}$	$\sum z_{1,t-i}$	$\sum \dfrac{P^0}{P_{t-i}}$	$\dfrac{\bar{R}^2}{DW}$
		4 lags	12 lags	6 lags	3 lags	
(1)	− 0.79	0.88	797.55	− 110.08	− 87.02	0.43
	(− 3.40)	(1.50)	(2.30)	(− 2.36)	(− 2.74)	1.98
		4 lags	8 lags	8 lags	4 lags	
(2)	− 0.68	0.78	656.33	− 107.45	− 95.52	0.46
	(− 0.86)	(1.41)	(3.38)	(− 2.33)	(− 2.83)	1.83

Germany	$\hat{e}_{t-1}$	$\sum \dfrac{TB}{P}_{t-i}$	$\sum z_{t-i}$	$\sum z_{1,t-i}$	$\sum y_{t-i}$	$\sum y^*_{t-i}$	$\dfrac{\bar{R}^2}{DW}$
		4 lags	6 lags	6 lags			
(3)	− 0.18	0.47	15.70	− 0.26			0.28
	(− 2.42)	(1.21)	(0.29)	(− 0.01)			2.04
		4 lags	6 lags	6 lags	2 lags	2 lags	
(4)	− 0.08	0.36	82.76	− 2.55	− 193.9	130.9	0.34
	(− 1.04)	(0.95)	(1.44)	(− 0.14)	(− 2.13)	(2.59)	2.19

US	$\hat{e}_{t-1}$	$\left(\dfrac{TB}{P}\right)_{t-4}$	z_{t-8}	y_{t-3}	y^*_{t-3}	$\dfrac{\bar{R}^2}{DW}$
(5)	− 0.26	0.42	32.16	158.8	− 133.5	0.41
	(− 2.81)	(3.73)	(2.35)	(2.25)	(2.07)	1.96

Notes: $\hat{e}$ is the residual from the cointegrating equation (see Appendix). All variables, including the dependent variable and except for $\hat{u}$, are first differences of the original series. When applicable, entries refer to the sum of the lagged coefficients. *t*-statistics in parentheses. The constant is not reported. Sample period: (1) 73:2–89:1; (2) 72:1–89:1; (3) and (4): 71:4–89:1; (5): 77:2–78:1.

materials, our two measure of exchange rates, and output. To account for growth, we add a measure of labour productivity changes and use the unemployment rate instead of output.

As can be seen in the Appendix and in Table 6.4, the inflation rate is co-integrated with wage and labour productivity growth in both France and Germany.[17] In principle, with a Cobb–Douglas technology, we should find unit coefficients on both terms, reflecting the long-run constancy of the labour share. Clearly, this is not the case. This may indicate that the Cobb–Douglas function is ill-suited, at least for aggregate data. More unsatisfactory is the fact that the coefficients for wage and

Table 6.6. *Inflation equations*
Dependent variable: CPI inflation

France	$\hat{e}_{t-1}$	π_{t-1}	π_{t-4}	u_{t-4}	z_{t-1}	$z_{1,t-1}$	$\dfrac{\bar{R}^2}{DW}$
France	− 0.09	0.55	− 0.28	− 1.30	− 4.95	4.91	0.43
72:3–88:1	(− 1.63)	(5.18)	(− 2.79)	(− 3.09)	(− 1.13)	(2.44)	1.90
Germany	− 0.06	0.35	− 0.18	− 0.46	− 3.61	2.84	0.26
72:2 − 89:4	(− 1.43)	(3.06)	(− 1.67)	(− 2.16)	(− 1.01)	(2.00)	2.07
US	− 0.14	0.51[a]		− 0.08[b]		3.94[c]	0.38
76:2–88:3	(− 2.17)	(2.92)		(− 0.60)		(1.37)	1.97

Notes: $\hat{e}$ is the residual from the cointegrating equation (see Appendix). All variables, except $\hat{e}$, including the dependent variable, are first differences of the original series. t-statistics in parentheses. The constant is not reported. (a): sum of first four lags; (b): first lag; (c): fourth lag of US real effective exchange rate (MERM from *International Financial Statistics*).

productivity growth should be of the same order of magnitude and of opposite signs. The signs are correct, but productivity growth enters with a surprisingly small, if significant, coefficient.[18]

The corresponding error correction equations are presented in Table 6.6. Although we started with a generous lag structure for the error-correction equations, the inflation rates seem to obey a much simpler process than the trade balance. The only significant variables are the first lags, occasionally the fourth lag. The results are fairly clear-cut and quite similar for both countries. The EC exchange rate affects inflation in a perverse way, as a real depreciation seems to produce disinflation. This effect is never statistically significant, though. On the other side, the non-EC exchange rate significantly affects inflation in the expected direction.[19]

4.4   Results from simulation studies

Because we obtain some wrong-signed and statistically non-significant estimates for the parameters of interest, we cannot compute the ratios of relative trade and price effects (a/h and a_1/h_1) as suggested by our theoretical model. We turn in this section to some popular macromodels for more evidence. Indeed, by simulating exchange rate changes, these models produce 'reduced form' values for the coefficients of interest.

For this purpose, we turn to the collection of simulations gathered in Bryant *et al.* (1988). Unfortunately, of the twelve models considered there, only one, the OECD's Interlink model, provides the detail required

Table 6.7. *Coefficients implied by OECD's Interlink model*

	Effect of a US dollar depreciation ($\Delta z_1 = 10\%$)		Effect of a country's depreciation ($\Delta z = \Delta z_1 = 10\%$)		Implied ratios	
	TB	π	*TB*	π	a/h	a_1/h_1
France	2.6	1.4	9.6	5.4	0.57	0.54
Germany	3.9	2.2	18.3	8.9	0.46	0.56
Italy	1.0	2.4	5.4	9.9	1.70	2.40
UK	2.4	2.1	12.9	4.7	0.25	0.88

Notes: The effects of a nominal dollar depreciation are drawn from Bryant *et al.* (1988), simulation F, p. 278, supplement volume. The effects of a single country's depreciation are from Richardson (1987), Table 9. The reported effects are measured five years after the initial exchange rate change. See text for explanation.

to separate out the effects of EC exchange rates from those of non-EC rates. Bryant *et al.* report the effect of a joint depreciation of all currencies *vis-à-vis* the US dollar. If we are willing to think of the US as representing the rest of the world, we thus observe the case where $z(t)$ is held constant while $z_i(t)$ is changed for each currency. This gives us the values of h_1 and a_1 in (2) and (3). On the other hand, Richardson (1987) reports on simulations with the same model where each country's currency depreciates *alone vis-à-vis* all other currencies. This is interpreted as a simultaneous and equal change in $z(t)$ and $z_1(t)$ and the results provide estimates of $a + h$ and $a_1 + h_1$. The results are shown in Table 6.7. It should be emphasized that the simulations concern *nominal* exchange rate changes, while in principle we look for the effects of *real* exchange rate changes. It would probably be seriously misleading to attempt to recover from those simulations the size of real exchange rate change effects. This should serve, however, as a caveat in the interpretation of these numbers.

For France and Germany the ratios a/h and a_1/h_1 are so close that any sharp interpretation would be hazardous. The figures for the two other EC countries modelled in Interlink, Italy, and the UK, provide much more clear cut evidence that h can be large enough in the EC to warrant the interpretation suggested in the previous section.

5   Policy interpretation

We read the evidence as suggesting that, in France and Germany, and possibly also in other EC countries, the trade effect of EC exchange rate

Table 6.8. *Standard deviations of real exchange rates, 1970–89*
(percent quarterly rates of change, 1970:2–1989:4)

	Real exchange rates *vis-à-vis*	
	EC countries	Non-EC countries
Belgium	1.46	4.77
Denmark	1.73	4.66
Ireland	2.27	4.46
Netherlands	1.19	4.81

Note: For details, see Table 6.1.

changes is large relative to the price effect, as compared to the effects of non-EC exchange rate changes, in the sense of the model presented in Section 3 (see Table 6.8). Then, our analysis implies that, in the presence of a symmetric supply shock, both countries will undertake insufficient monetary and fiscal policies, out of misguided concern for their bilateral real exchange rate.

These results can be used to shed light on the experience of the eighties and, maybe, to conjecture about some implications of the monetary union. We first recall the dramatic contrast between the wide fluctuations of the dollar and the remarkable stability of the DM–FF real rate over the eighties. This evolution is undoubtedly related to active monetary and fiscal policies in the US, with a more sober stance in Europe (with the noted exception of France in 1981–2, and possibly Italy). Our estimates for the US, as well as the coefficients derived from Interlink in Table 6.7 are not directly comparable to those for France and Germany because there is no comparable meaningful distinction between z and z_1. They confirm, however, that both price and trade effects are also at work in the US case. This indicates that the conclusion of Sachs (1983) that appreciation is always desirable in the face of a supply shock is not robust.

Blanchard (1987) also concluded that Europe would have been well advised to adopt policies more in line with the Reagan–Volcker mix. Sachs (1985) notes that the option of appreciating one's currency to bring down inflation at no output cost cannot be pursued by all countries at the same time without generating inefficiently over-active policy mixes everywhere. The implication is that Europe, by adopting insufficiently active policies, has allowed the US to score easy success through beggar-thy-neighbour action. Our interpretation is that this is the outcome of *optimal* policy-making by closely integrated countries in the absence of co-ordination. In this view, the remarkable stability of the DM–FF real exchange rate may be the equilibrium outcome of symmetric shocks in similar countries. If this interpretation is correct, the implication is that the EMS *per se* has not worked as an additional external constraint. What has been a constraint is the lack of policy coordination.

This brings us naturally to the effect that a monetary union might have on the external constraint. In our framework of Section 3, we interpret a monetary union as delivering monetary coordination, but not fiscal coordination. Under such conditions, monetary policy is more accommodative, while fiscal policy remains insufficiently active. We can then speculate on the foreseeable shock of the nineties. A likely possibility is that the dollar depreciates as the US budget deficit is brought under control. What difference would the monetary union make? Contrary to the first round of dollar depreciation over 1985–6, when both monetary and fiscal policies remained relatively passive, a monetary union would allow Europe to lessen its internal exchange rate constraint and limit the scope of another round of US beggar-thy-neighbour policies.

Appendix   Cointegrating equations

All data are from the *International Financial Statistics* tape. The trade balance is deflated by the GNP/GDP deflator. The foreign GNP is proxied by the world index of industrial production. Both price (π) and wage (dw) inflation are measured as percentage change over the same quarter of the previous year. The same applies to productivity growth ($d\psi$), where productivity is the ratio of real GNP/GDP over employment.

France

Trade balance
$$TB/P = 1,166.4 \quad - 139.4 \log(y) + 104.1 \log(y^*)$$
$$(4.86) \ (-4.91) \qquad\qquad (3.62)$$

1970: 1–89: 1. Nobs: 77. $DW = 0.81$. $\bar{R}^2 = 0.36$. $SEE = 9.15$.

Inflation
$$\pi = 2.54 + 0.52 \ dw - 0.09 \ d\psi$$
$$(4.81)(12.58) \quad (-1.64)$$

1971: 1–88: 1. Nobs: 69. $DW = 0.41$. $\bar{R}^2 = 0.70$. $SEE = 1.79$.

Germany

Trade balance
$$TB/P = 629.5 \quad - 80.7 \log(y) + 101.3 \log(y^*)$$
$$(2.24) \, (-2.16) \qquad (3.30)$$

1970: 1–89: 4. Nobs: 80. $DW = 0.42$. $\bar{R}^2 = 0.44$. $SEE = 6.24$.

Inflation
$$\pi = 0.71 + 0.58 \, dw - 0.11 \, d\psi$$
$$(1.57) \, (8.42) \quad (-1.95)$$

1971: 1–89: 4. Nobs: 76. $DW = 0.24$. $\bar{R}^2 = 0.49$. $SEE = 1.48$.

US

Trade balance
$$TB/P = 1{,}360.3 \quad - 167.6 \log(y) + 73.8 \log(y^*) + 18.9 \, z$$
$$(3.64) \, (-3.72) \qquad (1.59) \qquad (3.39)$$

1975: 1–89: 1. Nobs: 57. $DW = 0.65$. $\bar{R}^2 = 0.82$. $SEE = 5.44$.

Inflation
$$\pi = 0.44 + 0.78 \, dw - 0.41 \, d\psi + 5.74 \, z$$
$$(0.70)(10.38) \quad (-2.59) \qquad (3.47)$$

1975: 1–89: 4. Nobs: 60. $DW = 0.36$. $\bar{R}^2 = 0.75$. $SEE = 1.57$.

NOTES

We have benefited from comments and suggestions by George Alogoskoufis, David Currie, Juan Dolado, and conference participants. This paper is part of the CEPR programme in international economics, supported by grants from the Ford and Sloan Foundations. Support to the authors from the Commissariat General du Plan, from the EC's SPES Programme and from INSEAD is gratefully acknowledged.
 1 For a discussion of France over the first half of the eighties, see Sachs and Wyplosz (1986). For the German case, see Fels and Froehlich (1986) and Hellwig and Neumann (1987).
 2 See, e.g., De Grauwe (1987), Cohen and Wyplosz (1988), Fratianni and von Hagen (1989), Wyplosz (1990).
 3 The other advanced countries are Australia, Canada, Japan, and the USA. It is quite clear that the US dollar dominates this measure.
 4 We use changes because, as shown below, the levels are not stationary.
 5 Sachs (1985) emphasizes that the superior inflation–output performance of the US in the early eighties is out of line with previous experience. His interpretation, emphasizing the role of the dollar appreciation, is related to ours. His

prediction that this gain will have to be given back later on has not materialized yet. But nor has the US trade balance returned to equilibrium.

6 We deal here only with transitory shocks because in this case there is no proper dynamics to worry about. This is made clear in the next section.

7 The precise criterion by which h is large is $a/h < a_1/h_1$.

8 With h relatively small and asymmetric shocks, we are back in the case of insufficient policy action: a 'reversal of the reversal'.

9 For a discussion of European reactions to dollar swings, see Melitz (1987) and Wyplosz (1990).

10 In the estimation below we use the log for these rates, without changing the notation, though.

11 The critical values are drawn from Engle and Yoo (1987) for AR(1, 1) and from Engle and Granger (1987) for AR(1, 3).

12 If the variables themselves are statistically integrated of order one, *a priori* there is no ground for worrying about serial correlation.

13 See, for example, the derivation of a similar equation in Rose and Yellen (1989).

14 All variables enter as first differences, which have been shown to be stationary.

15 For example, in regression (2) for France, the eight lags are as follows, for i increasing from 1 to 8 (t-statistics in parentheses):

z_{t-i}: 64.46 (1.10), 124.79 (2.25), 34.24 (0.59), 104.85 (1.81), 37.43 (0.66), 123.56 (2.24), 52.46 (1.00), 114.54 (2.11).

$z_{1,t-i}$: -40.00 (-1.73), -11.00 (-0.42), 4.04 (0.12), 15.63 (0.50), 15.64 (0.60), -59.51 (-2.27), -17.05 (-0.62), -15.20 (-0.57).

16 Some intermediate coefficients are not significant. We have refrained from purging them, adopting the rule of adapting the lag length to the last significant coefficient.

17 In contrast to the US, the real exchange rates do not appear to be co-integrated with inflation.

18 This may be due to the very rough measure of labour productivity adopted here (output divided by employment instead of marginal productivity). Data availability is limited by the need to use quarterly data. We may look for other series in subsequent versions of this chapter.

19 In the case of the US, we also find a perverse, not statistically significant real exchange rate effect in the error correction dynamics. This result is however of little importance given that the real effective exchange rate is co-integrated with inflation in the US.

REFERENCES

Blanchard, Olivier Jean (1987), 'Reaganomics', *Economic Policy* 2 (5), 15–56.
Bruno, Michael and Jeffrey Sachs (1985), *The Economics of Worldwide Stagflation*, Oxford: Basil Blackwell.
Bryant, Ralph, Dale Henderson, Gerald Holtham, Peter Hooper, and Steve Symansky (eds.) (1988), *Empirical Macroeconomics for Interdependent Economies*, Washington, DC: The Brookings Institution.
Calmfors, Lars and John Driffill (1988), 'Bargaining Structure, Corporatism and Macroeconomic Performance', *Economic Policy* 3 (6), 13–61.

Cohen, D. and C. Wyplosz (1989), 'European Monetary Union: an Agnostic Evaluation', in R.C. Bryant *et al.* (eds.), *Macroeconomic Policies in an Interdependent World*, Washington, DC: IMF.

(1990), 'Price and Trade Effects of Exchange Rate Fluctuations and the Design of Policy Coordination', CEPR Discussion Paper No. 440.

de Grauwe, P. (1989), 'Is the European Monetary System a DM Zone?', CEPR Discussion Paper No. 297.

Engle, Robert and C.W.J. Granger (1987), 'Co-Integration and Error Correction: Representation, Estimation, and Testing', *Econometrica* **55**, 251–76.

Engle, Robert and Byung Sam Yoo (1987), 'Forecasting and Testing in Co-Integrated Systems', *Journal of Econometrics* **35**, 143–59.

Fels, Gerhard and Hans Peter Froehlich (1986), 'Germany and the World Economy: a German View', *Economic Policy* **2** (4), 177–206.

Fratianni, M. and J. von Hagen (1989), 'Asymmetries and Realignment in the EMS', University of Indiana, Bloomington, Discussion Paper No. 429.

Giavazzi, Francesco and Alberto Giovannini (1989), *Limiting Exchange Rate Fluctuations: the EMS*, Cambridge MA: MIT Press.

Hellwig, Manfred and Manfred Neumann (1987), 'Economic Policy in Germany: Was There a Turnaround?', *Economic Policy* **2** (5), 103–45.

Melitz, Jacques (1987), 'Germany, Discipline and Cooperation in the EMS', in Francesco Giavazzi, Stafano Micossi, and Marcus Miller (eds.), *The European Monetary System*, Cambridge University Press.

Miller, Marcus and Mark Salmon (1985), 'Policy Coordination and Dynamic Games', in Willem Buiter and Richard Marston (eds.), *International Economic Policy Coordination*, Cambridge University Press.

Richardson, Pete (1987), 'A Review of the Simulation Properties of OECD's Interlink Model', OECD Working Papers No 47, July.

Rose, Andrew and Janet Yellen (1989), 'Is There a J-Curve?', *Journal of Monetary Economics* **24**, 53–68.

Sachs, Jeffrey (1983), 'International Policy Coordination in a Dynamic Macroeconomic Model', NBER Working Paper No. 1166.

(1985), 'The Dollar and the Policy Mix: 1985', *Brookings Papers on Economic Activity* **1**, 117–98.

Sachs, Jeffrey and Charles Wyplosz (1986), 'The Economic Consequences of President Mitterrand', *Economic Policy* **1** (2), 261–322.

Stiehler, Ulrich (1987), 'Price Determination in the Major Seven OECD Countries in Interlink', OECD Working Papers No 44, July.

Wyplosz, Charles (1990), 'The Swinging Dollar: Is Europe Out of Step?', in Stefan Gerlach and Peter Petri (eds.), *The Dollar Cycle*, Cambridge, MA: MIT Press.

Discussion

DAVID CURRIE

This chapter by Daniel Cohen and Charles Wyplosz provides an elegant analysis of the nature of the exchange rate constraint within the Exchange Rate Mechanism. The first part of the chapter starts from the observation that the intra-EMS real exchange rate has been fairly stable, in contrast to the extra-EMS real exchange rate. This is rationalized in terms of a theoretical model in which, under certain conditions, European governments adopt too contractionary a fiscal stance, because of their failure (in the absence of coordination) to internalize the intra-European trade externality. Empirical work is then carried out to determine whether these conditions are satisfied, and the evidence, though recognized to be mixed, is argued to be broadly supportive. The end conclusion is one supportive of European Monetary Union: by coordinating monetary (though not fiscal) policy through a single European monetary authority, EMU gives a more efficient outcome relative to the EMS, and the resulting welfare gains are part of the case for EMU.

This is an interesting line of argument, and one that merits serious consideration. It is certainly one possible case for EMU, but not, I think, the best possible one. Indeed, as I shall argue, the line of argument of the chapter does not quite come off. The theoretical model is elegant and simple and goes straight to the point, as one would expect from this pair of authors. The model is of two countries, France and Germany, though clearly it can be readily generalized to more countries without altering the substance of the results. Fiscal policy affects absorption and thereby the trade balance; monetary policy is taken to determine, and is therefore defined as, the inflation rate; and the exchange rate and output are solved from the relationship linking inflation to output and the exchange rate and the identity that equates the trade balance (determined by the exchange rate) to the difference between output and absorption. A feature of this set-up is the heterodox definition of monetary policy: in a completely specified model, fiscal policy influences output and demand, and thereby inflation. Defining monetary policy as a constant inflation rate, as Cohen and Wyplosz do, implies offsetting changes in monetary aggregates in the face of fiscal changes or other disturbances. I am entirely comfortable with this approach, and indeed in a world in which monetary aggregates are less reliable because of the financial innovation associated with greater monetary integration in Europe, it is one that is generally more operational for policy purposes.

The two governments minimize welfare loss functions defined on deviations of output, fiscal policy, and inflation from a desired level. In the face of symmetric inflation shocks, the intra-EMS exchange rate necessarily remains unchanged. With cooperation, the optimal joint response is to engage in Reaganomics: relaxing fiscal policy, while tightening monetary policy, resulting in an appreciation of the extra-EMS exchange rate. If the intra-EMS exchange rate has a comparative advantage with respect to inflation, while the extra-EMS rate has a comparative advantage with respect to the trade balance, then each country has an incentive to engage in unilateral Reaganomics. But if, as Cohen and Wyplosz argue, the opposite is the case, so that the intra-EMS exchange rate has a comparative advantage with respect to trade, then governments will tend not to expand fiscal policy. In this case, the potential benefits of an appreciation of the European exchange rate will be lost. If EMU is the sole means of coordinating policy then the benefits of manipulating the European exchange rate must be adduced in favour of EMU.

The key condition in the analysis is whether the intra-EMS exchange rate has a comparative advantage with respect to trade or inflation. *A priori*, it is not clear to me that one should have any strong expectations on this point. Increased integration of European markets as a result of the 1992 process will certainly make trade flows more responsive to the intra-EMS exchange rate, but it will also make the pricing decisions of firms more responsive to overseas competition and hence to the intra-EMS exchange rate. It would have been possible to develop a model with greater microeconomic foundations to investigate this issue. Instead, Cohen and Wyplosz prefer to examine the issue empirically. They rely on evidence of two types: the evidence from OECD Interlink; and the evidence, using cointegration techniques, from estimation of direct reduced form trade and inflation equations for France and Germany.

Unfortunately the evidence is somewhat mixed. To be sure, from the reduced form equations, the intra-EMS exchange rate enters the trade equations with significant and correct signs, while the extra-EMS rate does not. Moreover, the extra-EMS exchange rate influences inflation with the expected sign, while the intra-EMS rate has an apparently perverse, though insignificant, sign. However, I have doubts as to whether these relationships are well specified: the experience of estimating reduced form equations of this type, particularly for the trade balance, is that they frequently display instability. It is for this reason that macromodellers are usually forced to adopt a more structural approach to modelling these relationships. It is therefore a pity that Cohen and Wyplosz do not report the standard panoply of stability tests and out-of-sample forecasting tests that are usual to test the robustness of such relationships.

The evidence from OECD Interlink is equally mixed. This shows that neither the intra-EMS nor the extra-EMS exchange rate has a comparative advantage with respect to the trade balance. From the theory, this would presumably suggest that uncoordinated policy actions are just about right. Cohen and Wyplosz point to the evidence for Italy and the UK which suggests that the intra-EMS rate has a comparative advantage with respect to trade, supporting their argument. But the marked fluctuations in the real exchange rate of the UK, in contrast to the experience of France and Germany, surely raise doubts about this argument.

Indeed, this point leads one to question the central supposition of the chapter. The argument appears to be that the stability of the French and German real exchange rate is attributable to optimal policy responses, and not to the constraints placed on policy by the Exchange Rate Mechanism. Thus the ERM plays no role whatever within the analysis. I am doubtful about this. Surely it is the case that France and Germany have experienced asymmetrical shocks within the EMS (for example, the Mitterrand experiment), which on Cohen and Wyplosz's analysis would lead one to expect variations in the French/German real exchange rate. I would prefer an analysis that puts much greater weight on the ERM itself as a constraint that limits intra-EMS exchange rate variation. To understand why governments accept such a constraint, one needs to consider the credibility benefits that accrue from such an arrangement.

Finally, the chapter takes it for granted that the optimal policy response for Europe in the 1980s was to match Reagonomics with its own expansionary fiscal policy. I am less sure of that. It is true that the outcome would have been better had the US responded to European fiscal expansion by cutting the Federal deficit. But the complexities and rigidities of US fiscal decision-making mean that such a response may not have been forthcoming. In that case, world real interest rates would have been even higher than they have been in the 1980s. This would have had important supply-side effects that could have been still more damaging for Europe than the actual outcome.

At the end, therefore, I am sceptical about the case advanced by Cohen and Wyplosz, and do not see it as a strong reason for European Monetary Union, for which there are much better arguments.

7   The external constraint in the UK

CHARLES R. BEAN

1   Introduction: some economic history

External considerations have frequently played a role in determining the direction of British macroeconomic policies. During the twenties, economic policy was directed at returning sterling to its prewar gold parity to the almost complete exclusion of domestic objectives. The fifties and sixties were characterized by an endemic balance-of-payments weakness and frequent sterling crises, with policy lurching from stop to go and back to stop. The attempt to circumvent this balance-of-payments weakness by devaluation in 1967 and again after the end of Bretton Woods, signalled the beginnings of Britain's inflationary problems in the seventies, which culminated in the Labour government's resort to IMF assistance in 1976. North Sea oil and the deep recession of 1980–1 for a time moved the balance of payments out of the limelight. However, external considerations are once again to the fore, with Britain currently running her largest-ever current account deficit during peace time.

It is easy to become obsessed with current events and in particular whether and for how long Britain's present current account predicament is sustainable. This is a topic I shall return to at the end of the chapter, but for the most part I shall try to take a somewhat wider perspective on the role and nature of the external constraint. Accordingly, the upper panel of Figure 7.1 presents data on the current account as a proportion of GDP (the solid line) from the middle of the last century through to the present. Also plotted in this figure is the current balance excluding net interest income from abroad (the dashed line). Finally, the lower panel of the same figure reports the unemployment rate which may be helpful in assessing the effect of domestic cyclical influences on the current account position. All historical data used here are drawn from Mitchell (1988) unless otherwise noted.

193

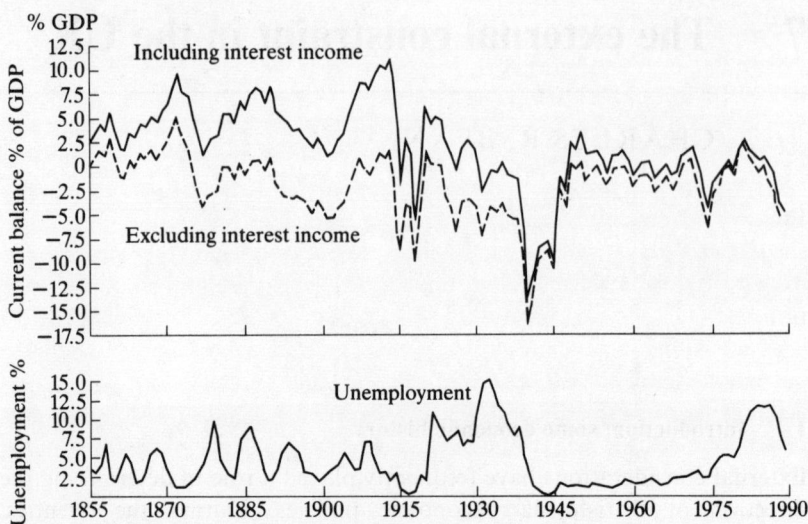

Figure 7.1   UK current account, 1855–1989 (% of GDP)

1.1   The pre-1914 period

Prior to the First World War the United Kingdom consistently ran a healthy surplus on the current account averaging around 5% of GDP. Superimposed on this are three long swings peaking in 1873, 1890, and 1913, apparently originating in fluctuations in world rather than domestic activity. Underlying this apparently satisfactory performance, however, was a steady decline in the balance on visible and invisible trade. This was offset by the increased importance of net property income from abroad, which reached a peak of almost 10% of GDP prior to the outbreak of war. The immediate causes of this deteriorating trade performance, especially after 1873, seems to have been a reduction in the rate of growth of productivity in textiles – which accounted for half of all exports in the mid nineteenth century – together with increased competition from producers in Western Europe and the United States (see Matthews et al., 1982, Chapter 5).

Of course these can only have been the proximate causes because ultimately the overall competitiveness of British industry is determined as the outcome of the interaction of a variety of forces in a full intertemporal general equilibrium. Adopting a neoclassical standpoint which views the current account as simply the mechanism through which international differences in savings and investment behaviour are reconciled, the deterioration in the trade balance was merely a reflection of the need to accommodate the increase in interest income resulting from the net accumulation of foreign assets. Under the gold standard this required that deterioration in competitiveness should come about automatically as specie movements lead to upward pressure on British demand and prices relative to incomes and prices abroad.

At this juncture it is useful to present the information contained in Figure 7.1 in a slightly different manner, viz, the net external position of the United Kingdom. Unfortunately continuous data on net foreign assets are only available from the end of 1957. This leaves us with the problem of estimating net overseas assets prior to this date. Since the flow accumulation of net foreign assets should be identically equal to the current account surplus, one possibility is simply to cumulate the current account balance and then adjust the overall level to coincide with some benchmark year in the post-1957 period. However, as well as attributing the large residual error in the balance of payments statistics entirely to the capital account, revaluations of the existing stock due to changes in asset prices, exchange rates, defaults, and depreciation are all ignored. We therefore adopt an alternative strategy of dividing the flow of net property income by a representative interest rate, in this case the American AAA corporate bond rate (railroad bonds pre-1919).[1]

Of course even this is very imperfect. Both assets and liabilities are in practice subject to a variety of different interest rates. Nevertheless the resulting series should hopefully provide a rough guide to the underlying trends in the overseas asset position. Fortunately Matthews *et al.* (1982, Table 5.2) report estimates for isolated years prior to 1958 which can be used to provide a check on our estimates.[2] Our constructed series (solid line); the official data post-1957 (dashed line) and the Matthews *et al.* historical estimates (indicated by crosses) are plotted together in Figure 7.2 (all measured as a percentage of GDP). Happily the main trends in the constructed series match those revealed by the Matthews *et al.* point estimates very well, with the exception of the 1951 observation.[3] Overall this seems rather encouraging. The figure shows the country steadily accumulating net foreign assets throughout the period reaching an all-time peak of two and half times GDP shortly before the outbreak of war.

Were there any balance-of-payments crises during this time? With the exception of a minor crisis in 1866 when the Bank Rate was raised to 10%, the answer appears to be no. Although the Bank of England was obliged to maintain the parity against both gold and other currencies, short-term capital movements brought about through quite modest variations in interest differentials were generally sufficient to maintain balance-of-payments equilibrium. This was despite the fact that the Bank

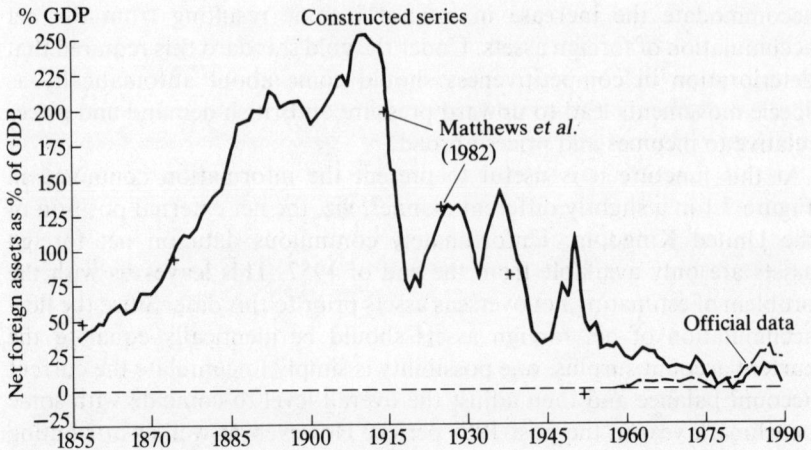

Figure 7.2   Imputed net foreign assets, 1857–1989

of England's reserves were typically equivalent to only about two weeks imports. The absence of balance-of-payments crises hardly seems surprising in view of the healthy net overseas asset position – national solvency can hardly have been at issue – although Matthews *et al.* prefer to attribute it to a self-perpetuating belief that, if necessary, the Bank of England *would* defend its own gold reserves by squeezing the monetary base.

1.2   The interwar years

Intertemporal models of the current account predict that temporary increases in government spending due to wars should be associated with a temporary worsening of the current account as households seek to maintain consumption levels in the face of the increased competition for output from the government (see, e.g., Frenkel and Razin, 1987). Both the major conflicts display this feature with roughly a ten percentage point deterioration in the current account in each case (see Figure 7.1). Associated with this is a significant decline in overseas assets (Figure 7.2).

However, the interwar years themselves were also a period of a weakening of the trade and current account positions and declining foreign assets. This was despite a very depressed level of domestic activity, with a high level of unemployment throughout the interwar period. The immediate causes of this were both the slow growth in world demand due to depressed activity in Northern Europe in the early 1920s and worldwide in the 1930s, and to the slowdown in the growth of world trade relative to world output because of increased protectionism and an increased con-centration of world output in the relatively self-sufficient United States. World trade grew by only 2.9% per annum over 1913–29 as opposed to 4.9% over the first part of the century. Furthermore, a shortage of industrial imports during the war led to the forced industrialization of some of the world's less-industrialized countries resulting in increased competition for what markets were available. Finally, the ill-fated attempt to return to, and maintain, the prewar parity of $4.86 inevitably led to at least a short-term adverse movement in competitiveness. As a result, the volume of British exports, which grew by 2.8% per year over 1899–1913, fell by an average 1/2% between 1913 and 1929.

The decision to leave the gold standard in September 1931 in the face of a run on sterling was a traumatic event, marking the final nail in the coffin of the interwar experiment with fixed exchange rates. However, its sig-nificance in understanding the role of the external constraint is probably limited. Macroeconomic developments had put the gold standard under severe pressure for some time, and a number of other countries had already suspended gold convertibility before Britain. The reasons for this are still a matter of debate; Eichengreen (1989) considers four competing explanations, some of which focus on structural deficiencies, others on misguided policies, and cites a number of relevant references. He also discusses the role the gold standard may have played in exacerbating the depression by enforcing restrictive monetary policies at a time when maintaining the liquidity of financial institutions should have been para-mount. However, none of the competing explanations – inadequate leadership, inadequate cooperation, a failure to play by the rules of the game, and structural inadequacies – suggest that issues of solvency, etc, were important in precipitating the September 1931 run on sterling. Rather what was at issue was the credibility of the government's willing-ness to carry through the monetary (and other) policies necessary to underpin a fixed exchange rate regime.

1.3   The post-war period

The years after 1945 are perhaps the most relevant to the topic in question, not merely because of their proximity to the present, but also because the state of the balance of payments increasingly became a central issue in economic policy-making. In the immediate aftermath of the war policy-makers were preoccupied by the need to move a fully mobilized wartime economy on to a peacetime footing. The major concern was to avoid a demand-induced inflation in an economy where the supply of non-military goods was limited, and to avoid accompanying balance-of-payments difficulties by reducing domestic absorption. However, by 1946 there was already concern about the possibility of unemployment emerging in two or three years time, taxes were reduced and a lax monetary policy instituted. A large current account deficit of 2.25% of GDP in 1947 ensued, together with a loss of dollar reserves, but the Government delayed action until it was forced to introduce crisis measures to reduce demand in a special Autumn budget. At the same time the convertibility of the pound, briefly reintroduced after the end of the war, was suspended. These events were partly instrumental in leading to the introduction of the Marshall plan by the United States, designed to aid European reconstruction.

The new era of austerity, accompanied by appeals for wage and dividend restraint, led to some improvement, but in 1949 there were further balance-of-payments problems as the United States experienced a recession, ultimately forcing a 30% devaluation of sterling. The resulting improvement in the trade balance was, however, shortlived as the Korean war forced a diversion of production to military ends and the accompanying inflation in raw material prices led to a deterioration in the terms of trade.

The macroeconomic history of the period until 1964 is one of repeated attempts to expand the economy being thwarted by large balance-of-payments deficits. Expansionary budgets in 1953, 1959, and 1963 increased output and reduced unemployment, only to be accompanied by deficits in foreign trade as domestic absorption increased and the increased pressure of domestic demand led to increased wage demands and a deteriorating international competitive position. These deficits in turn necessitated a reversal of policy and the adoption of deflationary measures.

The expansionary phases of these 'stop-go' cycles generally coincided with the run-up to an election which gives some credence to the notion of a politically induced business cycle. However, a less Machiavellian explanation lies in an inadequate allowance for the time lags between changes in policy and their effect on the economy. This is particularly true of both investment in fixed capital where gestation times are long, and investment in inventories where increases in demand may be initially offset by destocking by firms. Dow (1964), for instance, in his reappraisal of economic policy in this era, concludes that although policy was usually in the right direction it was almost always a case of too much, too late. This judgement that policy was actually destabilizing is broadly consistent with the later study of Caves et al. (1968).

The average growth rate over this period was around 3%, which, coupled with an average unemployment rate of 1.5% over 1953–64, was excellent by historical standards. However, the growth rate was low by comparison with the other major industrial countries (e.g., France 5.3%; West Germany 6.5%; Italy 5.5%; Japan 9.3%). Only the United States achieved a comparable growth rate, but American per capital income was already twice as high. These countries also displayed a much higher growth in productivity.

Increasingly, the problems of a weak balance of payments, low output growth, and low productivity growth were seen to be interrelated. Policy-makers aspired to a 'virtuous circle' in which raipd demand growth put pressure on capacity leading to increased investment, and promoted total factor productivity growth through 'learning by doing' (e.g., Kaldor, 1966). The consequent increase in productivity would lower unit costs, improve competitiveness, and thus relax the balance-of-payments con-straint. The question was how to get such a process started.

The new Labour administration which took office in October 1964 were among those who subscribed to the 'virtuous circle' theory. They were determined to avoid a continuation of earlier 'stop-go' policies. Inheriting a balance-of-payments deficit, rather than deflate, they introduced an import surchange and relied on UK drawing rights from the IMF to finance the deficit. In the longer term industrial policy and economic planning would foster increased productivity, while a (voluntary) incomes policy would hold down wages, thus leading to a fundamental improve-ment in the competitive position of the UK.

The government's National Plan of 1965 envisaged an average annual growth rate over the ensuing five years of no less than 3.8%. It was, however, short-lived. By July 1966 severe balance-of-payment difficulties had developed as a result of the rapid growth of demand and attempts to maintain competitiveness by voluntary restraint on wages had failed. The government was forced to abandon its original strategy and deflate. The deflationary measures were accompanied by a statutory freeze on wages for six months, which was followed by a period of severe restraint. Despite an initial improvement in the trade balance, the slow down in world trade and a dock strike in 1967 made a devaluation of sterling – from $2.80 to $2.40 – virtually unavoidable. Policy from then until the end of the decade was directed at making sure the devaluation was effective with continued domestic deflation, and a strict incomes policy. By 1970 a surplus on the trade account of 2% of GDP had developed, but this was at a cost of a growth rate of only 2.2% over the life of the National Plan. The attempt to maintain the improvement in competi-tiveness was not entirely successful, however, since by 1971 only about half of the original gain in competitiveness (as measured by normal unit labour costs) remained. Electoral defeat followed.

In 1972 the new Conservative government resolved to make a further 'dash for growth' by introducing massive income tax cuts. At the same time sterling was allowed to float in order to relax the balance-of-payments constraint and permit the pursuit of an independent monetary policy. Monetary policy was deliberately lax – broad money (£M3) grew by 26% in 1973 (although the growth of M1 was only 5%). By postwar standards unemployment seemed high at 3% and the inflationary implications of the monetary and fiscal expansion were believed to be minimal.

The consequence of these policies was an unsustainable growth in output of 7% in 1973, coupled with a current account deficit of 1.5% of GDP and a sterling depreciation. To maintain the improvement in competitiveness brought about by the depreciation, there was a statutory incomes policy in force from 1972–4. However, the commodity price inflation engendered by the high level of world demand coupled with the sterling depreciation led to a rapid rise in input prices. The high level of domestic demand enabled this to be translated into a 16% increase in retail prices in 1974. This in turn placed the incomes policy under severe strain, leading to industrial confrontation between the miners and the government, and ultimately the electoral defeat of the latter.

Simultaneously there was, of course, the quadrupling of oil prices in 1974, necessitating a shift in real incomes from oil consumers to producers. Even if the original Conservative strategy had been successful, it would certainly have faced major problems as a result of the rise in oil prices. The new Labour administration initially resisted deflation and allowed wages to rise in line with prices. Given the previous expansion in the money stock it was not surprising that inflation reached 26% in 1975, while the current account deficit rose to 4.5% of GDP.

In the face of both the high level of inflation and the large current account deficit, the government were obliged to adopt deflationary measures in return for a loan from the IMF. Control of inflation rather than unemployment became the central objective of policy, and monetary targets became an important part of the apparatus of economic policy-making for the first time. A 'Social Contract' with the trade unions helped to limit wage demands and keep unemployment to high but almost tolerable levels. Under this regime inflation fell to 8% by 1978, and balance in the current account was achieved with the aid of North Sea oil, production of which was now significant. Real wages fell by 12% and there was a 10% improvement in labour cost competitiveness between 1975 and 1977. All of this was undone, however, when the government was unable to obtain continued pay restraints and wages rose more than 18% between mid 1977 and mid 1978 while inflation was only 5%. A winter of industrial strife and large pay rises in the winter of 1979 spelt the end of the Labour administration and ushered in a new era of economic policy-making in the shape of Mrs Thatcher.

Since then the balance of payments has, until recently, tended to play a rather minor role in economic policy-making. Despite a 25% appreciation of the effective exchange rate between the beginning of 1979 and the end of 1980 the current account improved dramatically, reaching a surplus of 3% of GDP in 1981. Two factors are of course involved here: the worst recession since the interwar years, and the exploitation of North Sea oil which saw Britain become a net exporter of oil.[4] Since the latter is a temporary phenomenon, consumption-smoothing dictates that indeed it should have been associated with a temporary surplus. However, the recovery which started in 1981, coupled with a gradual decline in the relative importance of oil has been associated with a steady deterioration in the current account position culminating in the rapid deterioration since 1987 and the present deficit of nearly 4.75% of GDP.

1.4   The rest of the chapter

What is immediately apparent from this rapid tour of British economic history is the central role played by income from foreign assets in ensuring a strong current account performance during the Victorian and Edwardian eras, and by the two world wars in virtually eliminating that healthy buffer. While trade performance has in fact improved somewhat over this time, it has offset the fall in interest income to only a very limited extent. At the same time, British economic policy has apparently been increasingly constrained by external considerations.

In the next section we examine the possible link between the decline in the net foreign asset position and the apparent increasing prevalence of balance-of-payments difficulties in more detail. We begin with a discussion of national solvency and then go on to evaluate the extent to which there is an 'external constraint' over and above this. Perhaps surprisingly our econometric results do not seem to suggest that the 'external constraint' tightened significantly in the postwar period. The final section then briefly discusses conflicting explanations for the present deterioration in the current account and the prospects for the near future.

2   The external constraint: is it just a solvency requirement?

The phrase 'external constraint' is open to a variety of interpretations. It is here construed narrowly as reflecting the country's ability to borrow to cover a current account deficit. If the opportunities for borrowing at the 'world' interest rate are unlimited then this would amount (at most) to an intertemporal solvency condition. With imperfect international capital markets, however, there may be an additional period-by-period borrowing constraint. A wider interpretation is certainly possible; for instance expectations of future monetary expansion, or the need for future real depreciation to satisfy intertemporal solvency, may precipitate an attack on the currency now and make it difficult, or even impossible, to maintain the current level of the exchange rate. However, we prefer to think of this as a 'credibility constraint' brought about by a lack of credibility of the commitment to maintaining an appropriately tight monetary policy in the future, rather than the operation of an 'external constraint'.

We start by asking whether the data in Figures 7.1 and 2 are consistent with the usual intertemporal solvency requirement that would obtain with perfect capital markets, namely

$$A_t + \sum_{j=1}^{\infty} \left\{ \prod_{i=1}^{j} [1/(1 + r^*_{t+i})] \right\} \tilde{S}_{t+j} \geq 0 \tag{1}$$

where A_t is the net stock of foreign assets at the end of period t, $\tilde{S}_t$ is the trade surplus in period t (strictly the current account exclusive of net property income), and r^*_t is the world interest rate in period t. In a growing economy it is more convenient to write this as

$$a_t + \sum_{j=1}^{\infty} \left\{ \prod_{i=1}^{j} [(1 + n_{t+i})/(1 + r^*_{t+i})] \right\} \tilde{s}_{t+j} \geq 0 \tag{1'}$$

where n_t is the rate of growth of the economy in period t, and a_t and $\tilde{s}_t$ are the net asset–output ratio and trade surplus–output ratio respectively.

If we can assume that there is a τ such that for all $s > \tau$, $r^*_s > n_s$ the growth-corrected discount factor will be non-explosive and Ponzi games will not be feasible.[5] Furthermore, if (1)/(1') hold with strict inequality then the national consumption path would be lower than it need be, i.e. it is inefficient, and furthermore the rest of the world must be simultaneously violating its intertemporal solvency condition. Hence (1)/(1') should hold with equality. Hence if s_t follows a stationary stochastic process then so must a_t. Following Hamilton and Flavin (1986) we may use this result to test whether the solvency condition is satisfied.

Using the data for net foreign assets constructed for Figure 7.2 we obtained the following regression results for autoregressions of a_t and s_t

$$\Delta a_t = 0.025 - 0.03 \, a_{t-1} + 0.16 \, \Delta a_{t-1} + 0.178 \, \Delta a_{t-2} \tag{2}$$
$$\quad (1.22) \quad (1.58) \qquad (1.83) \qquad \quad (2.02)$$

Sample period: 1860–1989; Standard error = 0.131; $\bar{R}^2 = 0.051$; $DW = 2.04$ and

$$\Delta \tilde{s}_t = -0.0049 - 0.212\ \tilde{s}_{t-1} + 0.012\ \Delta \tilde{s}_{t-1} - 0.059\ \Delta \tilde{s}_{t-2} \qquad (3)$$
$$\phantom{\Delta \tilde{s}_t = } (2.22) \quad\ (3.47) \qquad\ (0.13) \qquad\qquad (0.67)$$

Sample period: 1860–1989; Standard error = 0.021; $\bar{R} = 0.095$; $DW = 1.97$ where Δ is the difference operator and t-statistics are in parentheses. Using the tables in Dickey and Fuller (1979) to evaluate the significance of the t-statistic on a_{t-1} in (2) and $\tilde{s}_{t-1}$ in (3) the results suggest that, while the trade balance is stationary, the process for net foreign assets is not, which apparently implies violation of the intertemporal solvency condition.

However, as described by Dolado and Viñals in this volume, the approach of Hamilton and Flavin suffers from a number of defects. An alternative, and more general, approach has been advanced by Wilcox (1989) which requires working with the discounted values of net assets and the trade surplus. A necessary condition for solvency is then that the discounted net asset position is a stationary process with zero drift. Following Wilcox, we obtain

$$\Delta a^d_t = 0.039 - 0.035\ a^d_{t-1} + 0.153\ \Delta a^d_{t-1} + 0.179\ \Delta a^d_{t-2} \qquad (2')$$
$$ (1.36) \quad\ (1.72) \qquad\ (1.74) \qquad\qquad (2.03)$$

Sample period: 1860–1989; Standard error = 0.19; $\bar{R}^2 = 0.051$; $DW = 2.04$ where

$$a^d_t \equiv \prod_{i=1860}^{t} [(1 + n_i)/(1 + r^*_i)]a_t$$

Once again there is little evidence that intertemporal solvency is satisfied. However, this is not quite as disturbing as perhaps it seems. To begin with the characterization of the process driving the data for the current account in Figure 7.1 as a single time-invariant stochastic process seems doubtful. Clearly there are major shifts corresponding to the onset of wars, and it does not seem very reasonable to regard these as random draws from some fixed distribution. Furthermore, a failure of the test can only tell us that the intertemporal solvency condition is not satisfied for the particular in-sample stochastic process driving the trade balance. It does not prohibit out-of-sample changes in that process, or default on some or all of foreign debt, to ensure solvency is satisfied *ex-post*. At best it gives an indication that something may have to give in the future.

If we grant that intertemporal solvency must ultimately be satisfied, what other external constraints are present? These are likely to take the form of period-by-period borrowing constraints, perhaps depending on the country's net asset position or the current account deficit, or a rising supply price of foreign debt.

To fix ideas consider the following simple open economy growth model in which a representative consumer maximizes the expected value of an intertemporally additive utility function $u(C_t)$ defined over consumption, C_t, with discount factor β. Labour is supplied inelastically and normalized to unity. The economy's production possibilities are given by a well-behaved technology $f(K_{t-1}; V_t)$, where K_t is the end-of-period stock of physical capital and V_t is a technology shock. Finally there is a government which levies taxes and borrows to finance a given level of government expenditure, G_t, which yields no direct utility to consumers. G_t is therefore best thought of as defence expenditures, rather than total government spending, a part of which presumably does yield utility to private citizens.

Product, factor, and domestic capital markets are perfect which ensures both that Ricardian neutrality holds (so that the government's financing decision is immaterial) and that the competitive equilibrium may be found as the solution to a social planning problem. The international capital market, however, may not be perfect.[6] This is summarized in a rising supply price of foreign debt, $\tilde{r}^*_t$

$$\tilde{r}^*_t = r^*_t + g(A_t, A_{t-1}) \qquad (g_1, g_1 + g_2 \leqslant 0) \qquad (4)$$

where r^*_t is the interest rate on prime assets in foreign capital markets and $g(A_t, A_{t-1}) \geqslant 0$ reflects the premium that the domestic country has to pay for overseas borrowing, with $g(0, 0) = 0$. The presence of A_t and A_{t-1} allows both the level and the rate of change of net foreign assets, i.e., the current account, to affect the borrowing premium. Note that quantity rationing can easily be accommodated in this formulation by interpreting $\tilde{r}^*_t$ as the *virtual* supply price of foreign debt, i.e., the interest rate at which the *observed* asset position would be freely chosen in the absence of any quantity restrictions.

The sequence $\{r^*_s, G_s, V_s\}$ is uncertain and follows a given stochastic process whose realization in period t is known at the start of the period. The competitive equilibrium then solves the program

$$\max_{\{C_s, K_s, A_s\}} E_t \left[\sum_{s=t}^{\infty} \beta^{s-t} u(C_s) \right] \qquad (5)$$

subject to (for all $s \geqslant t$)

$$A_s - A_{s-1}(1 + \tilde{r}^*_s) + K_s - K_{s-1} + C_s + G_s = f(K_{s-1}) \qquad (6)$$

The first-order conditions are then

$$E_t[\beta u'(C_{s+1})\{1 + f'(K_s)\}] = E_t[u'(C_s)] \qquad (7)$$

$$E_t[\beta u'(C_{s+1})\{1 + \tilde{r}^*_{s+1} + A_s g_2(A_{s+1}, A_s)\}]$$
$$= E_t[u'(C_s)\{1 - A_{s-1} g_1(A_s, A_{s-1})\}] \qquad (8)$$

together with a transversality condition that ensures intertemporal solvency is satisfied. For the purposes of the empirical work below it is convenient to combine (7) and (8) to give, for $s = t$

$$E_t[Y_{t+1}] \equiv E_t[u'(C_{t+1})\{f'(K_t) - r^*_{t-1}\}/u'(C_t)]$$
$$= E_t[u'(C_{t+1})\{g(A_{t+1}, A_t) + A_t g_2(A_{t+1}, A_t)\}/u'(C_t)$$
$$+ A_{t-1} g_1(A_t, A_{t-1})/\beta]$$
$$\equiv Z_t, \quad \text{say} \qquad (9)$$

When the country is a debtor ($A < 0$) and there is a borrowing premium, Z_t is positive. When the country is a creditor or international capital markets are perfect, Z_t is zero and (9) is simply the appropriate consumption risk-adjusted real interest parity condition for this economy.[7] The role of the current account is then simply to facilitate consumption-smoothing in the face of shocks to output, government spending, etc. as in the intertemporal models of the current account of Sachs (1981), Svensson and Razin (1983), Persson and Svensson (1985), and Frenkel and Razin (1987).

Before proceeding to the evaluation of departures from this model by measuring Z_t, it is useful to ask whether this way of looking at the current account is even remotely useful. As evidence that it is, consider the implications of various sorts of shocks in this model. Permanent shocks to income should not lead to a change in the current account since consumption should simultaneously increase. By contrast temporary shocks to output, e.g., due to strikes, or to government spending, such as, due to wars, should be associated with a current account deterioration. Finally, permanent shocks to the marginal product of capital should be associated with increases in both consumption (as permanent income has risen) and investment; thus the current account deteriorates. The historical evidence does seem to be roughly in accord with this interpretation as the following regression of the current account, s_t, on the change in consumption, Δc_t, the level of gross private investment, i_t, and the level of government defence spending, g_t (all measured as a proportion of GDP) attests

$$s_t = 0.037 - 0.055 \, \Delta c_t - 0.173 \, i_t - 0.098 \, g_t + 0.615 \, s_{t-1} \qquad (10)$$
$$\quad (4.7) \quad (0.56) \quad\quad (4.26) \quad\quad (4.81) \quad\quad (9.77)$$

Sample period: 1858–1989; Standard error = 0.02; $\bar{R}^2 = 0.77$; $DW = 1.79$. Lagrange Multiplier test for second-order serial correlation $\chi^2(2) = 2.55$. The coefficient on the change in consumption (a proxy for permanent shocks) is small and insignificant while investment (essentially a proxy for anticipated future shocks to income) and defence spending (a transitory shock to demand) are both highly significant.

Let us now return to the issue of estimating Z_t which captures limitations on foreign borrowing. Our strategy here is to parameterize the utility function by assuming constant relative risk aversion $u(C) = C^{1-\theta}/(1 - \theta)$, and then construct Y_{t+1} for different values of θ. Under the assumption of rational expectations, an estimate of Z_t can then be obtained by a generalized least squares projection of Y_{t+1} on information available at date t, X_t.

Of course the projection of Y_{t+1} on X_t is a noisy measure of Z_t so we also need to derive estimates of the associated standard errors.[8] First write

$$Z_t = X_t \beta + v_t \tag{11}$$

where v_t reflects omitted variables and is assumed serially uncorrelated with $\mathrm{Var}(v_t) = v_t^2$. Second, rational expectations implies

$$Y_{t+1} = E_t[Y_{t+1}] + e_t \tag{12}$$

where e_t is orthogonal to X_t and v_t and $\mathrm{Var}(e_t) = \epsilon_t^2$. Then by (9)

$$Y_{t+1} = X_t \beta + v_t + e_t \tag{13}$$

The estimate of Z_t, $\hat{Z}_t$ is given by

$$\hat{Z}_t = X_t(X' \Omega X)^{-1} X' \Omega Y \tag{14}$$

where $X' = \{X_1', X_2', \ldots, X_t', \ldots\}$, etc., and $\Omega = \mathrm{diag}(\epsilon_t^2 + v_t^2)^{-1}$. Thus

$$\begin{aligned} \mathrm{Var}(\hat{Z}_t - Z_t) &= E[\{X_t(X' \Omega X)^{-1} X' \Omega(v + e) - v_t\}^2] \\ &= (1 - 2\rho_t)X_t(X' \Omega X)^{-1} X_t' + \rho_t(\epsilon_t^2 + v_t^2) \end{aligned} \tag{15}$$

where $\rho_t = v_t^2/(\epsilon_t^2 + v_t^2)$. Of course ρ_t is unknown, but since $0 \leqslant \rho_t \leqslant 1$ it is possible to obtain the following bounds[9] on $\mathrm{Var}(\hat{Z}_t - Z_t)$

$$X_t(X' \Omega X)^{-1} X_t' \leqslant \mathrm{Var}(\hat{Z}_t - Z_t) \leqslant \epsilon_t^2 + v_t^2 - X_t(X' \Omega X)^{-1} X_t' \tag{16}$$

When most of the residual variance in (13) is due to expectational errors, ρ_t will be small and the variance of the estimated value of Z_t will be close to its lower bounds; on the other hand if the proxies for Z_t are poor and v_t^2 is correspondingly large, ρ_t approaches unity and the variance of $\hat{Z}_t$ about its unobserved true value will be closer to the upper bound. Both the absolute and relative importance of these two sources of error are likely to vary over the sample; thus we allow for heteroscedasticity in the error term in equation (13). Expectational errors are, however, likely to be relatively more important during floating rate periods and certainly for the most recent past one would expect the lower bound to give a better guide to the true variance.

Table 7.1. *Estimates of equation (9)*
Dependent Variable: $Y_{t+1}(\theta)$; Sample period: 1892–1988

	$\theta = 1$	$\theta = 20$
Constant	− 0.527	0.565
	(0.25)	(0.20)
Y_t	0.162	− 0.130
	(1.15)	(0.98)
ΔY_t	0.331	0.187
	(3.18)	(1.17)
$r_t - \bar{r}^*_t$	0.623	0.177
	(1.12)	(0.25)
$\Delta(r_t - \bar{r}^*_t)$	0.848	1.140
	(0.89)	(0.93)
$\Delta^2(r_t - \bar{r}^*_t)$	− 0.478	− 1.022
	(0.94)	(1.55)
d_t	− 0.005	− 0.012
	(0.51)	(0.91)
Δd_t	0.024	0.093
	(0.36)	(0.97)
$\Delta^2 d_t$	− 0.030	− 0.209
	(0.40)	(1.90)
a_t	0.001	− 0.010
	(0.03)	(0.44)
Δa_t	0.066	0.078
	(1.03)	(0.87)
$\Delta^2 a_t$	0.019	0.040
	(0.38)	(0.59)
Standard error	6.142	8.609
$\bar{R}^2$	0.179	0.022
DW	2.265	2.026
F-test of H_0: $Z_t = 0$	3.209	1.349
ARCH parameter	0.339	0.010

Table 7.1 provides estimates of equation (13) for two values of the coefficient of relative risk-aversion parameter: $\theta = 1$ and $\theta = 20$. Previous work on the intertemporal elasticity of substitution in consumption (e.g., Bean, 1986; Hall, 1988; Hansen and Singleton, 1983) suggests that a value of θ between 0 and 2 is appropriate and $\theta = 1$ corresponds to the special case of logarithmic preferences which has been used frequently in theoretical work on economic fluctuations. However, this form of preferences is very restrictive in constraining the reciprocal of the elasticity of

substitution in consumption and the coefficient of relative risk-aversion to be the same. Empirical work on portfolio allocation suggests that the degree of risk-aversion is very much higher. Recent work has attempted to relax this constraint between attitudes to risk and to intertemporal substitutability of consumption by introducing more flexible preference structures such as those of Selden (1978) and Kreps and Porteous (1978). It turns out that when these more general preference structures are employed an equation similar to (9) in all important respects can be derived,[10] except that the coefficient θ describing preferences now uniquely characterizes attitudes to risk and has no bearing on intertemporal substitution in consumption (see Attanasio and Weber, 1989). A value of $\theta = 20$ accordingly is consistent with empirical work on both the allocation of consumption over time and portfolio allocation.

In order to construct the dependent variable in this regression we also need a measure of the *ex-post* real interest differential, $f'(K_t) - r^*_{t+1}$. The domestic interest rate – which in the model is identically equal to the marginal product $f'(K_t)$ – is measured by the three-month Treasury Bill rate, while the foreign interest rate is the sterling return on three-month US Treasury Bills, i.e., adjusted to take account of capital gains or losses due to exchange rate changes. The information set, X_t, includes two lags of the dependent variable, plus three lags each of: the raw interest differential, i.e., not adjusted for exchange rate changes, $r - \tilde{r}^*$; the net foreign assets–output ratio, $\tilde{a}$; and the public sector debt–output ratio, d. This last variable is included because, arguably, the level of sovereign debt is more important in leading to borrowing constraints. The lags have been reparameterized as levels, differences, and second differences to produce a more orthogonal regressor set which can be more readily interpreted. Finally, the estimates allow for autoregressive conditional heteroscedasticity (ARCH) of order one. This is highly significant for the low risk-aversion ($\theta = 1$) case ($\chi^2(1) = 12.79$), but is trivial and insignificant in the high risk-aversion ($\theta = 20$) case ($\chi^2(1) = 0.05$).

One can test the hypothesis that $Z_t \equiv 0$ for all t by evaluating the joint significance of all the regressors, including the constant. The appropriate test statistic, distributed as $F(12, 85)$, is 3.21 for the low risk-aversion case, and 1.35 for the high risk-aversion case. Thus one can reject the assumption of perfect capital markets for the low risk-aversion case, but not for the high risk-aversion case. However, even for the former, the external position as reflected in either net foreign assets or the current account seems to play a relatively minor role in generating departures from risk-adjusted interest parity, the most significant variable by far being ΔY_t.

However, it is not the coefficients themselves that are of prime interest

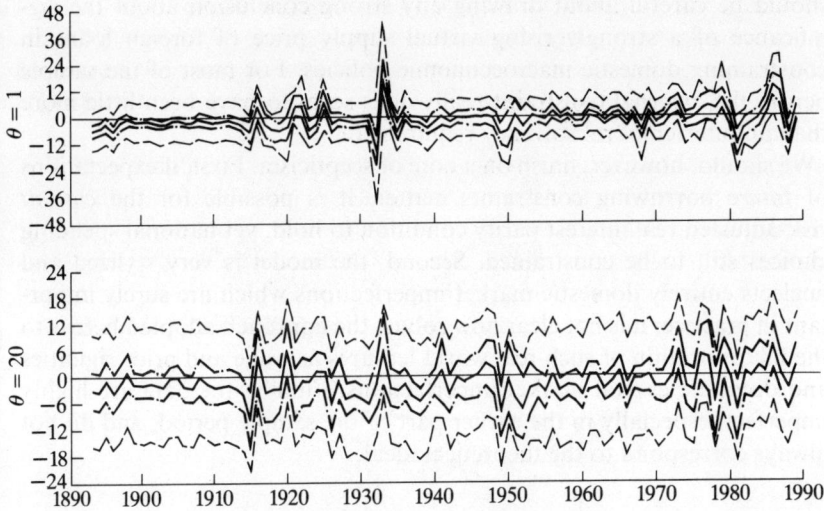

Figure 7.3 $\hat{Z}_t$ and minimum and maximum 90% confidence bands

here; rather it is the implied estimates of Z_t which measures period-by-period departures from risk-adjusted real interest parity. These are plotted in Figure 7.3 for $\theta = 1$ (upper panel) and $\theta = 20$ (lower panel), together with the minimum and maximum 90% confidence bands. In keeping with the results in Table 7.1, the confidence bands for the high risk-aversion case are rather wide and the zero line is always within the maximum 90% confidence interval, and almost always within the minimum 90% interval. By contrast the confidence bands for the low risk-aversion case are rather tighter. With respect to the maximum 90% confidence interval, $\hat{Z}_t$ is significantly below zero in 1981 and significantly above zero in 1986. With respect to the minimum 90% confidence interval it is significantly below zero in 1893–6, 1899–1900, 1902–3, 1906–7, 1910, 1914–15, 1918–19, 1923–4, 1929–30, 1932, 1935, 1937–9, 1949, 1963, 1966, 1968, 1970, 1981–2, and 1988, and significantly above zero in 1922, 1925, 1933, 1973, 1979, and 1986–7.

  In interpreting these results it is useful to recall the periods when sterling came under particular pressure in the foreign exchange markets and/or balance-of-payments considerations apparently played a role in determining the direction of macroeconomic policy. Apart from the float of 1931, these would seem to be 1947, 1955, 1960, 1964–5, 1967–8, 1974–5, 1979(?), and 1988–9. For the most part these are not periods when $\hat{Z}_t$ is low, but the matching between periods of relatively high $\hat{Z}_t$ and periods of external pressure are considerably less than perfect. It seems therefore that one should be careful about drawing any strong conclusion about the significance of a strongly rising virtual supply price of foreign loans in constraining domestic macroeconomic policies. For most of the sample period the external constraint really does seem to have been little more than an intertemporal solvency requirement.

We should, however, finish on a note of scepticism. First, if expectations of *future* borrowing constraints matter, it is possible for the *current* risk-adjusted real interest parity condition to hold, yet national spending choices still to be constrained. Second, the model is very stylized and neglects entirely domestic market imperfections which are surely important in practice; it is not clear how robust the approach adopted here is to the incorporation of such real world features as wage and price rigidities and domestic capital market imperfections. Finally, the data are highly imperfect, especially in the earlier part of the sample period, and do not always correspond to the theoretical ideal.

3   Prospects for the future

We conclude with a brief discussion of Britain's present balance-of-payments problems and a prognosis for the future. What is the root cause of the present current account deficit of 4.75% of GDP? Is it sustainable, and is it anything to worry about? If it is not sustainable what factors are likely to adjust and is that adjustment process likely to be smooth? The official line has been that the current account deficit is temporary, reflects (partly) an investment boom, can easily be financed, and in any case is the consequence of private sector decisions and is for the most part nothing to worry about.

Table 7.2 presents some raw data on public and private sector balances, together with a breakdown of the latter into savings and investment components. There has indeed been some recovery in investment during the second half of the eighties, but much of this is due to increased stock-building. The most remarkable feature is the marked reduction in personal savings. While the latter has been offset to some degree by increased public sector saving, this is surely a largely automatic response reflecting the level of activity in the economy and the associated increase in tax receipts and reduced transfer payments.

So what has caused the fall in private savings? There are at least three main hypotheses that have been advanced. First, increased consumption may reflect the greater availability of credit in the wake of financial market deregulation, especially allowing mortgages for purposes other than house purchase. Second, a succession of tax-cutting budgets and the relatively rapid growth of real income in recent years may have raised

Table 7.2. *Sectoral balances, 1982–8*
(% of GDP)

	1982	1984	1986	1988
Personal saving	9.5	8.6	6.2	3.1
Other private saving	10.4	13.4	13.3	14.8
Private investment	15.0	16.9	16.9	22.4
Private sector balance	4.9	5.1	2.5	− 4.5
Public sector balance	− 3.2	− 4.6	− 2.4	1.3
Current account deficit	− 1.9	− 0.7	0.0	3.7
Balancing item	0.2	0.2	− 0.1	− 0.5

Source: National Income and Expenditure (1989).

households' assessment of their permanent income. Third, the house price boom has made consumers feel wealthier and thus raised the propensity to consume (Muellbauer and Murphy, 1990). Of course these hypotheses are not necessarily mutually exclusive. In particular increased consumption because of more optimistic expectations of future incomes might only have been feasible with the changes in financial markets that have occurred over the last decade.

The problem with the first explanation *on its own* is that it is difficult to see why it should have taken so long for the rapid growth in consumption to occur when many of the changes in financial markets occurred early in the decade. However, the freeing-up of the lending operations of Building Societies occurred with the 1986 Building Society Act, and this no doubt acted as a spur to other financial intermediaries to increase their lending. So it seems reasonable to attribute some role to financial market liberalization.

On the assumption that the liberalization is a permanent feature of financial markets, what should we expect about the behaviour of consumption in the future? Liberalization has allowed previously constrained consumers, e.g., those early in the life-cycle, to borrow. This will result in a redistribution of consumption over their lifetimes for these households, with their future consumption being *lower* than it would otherwise have been. Thus it is not clear that in the new steady state the aggregate savings ratio will be any lower than prior to liberalization. The only difference will be that the net worth of the private sector will be lower than it would otherwise have been.[11] All that is involved is a once-off stock shift. Unless government savings increases to offset this, there will be an associated deterioration in the overall national net asset position. However, provided the transition, involving a period of current account deterioration, can be financed without any significant increase in domestic interest rates there seems to be no compelling welfare reasons for being worried about this.

Turning to the second hypothesis – increased optimism on the part of consumers – the objection voiced here is frequently that the tax cuts, which amounted to only a few billion pounds in 1987 and 1988 respectively, are completely dwarfed by the size of the increase in consumers' expenditure (£28 billion between 1986 and 1988). However, this ignores the fact that an increase personal disposable income may have considerably more than a one-for-one effect on consumption to the extent that the increase is both permanent and engenders expectations of further income increases. Between 1985 and 1988 real personal disposable income grew at an annual rate of 4.0%, very high by historical standards. Rapid productivity growth and government pronouncements of a British 'economic miracle' may well have led consumers to expect such rapid growth to continue. To see how significant this could be, consider a consumer who obeys the permanent income hypothesis. His average propensity to consume will be inversely proportional to the growth-corrected real interest rate. With a fixed real interest rate of, say, 5%, a permanent increase in the growth rate from 2% to 2.5% would lead to a reduction in the personal savings ratio of 20 percentage points! Obviously real world complications like credit market imperfections will attenuate this, but it does demonstrate the potentially important role even quite modest changes in the anticipated growth rate of income could have.

Whether income expectations are fulfilled or not, any current account deficit resulting from this source should be essentially self-correcting. On the one hand if expectations are correct and rapid output growth continues, then domestic supply will in due course outstrip absorption and produce compensating current account surpluses. On the other hand if, as now seems likely, consumers have been over-optimistic, high personal debt levels will force them to cut their coat according to their cloth and reduce expenditure accordingly. A return to the original growth path would then be associated with a return to original asset–income ratios and a period of current account surpluses. The counterpart to this is likely, however, to be a domestic recession.

It is unclear to what extent the third story advanced above – an increase in housing wealth – really is an independent hypothesis because house prices are an endogenous variable. Thus an increase in permanent income should raise the demand for housing services and, in the short run at least, push up house prices (the long-run effect of course depends on the elasticity of the supply of new housing). Muellbauer and Murphy argue that tax distortions to encourage owner occupation may have further raised prices, but it is difficult to see why this should have a major effect on consumption unless consumers expect to trade down to inferior houses and thus liquidate some of their housing equity.

It thus seems that a combination of financial deregulation and optimistic income expectations are likely to be at the root of the fall in savings. However, in both cases this is likely to be largely temporary implying the current account deficit should be self-correcting. The question is whether such a temporary deficit can be financed. Net external assets (on the official measure) currently stand at a little under 20% of GDP, so a continuation of the deficit at existing levels would turn the United Kingdom into a net debtor by 1994. However, given both the empirical results above, and the United States experience there does indeed seem to be no obvious difficulty in financing a considerable deficit for even longer if necessary. (This is not to deny that contractionary policies may be appropriate on counter-inflationary grounds.)

There remains the question of whether the government should be worried about the current account deficit. We already argued above that, provided the crowding-out effects via higher real interests are minimal, i.e., the period-by-period external borrowing constraint is not significant, the welfare grounds for intervention to squeeze consumption seem dubious. The one exception is where income expectations are overly optimistic in which case intertemporal smoothing of consumption and the deficit would raise welfare. This is only possible *ex ante* however; it is no use trying to shut the stable door after the horse has bolted.

Finally, let us note that, if the government *does* for some reason want to influence the national savings rate, the correct way to do this is surely with the aid of fiscal policy – and in particular higher taxes or incentives to savers – rather than primarily via monetary policy as at present. Financial deregulation may have monetary consequences but it is surely a *real* shock, not a nominal one.

NOTES

I am grateful for helpful comments from my discussant Mike Artis, as well as other participants at the Conference. The Centre for Economic Performance is financed by the Economic and Social Research Council.

1 From 1886 the data on interest from abroad in Mitchell (1988) are based on Inland Revenue returns. Prior to the passing of the 'Coupon Act' in 1885 no such information is available, and the data are constructed by applying a 'representative' interest rate to the cumulated current account surplus (see Imlah, 1958, pp. 59–67). For the early part of the sample our procedure thus merely recovers (roughly) the underlying cumulated current account balance.

2 These benchmark estimates are based on a variety of sources including both data on interest from abroad (see footnote 1), and information on the placement of securities. See Imlah (1958, pp. 68–81) for a fuller discussion.

3 The overprediction of the constructed series relative to the benchmark (and

official data later in the decade) seems to be associated with differences in the maturity structure of assets and liabilities, with a greater proportion of gross assets being in the form of relatively high-yielding, long-dated debt. This illustrates rather clearly the difficulty of finding a 'representative' interest rate for net foreign assets.

4 For a discussion of the role of oil in the appreciation of sterling see Bean (1987).

5 This is only a sufficient condition to rule out Ponzi games of course.

6 This asymmetry may seem very peculiar, but is helpful in focusing on the issues at hand.

7 It may seem odd that we develop a model in which there is a borrowing premium only when the country is a debtor and then proceed to apply it to a country that has for virtually all of the sample period been a net creditor! However, in practice some agents are borrowing while others are lending abroad, and borrowing restrictions may begin to bite even through the country as a whole is a net creditor. Formally modelling this requires departing from a representative agent model which complicates matters considerably. However, something like the generalized interest parity condition (9) will still hold in an economy with heterogeneous agents. The key feature of (9), and in the empirical tests below, is that, when borrowing constraints bite, the intertemporal terms of trade within the country are pushed above the intertemporal terms of trade in the rest of the world; this should be a robust property that holds in most environments.

8 For a very similar approach see Mishkin (1984).

9 For all sample observations except 1940 and 1941 ($\theta = 20$) it turns out that $X_t (X' \Omega X)^{-1} X_t' < 1/2$. For these two observations the bounds need to be interchanged.

10 This is one reason why we estimate (9) rather than (8) which might seem more direct. In the more general framework (8) contains a number of additional terms that are awkward to deal with.

11 In a growing economy the aggregate savings ratio would in fact need to be slightly lower as the proportion of young indebted households would be higher.

REFERENCES

Attanasio, O. and G. Weber (1989), 'Intertemporal Substitution, Risk Aversion and the Euler Equation for Consumption', *Economic Journal* **99** (Supplement), 59–73.

Bean, C. (1986), 'The Estimation of "Surprise" Models and the "Surprise" Consumption Function', *Review of Economic Studies* **53**, 497–516.

(1987), 'The Impact of North Sea Oil', in R. Dornbusch and Layard, R. (eds.), *The Performance of the British Economy*, Oxford: Clarendon Press.

Caves, R. *et al.* (1968), *Britain's Economic Prospects*, London.

Dickey, D. and W. Fuller (1979), 'Distribution of the Estimators for Autoregressive Time Series with a Unit Root', *Journal of the American Statistical Association* **74**, 427–31.

Dolado, J. and J. Viñals (1990), 'Macroeconomic Policy, External Targets and Constraints: The Case of Spain', this volume.

Dow, J. (1964), *The Management of the British Economy 1945–60*, National Institute of Economic and Social Research, London.

Eichengreen, B. (1989), 'International Monetary Instability between the Wars: Structural Flaws or Misguided Policies?', Centre for Economic Policy Research, Discussion Paper No. 348.

Frenkel, J. and A. Razin (1987), *Fiscal Policies and the World Economy*, Cambridge MA: MIT Pres.

Hall, R. (1988), 'Intertemporal Substitution in Consumption', *Journal of Political Economy* 96, 339–57.

Hamilton, J. and M. Flavin (1986), 'On the Limitations of Government Borrowing: A Framework for Empirical Testing', *American Economic Review* 76, 808–19.

Hansen, L. and K. Singleton (1983), 'Stochastic Consumption, Risk Aversion and the Temporal Behaviour of Asset Returns', *Journal of Political Economy* 91, 249–65.

Imlah, A. (1958), *Economic Elements in the Pax Britannica*, Cambridge, MA.

Kaldor, N. (1966), 'Causes of the Slow Rate of Economic Growth in the United Kingdom', Inaugural Lecture, Cambridge University.

Kreps, D. and E. Porteous (1978), 'Temporal Resolution of Uncertainty and Dynamic Choice Theory', *Econometrica* 46, 1429–45.

Matthews, R., C. Feinstein, and J. Odling-Smee (1982), *British Economic Growth 1856–1973*, Oxford: Clarendon Press.

Mishkin, F. (1984), 'The Real Interest Rate: A Multi-Country Empirical Study', *Canadian Journal of Economics* 17, 283–311.

Mitchell, B. (1988), *British Historical Statistics*, Cambridge University Press.

Muellbauer, J. and A. Murphy (1990), 'Is the UK Balance of Payments Sustainable?', *Economic Policy* 5 (11), 347–95.

Persson, T. and L. Svensson (1985), 'Current Account Dynamics and the Terms of Trade: Harberger-Laursen-Metzler Two Generations Later', *Journal of Political Economy* 93, 43–65.

Sachs, J. (1981), 'The Current Account and Macroeconomic Adjustment in the 1970s', *Brookings Papers on Economic Activity* 1, 201–68.

Selden, L. (1978), 'A New Representation of Preferences over "Certain–Uncertain" Consumption Pairs', *Econometrica* 46, 1045–60.

Svensson, L. and A. Razin (1983), 'The Terms of Trade and the Current Account: The Laursen-Harberger-Metzler Effect', *Journal of Political Economy* 91, 97–125.

Wilcox, D. (1989), 'The Sustainability of Government Deficits: Implications of the Present-Value Borrowing Constraint', *Journal of Money, Credit and Banking* 21, 291–306.

Discussion

MICHAEL J. ARTIS

Charlie Bean's chapter falls into three parts. The first reviews the qualitative evidence for an external constraint in the British case, in a broad sweep from the mid nineteenth century onwards. The second suggests a means of estimating the presence of an external constraint. The third looks at the present situation in the United Kingdom where the current account deficit, as a proportion of GDP, at least when measured inclusive of interest income, is at an all (peace-) time high. Aside from the reference in each section to the British case, the treatment is bound together by reliance on the modern intertemporal theory of the balance of payments (Sachs, 1981; Frenkel and Razin, 1987) as the 'bedrock' model.

By 'external constraint' is implied something over and above the solvency constraint; in some sense this is not a constraint at all any more than the individual's budget constraint, despite the terminology, counts as a constraint when one is discussing the effect on consumer behaviour of credit market imperfections. The external constraint then arises, in principle, from world capital market imperfections, though its shadow may be cast forward by anticipation: for example, if a liquidity constraint does exist, it could be anticipated that an *ex ante* 'excess' current account imbalance must be cleared by asset price adjustment (the exchange rate and/or interest rates). Anticipation of a contact with the external constraint may thus have immediate effects (on government policy as well as on a private sector behaviour).

One of the problems with the trawl for external constraint 'contacts' is thus that the constraint may remain latent. The desire to avoid the constraint may discipline government policies, so that the constraint certainly bites, yet without evidence of contact. The fact that reaction function studies generally find the current account to be an important argument suggests that the external constraint may be (or may have been) more important than either the qualitative review in the first section of the chapter or the more systematic search in the second part would suggest.

The argument of the first section of the chapter is greatly enlightened by reference to a long-run series of net foreign assets (depicted in Figure 7.2). Whilst such series have sometimes been constructed by simply cumulating current account balances, Bean pursues the alternative route of capitalizing the stream of net property income. Either approach contains deficiencies as the author notes and in this light a detailed comparison of the two alternatives might have been instructive. What the series shows, however, is both plausible and dramatic. The influence of the two world wars stands out, indicating the 'tax-smoothing' paradigm (see Roubini, 1988): in these periods, the huge rise in taxes is smoothed by (in effect) overseas borrowing. Then the analysis focuses on periods when policy-makers and others apprehended the presence of an external constraint.

All of this seems well recounted, though the account of the position in 1976 might be amplified. One of the striking features of the foreign exchange crisis in this year was that it went against the fundamentals – inflation was falling, the current account improving, and deflationary measures were undertaken before the IMF loan was applied for. The facts that not all of the loan was used and that sterling rebounded immediately after the stabilization agreement was signed and long before any measures could be effective, suggest that this was a confidence crisis which, if driven initially initially by doubts about the macroeconomic policies of the government, was amplified by speculative behaviour.

The centre section of the chapter presents, *inter alia*, a statistical con-firmation of the tax smoothing hypothesis (represented as 'g' smoothing in equation (10)) and is an exhibit that deserves more stress. By contrast, the value of running stationarity tests (equations (2), (2'), and (3)), is undermined by the graphical evidence of the behaviour of the trade account and net foreign assets series, where the story of the accumulation before the First World War and the huge shocks inflicted in both this and the Second World War stand out. The main purpose of this part of the chapter, however, is to generate a measure of the external constraint departures from real interest parity (adjusted for risk). The estimates, produced from the regression equation derived from the model, presented in equations (4)–(9), with imposed parameter values to measure relative risk-aversion, do not seem to track the episodes of external constraint contact identified in the first section. This might cast doubt on the model, or on the identification exercise, or both. The model might be misleading for a number of reasons. It assumes Ricardian equivalence and so sweeps the government out of sight; aside from anything else, the assumption that all domestic markets are perfect chimes oddly with the assumption that the world capital market is imperfect (the author acknowledges this awkwardness in a note). The identification exercise may produce a misleading sample if governments have for most of the time been success-ful in avoiding external constraint contacts. But despite these quali-fications, the exercise is nevertheless a stimulating one; long-run balance of payments and related data represent practically virgin territory for the applied econometrician and this original foray represents an encouraging attempt to make sense of them.

In the final section of the chapter, Bean discusses current British balance-of-payments problems. Given an assumption of substantially 'perfect' world capital markets, the episode is to be explained in terms of the intertemporal theory of the balance of payments. A financial liberalization effect and excessive upward revisions of permanent income are prime candidates, the housing market-driven increase in wealth providing a link between the two. On this basis consumption has been increased temporarily and the prognosis is for a built-in correction. It is sobering that the balance-of-payments figures have caused so *little* disturbance to the markets. This, and the contrast with the position as it would surely have been, say, twenty years ago, suggest to me that the conditions for the modern intertemporal theory of the balance of payments *are* now substantially met, which was not the case before.

There is, however, an alternative explanation which has the benefit of having been used by proponents to make successful predictions of the balance-of-payments deficits (House of Lords, 1985). This alternative position can be seen as proceeding from the absorption theory of the balance of payments, which sees the current account as the residual of supply and demand and as emphasizing the destruction of the supply capacity of the British economy in the early 1980s as the proximate and predictable cause of our current deficits. The balance of payments is an identity capable of being manipulated to highlight alternative approaches; the well-worn elasticities approach for example is focused by looking at the balance of payments directly as the difference between exports and imports, whilst, by incorporating the national accounts identities, the balance of payments can alternatively be manipulated to focus the absorption approach or the savings-investment (intertemporal) approach. Identities are correct so there is a sense in which all the approaches are correct. What makes one superior to the others is that it should have a cutting edge in descriptive power or constructive policy implications that the others lack. Implicit in Bean's account is that the intertemporal theory has such a superior leverage.

REFERENCES

Frenkel, J. and A. Razin (1987), *Fiscal Policy in the World Economy*, Cambridge, MA: MIT Press.
House of Lords (1985), *Report from the Select Committee on Overseas Trade*, London: HMSO.
Roubini, N.L. (1988), 'Current account and budget deficits in an intertemporal model of consumption and taxation smoothing. A solution to the Feldstein–Horioka puzzle?', National Bureau of Economic Research Working Paper No. 2773.
Sachs, J. (1981), 'The current account and macroeconomic adjustment in the 1970s', *Brookings Papers on economic Activity* 1, 201–68.

8　Savings, investment, government finance, and the current account: the Dutch experience

HUGO A. KEUZENKAMP and FREDERICK
van der PLOEG

1　Introduction

Apart from a very short interval in 1982 the Netherlands have been governed by a centre-right coalition since 1978. During the first four years Mr van Agt was prime minister. This coalition was supported by seventy-six of the 150 seats in parliament. This period was marked by a sharp increase in unemployment and quickly deteriorating government finances. Halfway during its term, the Minister of Finance, Frans Andriessen, left after a quarrel in which he insisted on further restrictions on government spending, but his colleagues did not give him sufficient support. In 1982 a centre-left government took over, but was unable to agree on its policies. Government finances deteriorated further and so did unemployment. New elections in 1982 brought a gain of ten seats for the conservative–liberal party, VVD, and a small loss for the centrist Christian Democrats (CDA). They formed a new coalition under Mr Ruud Lubbers as prime minister and former banker Dr Onno Ruding as Minister of Finance. The program of this government strongly emphasized the need for sound government finances, and recovery of the market sector to beat the unemployment problem. The Lubbers government was more convinced and convincing on its goals than its two predecessors. Hence, Mr Lubbers secured a second term of office after the election on 21 May 1986 and was able to continue to focus on his policy of sound government finance. In this election the CDA gained nine seats and became the largest political party with fifty-four seats. Despite the fact that the VVD lost nine seats (a return to twenty-seven seats), a CDA–VVD coalition government continued. However, some fatigue with this policy started to occur as budget discipline deteriorated during the course of the second government of Lubbers and Ruding. The Labour party was with fifty-two seats the second largest political party, but again remained out of office.

On the night of 2 May 1989 the VVD forced a break in the coalition over the finance of the National Environment Plan: this was probably the last straw as there had already been a period of dissatisfaction of the VVD members of parliament with their ministers who had lost sight of some VVD principles and were selling their liberal souls to the CDA, and Mr Lubbers in particular, on too many occasions. Given almost twelve years of being out of the office the leader of the PvdA, Mr Wim Kok, can be forgiven when he joked that from now on the PvdA will celebrate the second, rather than the first day of May. The election results of 6 September indeed show a loss for the VVD–CDA coalition: although the CDA kept its fifty-four seats, the VVD lost five seats which gives only a one-seat majority in parliament to these two parties. The result was a CDA–PvdA coalition with Mr Lubbers as prime minister and Mr Kok as Minister of Finance. This coalition still faces a number of unpleasant constraints to devise a new unemployment policy and to face up to the problem of the environment at a time when government finances are in a deplorable condition.

There are many constraints for Dutch unemployment policy, but the main ones are financial constraints and the associated lack of government investment (cf., Keuzenkamp and van der Ploeg, 1990a, b). We strongly believe that there are possibilities for an effective reduction of unemployment despite perceived financial and other constraints. This is an issue that has occupied the minds of politicians, journalists, and economists in the Netherlands during the last decade. Section 2 reviews the debate, pin-points the areas of concern for the future development of the Dutch economy, and pays attention to the composition of the pool of unemployed and hysteresis phenomena, which together with the bad state of government finances are the main problems facing the Dutch economy. Generally speaking, it reviews the development of the Dutch economy in the eighties. Section 3 uses the theory of tax smoothing to derive ten rules for sound government finance and argues that most of these have been violated by Dutch governments of the last decade. In fact, formation of productive government assets has not kept up with the explosion of government debt so that the net worth of the public sector has declined since 1982. Deficits have thus been used to finance transfers and other forms of government consumption rather than government investment. This has been the unfortunate political reality of budget cuts in the Netherlands.

Section 4 discusses the policies conducted by De Nederlandsche Bank. The rigid pegging of the guilder to the Deutschmark has bought an excellent reputation for monetary discipline. Inflation is now the lowest in the OECD, but this may have been at the expense of an explosion of government debt. The trade-off between discipline and giving up an independent instrument of monetary policy is discussed. Section 5 points out that, given that capital markets in the Netherlands are fully integrated with world capital markets, investment should be financed through the current account of the balance of payments. In general, smoothing of consumption means that temporary falls in income must be accommodated through current account deficits, i.e., borrowing from the rest of the world. Unfortunately, Section 6 shows that there is little empirical evidence of consumption smoothing for the Netherlands, since investment seems to be constrained by domestic saving. This worrying state of affairs may be due to institutional restrictions or, alternatively, due to the 'structural budget deficit' rule advocated and implemented by Zijlstra in the fifties and sixties. Section 7 concludes the chapter.

2   The Dutch economy in the 1980s

In our introduction we already mentioned the most salient facts of the Dutch economy in the last decade. High unemployment, a high government budget deficit, a steady surplus on the current account, very low inflation, and a stable exchange rate *vis-à-vis* the Deutschmark characterized the Dutch economy. Let us first turn to unemployment. Figure 8.1 shows unemployment percentages (national definition) and the ratio of long-term unemployed to total unemployment in one graph. The international economic depression that started with the second oil crisis and the tight monetary policy in the US in 1979 led to an unprecedented rise in unemployment. The Dutch economy is more vulnerable to external shocks than nearly any other Western economy. Moreover, it relies heavily on petrochemical industries (Rotterdam). Furthermore, profitability of the private sector had weakened during the seventies. Figure 8.2 shows how the profit share in the economy steadily decreased during the seventies and picked up in a spectacular fashion during the eighties. Unemployment soared to a peak in 1983 of 12% of the labour force (standardized OECD figure). This was well above the EEC or OECD average, despite very low participation rates (especially for women). In the mean time, long-term unemployment started to increase. The tide turned in 1985 with the recovery of the international economy. As Figure 8.1 shows, unemployment decreased but long-term unemployment stayed at a high level. In fact, the minor decrease is due to the fact that a large proportion of the long-term unemployed are close to retirement age, hence time is an important factor in the solution to the long-term unemployment problem. The main point, however, is that due to crowding out on the labour market the long-term unemployed are mostly not

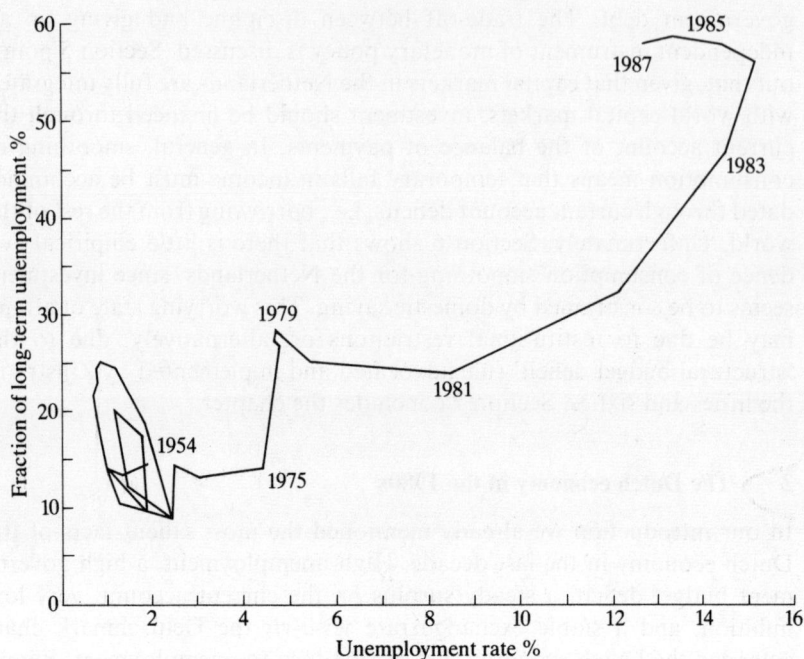

Figure 8.1   The unemployment rate and long-term unemployment in the Netherlands, 1954–87

very skilled and have become alienated. They no longer exercise down-ward pressure on wages. The appropriate response to such hysteresis phenomena is to provide training and schooling programmes, but the self-imposed financial straight-jacket for government finances has not allowed this.

The government's response to the unemployed problem was one of 'benign neglect'. A centrist–conservative coalition was in power from 1978 to 1989 (except for the year 1981). The policy agenda had a reduction of the share of government in the national income and of the government budget deficit as a top priority, the labour market was expected to solve its own problems. The government urged that wage moderation should play a leading role in this process. As a result, within a decade the share of labour in value added fell by almost 15%. Unemployment benefits remained relatively generous, however, and had a near open-ended character so that government finances deteriorated rapidly. Furthermore, the Dutch government was opposed to active labour market intervention by means of training and schooling or school-leaver programmes. Public spending on such items was negligible, also, when

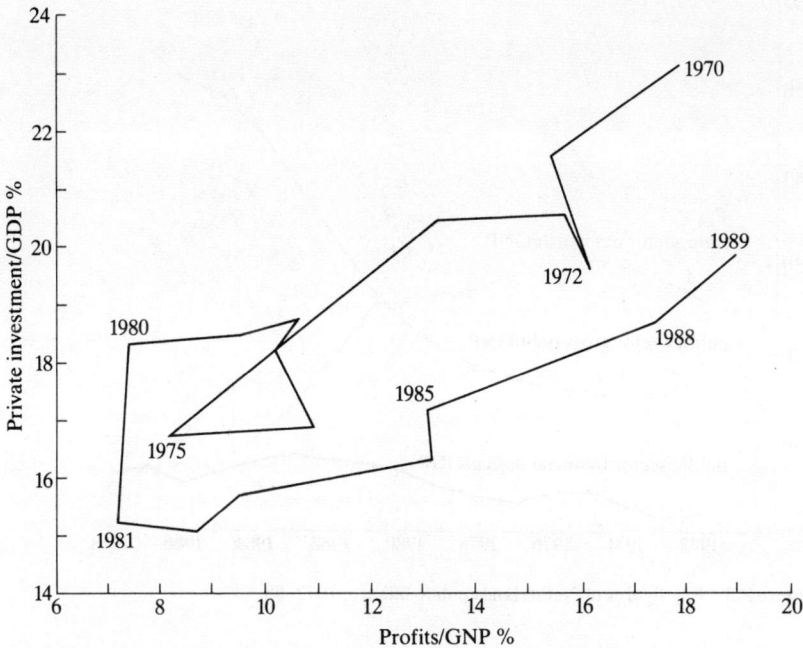

Figure 8.2 The profit share and investment in the Netherlands, 1970–89

compared with other European countries (Keuzenkamp and van der Ploeg, 1989, 1990a). As a result of these factors, the long-term unemployed became more and more alienated from the labour market. Their downward wage pressure became less important, so that endogenous wage moderation became mere wishful thinking (see also Graafland and Huizinga, 1988).

Reduction of both the share of the public sector and the budget deficit was the single most important policy goal of the eighties. However, this policy was not too successful. Figure 8.3 depicts the government debt, net worth and the financial deficit of the public sector as percentages of GNP. The improvement of world trade and hence the Dutch economy since the mid eighties led to a slight increase in the deficit, but the debt–GDP ratio is still rising. Worse, if we take a look at the government balance sheet, we see that the net worth of the Dutch state has collapsed since 1982 (Figure 8.3). Effectively, government debt exploded without a corresponding increase in productive government assets. The reason is that the financial deficits of the government were used for transfers and other consumption purposes rather than for investment. Government investment halved between 1970 and 1989 (from 4.7% of GNP in 1970 to 2.3% in 1989)!

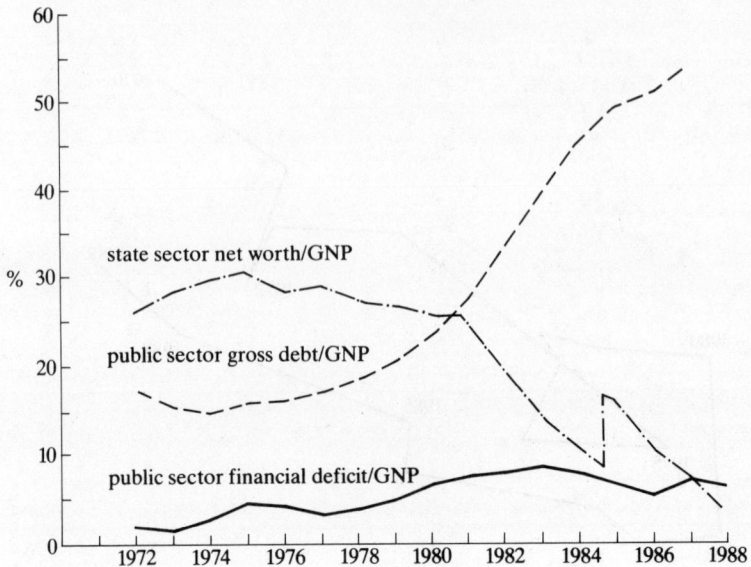

Figure 8.3   Key figures of Netherlands public finance, 1972–88

The excessive financial deficits violate public finance principles such as tax-smoothing. The collapse of government investment erodes the long-term strength of the Dutch economy (see Keuzenkamp and van der Ploeg, 1990b). Another potential distortion caused by the government's burden on the capital market could be crowding out of private investment. However, as real interest rates are due to the presence of fully liberalized capital markets, tied to foreign and in particular German real interest rates, this distortion cannot be blamed that easily on bad policies of Dutch governments.

The share of government in the economy (consumption, investment, and wages, excluding credits and debt repayments) rose from 29.7% in 1971 to 35.9% in 1980 and a prospective 37% of NNP in 1990. The increase has been slowed down or stopped, on the one hand (as mentioned before) as a result of decreasing investment spending and on the other hand due to autonomous wage moderation in the public sector. Whether this wage moderation is still sustainable is an open question: for example, currently tensions are building up in the health care sector where it is hard to attract new entrants to the work force.

One motivation for the would-be policies of 'sound government finance' has been fear of international insolvency or a credibility crisis. The solvency argument is for the Netherlands rather far-fetched, however. Even

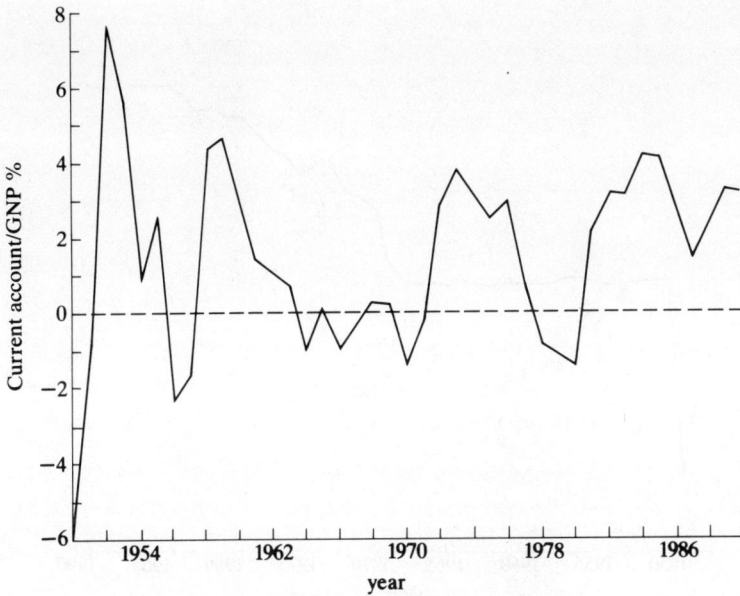

Figure 8.4   The Netherlands surplus on current account, 1953–88

though government net worth plummeted, the government is far from insolvent (see again the very conservative estimate of net government worth in Figure 8.3). Furthermore, from an international perspective the Netherlands are in a favourable situation of considerable surpluses on the current account of the balance of payments (Figure 8.4). Insolvency of the Dutch economy seems to be the very last problem to worry about. Exchange rate stability and inflation are other items on which the Dutch economy scored well. Inflation is among the lowest in the world, and the guilder–Deutschmark rate is close to becoming a natural constant (Figure 8.5). Between 1980 and 1989 the guilder depreciated slightly *vis-à-vis* the Deutschmark and the dollar. The dollar appreciated strongly between 1980 and 1985, but since then the bubble has burst. The yen appreciated by nearly 75%, the pound sterling and the French franc depreciated 25% to 30%.

In the area of unit labour costs the Dutch economy has scored extremely well during the last decade. Figure 8.6 shows how, during the seventies, unit labour costs (measured in national currencies) in the Netherlands rose slightly more than in Germany and the US, but since 1980 this has been reversed. Competitiveness with Japan has also improved, given the appreciation of the yen.

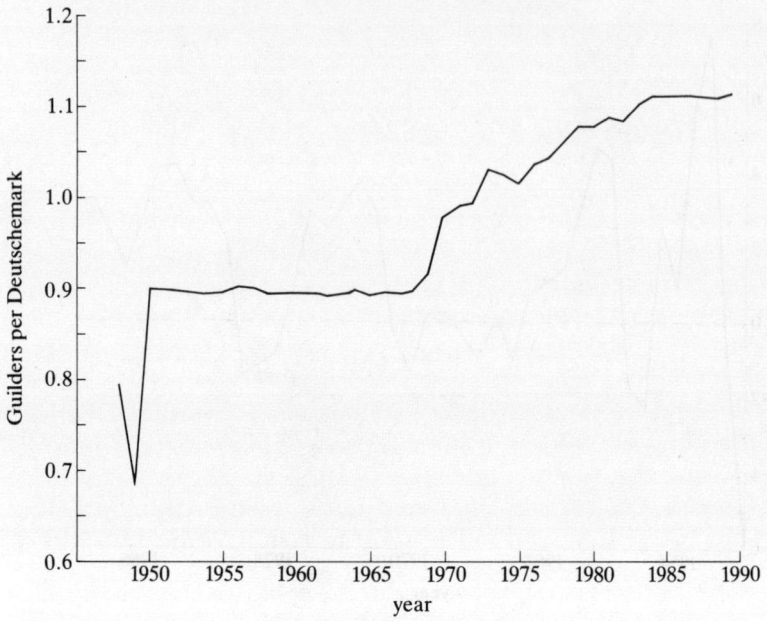

Figure 8.5   The Deutschmark–guilder exchange rate, 1948–89

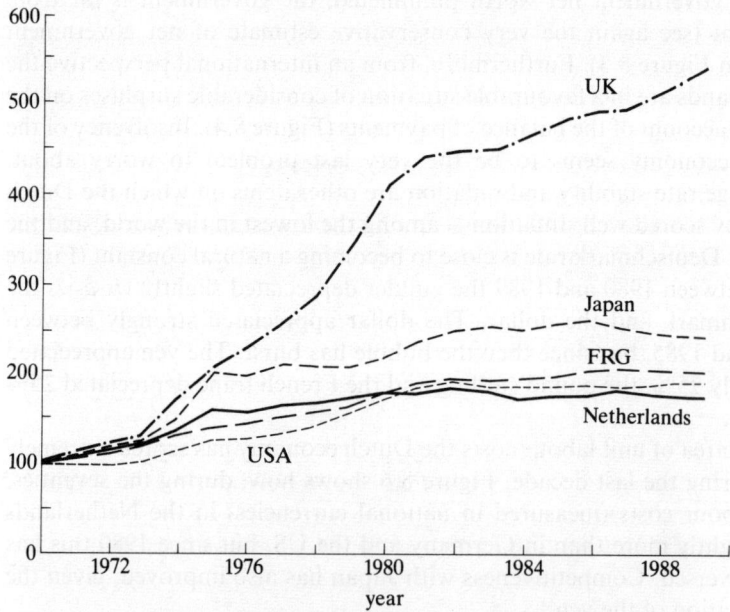

Figure 8.6   Unit labour costs of the Netherlands and some competitors, 1970–89

The economic agenda for the nineties is somewhat different from the last decade, as a centrist–left-wing coalition took over at the end of 1989. The social-democrats, the PvdA, had a program of 'investing in the future', by which it meant to restore government investment as well as recovering human capital lost through long-term unemployment. Still, the new coalition faces severe budget constraints, the government accounting system does not distinguish consumption and investment spending. Furthermore, fears of crowding out private investment by government borrowing are not yet gone. One of the issues we discuss in our contribution is to see if these fears are warranted, given the opening of international capital markets. We will conclude that it is very hard to make a strong case for the imposition of such a self-imposed external constraint.

Another item high on the policy agenda is further monetary and economic integration. To see whether monetary integration imposes an external constraint, we evaluate the policy of the recent past, of tying the guilder to the Deutschmark. Furthermore, we discuss how economic integration may lead to international tax wars, not unlike the devaluation wars that characterized the 1930s.

3   Short-sightedness in the budgetary policies of Dutch governments

3.1   Financial constraints in the Netherlands

During the last twelve years public sector deficits have led to a steady rise in government debt and in debt service, as Figure 8.3 shows. After the fall of the Christian Democrat–Labour coalition in 1977, government finances started to deteriorate. The second oil crisis did not help to improve government finances. Basically, increasing gas profits did not outweigh the decline in tax revenues. Also remarkable is that the first Lubbers government apparently was more successful in turning the tide than the second one; from 1983 to 1986 the deficit decreased but afterwards the government seemed to lose grip on its expenditures. Some further details on government finance can be summarized as follows:

the public sector financial deficit fluctuated around 3% of NNI until 1978, from this year onward the deficit rose steadily to 9.4% in 1983. In 1988 the deficit still is twice as much as the average for the early seventies. The public sector borrowing requirement includes repayment of debt and has increased even more dramatically: from 1.6% of NNI in 1970 to 11.1% in 1987 and 10.5% in 1988.

As a result, government debt increased from a steady 40% during 1973–7, to nearly 80% of NNI in 1987 (the most recent available figure).

Interest payments on government debt therefore rose from roughly 2% to

Table 8.1. *Alternative scenarios for the Netherlands government debt, 1988–2005*
(as a percent of GNP)

	1988	1990	1991	1992	1993	1994	1995	2005
Financial deficit $\pi + n = 4.5\%$								
(i) $5\frac{1}{4}\%$ from 1994	69.1	73.7	75.4	77.0	78.5	80.0	81.4	92.5
(ii) $3\frac{1}{4}\%$ from 1994	69.1	73.7	74.9	75.5	75.6	75.2	74.8	71.8
(iii) $2\frac{1}{4}\%$ from 1994	69.1	73.7	74.6	74.8	74.2	72.8	71.5	61.4
Financial deficit $\pi + n = 2.5\%$								
(i) $5\frac{1}{4}\%$ from 1990	69.1	75.1	78.1	81.0	83.9	86.7	89.4	113.4
(ii) $3\frac{1}{4}\%$ from 1994	69.1	75.1	77.6	79.5	81.0	81.8	82.7	90.2
(iii) $2\frac{1}{4}\%$ from 1994	69.1	75.1	77.3	78.8	79.5	79.4	79.3	78.5

Source: Studiegroep Begrotingsruimte (1989).

about 7% of NNI. For comparison, this amounts to 60% of the government wage bill, and there is a serious threat that other expenditures will be crowded out as a result of debt servicing.

It is therefore no surprise that a consensus has emerged in the Netherlands to stabilize the government debt as a percentage of national income, so that the fall in debt service allows more room for productive government expenditures. But the way in which this has been implemented has, in our view, not been thought through very well. First we will take a look at the proposals made by the Studiegroep Begrotingsruimte. According to the 1986 Government Agreement the financial deficit should drop to $5\frac{1}{4}\%$ by 1990. Afterwards, three possibilities can be considered: (i) no further reduction in the financial deficits, (ii) further gradual cuts towards $3\frac{1}{4}\%$ by 1994, (iii) further gradual cuts towards $2\frac{1}{4}\%$ by 1994. Roughly speaking, these three alternatives correspond to a PvdA, CDA, and VVD view, respectively. A real growth rate (n) of 2.5% and an inflation rate (π) of 2% are assumed. Table 8.1 then shows that a reduction in the financial deficit of 0.5%–0.75% points per year is a necessary requirement for the ratio of government debt to national income to start falling during the period 1990–4. However, if there is no inflation and nominal interest rates remain the same, the rise in the government debt ratio will not be reversed unless the financial deficit is eventually cut to $2\frac{1}{4}\%$. The Studiegroep Begrotingsruimte (1989) therefore makes a strong plea for the financial deficit to drop to 2%–3% of the national income. It also argues for forcing these cuts in financial deficits through something similar to the Gramm-Rudman-Hollings law for the US.

One can make a number of critical remarks about these proposals. To put them in perspective, consider a simple version of the government budget constraint

$$\dot{d} \equiv f - (\pi + n)d, \quad f \equiv g - \tau + id - z_I \tag{1}$$

where d and f denote government debt and the financial deficit, g and τ denote government expenditures (excluding debt service) and taxation, i denotes the nominal interest rate on government debt, z_I denotes the return on government investment, π denotes inflation, and n denotes the real growth rate. The first criticism of the proposals to reduce f is very basic: there is no theoretical consensus on how important deficits really are. Romer (1988) investigates the costs of excessive deficits for the USA, and lists some views on the possible effects of government deficits. On the one extreme is the supply-side and Reaganomics view, according to which deficits resulting from reducing marginal tax rates are highly desirable as they reduce distortions and will probably pay themselves back in the long run thanks to higher incentives for economic growth. Then there is the Ricardian view, according to which deficits are rather unimportant. Rational agents anticipate higher future taxation resulting from an increase in current deficits and there will therefore be no net effect on total spending, because the decline in human wealth exactly offsets the increase in non-human wealth. The reason is that the present value of future taxes is exactly equal to the rise in current taxes that would have been necessary if the government had not let its deficit rise today, so that the size of the deficit does not distort the behaviour of private sector agents. Alternatively, agents save more in order to meet future tax claims. Incidentally, the Ricardian view does not tell us anything about the size of the government sector, only about indifference between tax and debt finance. Finally, there is the view that excessive deficits are distortionary, as a current deficit places a burden of taxation on future generations which seems 'immoral'. This argument (among others defended by Buchanan) is rather hard to understand, unless the deficits are primarily used for current consumption and thus crowd out investment in human or physical capital. What seems to be most important is the effect of government spending on economic growth, an issue that remains somewhat neglected in the discussion about optimal government deficits. Study of this issue can also appraise the possibly beneficial effect of running counter-cyclical deficits on long-term economic prospects and growth.

These points lead to the second problem of the proposal of the Studiegroep Begrotingsruimte. That is, the analysis fails to take account of the intertemporal aspects of the government budget constraint (e.g., Buiter,

1985). The returns on assets have to be taken care of. Solvency of the government finances and (1) yields

$$
d(t) + \int_t^\infty [g_c(s) + g_I(s)] \exp\left[\int_t^s -r(s')\,ds'\right] ds
$$

$$
= k_G(t) + \int_t^\infty [\tau(s) + z_I(s)] \exp\left[\int_t^s r(s')\,ds'\right] ds \tag{2}
$$

where $r \equiv i_d - \pi - n$ denotes the growth-corrected real interest rate, g_c denotes government consumption, g_I denotes government investment, z_I denotes the return on government investment and k_G denotes the public stock of capital. The point is that, as far as government investment has the same return as the market rate of interest, it can be netted out of the intertemporal government budget constraint (2). The recommended reduction of the financial deficit to $2\frac{1}{4}\%$ (Studiegroep Begrotingsruimte, 1989) does not take full account of this point; it makes a lot of difference whether the cut in the deficit is achieved through cuts in government consumption, through cuts in government investment or through tax increases. In practice, the cut in the Dutch financial deficit has been accompanied by cuts in government investment, which seems a rather short-sighted policy. It is a pity that since 1977 Dutch government accounting has not made a clear distinction between government consumption and government investment. The political reasons are that ministers will try to claim that all their expenditures are investments, so that budgetary control may become more difficult. However, in practice government investment has fallen dramatically since 1977 (see Table 8.2). Many economists in the Netherlands now advocate the 'golden rule of government finance', which says that firstly the government is allowed to borrow for investment purposes only to the extent that they bear the market rate of return and secondly that the amount of tax levied should be high enough to finance government consumption and the interest payments on the initial government debt $(g_c(s) + i(s)\,d(s) = \tau(s), \; s \geq t)$. The desired or sustainable financial deficit is thus $id + g_I - z_I$. Table 8.3 provides some information on government interest payments, capital income and government investment. Since an important part of the proposed new government expenditures in the Netherlands is investment, witness the National Environment Plan, it is of the utmost importance that investigations into the intertemporal features of the government budget constraint are initiated. Ideally, one would like to calculate an estimate of the permanent deficit for the Netherlands (Buiter, 1985). This is the real perpetuity equivalent of the discrepancy in the government's *ex-ante* comprehensive balance sheet, i.e., the annuity value of the present

Table 8.2. *Investment in the Netherlands, 1970–90*
(*% GNP*)

	1970	1975	1980	1975	1988	1989	1990
Private investment	23.1	16.7	18.3	17.1	18.7	19.2	19.2
Government invetment	4.7	3.9	3.3	2.6	2.3	2.3	2.3

Source: Central Planning Bureau, CEP 1989 and 1990 (Table B.1).

value of spending plans minus the net worth of the public sector, where net worth equals public sector assets minus public sector debt plus the present values of taxes and seigniorage and public sector capital formation. Privatization of public assets, such as the Dutch State Mines, or privatization of student loans does not affect net worth if the revenues of the sale ($-\Delta k(t)$) exactly match the discounted value of the future incomes associated with these assets ($-\int_t^\infty \Delta z_t(s) \exp[-\int_t^s r(s')ds']ds$). The Ministry of Education provides a very sad example of how to reduce the financial deficit in the wrong way. Education has been successful, since more people have participated in education in recent years. The total budget has been the same, so the sum available per student has gone down. This seems short-sighted, because education can be seen as an

Table 8.3. *Government interest payments, capital income, and investment in the Netherlands, 1977–87*
(*billion guilders*)

	NNP	Government interest payments	Government capital income	Government investment
1977	251.2	8.4	10.9	9.3
1978	269.7	9.3	10.9	9.6
1979	285.9	10.3	12.8	9.8
1980	303.6	12.5	15.9	11.0
1981	316.3	15.7	21.1	11.1
1982	330.6	19.0	22.0	10.6
1983	342.4	21.7	23.6	10.2
1984	358.6	23.9	25.8	11.2
1985	376.0	26.1	29.0	10.9
1986	385.4	26.6	22.7	10.2
1987	386.5	26.4	15.7	10.0

Source: Columns 3 and 4: *CBS, National Accounts* 1983, Table 12, 1987, Table R.5. Column 5: CBP, CEP 1989, B.1.

investment in human capital which to a large extent repays itself. Even more serious has been the 40% discounts given when student loans from the past are immediately repaid. The idea is to help cut the financial deficit, but it completely ignores that a future Minister of Education no longer receives repayments. Such short-sighted measures fail to distinguish between cash-flow and assets and illustrate the lack of financial discipline that began to prevail under the second Lubbers administration.

Thirdly, it seems odd that the desired financial deficit is independent of the achieved inflation rate. Given that the De Nederlandsche Bank maintains a fixed parity of the guilder versus the Deutschmark, an increase in inflation in Germany will eventually lead to higher inflation in the Netherlands. For example, if inflation rises to 4.5%, then equation (3) shows that a financial deficit of 5.6% is warranted when one wants to stabilize the ratio of government debt to national income at, say, 0.8. Hence, it seems more sensible to advocate guidelines for the inflation-corrected financial deficit, $\bar{f} \equiv f - \pi d$, of, say, $\bar{f} = nd = 2\%$. If one substitutes f in (1), one obtains

$$\dot{d} = (i - \pi - n)d + g_c + g_I - \tau - z_I \tag{3}$$

From this it is clear that the impact of inflation on the debt ratio is zero as long as the real interest rate, $i - \pi$, and the ratios of government spending and taxes do not change with inflation. However, there is a negative correlation between the real interest rate and inflation, particularly on a world scale (the Mundell effect) and thus higher inflation may, for a given debt–GDP ratio, sustain a higher ratio of the primary deficit to national income, $g_c + g_I$. In addition, higher inflation may make it easier to cut the ratio of government spending to national income. Government debt is not indexed in the Netherlands. An unexpectedly low inflation therefore leads to excessive gains for capital owners. The current low rate of inflation leads to redistribution from tax payers to owners of government debt. These owners coincide partly with the common taxpayer (pension funds own large sums of government debt), but the extra gain for wealthy persons may be substantial.

Finally, it is true that the Netherlands have experienced a larger explosion in government debt than most other OECD countries (see Table 8.4). Only Belgium, Italy, and Ireland now have a greater debt–GDP ratio than the Netherlands. However, the debt–GDP ratio in most other countries is under-estimated because no provision is made for future pensions to be paid by the government. For the Netherlands the government pension fund, ABP, has assets of 145 billion guilders (and a future actuarial liability of the same amount), which would reduce the debt–GDP ratio by almost 40 percentage points. When one takes account of this difference,

Table 8.4. *International comparison of government debt, 1980–90*

	Gross debt (% of GDP)			Net debt (% of GDP)		
	1980	1986	1990	1980	1986	1990
Belgium	77	122	127	69	114	119
Italy	59	88	100	54	86	98
Netherlands	46	74	90	25	48	64
Canada	45	67	71	12	34	38
Japan	52	69	65	17	27	23
US	38	51	50	20	30	29
Sweden	45	68	50	− 14	16	− 2
Spain	19	48	49	8	30	31
Denmark	34	59	49	7	28	17
France	37	46	48	14	25	28
West Germany	33	42	45	14	22	25
UK	55	53	39	48	46	32
Norway	56	38	34	7	− 16	− 20
Total	42	56	55	22	33	33

Source: OECD, *Economic Outlook*, December 1988.

the debt–GDP ratio for the Netherlands does not seem so high compared with the other OECD countries.

Apart from the question what the optimal size of government debt would be, there remains the question what caused the recent increase in government debt. In an international comparison, Roubini and Sachs (1989) analyse this question. One of their conclusions is that difficulties of political management in coalition governments account for some of the growth of government debt ratios. Lack of consensus on economic policy may have accounted for the increase in the debt ratio in the late seventies and early eighties. Indeed, the first Van Agt-coalition (VVD and CDA) and the short-lived second one (CDA and PvdA) lacked consensus on financial policies. These governments also experienced the highest increase in government debt. Only the first Lubbers administration was strongly directed to reducing the deficit. The second Lubbers coalition suffered from the loss of the VVD at the elections, perhaps this loss of popularity induced VVD ministers to support some popular expenditures thus leaving the task of improving government finance to the CDA Minister of Finance, Mr Ruding. Despite popular belief he lost his grip on government finance. The last years of the CDA–VVD coalition witness a remarkable lack of financial discipline, which can also be seen from the fact that government spending is now already 9 billion guilders (2% of

NNI!) higher than planned in the Budget of September 1988 (Sterks *et al.*, 1989; see also the resulting discussion between them and Ruding in *Economische Statistische Berichten*).

We conclude that cuts in the financial deficit are desirable, but that in practice the cutbacks have worsened the mix of government spending at the expense of public investment in infrastructure, the environment, and education. The worsening of the mix already occurred before 1977, when the revenues from Dutch gas exploration were mainly used for consumption purposes. The 'government budget constraint' has never been a real constraint in the sense of being binding. Solvency is not a problem for the Dutch government; crowding out (of productive and other useful expenditure by interest payments) is. Sound government finance is a necessary condition for being able to implement environmental policies, labour market programs for reducing (long-term) unemployment, and so on.

The second link between government finance and the labour market goes via taxation. From 1 January 1990 a simplification of the Dutch tax system ('Plan Oort') will come into force. The main ideas are to reduce the bureaucracy of filling in tax forms, to reduce the number of tax brackets from nine to four, to combine the national insurance contributions rate with the first tax bracket at a rate of 35% and a top bracket of 60%, and to abolish a number of tax-deductable expenses. In addition, the plan is to implement tax cuts of the order of 4.1 billion guilders or almost 10% of the total tax bill, but this may be less when the Labour party gains a new coalition government and in any case a substantial part of it is meant to be financed by cutting tax-deductable expenses.

Table 8.5 shows that the wedge between producers' and consumers' wage is the highest in the OECD and this explains why Dutch governments have been very keen to reduce it. Due to the enormous scope for tax-deductable expenses, the average tax rate in the Netherlands is low compared with the rest of Europe (but higher than for the US and Japan). Marginal tax rates, however, are very high in the Netherlands and the proposed reform of the system will remove a large number of tax distortions. The problem is that due to the very generous pension system the premiums are extremely high compared with abroad, but then these lead to tangible benefits for those who pay for it.

Table 8.5 shows that both the marginal and the average wedge have risen since the sixties. The marginal wedge for a married employee with two children was about 73% when in Germany and the OECD it was only about 56%. However, the average tax wedge (excluding social premium) was only 37.5% in the Netherlands, compared with 39% for the OECD.

Table 8.5. *An international comparison of taxes and contributions on labour income (%)*

	Taxes and social premiums (% of GDP)		Average tax rate 1983	Total marginal tax wedge* 1983	Top income tax rate	
	1965	1983			Actual	Proposed
Sweden	36	50	61.7	73	75	60
Netherlands	34	47	37.5	73.5	72	60
Norway	33	47	50.4	63	56	
Belgium	31	45	48.1	61.7	72	55
France	35	45	47.6	59.7	56.8	
UK	31	38	39	54.5	40	
Germany	32	37	36.6	57	56	53
US	26	30	28.2	42.6	28	
Japan	18	28	19.1	39.9	88	66
Total OECD	27	37	39	55.8		

Note: * Married worker with two children, including indirect taxes and employers' contributions.
Source: OECD Economic Studies, Nos. 7 and 8.

3.2 Ten rules for sound government finance

Dutch governments have traditionally given up an independent monetary policy, because the guilder is firmly tied to the Deutschmark. In practice, this means that Dutch inflation (π) tracks German inflation (π^*) very closely. The disadvantages of tying one's hands to the policies conducted by the Bundesbank are that the Netherlands cannot use monetary policy for macroeconomic stabilization and cannot use inflation taxes as a source of government revenue. The advantages are that the Netherlands ties its hands to the Bundesbank, so that it never uses an unanticipated inflation tax to accommodate demands for higher wages or to erode the real value of nominal government debt. The result is that in equilibrium inflation is lower than it would otherwise be. Recently, some commentators have been sceptical about the independence of the Bundesbank and thus some have argued that the Netherlands should not follow increases in interest rates at all times.

Tax smoothing follows from minimizing the costs of tax collection subject to the present-value budget constraint

$$\underset{\tau(s)}{\text{Min}} \int_t^\infty \tau(s)^2 \exp\left[-\int_t^s r(s')\,ds' \right] ds \qquad (4)$$

subject to (2) and (3) (cf. Barro, 1979). If government investment bears a market rate of return, one has

$$\tau = r[d - k_G] + g_c^P \tag{5}$$

$$\dot{d} = (g_c - g_c^P) + g_I - z_I + rk_G \tag{6}$$

$$f = (g_c - g_c^P) + g_I - z_I + rk_G + (\pi + n)d \tag{7}$$

where the permanent level of government spending is defined as

$$g_c^P(t) = r(t) \int_t^\infty g_c^P(s) \exp\left[- \int_t^s r(s')\,ds' \right] ds \tag{8}$$

On the basis of the above equations, one can formulate ten rules of thumb for sound government finance:

(1) The amount of government debt is only of historical interest. The interest burden on existing debt does not crowd out other public expenditure, as a high ratio of debt to GDP implies a high tax rate and a high deficit.
(2) If policy-makers choose to continue the current level of primary expenditures (total expenditure minus interest and repayments of principal), and if they do not want to make new investments, then it is optimal to stick with the current debt–GDP ratio ($\dot{d} = 0$). The deficit will be equal to the inflation-cum-growth-tax on existing debt ($f = (\pi + n)d$).
(3) Applying the theory leads to the result that a permanent decrease of primary expenditures lead to an immediate decrease of the tax rate without any effect on the deficit or debt–GDP ratio. This means a balanced decline of the public sector.
(4) If expenditures are temporarily above normal (for example resulting from unemployment due to a decrease in world trade), then it will be optimal to leave the tax rate unaltered, running a higher than normal deficit, increasing the debt rate ($s > 0$). This is not the result of counter-cyclical Keynesian policy, although it is similar to it, but follows from a tax smoothing policy. From this point of view, the rising debt–GDP ratio around 1980 might have been a sensible policy.
(5) If, however, changes turn out to be permanent (for example, due to the alienation of the long-term unemployed), then taxes must immediately rise, whilst the growth in the debt–GDP ratio must immediately be stopped ($\dot{d} = 0$). This pessimism seems to underlie the recent recommendations of the IMF to increase taxes in the Netherlands.

(6)   If policy-makers choose to increase permanent spending in the future, they will retire debt now, in order to create financial room for later years. This may lead to political business cycles (see, e.g., Persson and Svensson, 1989).

(7)   Investment carrying a market rate of return can be netted out of the government budget constraint. There is no reason why a government should restrict investment expenditures in bad times, as happened in the Netherlands (see Table 8.2). In fact, the political economy of budget cuts is such that it is easier to cut government investment than to cut government current transfers.

(8)   If policy-makers want to reduce primary expenditure, g, by $100x\%$ per year, then one can show that the permanent level of g, g^P, lies below the actual level: $g^P = g[(r - n)/(r - n + x)] < g$. Hence, optimal policy is to slow down the decrease in tax rates and to run above-normal deficits.

(9)   If real interest rates are temporarily high (which seems to be the current situation), than it will be optimal to finance the extra costs by debt creation.

(10) From a pure financial point of view, it does not make sense to sell government assets in order to improve government finances.

3.3   The political economy of budget cuts

The main feature of Dutch government finance has been that tax smoothing policies have not been used. The main result is that in the process of making the government's finances healthy, it has been easier for politicians to cut investment than to cut transfers or government consumption. The result is that the formation of productive government assets has not kept up with the explosion of government debt, so that the net worth of the public sector has declined since 1982, the year in which the process of budget cutting under CDA-leadership was meant to start (see Figure 8.3).

In other words, the financial policy of the Dutch government has been characterized by an extreme degree of short-sightedness. One of the reasons is, of course, that politicians are motivated by short-term re-election considerations and thus prefer to spend rather than to invest. The minister of finance, Mr Ruding followed by Mr Kok, is faced with a large group of spending ministers and has not got enough power to force a healthy, far-sighted financial policy. This is why some people in the Netherlands now argue for a nucleus-cabinet consisting of the prime minister and the minister of finance, who can force such a number of spending ministers to take a longer-run view. Such a reorganization of ministers and departments can, of course, only happen at the time a new coalition government is being formed.

An alternative proposal is to distinguish sharply between the current account and the capital account in the government budget and to adopt a 'golden' rule of government finance: tax for permanent streams of government spending and borrowing for temporary increases in government spending such as productive investment projects. The problem is that all kinds of definitional problems will arise, because each spending ministry will claim its expenditures as a productive investment. Some investments are unproductive (missiles, road in Drente), whilst some consumption can be productive (education). The point is that it seems best to overcome short-run political restrictions and implement the rules of Section 3.2. This requires *either* a nucleus-cabinet *or* an independent accounting body which checks whether projects have a market rate of return and thus warrant government borrowing.

4   Monetary discipline and the advantages of a firm EMS anchor

4.1   Monetary policy in the Netherlands

The latest annual report of De Nederlandsche Bank expresses satisfaction that the Delors Committee argues for a European System of central banks and eventually economic and monetary union that differs very little from the institutional structure of the Dutch central bank. On the whole all the main Dutch political parties are strongly in favour of increasing the progress towards monetary unification in Europe and of establishing a European Central Bank that is independent of the fiscal authorities. De Nederlandsche Bank and the Bundesbank enjoy, in contrast to the Bank of England and the Banca d'Italia, autonomy in the sense that they conduct a policy quite independent of the fiscal authorites. In other words, De Nederlandsche Bank will never allow finance of the public sector deficit by printing money and, indeed, seigniorage revenues in the Netherlands have been either negligible or non-existent. This is in sharp contrast to the countries of southern Europe. For example, central bank loans to the Treasury as a percentage of total debt are in 1987 14.6%, 7.2%, 7.2%, and 32.8% for Greece, Spain, Italy, and Portugal, respectively, and non-existent for the Netherlands and Germany (Giavazzi and Pagano, 1989).

This is reflected in the fact that the main goal of De Nederlandsche Bank is laid down by constitutional law to be a stable price level and thus zero inflation. Table 8.6 shows that from this narrow perspective De Nederlandsche Bank has scored extremely well. Inflation has been less than 1%

Table 8.6. *Annual inflation rates in the consumers' price index, 1983–8 (%)*

	1983	1984	1985	1986	1987	1988
Belgium	7.7	6.3	4.9	1.3	1.6	1.9
Denmark	6.9	6.3	4.7	3.6	4.0	4.5
Germany	3.3	2.4	2.2	− 0.2	0.2	1.6
Greece	20.2	18.4	19.3	23.0	16.4	14.0
Spain	12.2	11.2	7.8	8.8	5.3	5.9
France	9.6	7.3	5.9	2.7	3.1	3.1
Ireland	10.4	8.6	5.4	3.8	3.1	2.7
Italy	14.7	10.8	9.2	5.8	4.8	5.4
Luxembourg	8.7	6.5	4.1	0.3	− 0.1	1.9
Netherlands	2.7	3.2	2.3	0.3	− 0.2	1.0
Portugal	25.1	28.9	19.6	11.8	9.3	11.7
United Kingdom	4.6	5.0	6.1	3.4	4.1	6.8
Europe (12)	8.6	7.4	6.1	3.6	2.9	4.4
US	3.2	4.3	3.6	1.9	3.7	4.4
Japan	1.8	2.4	2.0	0.7	0.0	0.9

Source: European Economy, January and February 1989.

and even lower than in Germany. Together with Japan, the Netherlands has the lowest inflation rate in the OECD. De Nederlandsche Bank is very much concerned about higher inflation because prices of non-energy raw materials rose by more than 20%, strikes and other labour disputes are on the increase, capacity limits are being reached, and productivity growth is levelling out. However, one can seriously ask whether a policy of near-zero inflation is not a mixed blessing. It may be that some inflation, as long as it does not get out of hand, may be desirable as this may lead to less unemployment (as an incomes policy may be easier to conduct) and as the stabilization of the debt-GDP ratio may be easier due to erosion of the real value of nominal government debt, bracket creep in a progressive tax system, and incomplete indexation of benefits and salaries of civil servants (also see Section 3). Dornbusch (1989) discusses the unpleasant side effects of the cut in inflation achieved in Ireland and some of these may also be relevant for the Netherlands. It is clear that to a certain extent the optimal rate of inflation is a political choice and may be different from zero. In any case, due to the emerging dangers of inflation (witness the rise of bank credit by 14% in 1988 and the rise of M2 in 1988, see Table 8.7), De Nederlandsche Bank has raised interest rates and has even imposed a new (more subtle) version of the old instrument of quantitative limits on bank lending. This may be a bit over-cautious, because Dutch consumers

Table 8.7. *Annual growth rates in money stocks, 1983–8 (%)*

	1983	1984	1985	1986	1987	1988
Belgium (M2)	8.7	5.9	7.6	11.5	10.5	8.1
Denmark (M2)	25.5	17.8	15.8	8.4	4.4	1.9
Germany (M3)	5.3	4.7	5.1	6.8	6.0	6.8
Greece (M3)	20.3	29.4	26.8	19.0	24.8	24.6
Spain (ALP)	15.9	13.2	12.8	11.4	14.0	10.9
France (M2)	13.7	9.8	6.0	4.1	4.3	4.2
Ireland (M3)	5.6	10.1	5.3	− 1.0	10.9	4.6
Italy (M2)	13.3	12.1	10.8	9.4	8.3	8.4
Netherlands (M2)	10.7	6.8	10.5	4.5	3.9	10.7
Portugal (L)	16.8	24.6	28.9	25.9	16.8	15.0
United Kingdom (LM3)	11.1	10.1	13.4	19.1	22.9	20.3
Europe (12) (m)	11.4	9.8	9.6	9.7	10.1	9.8
US (M2)	11.7	8.2	8.1	9.1	3.4	5.6
Japan (M2)	7.3	7.8	8.7	9.2	10.8	10.4

Source: European Economy, January and February 1989.

have on average a personal debt for consumption purposes of 1,700 guilders whilst German and US consumers have a personal debt of 4,000 and 6,000 guilders, respectively. Lack of credit availability for consumption and investment purposes may slow down the expected increase in economic growth. Given the fact that capacity in the Netherlands is lower than needed for full employment, it is rather odd that investment should be slowed down in this way. Credit constraints are unwarranted. A somewhat higher rate of inflation is the least important economic problem that the Netherlands currently has to fear, and anyway the higher German inflation will gradually be followed by higher Dutch inflation unless De Nederlandsche Bank is willing to appreciate the guilder *vis-à-vis* the Deutschmark.

This, however, conflicts with the secondary goal of De Nederlandsche Bank, which is to maintain a stable exchange rate between the guilder and the Deutschmark (see Figure 8.5). This is why in practice, the monetary policy of De Nederlandsche Bank has followed very much the policy of the Bundesbank and therefore cannot be conducted in an independent fashion. The main reason is that the Dutch economy has liberalization of capital markets, so that interest-rate differentials in favour of Germany would lead to a flight of capital out of the Netherlands and this would lead to downward pressure on the guilder and thus eventually violate the exchange-rate target. Italy and France have traditionally had capital controls and have thus been able to conduct a somewhat more independent monetary policy. However, since 1st July 1990 their capital markets have been fully liberalized, and from then on one would expect a convergence of offshore and onshore interest rates. Obviously, this asymmetry or German hegemony in the EMS means that Dutch monetary policy and, eventually, inflation are determined by the Bundesbank. The payments imbalances in Europe (deficits in Italy, Spain, and now France, and surpluses in the Netherlands and Germany) cause tensions in EMS parities, hence some argue that a convergence of budgetary policies is necessary for stable intra-European exchange rates. If headway is made on the proposals for economic and monetary union made by the Delors Committee, then exchange rates will be fixed and binding restrictions on national budget deficits will hold. Hence, regional imbalances in Europe will persist for longer as neither the exchange rate nor the budget deficit can be used for stabilization purposes. It follows that Brussels will have a greater role to play in alleviating regional imbalances, so that one of the prices one pays for monetary unification is greater intervention on an EEC level. Given these interactions between monetary and fiscal policies for Europe in the future, many Dutch politicians are concerned about delegating responsibility for these matters to a European System of central banks when the European Parliament and thus democracy still has relatively little to say in these matters.

We already mentioned in short the policy of De Nederlandsche Bank to stabilize credit. In our view such a policy is out of place in the current situation. Stiglitz and Weiss (1988) study the importance of credit. Even with an accommodating credit policy of the Dutch central bank there remain special problems in the Dutch economy that may make credit constraints binding in significant parts of the economy. Table 8.8 shows the development of consumer credit since 1980. In real terms, in 1988 credit was still 10% lower than eight years before.

4.2 Unanticipated inflation and nominal government debt

We now want to discuss why it is advantageous for the Netherlands to tie its hands so much to the policies of the Bundesbank. A change in German interest rates usually leads to a change in Dutch interest rates on the same day and consequently the guilder–Deutschmark rate is kept within very small bounds and Dutch inflation is very close to German inflation. The best way is to contrast three outcomes: (i) a dependent central bank which is not committed to the EMS and is forced to the discretion outcome (D); (ii) an independent central bank which is not a follower in the EMS and can benefit from rules (R); and (iii) an independent central bank firmly committed to the EMS (E). Case (i) corresponds to Britain, case (ii)

Table 8.8. *Consumer credit in the Netherlands, 1979–89*
(billion guilders)

	1979	1980	1981	1982	1983	1984	1985	1986	1987	1988	1989
Provided by banks	4.4	4.4	4.4	4.4	4.5	4.4	4.7	5.2	5.7	5.9	6.1
Other	7.6	8.1	7.9	7.4	7.0	6.6	6.5	6.8	7.4	7.7	8.5
Total	11.9	12.5	12.3	11.8	11.5	11.0	11.2	12.1	13.1	13.6	14.6
In real terms (1980 = 100)	101	100	93	84	80	75	74	80	87	90	96

Source: De Nederlandsche Bank *Annual Report* 1989, Table 2.3. Price index: CPB.

to Germany and case (iii) to the Netherlands. Ignoring investment, the government budget constraint can be written as

$$\dot{d} = (r + \pi^e - \pi)d + g_c - \tau - (\pi + n)m \tag{9}$$

where r denotes the *ex-ante* (growth-corrected) real interest rate (given by tastes and technologies) and m denotes the constant money–GDP ratio. Effectively, the quantity theory of money and the Fisher hypothesis have been assumed so that inflation is the excess of monetary over real growth and nominal interest rates go up and down together with expected inflation. The government solves the public-finance problem (cf. Mankiw, 1987)

$$\operatorname*{Min}_{\pi, \tau} \int_t^{\infty} [\tau(s)^2 + \beta \pi(s)^2] \exp \left[- \int_t^s r(s') ds' \right] ds \tag{10}$$

subject to (9). Hence, the government minimizes the dead-weight losses caused by conventional taxation and by inflation taxes but both are needed to finance a given stream of public goods.

Case (iii) was discussed in Section 3.2; $\pi_E = 0$ and $\tau_E = rd + g_c^P - nm$. Case (i) implies that the central bank is unable to manipulate the expectations of the private sector and thus must take π^e as given. In equilibrium expectations are not falsified, $\pi = \pi^e$. Discretion yields $\beta \pi_D = (m + d) \tau_D$ and $\dot{\tau}_D = 0$. Tax and seigniorage revenues are smoothed over time and go up and down together. Substitution into the present-value budget constraint gives

$$\tau_D = \left(\frac{\beta}{\beta + m(m + d)} \right) (g_c^P + rd - nm) < \tau_R < \tau_E \tag{11}$$

$$\pi_D = \left(\frac{m + d}{\beta + m(m + d)} \right) (g_c^P + rd - nm) > \pi_R > \pi_E = 0 \tag{12}$$

Under rules the central bank has sufficient reputation and can thus assume $\pi = \pi^e$ when it optimizes. Discretion leads to higher inflation and lower taxes than rules, because the private sector knows the central bank has an incentive to renege by levying a surprise inflation tax and wiping out the real value of debt service and thus assumes that the central bank will extract more seigniorage. Hence, rules yield higher welfare than discretion.

The crucial comparison is between outcomes (i) and (iii). The latter, i.e., tying the hands of De Nederlandsche Bank to the Bundesbank, yields higher welfare than the former, the case of a dependent central bank, if $(\beta - m^2)d > (\beta + m^2)m$ (Gros, 1988). One is more likely to be a committed member of the EMS when one has a high level of public debt (as then the incentive to impose a surprise inflation tax is large) and when the priority one attaches to fighting inflation relative to the costs of tax collection is high. Both of these conditions are satisfied for the Netherlands, hence it is no surprise that the Dutch are such loyal members of the EMS. Even though the monetary discipline argument has been made with reference to the real value of nominal government debt, it could have been made just as easily for the real value of nominal wage contracts (Giavazzi and Pagano, 1988). The story can also be extended to analyse the case for an independent EuroFed (van der Ploeg, 1990).

5   Investment, government deficits, and the current account

5.1   Saving and consumption

Table 8.9 shows the relative performance of the Dutch economy as far as real growth is concerned. Average growth during the period 1982–8 was 1.7% (excluding energy revenues about 0.2% higher), but throughout the OECD it was 3% and throughout the European countries of the OECD growth it was 2.3%. It is thus considerably worse than the average performance for Europe and for the OECD and comparable with the modest performance of Germany. More recently, Dutch growth has been

Table 8.9. *Growth of real GNP/GDP in the OECD, 1981–9 (%)*

	1981	1982	1983	1984	1985	1986	1987	1988	1989
US	1.9	− 2.5	3.6	6.8	3.4	2.7	3.7	4.4	3.0
Japan	3.7	3.1	3.2	5.1	4.9	2.6	4.6	5.7	4.9
Germany	0.0	− 1.0	1.9	3.3	1.9	2.3	1.7	3.6	4.0
France	1.2	2.5	0.7	1.3	1.7	2.3	2.4	3.8	3.7
UK	− 1.2	1.8	3.7	2.2	3.5	3.6	4.7	4.5	2.3
Italy	1.1	0.2	1.1	3.2	2.9	2.5	3.0	4.2	3.2
Canada	3.7	− 3.2	3.2	6.3	4.6	3.1	4.5	5.0	2.9
Belgium	− 1.4	1.5	0.2	2.2	0.9	1.8	2.0	4.3	4.2
Denmark	− 0.9	3.0	2.5	4.4	4.2	3.6	− 0.6	− 0.2	1.1
Ireland	2.6	− 0.7	− 1.6	2.0	− 0.1	− 1.1	5.6	1.2	4.0
Luxembourg	− 0.2	1.5	3.0	6.5	3.8	4.4	2.8	4.3	3.5
Netherlands	− 0.7	− 1.4	1.4	3.2	2.4	2.7	1.1	3.0	4.3
Total OECD	1.6	− 0.4	2.7	4.9	3.4	2.7	3.5	4.4	3.6
OECD Europe	0.2	0.8	1.8	2.6	2.6	2.7	2.8	3.8	3.5

Source: OECD, *Economic Outlook*, December 1988 and June 1989.

Table 8.10. *Savings in the Netherlands, 1979–90*
(% of net national income at market prices)

	1981	1982	1983	1984	1985	1986	1987	1988	1989	1990***
Private sector	12.0	14.7	14.6	15.7	15.1	14.9	13.4	15.2	17.3	17.6
Public sector*	− 0.4	− 2.7	− 2.2	− 1.2	0.2	− 1.3	− 1.7	− 1.0	− 1.5	− 1.8
Current account	2.5	3.5	3.5	4.6	4.6	3.0	1.6	3.0	3.5	3.5
Capital account**	− 1.3	− 2.2	− 2.4	− 2.4	− 3.0	− 5.4	− 0.9	− 0.5	3.0	—

Source: Centraal Economisch Plan, 1989 and 1990.
Notes: * Including social insurance institutions.
        ** Private and public sector.
        *** Preliminary figures.

Table 8.11. *Current balances of OECD countries, 1985–9*
(% of GDP/GNP)

	1985	1986	1987	1988	1989
United States	− 3.0	− 3.6	− 3.5	− 2.6	− 2.0
Japan	3.7	4.4	3.6	2.8	2.0
Germany	2.6	4.4	4.0	4.0	4.4
France	− 0.1	0.3	− 0.5	− 0.4	− 0.4
United Kingdom	0.9	0	− 0.9	− 3.2	− 4.1
Italy	− 0.9	0.4	− 0.2	− 0.7	− 1.3
Belgium–Luxembourg	0.8	2.7	1.9	2.3	2.4
Denmark	− 4.6	− 5.5	− 2.9	− 1.6	− 1.3
Greece	− 9.8	− 4.3	− 2.6	− 1.8	− 4.8
Netherlands	4.1	2.6	1.4	2.4	3.1
Spain	1.7	1.7	0	− 1.1	− 2.9

Source: OECD Economic Outlook, June 1990.

picking up. Tables 8.10 and 11 show that this has been associated with relatively large current account surpluses for the Netherlands. The main reason is that savings of the private sector have risen from about 12% in 1981 to 18% in 1990 and this has more than off-set the borrowing of the public sector. Viewed in this light, the public sector deficits do not look too bad. A consequence of this has been very low growth in real private consumption; less than 1% per annum during the period 1980–9. The growth in real income during this period of 1.3% per year has been mainly achieved through a growth in real exports of 3.5%, but despite a decline in government investment of 3.5% per year during this period. This has been due to the disproportionate burden of government cuts on investment and due to a substantial improvement in the competitive position of the Dutch economy.

The contrast between the Dutch and the British economies in recent years is striking (see van der Ploeg, 1989). The UK has experienced a consumption-led boom leading to more than 4% growth recently, whereas the Netherlands has had very modest growth originating almost entirely from the substantial increase in exports arising from the recent recovery in world trade (see Table 8.12). Inflation in the Netherlands is very low, whereas in the UK inflation is now surging to above 8%. Private savings (including pension funds) in the UK are much lower than in the Netherlands, whereas the UK is now paying off government debt and the Netherlands still has substantial public sector deficits. Hence, the UK has substantial current account deficits and the Netherlands has substantial current account surpluses. It follows that there is considerable room for

Table 8.12. *Growth in the volume of world trade, 1977–90 (%)*

1977–9	1980	1981	1982	1983	1984	1985	1986	1987	1988	1989	1990
5–6	2.0	0.3	− 2.3	1.8	8.3	3.1	4.1	6.2	9.0	6.7	6.0

Source: Central Planning Bureau, CEP 1990.

demand expansion in the Netherlands, whereas the UK is a prime example of over-heating. The mirror image of the above picture is that the Netherlands invests a lot abroad, but this does not generate jobs at home.

5.2 Smoothing of private consumption

Let us now consider an economy, which attempts to use the current account to smooth consumption

$$\operatorname*{Min}_{c,j} \int_t^\infty [\bar{c} - c(s)^2] \exp\left[- \int_t^s r(s')\,ds' \right] ds \qquad (13)$$

subject to the present-value constraint for the nation as a whole

$$g_c^P + c^P + j^P \le y^P + ra \qquad (14)$$

the intensive-form production function, $y = f(k)$, and the capital accumulation equation

$$\dot{k} = j - (\delta + n)k, \qquad (15)$$

where $c, \bar{c}, a, j, y$, and k denote the actual and the desired value for private consumption, net foreign assets, private investment, national income, and the capital stock (all as percentages of GDP), respectively, and δ denotes the depreciation rate. Equation (14) requires solvency of the nation and follows from integration of the identity that the current account corresponds to the increase in wealth of the nation.

The result is that private consumption is smoothed over time, $\dot{c} = 0$, that the marginal product of capital equals the user cost of capital, $f'(k) = r + \delta + n$, and that the current account is in surplus when actual income exceeds permanent income or when the actual level of government spending is less than the permanent level, $ca = y - y^P + g_c^P - g_c - j$. When taxes are also smoothed over time (see Section 3.2), one obtained (Roubini, 1988)

$$ca = - def + (y - y^P)(1 - \tau) - j \qquad (16)$$

where *def* denotes the inflation-adjusted government deficit. Hence, private investment needs to be financed through a deficit on the current account of the balance of payments.

6   Capital mobility and the external constraint

In our review of the Dutch economy during the eighties we already claimed that an external 'solvency constraint' is currently not relevant for the Netherlands. The current account of the balance of payments shows a considerable surplus on average (Figure 8.4). If, however, capital markets are less open than casual inspection suggests, another external constraint may hamper the Dutch economy. We have already shown that the government budget deficit is excessively high (given the fact that debt is not allocated for investment spending), furthermore that private investment is relative low. If capital markets are closed, the deficit may have crowded out private investment. Hence, it is important to assess whether this has in fact been the case. Furthermore, Dutch central bankers worry about the fact that an increasing share of Dutch government debt may be held by foreigners. This fear is misplaced if international capital is mobile and individuals are forward-looking: in that case Ricardian Equivalence implies that whether a given stream of primary government spending is financed through taxes or debt is irrelevant and furthermore that placement of government debt abroad or at home is irrelevant. Finally, if capital is relatively mobile this has implications for the optimal structure of taxation.

Let us turn to the data. Figure 8.7 shows gross direct international flows. The solid line is direct Dutch investment abroad, the broken line is foreign direct investment in the Netherlands (both percentages of GNP). Both lines, in particular Dutch investment abroad, slope upwards. Figure 8.8 shows the total of net long-term capital streams (direct investment plus equity and bonds, figures presented for the non-monetary sector of the economy). Again both curves, volatile as they are, slope upwards. The recent increase of holdings of Dutch assets by foreigners is a result of a small positive interest differential between the Netherlands and Germany together with a strong guilder (low inflation). However, this effect may be attenuated somewhat due to the presence of a liquidity premium, because the capital market of the Netherlands is much smaller than that of Germany. The increases in direct investment seem to anticipate '1992'.

Other direct evidence on growing international capital mobility is available by comparing onshore and offshore interest rates. Figures 8.9 and 8.10 show onshore and offshore three-month interest rates for the Netherlands and Italy respectively. The message is quite clear: the Netherlands (where capital controls hardly exist) has nearly identical onshore and

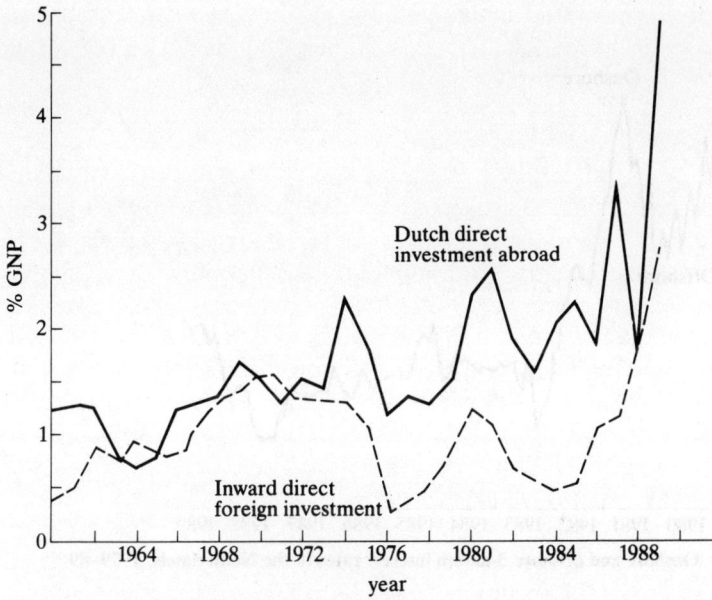

Figure 8.7 Direct international investment flows in the Netherlands, 1960–89. *Source:* Central Bank *Annual Report* 1989. Table 6.3.

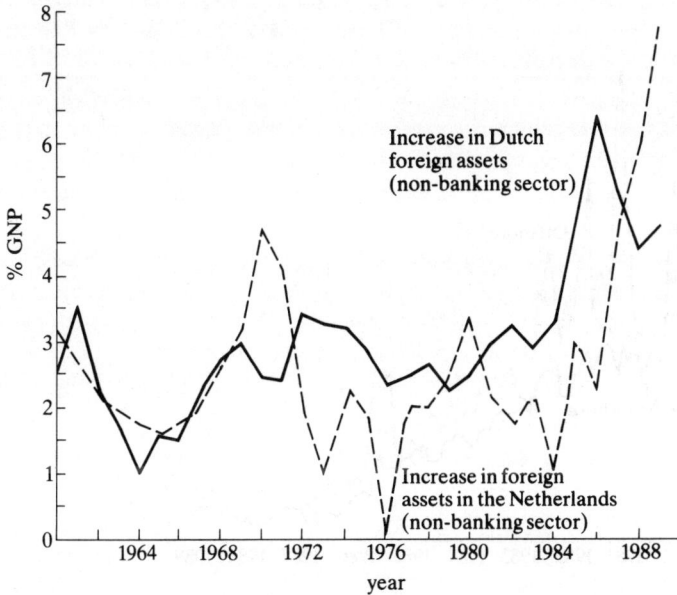

Figure 8.8 Long-term international investment flows in the Netherlands, 1960–89. *Source:* Central Bank *Annual Report* 1989. Table 6.3.

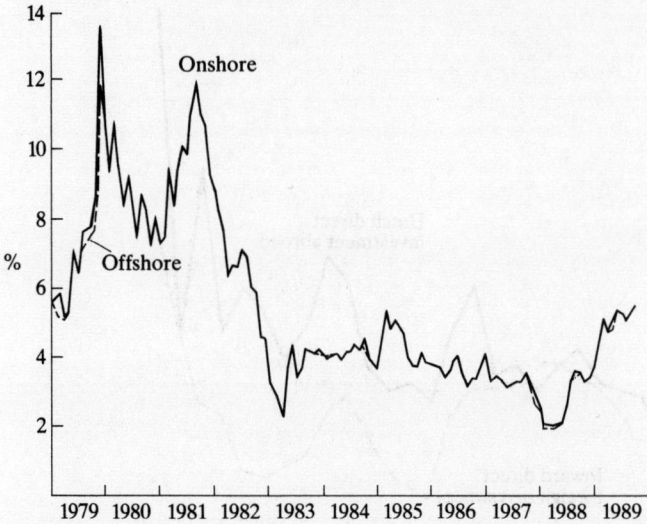

Figure 8.9   Onshore and offshore 3-month interest rates in the Netherlands, 1979–89

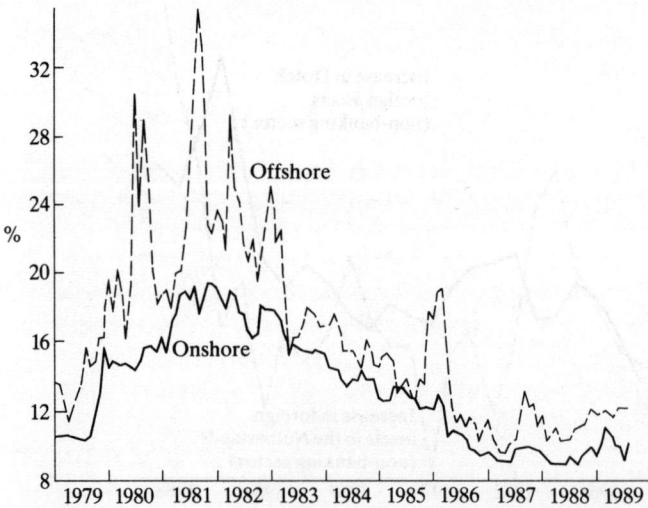

Figure 8.10   Onshore and offshore 3-month interest rates in Italy, 1979–89

offshore rates, whereas Italy (with strong capital controls) has large divergences. Increasing mobility need not necessarily lead to larger capital flows, but should eventually lead to convergence of rates of return on capital.

Despite these direct sources of evidence for increased openness of capital markets, there is an empirical puzzle known as the Feldstein–Horioka puzzle that contradicts this evidence (Feldstein and Horioka, 1980 (FH for short)). As argued in the previous section, perfect capital mobility together with forward looking behaviour of economic agents implies that the current account of the balance of payments is used as a smoothing device. Temporary fluctuations in income should not lead to significant changes in spending (consumption and investment), since these shocks are absorbed by the current account. A temporary fall in income thus leads to a trade deficit, rather than to a trade surplus as in the usual Keynesian story. A permanent (additive) shock to income should lead to an immediate adjustment of consumption, leaving saving and investment unaltered (hence, the current account is not affected by this shock). The implication of this theory is that consumption and investment for the economy as a whole should be uncorrelated. FH and Feldstein and Bacchetta (1989) find quite different empirical evidence, though. This does not necessarily contradict perfect capital mobility, as the intermediate case shows, that is, persistent productivity shocks will lead to higher savings and higher investment as long as capital becomes more productive. In this case, even under perfect capital mobility one can find positive savings–investment correlations.

Figure 8.11 presents the time series for gross savings, gross investment, and the current account. If the current account works as a smoothing device, then FH expect a value close to zero of the 'savings retention factor' or in the regression $I/Y = \alpha_0 + \alpha_1(S/Y)$. In fact, FH finds values of α_1 close to one using data for 16 OECD countries. Note, by the way, that if the null hypothesis of perfect capital mobility were true, investment should be the exogenous variable (determined by the international rate of return). Simultaneity is just one of the econometric problems that hampers the FH line of research (estimation by 2SLS does not lead to different findings, however). Other problems occur if one does not use cross-section data but time series (Ghosh, 1990). As the Dutch savings and investment ratios do not clearly show evidence of a unit root or cointegration, we ignore problems related to cointegration. Estimating with Dutch time series for 1951–89 provides a savings retention coefficient (α_1) of 0.90 (s.e. 0.15), with an $\bar{R}^2$ of 0.50 and a DW of 1.08. Estimation by 2SLS gives essentially the same results. A first problem of this result is the apparent dynamic misspecification. Furthermore, we expect a lower

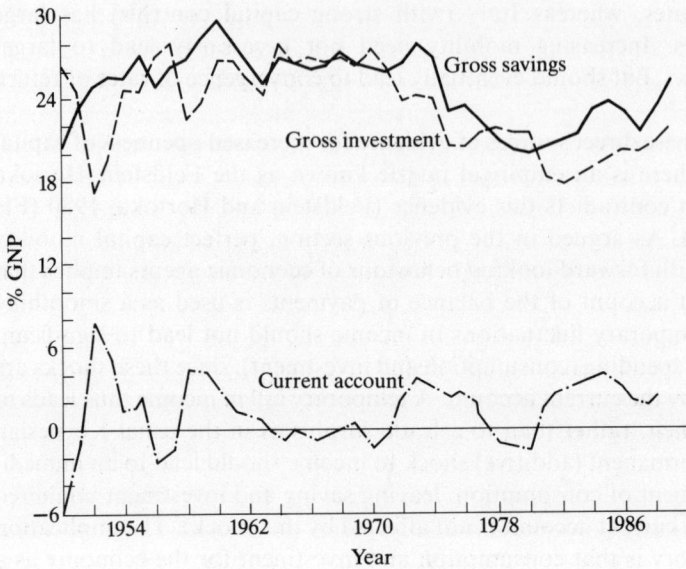

Figure 8.11   Savings, investment, and the Netherlands current account, 1950–89

value for α_1 in more recent periods than in the beginning of our sample. Estimating for subperiods leads to degrees of freedom problems. An alternative is to use a Bayesian updating procedure or recursive least squares (RLS) instead, which suggests an increase instead of a decrease of α_1 over time. This is surprising, because one would have thought that the increasing degree of liberalization of capital markets should with the passing of time have led to a fall in α_1.

A mirror image of the savings–investment correlation is the current account–savings correlation (as $S \equiv CA + J$). In the following, we will take investment as the independent variable (consistent with the null hypothesis of full capital mobility). If we regressed the current account on investment we obtain a coefficient of -0.44 (s.e. 0.09), very different from the expected value of minus one. Of course, this estimate is troubled by the same problems as our earlier findings. One possible way out is to differentiate between private and government behaviour. This also has the advantage that it will be possible to see if the government really crowds out private investment if it runs a deficit. If the permanent income hypothesis holds true, then private savings depend on the after-tax difference between current and permanent income. Government savings, or minus the government budget deficit, depend on either tax smoothing or explicit offsetting government policies. Roubini (1988) estimated equation

(16) which corrects for the government deficit, assuming that GNP is a random walk so that $y_t^p = y_t$. Our estimates are not significantly different (differences may result from the way of correcting the deficit for the inflation tax) and are -0.43 (s.e. 0.33) for the deficit term and -0.68 (s.e. 0.39) for the investment term ($\bar{R}^2 = 0.21$, $DW = 0.41$, estimation period 1971–85 as in Roubini). These results are closer to the perfect capital mobility prediction but still far from satisfying. Estimates using the complete sample period (1951–89) lead to estimated parameters somewhat closer to zero (not really surprising as the 1950s and 1960s had probably lower capital mobility than the years used by Roubini). Problems with dynamic misspecification (revealed by the DW statistics) and 'perverse' instability (revealed by updating or RLS regression) point out that we have not yet captured a satisfactory model for capital mobility in relation to savings and investment.

Let us proceed with an equation along the lines of (16), but drop the assumption that GDP follows a random walk. Instead, consider the case where GDP is an integrated AR(1) process

$$\Delta Y_t = \beta \Delta Y_{t-1} + \epsilon_t$$

In that case it can be shown that

$$Y_t - Y_t^P = - \frac{\beta \phi}{1 - \beta \phi} (Y_t - Y_{t-1})$$

where $\phi \equiv 1/1 + r$. Estimation with real GDP from 1956 to 1989 gives

$$\Delta Y_t = 5.38 + 0.30\ \Delta Y_{t-1} \qquad \bar{R}^2 = 0.06$$
$$\quad\ (1.55)\ \ (0.17) \qquad\qquad DW = 1.90$$

If we take $r = 0.025$ (hence $\phi = 0.976$), we obtain $Y_t - Y_t^P = -0.42$ $(Y_t - Y_{t-1})$. Estimating equation (16), using this result, gives

$$ca = 0.14 - 0.58\ J/Y - 0.12\ def - 1.15\ (1 - \tau)(Y - Y^P)/Y$$
$$\quad\ (0.03)\ \ (0.13) \qquad (0.13) \qquad (0.55)$$

$$\bar{R}^2 = 0.36;\ DW = 0.71;\ \chi^2(4) = 19.7;\ \text{sample } 1955\text{–}89$$

It is clear that these results do not improve upon the earlier findings. Dynamic misspecification is still a problem, the estimates for the coefficients are even worse than in an equation with a random-walk specification for income. There still are other ways to test for the existence of full capital mobility combined with forward-looking behaviour. Ghosh (1990), for example, shows that the current account should predict ('Granger cause') the change in net cash flow of a country ($\Delta NCF \equiv \Delta(Y - I - G)$), where G equals government spending. We will discuss the implications of government spending below. We were unable to find conclusive evidence for this hypothesis.

A possible explanation for the lower (in absolute value) than expected coefficient of the deficit in the current account regression is given by Summers (1988). He suggests that the government might have the explicit intention to fill the private savings–investment gap. In a cross-country study, Summers finds a coefficient of 0.72 in a regression of the deficit in the net savings gap: $DEF = 0.72 (S_{net} - I_{net})$. Hence, Summers argues that 72% of the savings gap is explicitly offset by the government's finance policy. Indeed, in the Netherlands there has been a well-known deficit rule due to Jelle Zijlstra (former minister of economic affairs, finance, prime minister, and central banker), known as the structural budget deficit rule according to which the government budget deficit should match the savings surplus of the private sector, minus 1.5% of GDP intended for capital transfers to Third World countries (development aid). Hence, if this policy has been pursued in practice indeed, we would expect

$$def = -0.015 + ca$$

Estimating this relation provides

$$def = 0.02 + 0.02 \ ca \qquad R^2 = 0.0$$
$$(0.005)(0.18) \qquad DW = 0.30$$

Various efforts to obtain better results by introducing dynamics did not lead to improvements. Furthermore, estimation for subsamples gave essentially the same result. Using instrumental variables also did not make much difference. A further test to infer whether the structural current account surplus determines the deficit or vice versa is to perform a 'Granger causality' test. Taking for granted the many well-known objections to interpreting this kind of test as a sign of (lack of) causality, we were unable to conclude either that the current account 'Granger causes' the deficit or the reverse. Our test is based upon Geweke et al. (1982). The first test is for 'causation' of the deficit by the current account

$$\frac{CA}{Y} = C_0 + \sum_{i=-4}^{4} \alpha_i \left(\frac{DEF}{Y}\right)_{t-i} + \sum_{i=1}^{4} \beta_i \left(\frac{CA}{Y}\right)_{t-i}$$

Estimating this equation for 1955 to 1985 and testing if the α_i, $i = -4$, ..., -4 jointly differ from zero leads to an F-Statistic $F(4.17) = 0.81$. Hence, there is no sign of 'Granger causation' of the current account on the deficit. Similarly, a test for the reverse 'Granger causation' leads to a F-Statistic of 0.34; again there is no sign of 'causation'.

Another reason for the counter-intuitive estimates of (16) is a violation of the tax smoothing policy by the Dutch government. Indeed, it is hard to argue that the financial policies during the eighties were even remotely consistent with a tax smoothing policy as argued in Section 3.

According to the various regression results presented above, the recurrent conclusion seems to be that, despite being an open economy, the Netherlands do not fully profit from international capital mobility. The current account does not seem to fulfill its role of a smoothing device. If this conclusion were warranted, then increases in government budget deficits would tend to crowd out investment. This is what Feldstein and Bacchetta argue as well. They estimate an investment equation with the budget deficit and private savings as independent variables for a panel of thirteen OECD countries. We did the same for the Netherlands, resulting in

$$J/Y = 0.00 - 0.70 \frac{DEF}{Y} + 0.86 \frac{PS}{Y}$$
$$(0.05) \quad (0.16) \qquad (0.18)$$
$$\bar{R}^2 = 0.46; \ DW = 1.06; \text{ sample } 1951\text{--}89$$

This result is very similar to Feldstein and Bacchetta. If we are satisfied with this result (and below we will argue that we are not), then the conclusion should be that, indeed, government deficits crowd out private investment. Still, how can it be that in such an open economy as the Dutch we are apparently faced with capital constraints? We have to stretch our imagination to find a satisfactory answer. FH mention a few capital market 'imperfections' that may cause less than perfect capital mobility. One factor they mention is nationalistic portfolio preferences, i.e., Dutch investors like to invest in the Netherlands. It is hard to see how such preferences can persist in an otherwise open and competitive market. Furthermore, some actors may have such preferences but the issue is what happens on the margin. If the marginal investor is more 'rational' then there is no external (capital mobility) constraint. The same holds for institutional rigidities. It is true that, for example, Dutch pension funds are not allowed to invest as much as they like abroad (similar constraints apply to other European pension funds). Table 8.13 shows that these funds have relatively few foreign assets and many government bonds. The civil servants' pension fund, ABP, invested about two-thirds of its capital in government loans, whilst private investors held nearly 40% of their funds in government stock. ABP invested only 2% in equities, but private pension funds reached nearly 8%. Apart from institutional barriers and forced saving, risk-aversion explains much of this investment behaviour. The situation is changing, though, as these funds are increasingly invested in equity as well as abroad (some institutional limitations will be dropped in the near future), on the other hand more foreign investors are starting to buy Dutch government bonds.

Table 8.13. *Investment behaviour of Netherlands pension funds and insurance companies, September 1988*
(billion guilders)

	Private sector loans and bonds	Private sector, equity	Building and mortgage	Foreign assets	Government	Total
Insurance Companies	27.4	10.2	42.1	9.3	37.5	126.5
Private Pension Funds	42.6	15.5	31.2	31.3	74.5	195.1
Civil Servants Pension Fund	30.0	3.1	15.7	4.3	92.9	146.0
Total	100.0	28.8	89.0	44.9	204.9	467.6
P.M. NNP 1988						401.2

Source: De Nederlandsche Bank annual report 1988, Table 2.2.

Let us now criticize the earlier findings. Things change drastically as soon as we control for the effect of world trade. Both private investment (PI) and the government budget are strongly correlated with growth in world trade (WT) (see Table 8.12), as the two following regressions clearly show

$$\frac{DEF}{Y} = 0.02 - 0.06 \; WT - 0.14 \; WT_{-1} + 0.82 \left(\frac{DEF}{Y}\right)_{-1}$$
$$(0.005)(0.05) \qquad (0.05) \qquad\qquad (0.08)$$

$$\bar{R}^2 = 0.76; \; \chi^2(1) = 0.26; \; \chi^2(4) = 3.1$$

$$\frac{PI}{Y} = 0.07 + 0.18 \; WT + 0.28 \; WT_{-1} + 0.51 \left(\frac{PI}{Y}\right)_{-1}$$
$$(0.02) \quad (0.07) \qquad (0.07) \qquad\qquad (0.09)$$

$$\bar{R}^2 = 0.65; \; \chi^2(1) = 0.22; \; \chi^2(4) = 3.5; \; \text{(both samples 1951–89).}$$

Hence, private investment and the government budget deficit are both affected by a third variable, world trade, leading to spurious regressions in earlier equations. If we include the deficit, we obtain

$$\frac{PI}{Y} = 0.05 + 0.15 \frac{DEF}{Y} + 0.19 \; WT + 0.30 \; WT_{-1} + 0.56 \left(\frac{PI}{Y}\right)_{-1}$$
$$(0.02) \; (0.12) \qquad (0.07) \qquad (0.07) \qquad\qquad (0.10)$$

$$\bar{R}^2 = 0.66; \; \chi^2(1) = 0.16; \; \chi^2(4) = 6.27$$

The impact of the deficit on private investment loses its significance and even changes sign. As we have seen from Table 8.2, there occurred a strong decline in both private and public investment, that started in the early seventies. Two major showdowns occurred just after the two oil crises. Private investment as a percentage of GNP was at an absolute minimum of 15% in 1982, after which a slow recovery started. Government investment has halved and remained in decline, even with a few grand projects (building new dikes) going on. The decrease in investment, in addition to an increase in labour supply, must have led to a decrease in the relative level of full capacity. If anything, government investment policy only made things worse. As mentioned in Section 3 the government budget constraint does not discriminate between consumptive and productive government expenditures. In times of budget cuts, it is easier to stop making new investments than to reduce government consumption (as sacking or cutting salaries of public servants invariably leads to strikes and political embarrassment).

Figure 8.2 portrayed the development of the share of profits and the share of investment in the national income. It is obvious that the last seven years of wage moderation by the trade unions have resulted in a dramatic fall of the share of labour from over 90% in 1982 to about 77% seven years later. The resulting increase in profits combined with the recent recovery in world trade and demand, has led to a recovery of investment during the last few years. This is consistent with a Kaleckian or Keynesian explanation of private investment behaviour. However, it is interesting to note that the recovery of profitability has not led to a full recovery of investment. This corresponds to a kind of hysteresis in investment. Nevertheless, if the Kaleckian story of investment holds true, there is only a limited role for the current account as a smoothing device.

7   Concluding remarks

The Dutch economy is making some progress towards making public sector finances more healthy, but this has been at the expense of too little fiscal stimulus. The Netherlands cannot expand demand unless the rest of Europe, in particular Germany, does the same, so the Dutch should be strongly in favour of a coordinated supply–friendly fiscal expansion for Europe. Since public investment has declined dramatically in the process of cutbacks, it is essential that the government invests more heavily in infrastructure, education, and the environment. Financial discipline has not been good, because government investment has fallen dramatically and actual spending has been much higher than planned spending. There is some evidence that monetary policy in the Netherlands is too tight and, given the large public debt, a slight increase of inflation to, say, 3 or 4% per year may not be as bad as De Nederlandsche Bank suggests. Since private sector savings in the Netherlands more than offsets public sector borrowing (witness the substantial current-account surpluses), there seems to be room for an expansion of demand. The growth in 1989 in the Netherlands has been substantial, but these extra jobs have been mainly of a low-quality and part-time nature and have not been enough to keep up with the increase in labour supply (resulting mainly from increased participation). As a result, unemployment in the Netherlands has remained persistently high. The growth in output and jobs has been mainly the result of the recovery in world trade, helped by the wage moderation that has taken place since 1983, so that one cannot give the credit to government policy. Wage moderation has been mainly forced through high unemployment, but given the alienation of the long-term unemployed and the presence of hysteresis it is not clear that wage moderation will continue in the future. There is a case for more government investment in permanent schooling and retraining programmes, especially as these may to a large extent be netted out of the government budget constraint. An application of the 'golden rule' of government finance would permit such policies. In addition, more attention should be paid to 'sabbatical leaves' and permanent schooling as they are a much more fruitful policy than the cuts in hours worked (advocated by part of the trade union movement). The Dutch direct tax system is highly inefficient, because it combines high marginal tax rates with low average tax rates. The proposed reform of the tax system will go some way towards remedying these inefficiencies. Social premiums are high in the Netherlands, but then these are offset by a generous pension system. It is not clear what the adverse effects of this on unemployment are.

It is not clear that investment in the Netherlands is financed through the current account. This may be due to legal constraints on foreign investment by pension funds, but more generally it is an indication that neither tax smoothing nor consumption smoothing has been of much importance in the Netherlands. In other words, the Netherlands is characterized by two self-imposed external constraints, a rigid guilder-Deutschmark rate and investment being too closely tied to domestic saving.

NOTE

We are grateful for comments to participants in the CEPR–Bank of Greece conference on Macroeconomics and the external constraint, and in particular to George Alogoskoufis for editorial advice.

REFERENCES

Barro, R. (1979), 'On the Determination of Public Debt', *Journal of Political Economy* **87**, 940–71.

Buiter, W.H. (1985), 'A Guide to Public Sector Debt and Deficits', *Economic Policy* **1**, (1), 13–79.

Dornbusch, R. (1989), 'Credibility, Debt and Unemployment: Ireland's Failed Stabilization', *Economic Policy* **4**, (8), 173–209.

Feldstein, M. and C. Horioka (1980), 'Domestic Saving and International Capital Flows', *Economic Journal* **90**, 314–29.

Feldstein, M. and P. Bacchetta (1989), 'National Saving and International Investment', NBER Working Paper No. 3164, Cambridge, MA.

Geweke, J., R. Meese, and W. Dent (1982), 'Comparing alternative tests of Causality in Temporal Systems', *Journal of Econometrics* **21**, 161–94.

Ghosh, A.R. (1990), 'International Capital Mobility and Optimal Current Account Behaviour: An Empirical Investigation', Princeton University Discussion Paper No. 50.

Giavazzi, F. and M. Pagano (1988), 'The Advantage of Tying One's Hands: EMS Discipline and Central Bank Credibility', *European Economic Review* **32**, 1055–82.

(1989), 'Confidence Crises and Public Debt Management', NBER Working Paper No. 2926, Cambridge, MA.

Graafland, J.J. and F. Huizinga (1988), 'Modelling a Wage Equation for the Netherlands: A Cointegration Approach', Central Planning Bureau Memorandum No. 51, The Hague.

Gros, D. (1988), 'Seigniorage versus EMS Discipline: Some Welfare Considerations', Working Document No. 38, CEPS, Brussels.

Keuzenkamp, H. and F. van der Ploeg (1989), 'Zeven verloren jaren? De mislukte sanering', *Intermediair* **25**, 5–11.

(1990a). 'Perceived Constraints for Dutch Unemployment Policy', in C. de Neubourg (ed.), *The Art of Full Employment: Unemployment Policy in Open Economies*, Amsterdam: North-Holland.

(1990b). 'Het Grote Onvermogen: Een kritiek op de gangbare analyse van financieringstekort, schuld en begrotingsruimte', *ESB* **75**, 608–12.

Mankiw, N. (1987), 'The Optimal Collection of Seigniorage: Theory and Evidence, *Journal of Monetary Economics* **20**, 327–41.

Persson, T. and L. Svensson (1989). 'Why a Stubborn Conservative Would Run a Deficit', *Quarterly Journal of Economics* **104**, 325–45.

Ploeg, F. van der (1989). 'Tien jaar van voorspoed en ongeluk: Mrs. Thatcher en de Britse economie (Ten years of progress and unhappiness: Mrs Thatcher and the British economy)', *Socialisme en Democratie* **6**, 191–95.

(1990), 'Budgetary Aspects of Economic and Monetary Integration in Europe', Discussion Paper No. 9037, CentER, Tilburg University.

Romer, D. (1988), 'What are the Costs of Excessive Deficits?' *NBER Macroeconomics Annual 1988*, Cambridge, MA: MIT Press.

Roubini, N. (1988), 'Current Account and Budget Deficits in an Intertemporal Model of Consumption and Taxation Smoothing. A Solution to the "Feldstein–Horioka Puzzle"?', NBER Working Paper No. 2773, Cambridge, MA.

Roubini, N. and J. Sachs (1989), 'Political and Economic Determinants of Budget Deficits in the Industrial Democracies', *European Economic Review* **33**, 903–33.

260 **Discussion by Christopher Martin**

Sterks, C.G.M., J. de Haan, and C.A. de Kam (1989). 'De erfenis van Ruding', *Economische Statistische Berichten*, 1898.
Stiglitz, J.E. and A. Weiss (1988), 'Credit Rationing, and Its Implications for Macro-Economics', unpublished manuscript.
Studiegroep Begrotingsruimte (1989), *Naar Gezonde Overheidsfinanciën*, presented to Parliament.
Summers, L. (1988), 'Tax Policy and International Competitiveness', in J. Frenkel (ed.), *International Aspects of Fiscal Policies*, NBER Conference Report, Chicago University Press.

Discussion

CHRISTOPHER MARTIN

Hugo Keuzenkamp and Rick van der Ploeg provide a lively, provocative discussion of the problems of fiscal and monetary policy in the Netherlands. Their analysis combines elements of high theory, such as continuous-time intertemporal budget constraints, with details of Dutch political life. This combination works well and their diagnosis is on the whole convincing. My only substantial reservation about their chapter concerns the lack of attention devoted to the central issue of this volume, namely the existence and effects of the external constraint. One can however infer something on the matter from this chapter and I shall attempt to do this.

The history of monetary and fiscal policy in the Netherlands is one of sharply contrasting fortunes. Monetary policy has been used with some success to peg the guilder closely to the Deutschmark. As a result, inflation has been kept low, lower indeed than in the FRG, and a reputation for monetary discipline has been earned. Fiscal policy, by contrast, is widely perceived as a failure; public sector debt has spiralled while public expenditure has resisted all attempts at control. In the wider economy, monetary discipline has led to sustained high interest rates and private sector expenditure has been carefully controlled. Unlike other European countries, there has been no boom in consumer spending in the Netherlands over the past decade. Unemployment is a severe problem and long-term unemployment is high. Despite this, and symptomatic of the dislocation of the Dutch labour market, certain workers are in short supply and indeed migrants from East Germany have been sought.

Keuzenkamp and van der Ploeg provide a thorough analysis of how this situation evolved, placing emphasis on the problems of budgetary control in coalition governments. If we consider the experience of other countries, it becomes clear that it is not coalition government in itself that leads to fiscal difficulties; the FRG, for example, faces no such problems. Rather, it appears that public debt problems arise in countries characterized by short-lived disunited coalitions, for example Italy and perhaps Israel. The narrative provided by Keuzenkamp and van der Ploeg makes it clear that the Netherlands also belongs in this category; for example they argue that periods of particularly sharp increases in public debt coincided with a lack of consensus within the administration over the course of fiscal policy. Recently, widespread political agreement on the need to reduce the level of public borrowing has merely led to a stabilization in its level. What reductions there have been were in the area of government investment in precisely those areas, education, infrastructure, and environmental policy, to which the Labour party, a major partner in the current coalition, is most committed. If, therefore, political pressures mount, further erosion of budgetary discipline can be expected.

In response to the budgetary problems, Keuzenkamp and van der Ploeg offer 'ten rules for sound government finance'. These seem perfectly sensible from the viewpoint of the economist and public finance theorist; for example, if expenditure rises, taxes should only rise if the increase is permanent, or 'investment carrying a market rate of interest should be netted out of the government budget constraint'. Indeed, many policy-makers would probably agree with these rules. However, while the rules provide a framework against which to measure actual fiscal conduct, I am not at all sure about their practical relevance. Since Keuzenkamp and van der Ploeg argue, persuasively, that the budgetary problems have arisen for political reasons, it seems that some form of decisive political action is at least necessary for their solution. As with other countries, the heart of the problem lies in the process of setting expenditure plans, which inevitably lead to pressure on the finance minister, pressure which is especially difficult to resist within unstable coalitions. It is not clear whether the authors believe that the deficit itself is too high or whether the real problem is that attempts at budgetary control have led to a squeeze on long-term capital (including human capital) formation by the public sector. I suspect they believe the latter. Some form of precommitment, for example the plan to put current and capital expenditure in clearly separate budgets may offer a way forward, but strong political will is needed.

The achievement in restraining inflation can be attributed to the success of de Nederlandsche Bank in keeping the guilder in line with the Deutsch-mark. The central bank has the constitutional duty of keeping inflation down, enjoys full independence from the fiscal authorities and so has been able to resist any pressure for excessive monetary expansion. As the authors note, this has led to the absence of seigniorage revenues. The central bank has shown itself to be very sensitive to any sign of inflationary pressure, relying on a mixture of high interest rates and direct controls on lending. Although the monetary authorities have achieved their aims and although there appears to be political consensus on the value of these aims, Keuzenkamp and van der Ploeg appear to have their doubts. They note the low level of personal debt and the fact that investment has been suppressed to the extent that available capacity may well not be sufficient for full employment (investment has however picked up somewhat recently as the share of wages in value added has been reduced). In this they make a valid point and indeed the relatively weak supply side may provide a role for selective state action.

We must now pose the central question of the conference. Is there an external constraint in the Netherlands and what form does it take? Unfortunately the authors do not really consider this question and we must infer what we can from their analysis. We can begin by asking whether monetary and fiscal policy would be different if the Netherlands were a closed economy (and if the fiscal authorities had greater control over the monetary sector). The low inflation and high unemployment rate, together with political pressure arising from the increasing difficulty in restraining wage growth, conspire to make some form of expansion tempting. If this were done, some fall in unemployment would probably result, albeit at the cost of some inflation. However, as the authors note, it is by no means clear that the socially optimal inflation rate is zero. Since the Netherlands is actually a small open economy, very dependent on external events, an expansion would in reality be less likely to succeed because of the induced pressure on the currency. It is unclear whether such a position would be sustainable but the political authorities might still judge the short-term gains to be sufficient to make the expansion worthwhile. The limits imposed by potential depreciation or current account deficits constitute the external constraint. In fact, it is almost certain that the central bank would not allow an expansion since this would put its constitutional duty of keeping prices stable at risk. However, if the Bundesbank were to sanction an expansion of the German economy, the Dutch would be able to follow suit, with probably beneficial results. The conclusion from this is that the Netherlands does indeed face an external constraint. Because of the institutional arrangements of the monetary sector, this constraint is never allowed to bite, nonetheless the constraint is real.

Finally, some empirical evidence is presented on the possible role of the current account in smoothing consumption as income varies and also on the more immediate question of whether the fiscal deficit crowds out private investment. Consumption smoothing occurs when consumers maintain consumption expenditure in the face of fluctuating income, allowing the current account to absorb the shocks. Such behaviour can occur when consumers look forward and when capital is fully mobile. It appears that since offshore and onshore interest rates are very close (cf. the chapter by Artis and Bayoumi in this volume), capital is mobile and indeed has been so for a number of years. The authors then investigate the applicability of the 'Feldstein–Horioka puzzle', which has been considered elsewhere in this volume, and indeed find that consumption and investment are related, apparently contradicting the evidence that capital is mobile. Keuzenkamp and van der Ploeg also find strong evidence that government deficits crowd out private investment. They do not infer that capital is immobile, rather they appear sceptical about the approach, rightly so in my opinion. The authors then add the level of world trade to the regressions, a sensible variable to use since the Netherlands is both small and open, and find their results to be much altered. In particular they find no evidence that the fiscal deficit crowds out private investment. All these regressions have really shown is that there are no simple relationships in macroeconomics and that there is no substitute for proper econometric modelling, guided by the appropriate theory. There are no short cuts.

9 Fiscal deficits, seigniorage, and external debt: the case of Greece

GEORGE S. ALOGOSKOUFIS and NICOS CHRISTODOULAKIS

One of the most significant developments of the 1980s in Greece has been the spectacular rise of external debt. External debt rose from $5.1 billion in 1979 (13% of GNP) to $20.6 billion ten years later (40% of GNP). Debt servicing as a percentage of current receipts from abroad has also more than tripled. It was 8% in 1979 and reached 24% in 1988. In addition, while for the rest of the OECD the 1980s have been a decade of disinflation, average consumer price inflation in Greece rose from 12.3% in the 1970s to 19.6% in the 1980s.

The 1980s have also witnessed a significant rise in the share of the public sector in Greece, a rise which has been accompanied by persistently high budget deficits and a rapid buildup of public debt. Public sector debt rose from 27.4% of GDP in 1979 to 91.5% in 1988. The estimates for 1989 put it at more than 100% of GDP. At the same time, total government expenditure rose from 33% of GDP in 1979 to 49.4% in 1988.

What is the relation between the rise in external indebtedness and these fiscal developments? What are the appropriate policies for stabilizing the external debt to GDP ratio? In particular, is the stabilization of the public debt to GDP ratio a sufficient condition for the stabilization of the external debt ratio, or are additional policy measures required? In other words, is the external constraint just the flip side of the government solvency constraint? What are the pros and cons of alternative ways of stabilizing the public debt ratio? Is a further rise in inflation in Greece going to help this process? What are the costs and benefits of joining the process of European Monetary Unification?

The purpose of this chapter is to investigate these questions. The focus is firmly on the medium-run implications of fiscal deficits for external debt and inflation. In the context of Greece we look at both the pattern of developments in the 1980s, and at the implications of the various options for stabilizing the ratios of public and external debt to GDP.

The model we use to address these questions is one of optimal private

264

sector savings, in which private households are forward-looking. This type of model is being increasingly used in both open economy macroeconomics and public economics, as it recognizes the role of intertemporal private sector responses to fiscal policy, something ignored by more traditional Keynesian models.[1]

The first question we seek to answer is whether the stabilization of the ratio of public debt to GDP is a sufficient condition for the stabilization of the external debt to GDP ratio. Additional questions relate to the implications for external debt of alternative ways of stabilizing the public debt to GDP ratio.

We argue that, if the private sector is forward-looking in its savings behaviour, stabilization of the public debt to GDP ratio will be sufficient to stabilize the external debt to GDP ratio as well. The reason is that the private sector, through its consumption pattern, stabilizes the ratio of its own assets to GDP.[2]

The authorities of a country in which the ratio of public debt to GDP is rising, like in Greece, have three options in trying to stabilize it at its current level. The first is to reduce government expenditure on goods and services, the second is to increase tax receipts, and the third is to increase revenues from money creation, i.e., seigniorage. The latter would substitute money finance for debt finance.

Our theoretical results suggest that stabilization of the public debt to GDP ratio at a given level through higher taxation will result in a higher external debt–GDP ratio than stabilization at the same level through a reduction in (non-interest) government expenditure. The same also applies to seigniorage. Public debt stabilization at a given level through higher seigniorage (monetary growth) will result in a lower external debt than if public debt were to be stabilized through higher taxation. The reason why tax increases result in higher external debt than expenditure reductions is that, for given pre-tax household income, higher steady-state taxation reduces disposable private sector income, thus causing a reduction in both private consumption and real household assets. For a given stock of government bonds, a reduction in private sector assets require a reduction in the stock of assets other than bonds, say money and foreign assets. Such effects do not arise if the government reduces government expenditure instead of raising taxes. On the other hand, a rise in steady-state seigniorage revenue reduces real money balances, through a rise in expected inflation and nominal interest rates. As a consequence, there is less of a reduction in the holdings of foreign assets by the private sector than in the case where the same revenue was raised by increased taxes.

We calibrate the model and provide alternative numerical estimates of the rise in taxes and reductions in government expenditure that would be required for stabilization of the public debt to GDP ratio at its 1989 level of approximately 100%. We also calculate the implications for external debt.[3]

Our results suggest that in the case of Greece there is no further scope for any increase in seigniorage revenue. At the 1989–90 inflation rates of 20%, seigniorage as a percentage of GDP is already at its maximum. In fact, the inflation rate slightly exceeds the seigniorage-maximizing rate, so, if anything, a reduction in steady-state inflation would be called for on seigniorage maximization grounds. We calculate that, if the public sector debt is to be stabilized at its current level of approximately 100% of GDP, the primary deficit (i.e. the deficit excluding interest payments) will have to fall to 0.3% of GDP from its projected ratio of 6.5% in 1990 and 5.1% in 1991. This assumes GDP growth rates of 2% per annum, inflation rates of 20% and 5% world real interest rates, numbers which are roughly in line with projections for the next two years in the June 1990 OECD *Economic Outlook*. These calculations show the order of the task facing the Greek authorities. They need to reduce the primary deficit by a further 5.5 percentage points of GDP per annum, in addition to the reductions envisaged in the plans prepared by the new government.

If Greece were to enter the exchange rate mechanism (ERM) of the EMS, and therefore adopt a steady-state inflation rate of approximately 5%, stabilization of public and external debt would require a primary surplus of 0.6% of GDP on the same assumptions. Thus, the seigniorage revenue loss associated with ERM membership would roughly require a further reduction in the primary deficit of about one percentage point of GDP. This appears to us a small price to pay for the credibility and other gains that would be associated with a more stable monetary policy and exchange rates in the EMS (see Giavazzi and Giovannini, 1989).[4]

The rest of the chapter is as follows: in Section 1 we examine macroeconomic developments in Greece in the last decade. We point to the fall in the average GDP growth rate, the rise in inflation and the unprecedented rise of the public sector and its deficits. The upshot has been a spectacular rise in public and external debt. In Section 2 we examine a simple medium-run model of deficits and debts to examine the relation between public and external deficits and debts. In Sections 3 and 4 we present a theoretical investigation of alternative methods for stabilizing a rising public debt to GDP ratio, and their implications for external debt and inflation. In Section 5 we turn to a detailed numerical investigation of the options for Greece by calibrating the model. We also examine the prospects for Greece in the context for monetary union in Europe. Section 6 contains conclusions.

Table 9.1. *Comparative macroeconomic developments in Greece, OECD and the EEC, 1970–89*

	1970–9	1980–9
Growth rate of GDP (%)		
Greece	5.4	1.5
OECD	3.5	2.8
EEC	3.3	2.1
Consumer price inflation (%)		
Greece	12.3	19.5
OECD	8.3	6.1
EEC	9.3	7.0
Current account (% in GDP)		
Greece	− 4.7	− 5.1
OECD	− 0.1	− 0.4
EEC	0.0	0.1
Unemployment rate (%)		
Greece	2.3	6.6
OECD	4.3	7.5
EEC	3.9	9.9
Growth of business investment (%)		
Greece	4.9	− 0.6
OECD	3.7	4.7
EEC	3.1	3.7

Source: OECD *Economic Outlook*, December 1989.

1 Macroeconomic developments in Greece in the 1980s

In this section we briefly review macroeconomic developments in Greece in the last decade. The performance of the economy in this decade has been rather disappointing in most respects. Some comparative data are presented in Table 9.1.

As can be seen from Table 9.1, the performance of the Greek economy in the 1980s has been much worse than in the 1970s. The average growth rate of GDP fell from 5.4% to 1.5%, average inflation rose to 19.5% from 12.3%, and the current account deficit deteriorated as a percentage of GDP. In addition, the average unemployment rate almost tripled, and the growth rate of business fixed investment has been negative. During the 1980s, the average growth rate of GDP fell below that of the OECD and the EEC, for the first extended period since the end of the Second World War. The average inflation rate has been almost three times as high as in the OECD and the EEC, and average unemployment has risen more steeply than in the other OECD and EEC economies.

However, the most spectacular deterioration has been in Greece's external position (Table 9.2). Total external debt has risen from about $5 billion in 1979 (13% of GNP) to about $20 billion in 1988 (40% of GDP). Debt servicing in 1988 required 24% of current foreign exchange receipts, three times the fraction of 1979. The situation in 1989 and 1990 may have deteriorated a lot more, as the stabilization programme of 1985–7 that slowed down the rise in external indebtedness was abandoned in 1988.

The rise in external indebtedness has gone hand in hand with a sharp deterioration in public finances (Table 9.3). The public sector borrowing requirement (PSBR) which was equal to 5.7% of GDP in 1979, remained persistently above 12% throughout the 1980s. The election years of 1981, 1985, and 1989 seem to have been crucial in this process, as the PSBR to GDP ratio peaked at elections.

The rise to 14.3% in 1981 was unprecedented. This was in the depths of the recession, and coincided with world real interest rates climbing to record levels. In 1981 external debt rose by 5 percentage points of GDP. Yet the spending spree and the deferral of taxes did not help the conservative government, and the socialists won power in a virtual landslide. The PSBR was reduced very little as a percent of GDP in the next three years, as the new government engineered significant rises in public expenditure, which took total government expenditure from 33.2% of GDP in 1980, to 47.8% in 1985 (Table 9.3). In fact, in 1985, another election year, the PSBR–GDP ratio shot up to 17.9%. External debt rose by 10 full percentage points of GDP in that year alone. The socialist government held on to power in the 1985 elections, but a few months later, in crisis conditions, negotiated a loan from the EC, and instituted a stabilization programme. This was based on a devaluation and a draconian incomes policy, but had little impact on the PSBR. The PSBR–GDP ratio was reduced only to 14% and 13.2% in 1986 and 1987 respectively, and, when the stabilization policy was abandoned in late 1987, it started climbing again, to 16.1% in 1988 and 21.5% in the election year of 1989.

We thus see a spectacular upward ratchet of the PSBR in successive elections. In between elections there were only weak attempts to reverse these rises. As a result, public debt rose from 27.4% of GDP in 1979 to 100% (possibly more) in 1989. A large part of the rise in public sector debt was due to government debt (Figure 9.1) which accelerated sharply as a percentage of GDP. External public sector debt more than quintupled as a percentage of GDP between 1979 and 1988, accounting for the lion's share of the rise in external indebtedness.

The major reason for the rise in public sector deficits and debts has been

Table 9.2. *Greece's external debt and its servicing, 1978–88*

	1978	1979	1980	1981	1982	1983	1984	1985	1986	1987	1988
						Billion US $					
Total external debt	4.5	5.1	6.4	7.9	9.5	10.6	12.3	15.7	17.1	21.0	20.6
of which medium- and long-term	3.8	4.1	5.4	6.2	7.3	8.7	9.8	12.8	14.7	19.2	18.4
Total external debt (% of GDP)	14	13	16	21	24	30	37	47	44	46	40
Debt servicing (% current receipts)	8	8	9	13	14	16	19	22	22	26	24

Source: OECD *Economic Surveys: Greece* (various issues).

Table 9.3. *Public sector deficits, public debt and external debt of Greece, 1979–89*
(% of GDP)

	1979	1981	1983	1985	1986	1987	1988	1989
PSBR	5.7	14.3	11.3	17.9	14.0	13.2	16.1	21.5
Public debt	27.4	39.7	54.2	76.9	79.4	84.5	91.5	100.0
Internal	21.8	26.9	32.2	40.5	43.0	49.9	58.5	—
External	5.6	12.8	22.0	36.4	36.4	34.6	33.0	—
External debt	13	21	30	47	44	46	40	—

Source: OECD *Economic Surveys: Greece* (January 1990)

the sharp rise in government expenditure (Table 9.4). The share of government expenditure in GDP rose by almost 50%, from 33.2% in 1980 to 49.4% in 1988. The rise has been concentrated on transfer and social insurance payments, government consumption, but more ominously on interest payments. The growth of these items has not been reversed by the stabilization program of 1985–7, which, as was suggested above, was mainly based on a devaluation and a draconian incomes policy.

The conservatives were returned to power in 1990, and have announced a gradualist approach to the reduction of public deficits. For example, the budget forecast for the PSBR–GDP ratio was 16% in 1990, with further

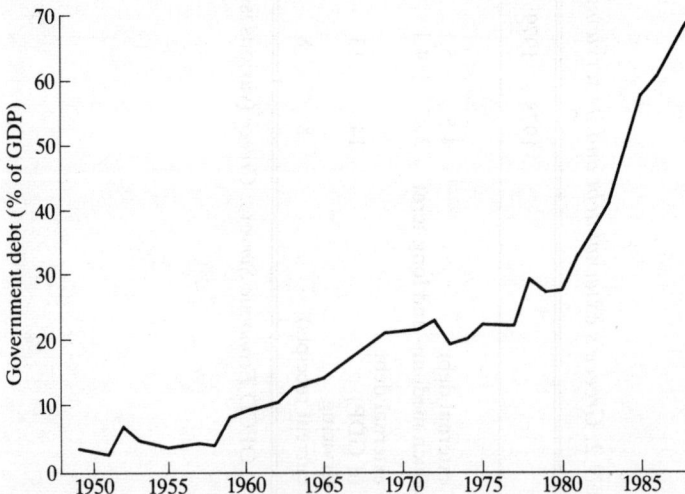

Figure 9.1   Greek government debt, 1949–88. *Source:* OECD *Economic Outlook*, June 1990.

Table 9.4. *Greek government expenditure and its structure, 1960–88 (% of GDP)*

	1960	1970	1980	1985	1988
Government consumption (excluding wages)	3.1	3.4	4.8	6.4	6.8
Government wage bill	8.6	9.3	11.4	14.0	13.8
Government investment	4.8	4.5	2.5	4.0	3.0
Subsidies	0.1	0.8	2.4	3.0	1.6
Social insurance and transfers	4.9	7.6	9.0	14.6	15.1
Interest payments	0.3	0.9	2.4	5.4	8.1
Grand total	21.8	26.5	33.2	47.8	49.4

Source: OECD *Economic Outlook* (December 1989).

gradual reductions until 1992, when the PSBR–GDP rate is forecast to fall to 13.5% (*Kathimerini*, 1 June 1990). Is such a program sufficient for stabilization of public and external debt? In the remainder of this chapter we turn to the medium-run implications of fiscal deficits for external debt and inflation, and for the various stabilization policy options open to the authorities in Greece.

2   A model of optimal savings, deficits, and debts

In this section we utilize a neoclassical long-run equilibrium model, which rests explicitly on the assumption of intertemporal optimization on the part of private households. The model belongs to a very wide class of models in this spirit, which assume that households have a finite horizon. The specific model we use is the Yaari–Blanchard model (Yaari, 1965; Blanchard, 1985), according to which each household is assumed to face a constant probability of death λ at each instant. In fact, we use a variant of the version due to Buiter (1988), which allows for both population and productivity growth.

2.1   Optimal savings by the household

Assume an economy consisting of a large number of households, born at different times in the past. All households are alike in all respects, apart from their date of birth. A fraction β of new households are added to the economy at each instant, and a fraction λ of old households die. The probability of death of a household is assumed constant and independent of the age of the household.

With a constant probability of death λ, and continuous time, the expected lifetime of a household is given by

$$\int_0^\infty t\lambda e^{\lambda t}dt = \frac{1}{\lambda}$$

The horizon of the household is thus equal to $1/\lambda$.

Under the assumption that individual utility is logarithmic, the household born at time s is modelled as maximizing the following expected utility function as of time t

$$E_t\left(\int_t^\infty \log[c_T(s, v)^\phi c_N(s, v)^{1-\phi}]e^{\delta(t-v)}dv\right); \quad \phi < 1 \tag{1'}$$

where E is the mathematical expectations operator c_T is household consumption of internationally traded goods, and c_N is household consumption of home (non-traded) goods. δ is the pure rate of time preference, and ϕ is a parameter.

Under the assumption that the only source of uncertainty is about the time of death, the problem of the household can be written as

$$\max_{\{c_T(s, v), c_N(s, v)\}} \int_t^\infty \log[c_T(s, v)^\phi c_N(s, v)^{1-\phi}]e^{(\delta+\lambda)(t-v)}dv \tag{1}$$

subject to

$$\dot{a}(s, v) = [r(v) + \lambda]a(s, v) + \omega(s, v) - c(s, v) \tag{2}$$

where α denotes the real assets of household s. A dot above a variable denotes its time derivative, r is the real interest rate, and ω is the real labour income of the household, assumed exogenous. All real variables, including the real interest rate, are expressed in terms of the price of home goods.

Households are allowed to take life insurance. At the time of their death their non-human wealth is transferred to insurance companies, who in return pay households an income stream consisting of instantaneous payments equal to a proportion λ of their non-human wealth. We assume (following Yaari, 1965) that the insurance industry is competitive. Also note that the effective discount rate of future instantaneous utilities is higher than the pure rate of time preference, as the household takes into account the probability of death.

The first-order conditions for a maximum of (1) subject to (2) are the following

$$\frac{c_T(s, v)}{c_N(s, v)} = \frac{\phi}{1-\phi}Q(v)^{-1} \tag{3a}$$

$$\dot{c}_N(s, v) = [r(v) - \delta]c_N(s, v) \tag{3b}$$

$$\dot{c}_T(s, v) = \left[r(v) - \delta - \frac{\dot{Q}(v)}{Q(v)}\right]c_T(s, v) \tag{3c}$$

where Q is the real exchange rate, defined as the relative price of traded goods.

The first-order conditions have a standard interpretation. Equation (3a) suggests that the household will seek to maintain a constant ratio between its consumption of traded and non-traded goods, and is a direct consequence of the Cobb–Douglas assumption. Equations (3b) and (3c) suggest that consumption of each good will be increasing if the corresponding real interest rate exceeds the rate of time preference, it will be constant if the two are equal, and it will be negative if the rate of time preference exceeds the real interest rate.

From the constant shares property of the Cobb–Douglas utility function we can use (3b) and (3c) to derive the equation of motion of total household consumption, c, which is given by

$$\dot{c}(s, v) = [r(v) - \delta]c(s, v) \tag{4}$$

where $c(s, v) = c_N(s, v) + Q(v)c_T(s, v)$.

Equations (2) and (4) are the equations of motion of non-human wealth and consumption (savings) respectively for the household born at time s.

2.2 Aggregation

Assume a birth rate equal to $\beta > 0$. Then, normalizing population at time 0 to unity, population at time t is given by

$$N(t) = \beta e^{-\lambda t} \int_{-\infty}^{t} e^{\beta s} \, ds \tag{5}$$

Under the assumption that all households receive the same labour income, it is straightforward to show (see Blanchard, 1985, or Buiter, 1988) that aggregate consumption, non-human wealth, and human wealth evolve according to

$$C(t) = (\delta + \lambda)[A(t) + H(t)] \tag{6a}$$

$$\dot{A}(t) = r(t)A(t) + \Omega(t) - C(t) \tag{6b}$$

$$\dot{H}(t) = [r(t) + \beta]H(t) - \Omega(t) \tag{6c}$$

where capital letters denote aggregate variables. C is aggregate consumption, A is aggregate non-human wealth of households, H is aggregate human wealth, and Ω is aggregate labour income.

Again (6a)–(6c) have a standard interpretation. According to (6a) consumption is a constant fraction of the sum of human and non-human wealth. Equations (6b) and (6c) are standard accumulation equations. The presence of β in (6c) reflects the fact that all surviving households, even the newborn, have the same human capital.

The production side of the economy will be assumed very simple. Labour is the only factor of production, and technology is linear in employment in both the traded and non-traded goods sectors. Both sectors are competitive. The equilibrium real exchange rate is thus given by relative marginal productivities of labour. In what follows relative marginal productivities will be assumed equal and the real exchange rate is thus normalized to unity.

However, following Buiter (1988), we shall assume that there is a constant instantaneous proportional rate of growth of productivity θ. By choice of units the level of productivity in both sectors at time 0 is equal to unity. With this additional assumption, the equations of motion of aggregate variables as a fraction of labour income Ω are given by

$$c(t) = (\delta + \lambda)[\alpha(t) + h(t)] \tag{7a}$$

$$\dot{\alpha}(t) = [r(t) - (\beta - \lambda + \theta)]\alpha(t) + 1 - c(t) \tag{7b}$$

$$\dot{h}(t) = [(r(t) + \lambda - \theta]h(t) - 1 \tag{7c}$$

where $x(t) = X(t)/\Omega(t)$ for $x = c, \alpha, h$

Eliminating human capital between (7a)–(7c), we end up with

$$\dot{c}(t) = [r(t) - (\delta + \theta)]c(t) - \beta(\delta + \lambda)\alpha(t) \tag{8a}$$

$$\dot{\alpha}(t) = [r(t) - (\beta - \lambda + \theta)]\alpha(t) + 1 - c(t) \tag{8b}$$

Equations (8a) and (8b) are the equations of motion of the consumption–labour income ratio and the wealth–labour income ratio. Their properties are familiar from the Yaari–Blanchard model.

To proceed any further we need to specify the forms in which non-human wealth is held, and introduce the government.

2.3   Public sector deficits and debts in a small open economy

Assume a small open economy in which there are only two assets: foreign bonds f, and government bonds b. Given the absence of risk in the model, other than the probability of death, the two types of bond are perfect substitutes for households (see Giovannini, 1988). In such an economy, given the structure of production assumed in the previous section, Gross Domestic Product (GDP) is equal to total labour income Ω. Thus, the variables in (8a) and (8b) are the consumption-GDP ratio and private assets-GDP ratio respectively.

Assume a government that spends an amount g on goods and services, levies lump sum taxes τ, and borrows by issuing government debt b. g, τ, and b are ratios to GDP, i.e., Ω. With the introduction of the government, (8a) and (8b) are amended to

$$\dot{c}(t) = [r(t) - (\delta + \theta)]c(t) - \beta(\delta + \lambda)\alpha(t) \tag{9a}$$

$$\dot{\alpha}(t) = [r(t) - (\beta - \lambda + \theta)]\alpha(t) + 1 - \tau(t) - c(t) \tag{9b}$$

$$\dot{b}(t) = [(r(t) - (\beta - \lambda + \theta)]b(t) + g(t) - \tau(t) \tag{9c}$$

$$\dot{f}(t) = [r(t) - (\beta - \lambda + \theta)]f(t) + 1 - c(t) - g(t) \tag{9d}$$

$$\alpha(t) \equiv b(t) + f(t) \tag{9e}$$

From (9c), the change in the public debt to GDP ratio is driven by the primary deficit of the government $g - \tau$, while from (9d) the change in the external debt to GDP ratio is driven by the trade deficit $c + g - 1$.

It is straightforward to see from (9a)–(9e) that the model can be first solved for the consumption and private asset ratios to GDP by using equations (9a) and (9b), and then it can be solved for the distribution of the private sector assets between foreign and government bonds.

The system of (9a) and (9b) is linear in consumption and external debt. It will be saddlepoint stable if $(r - \delta - \theta)(r - \beta + \lambda - \theta) < \beta(\delta + \lambda)$. Sufficient conditions for saddlepoint stability are that the real interest rate is no higher than either the growth rate of GDP $(\beta - \lambda + \theta)$, or the sum of the pure rate of time preference and productivity growth $(\delta + \theta)$. However, neither of these conditions is necessary. The economy could be saddlepoint stable if the birth and death rates, and the pure rate of time preference, were sufficiently high relative to the difference of the real interest rate from both the growth rate of GDP, and the sum of the rates of time preference and productivity growth. If the condition for saddlepoint stability is not satisfied, and the real interest rate is too high, then the aggregate consumption–GDP ratio would be increasing for ever. In what follows we exclude this pathological case, by assuming that the condition for saddlepoint stability is satisfied. In such a case there is a well-defined steady state.

The determination of the steady state and the associated saddlepath dynamics are depicted in Figures 11.2 and 11.3. The $\dot{c} = 0$ and $\dot{\alpha} = 0$ lines represent the particular solutions of (9a) and (9b) when the private consumption and asset ratios to GDP respectively are constant. The vertical arrows show the direction of change in consumption and the horizontal arrows show the direction of change of assets in the relevant

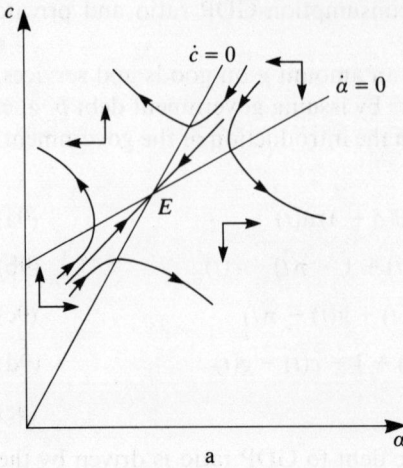

a

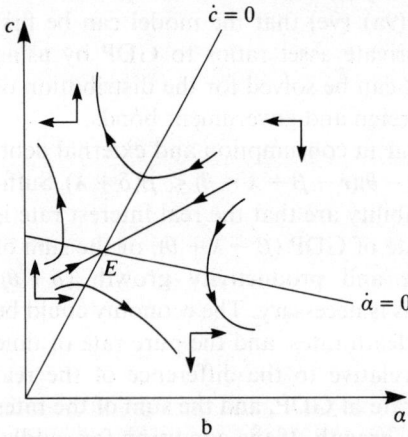

b

Figure 9.2   Equilibrium private consumption and assets $(r > \delta + \theta)$

quadrants. The slope of the constant consumption line will be positive if
the real interest rate exceeds the sum of the pure rate of time preference
and the rate of growth of labour productivity (Figure 9.2), and negative
if it falls below this sum (Figure 9.3). In the first case, steady-state private
non-human wealth will be positive, and in the second negative. The
$\dot{\alpha} = 0$ line will be positively sloping if the real interest rate exceeds the
growth rate of GDP, and negative sloping in the opposite case. Both types
of equilibria, with positive and negative private assets, will be assumed

$\dot{c} = 0$

c

E

$\dot{a} = 0$

a

a

$\dot{c} = 0$

c

$\dot{a} = 0$

E

a

b

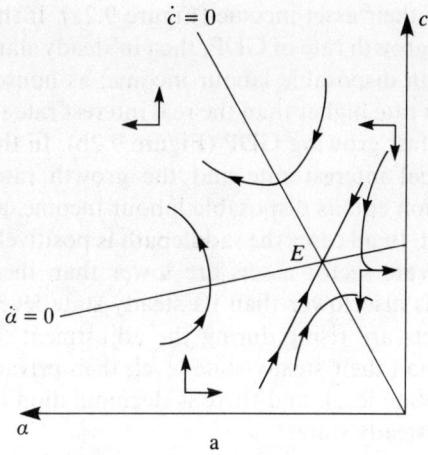

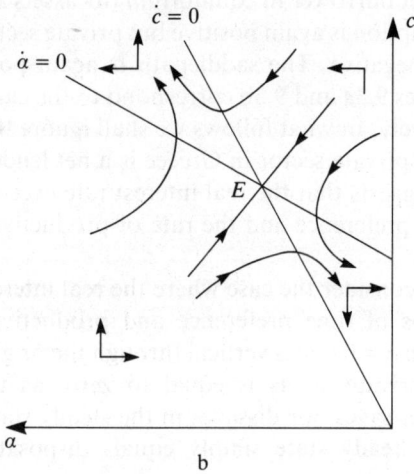

Figure 9.3   Equilibrium private consumption and assets $(r < \delta + \theta)$

saddlepoint stable and consumption is the variable that jumps to put the economy on the saddlepath.

Let us first consider the case in which the real interest rate exceeds the sum of the pure rate of time preference and the growth rate of productivity. This case is depicted in Figure 9.2. In steady state the private sector is a net lender, i.e., private sector assets relative to GDP are positive. If the real interest rate also exceeds the growth rate of GDP, then in steady state private consumption is higher than disposable labour income $(1 - \tau)$, as households also consume part of their asset income (Figure 9.2a). If the real interest rate falls short of the growth rate of GDP, then in steady state private consumption is lower than disposable labour income, as households must add to their assets at a rate higher than the real interest rate to maintain a constant ratio to the fast growing GDP (Figure 9.2b). In the case of equality between the real interest rate and the growth rate, steady-state aggregate consumption equals disposable labour income, as the $\dot{\alpha} = 0$ line would be horizontal. In all cases the saddlepath is positively sloping. This means that, if private sector assets are lower than their steady-state level, consumption is also lower than its steady-state level, ensuring that private sector assets are rising during the adjustment. If private sector assets are higher than their steady-state level, then private consumption exceeds its steady-state level, and there is decumulation of private sector assets towards the steady state.

If the real interest rate falls short of the sum of the pure rate of time preference and the rate of productivity growth ($r < \delta + \theta$), as in Figure 9.3, then the private sector is a net borrower in equilibrium (its assets are negative). In steady state, consumption is again positive but private sector assets (non-human wealth) are negative. The saddlepath is again positively sloping. The cases in Figures 9.3a and 9.3b correspond to the cases in Figures 9.2a and 9.2b respectively. In what follows we shall ignore this case, as the data suggest that the private sector in Greece is a net lender, which, in terms of our model, suggests that the real interest rate exceeds the sum of the pure rate of time preference and the rate of productivity growth.[5]

For completeness, let us briefly consider the case where the real interest rate equals the sum of the rates of time preference and productivity growth, $r = \delta + \theta$. In that case, the $\dot{c} = 0$ line is vertical through the origin, and the value of steady-state private assets is equal to zero, as the domestic household sector neither saves nor dissaves in the steady state. Aggregate consumption in the steady state simply equals disposable labour income.

The expressions for steady-state private sector assets and the consumption are given below

$$\bar{\alpha} = \frac{r - \delta - \theta}{\beta(\delta + \lambda) - (r - \delta - \theta)(r - \beta + \lambda - \theta)}(1 - \bar{\tau}) \tag{10}$$

$$\bar{c} = \frac{\beta(\delta + \lambda)}{\beta(\delta + \lambda) - (r - \delta - \theta)(r - \beta + \lambda - \theta)}(1 - \bar{\tau}) > 0 \tag{11}$$

A bar above a variable denotes its steady-state value. Note that the denominator in both expressions will be positive if the condition for saddlepath stability is satisfied. With saddlepath stability steady-state consumption will always be positive. Non-human wealth will only be positive if $r > \delta + \theta$, as suggested above.

We can now turn to one of the major concerns of this chapter, namely the implications of different ways of stabilizing a rising ratio of public debt to GDP.

3   Stabilizing a rising public debt–GDP ratio

We saw in Section 1 that the 1980s witnessed a significant and almost continuous rise in Greece's ratio of the public debt to GDP. What are the implications for tax revenue, government expenditure, and external debt if the government were to try to stabilize the public debt to GDP ratio? This section examines the theoretical aspects of the available options.

A rising public debt to GDP ratio occurs when the government is running public sector deficits which, as a percentage of GDP, exceed the product of the growth rate of GDP and the debt–GDP ratio. Consider equation (9c)

$$\dot{b}(t) = [r(t) - (\beta - \lambda + \theta)]b(t) + g(t) - \tau(t) > 0 \qquad (9c)$$

$\dot{b}$ will be positive if the sum of interest payments on public debt and non-interest government expenditure exceeds tax revenues and the growth induced reduction in the debt–GDP ratio. When $r > \beta - \lambda + \theta$ (i.e., when the real interest rate exceeds the growth rate) the process of public debt accumulation will be dynamically unstable. The ratio of public debt to GDP, b, will be rising for ever, unless there is some discretionary rise in tax revenues, or some discretionary fall in government expenditure to put a stop to this process. If $r < \beta - \lambda + \theta$, the public debt to GDP ratio will converge to a steady-state value, but, if it is currently rising, it will converge to a higher value than the current one.

The thought experiment we shall consider in this section and the next is the following: assume that the government faces a rising public debt to GDP ratio. What would happen if the government followed alternative discretionary actions to stabilize it at its current level?[6]

When the real interest rate exceeds the growth rate, the government can only stabilize the ratio of its debt to GDP by either producing a primary surplus, or using inflationary finance. If the growth rate exceeds the real interest rate it must reduce its primary deficit, but need not produce a surplus. In any case, ignoring inflationary finance for the moment, what is needed is either an increase in average taxation or a reduction in (non-interest) government expenditure. We shall examine these two options in turn.

3.1   Public debt stabilization through higher taxation

The steady-state relationship between taxes, debt, and government expenditure is given by the particular solution of equation (9c) for a constant b. Solving it for τ we get,

$$\bar{\tau} = (r - \beta + \lambda - \theta)\bar{b} + \bar{g} \tag{12}$$

Consider the following experiment: starting from steady state, the government increases the share of government expenditure and announces that it will stabilize the public debt to GDP ratio at a higher level through higher future taxes. The case where the real interest rate exceeds the growth rate is depicted in Figure 9.4.

The rise in steady-state taxation will cause a downward shift in the $\dot{\alpha} = 0$ curve, which will result in lower steady-state private consumption and private real assets (from point A to point C in Figure 9.4). Thus, external debt will increase on two counts. It will increase because of the substitution of government debt for foreign assets in the portfolios of households, and it will also increase because of the decumulation of assets that will occur in response to the higher steady-state taxation. The impact effect of such a program will be a sharp fall in private consumption (point B). This will be followed by further gradual falls in the average propensity to consume and decumulation of external assets (capital flight) along the saddlepath, as the private sector tends towards its new steady-state equilibrium with a lower non-human wealth to income ratio.

The case where the growth rate exceeds the real interest rate is similar in all respects, with the exception that public debt stabilization does not require a primary surplus but can be achieved with a primary deficit.

3.2   Public debt stabilization through lower government expenditure

If the government were to opt for a stabilization of the public debt through a fall in g from its current levels, the effects would be different.

Consider the following experiment. Starting from steady state, the government implements a (temporary) rise in the share of government exenditure, and announces that it will stabilize the public debt to GDP ratio at a higher level through a future fall in the share of government expenditure.

With such a program, neither steady-state private consumption nor private sector assets will change as a proportion of GDP. During the adjustment, public debt accumulation will be matched one-for-one by external asset decumulation, and the steady-state increase in external debt will thus be lower than in the case where future taxes go up. In the case of

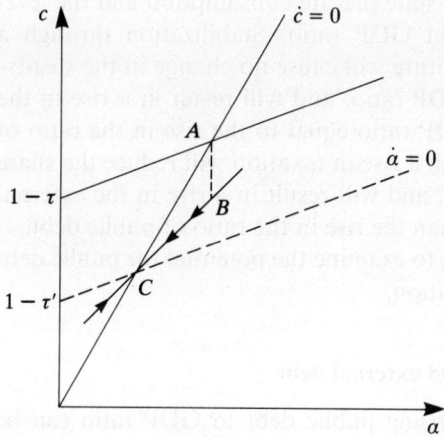

Figure 9.4   A tax-financed steady-state increase in the public debt–GDP ratio

stabilization through reductions in government expenditure the rise in the external debt to GDP ratio is the same as the rise in the public debt to GDP ratio. With stabilization through higher taxation the rise in the external debt to GDP ratio is higher than the rise in the public debt to GDP ratio, because private consumers also run down their assets as a proportion of GDP by accumulating foreign debt.

When the real interest rate exceeds the growth rate, the eventual reduction of the share of non-interest government expenditure to GDP will have to be higher than the original increase. In the opposite case it will be lower than the original increase.

3.3   Public debt and external debt stabilization

It is worth emphasizing something which is implicit in our discussion above, namely that stabilization of the public debt to GDP ratio is sufficient for the stabilization of the external debt to GDP ratio as well. No further action is needed on the part of the authorities. This is a direct consequence of the fact that the private sector, through its savings behaviour, stabilizes the ratio of its own assets to GDP, and the identity (9e) which states that private sector assets are the sum of government bonds and external assets.

In conclusion, stabilization of the public debt–GDP ratio will also stabilize the external debt–GDP ratio. In other words, the 'external constraint' in this model is just the flip side of the government solvency constraint. However, the manner in which the public debt–GDP ratio is stabilized will affect both steady-state private consumption and the level of the steady-state external debt–GDP ratio. Stabilization through a reduction in government expenditure will cause no change in the steady-state private consumption to GDP ratio, and will result in a rise in the steady-state external debt to GDP ratio equal to the rise in the ratio of public debt. Stabilization through a rise in taxation will reduce the share of private consumption in GDP, and will result in a rise in the external debt–GDP ratio that is higher than the rise in the ratio of public debt.

In the next section, we move on to examine the potential for public debt stabilization through higher inflation.

4   Seigniorage, public debt, and external debt

An additional way in which a rising public debt to GDP ratio can be stabilized is through an increase in seigniorage, i.e., government revenue from money creation. With a stable money demand function and a constant steady-state growth rate of GDP, an anticipated rise in the rate of growth of the money supply will result in higher expected and actual inflation.

4.1   Higher monetary growth and seigniorage

An anticipated increase in monetary growth may or may not increase seigniorage, as this will depend on the initial rate of monetary growth and the interest rate semi-elasticity of money demand. An increase in anticipated monetary growth will raise anticipated inflation and this will be reflected in higher nominal interest rates, which will reduce the proportion of money balances to GDP. To see this point, let us assume an interest-elastic demand for money function of the following form

$$\frac{M(t)}{P(t)} = k\Omega(t)e^{-\eta[r(t) + \pi(t)]} \tag{13'}$$

M is the nominal money supply, P the price level, π is expected inflation, and k is a constant. It is assumed that an increase in the nominal interest rate reduces money demand.[7]

Differentiating (13') with respect to time, assuming a constant real interest rate and a constant expected inflation rate, after some rearrangement we get

$$\pi = \mu - (\beta - \lambda + \theta) \tag{14}$$

where μ is the rate of growth of the money supply, $(\beta - \lambda + \theta)$ is the growth rate of GDP, and π is inflation. Thus, an anticipated permanent rise in μ will cause a rise in π in the same proportion. What will be the effect on steady-state seigniorage? To examine this it is worth writing money demand as a fraction of GDP. Dividing both sides of (14') by Ω we get

$$m = \frac{M}{P\Omega} = ke^{-\eta(r+\pi)} \tag{13}$$

where m is the ratio of money balances to GDP, and where the time index has been suppressed.

Steady-state seigniorage as a percentage of GDP is equal to

$$\sigma = \mu m \tag{15}$$

Using the money demand function (13) and the relation between money growth and expected inflation (14), we can see that

$$\frac{\partial \sigma}{\partial \mu} = (1 - \eta\mu)m = [1 - \eta(\pi + \beta - \lambda + \theta)]m \tag{16}$$

Whether seigniorage as a percentage of GDP rises or falls with a rise in the rate of growth of the money supply and inflation will depend on whether the product of the initial rate of monetary (or nominal income) growth and the interest rate semi-elasticity of money demand is less than or higher than unity. For low enough rates of monetary (nominal income) growth we are on the rising part of this 'Laffer curve' (see Figure 9.5). Maximum seigniorage is being extracted when the rate of monetary growth is equal to the inverse of the interest rate semi-elasticity of money demand. When the rate of monetary growth exceeds this threshold, seigniorage as a proportion of GDP falls with a rise in monetary growth.

4.2 The model with the addition of the money market

The model described in equation (9a) to (9e), with the addition of real money balances to real private sector wealth, the inflation tax, and seigniorage revenue, is amended as follows (money demand is given by (13)):

$$\dot{c}(t) = [r(t) - (\delta + \theta)]c(t) - \beta(\delta + \lambda)\alpha(t) \tag{9a}$$

$$\dot{\alpha}(t) = [r(t) - (\beta - \lambda + \theta)]\alpha(t) + 1 - \tau(t) \\ - [r(t) + \pi(t)]m(t) - c(t) \tag{9'b}$$

$$\dot{b}(t) = [(r(t) - (\beta - \lambda + \theta)]b(t) + g(t) - \tau(t) \\ - [\pi(t) + \beta - \lambda + \theta]m(t) \tag{9'c}$$

$$\dot{f}(t) = [r(t) - (\beta - \lambda + \theta)]f(t) + 1 - c(t) - g(t) \tag{9d}$$

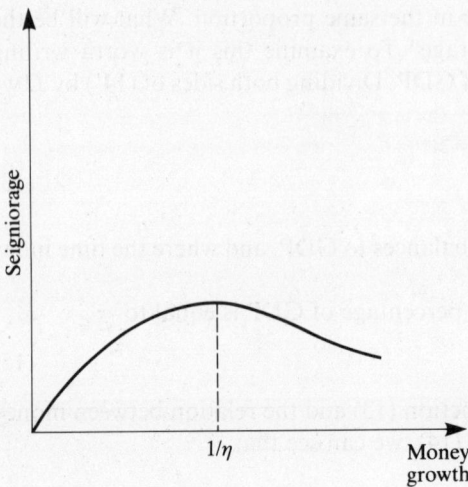

Figure 9.5   The seigniorage 'Laffer curve'

$$\alpha(t) = m(t) + b(t) + f(t) \tag{9'e}$$

The inflation tax as a percentage of GDP is equal to the nominal interest rate times the money–GDP ratio (9'b), while seigniorage as a percentage of GDP is equal to the growth rate of nominal income times the money–GDP ratio. The difference between the two is equal to the product of the money–GDP ratio and the difference between the real interest rate and the growth rate of GDP.

The steady-state solutions for consumption and private sector wealth are now as follows

$$\bar{\alpha} = \frac{r - \delta - \theta}{\beta(\delta + \lambda) - (r - \delta - \theta)(r - \beta + \lambda - \theta)}[1 - \bar{\tau} - (r + \pi)\bar{m}] \tag{10'}$$

$$\bar{c} = \frac{\beta(\delta + \lambda)}{\beta(\delta + \lambda) - (r - \delta - \theta)(r - \beta + \lambda - \theta)}[1 - \bar{\tau} - (r + \pi)\bar{m}] > 0 \tag{11'}$$

If the economy is to the left of the seigniorage 'Laffer curve', an increase in steady-state inflation will reduce private sector assets and private consumption as a proportion of GDP, as it will raise the share of the inflation tax.

4.3   Public debt stabilization through a rise in seigniorage

What are the implications of using a rise in steady-state monetary growth for public debt stabilization, private consumption, and external debt?

Public debt stabilization requires from (9'c) that

$$(\pi + \gamma)m = \mu k e^{-\eta(r + \mu - \gamma)} = (r - \gamma)b + g - \tau \tag{17}$$

where γ is the steady-state growth rate defined as $\gamma \equiv \beta - \lambda + \theta$.

Assume that the government opts for public debt stabilization through a rise in steady-state monetary growth. We shall again consider thought experiments similar to the ones examined before.

Starting from a steady state, consider a rise in government expenditure and public debt as shares of GDP, financed through higher seigniorage. We shall again start with the case when the real interest rate exceeds the growth rate. In fact, in this case, seigniorage must rise by enough to cover both the higher primary fiscal deficit and the part of interest payments on the increased public debt which is not paid for by economic growth. This case is depicted in Figure 9.6.

The rise in steady-state seigniorage will cause a downward shift in the $\dot{\alpha} = 0$ curve, as it will be associated with an increase in the inflation tax. This, as in the case of the increase in tax rates, will reduce steady-state private consumption and private real assets. External debt will increase if the reduction in the private asset–GDP ratio exceeds the reduction in the money–GDP ratio brought about by higher steady-state inflation. In any case, external debt will increase by less than in the case of higher taxation. The reason is that part of the reduction in private sector assets is achieved through the reduction in real money balances implied by higher nominal interest rates. Thus, there is less of a need to reduce foreign assets.

In conclusion, public debt stabilization through inflation will result in the same reduction in private consumption as public debt stabilization through higher taxation, and the same reduction in private sector assets. However, there will be less of an increase in the external debt to GDP ratio than in the case of tax finance, because inflationary finance also causes a reduction in real money balances as a percentage of GDP.

4.4   The trade-off between inflation and external debt

The above analysis suggests that to stabilize the public debt to GDP ratio at a given value, there is a trade-off between steady-state external debt and inflation. The higher the weight of monetary finance, the lower the external debt to GDP ratio. The trade-off is depicted by the convex curve in Figure 9.7. The equilibrium inflation rate and external debt to GDP ratio will be determined at the point of tangency of this curve and the government's indifference curves, assuming that the government dislikes both inflation and external debt.

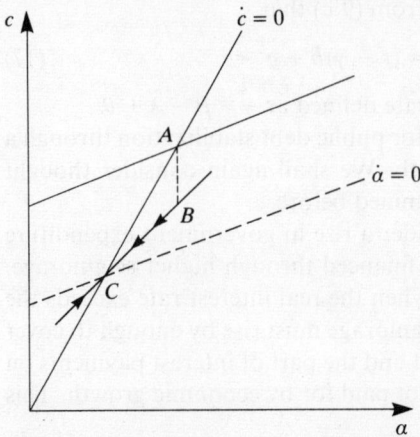

Figure 9.6   A seigniorage-financed steady-state increase in the public debt–GDP ratio

Figure 9.7 can be used to analyse what would happen to external debt and inflation following a permanent rise in government expenditure accompanied by a steady-state rise in the ratio of public debt to GDP. Such a policy would shift the trade-off to the right, and the government has two options in trying to stabilize the higher public debt to GDP ratio. The first is to raise taxes, which would result in high external indebtedness, and the second is to raise seigniorage, which would result in lower external indebtedness, but higher steady-state inflation. If the government dislikes both inflation and external debt, it will opt for a mix of tax and inflationary finance (Mankiw, 1987; Grilli, 1989). The economy will move from E to E'. Thus, in the new equilibrium, both the external debt to GDP ratio and the inflation rate will rise.

4.5   External versus public debt targets and inflation

We have concentrated up to now on the case where the government stabilizes the public debt to GDP ratio through different means, allowing the external debt to GDP ratio to settle at whatever level is required. Alternatively, the government could choose to stabilize the external debt to GDP ratio at its current level, or, more generally, it could have an external debt to GDP target. To see the effects on policy options and the public debt from some targets, we can use (9'e), (10″), and (18) to arrive at

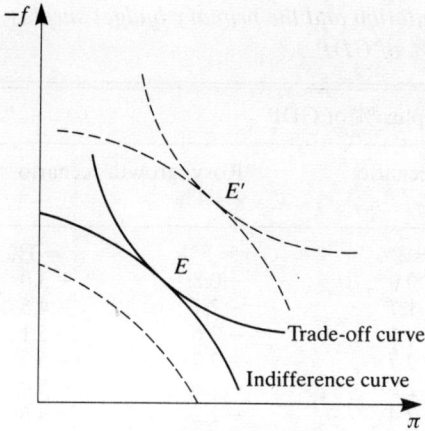

Figure 9.7   The trade-off between inflation and external debt

the following relation between the external debt target, inflation, tax-ation, and government expenditure

$$(r + \pi)\psi m = (r - \gamma)(-\bar{f}) + g - \psi\tau \qquad (18)$$

where $\psi = \dfrac{\beta(\delta + \lambda)}{\beta(\delta + \lambda) - (r - \delta)(r - \gamma)}$.

For given government expenditure, equation (18) provides long-run combinations between income tax and inflation which are long-run com-patible with external debt targets. With external debt targets, the rise in inflation and taxes reduces private sector wealth in a similar way as with public debt stabilization. However, in this case, because the government has an external debt target, the private sector will arrive at its optimal wealth to GDP ratio by off-loading government bonds rather than external assets. Thus, if the government is trying to stabilize a rising external debt to GDP ratio, it will reduce the public debt GDP ratio below its current level. Accordingly, the required seigniorage will be lower for given taxes and government expenditure.

Having analysed the alternative options, we turn to the details of the Greek case.

5   Public and external debt stabilization in Greece

We have seen in Section 1 that the rise in Greece's external indebtedness went hand in hand with the rise in inflation and the GDP shares of

Table 9.5. *The trade-off between inflation and the primary budget surplus for public debt stabilization at 100% of GDP*

Inflation %	Primary budget surplus % of GDP			
	'Gloomy' growth scenario $\gamma = 2\%$		'Rosy' growth scenario $\gamma = 4\%$	
	$r = 5\%$	$r = 3\%$	$r = 5\%$	$r = 3\%$
0	2.1	0.0	− 0.8	− 3.0
5	0.6	− 1.7	− 2.1	− 4.5
10	− 0.1	− 2.5	− 2.6	− 5.1
15	− 0.3	− 2.7	− 2.7	− 5.2
20	− 0.3	− 2.6	− 2.6	− 5.0
25	0.0	− 2.4	− 2.2	− 4.6
30	0.3	− 2.0	− 1.9	− 4.2
40	1.0	− 1.3	− 1.1	− 3.4

Notes: These numbers have been obtained by calibrating the model with the following parameter values: $\delta = 2.5\%$, $\beta = 1.7\%$, $\lambda = 1\%$, $k = 60\%$, $\eta = 5.6$. See the text for a justification of these choices.

government expenditure and public sector debt. In this section we are concerned with the implications of alternative options for public and external debt stabilization.

To get beyond the theoretical arguments contained in the previous section, we calibrate the model by using appropriate numerical parameter values corresponding to the Greek economy. The parameters we chose are summarized in Table 9.5 and its footnote.

The parameter of 2.5% for the pure rate of time preference has been taken from Alogoskoufis and Nissim (1981). λ has been assumed equal to 1%, which is approximately equal to the inverse of life expectancy in Greece (73 years). β, the rate of birth of new households, has been calculated by adding λ to the rate of growth of population of age 15–64, which was equal to 0.7% per annum on average for the 1960–88 period. η has been assumed equal to 5.6. This is our best estimate of the interest rate semi-elasticity of money demand using annual data (see Appendix 9.2). k has been assumed equal to 60%. This has been calculated from the estimates of the money demand function (Appendix 9.2), noting that recent velocity at 20% inflation rates was equal to about 5. With regard to the other parameters of the model we have examined two growth scenarios, a 'gloomy' one ($\gamma = \beta - \lambda + \theta = 2\%$ per annum), which happens to be in accordance with OECD projections for 1990 and 1991, and a 'rosy' one ($\lambda = 4\%$ per annum). We also examine two real interest rate scenaria (3% and 5%).

Note that, with an estimate of the interest rate semi-elasticity of money demand equal to 5.6, the seigniorage-maximizing nominal income (monetary) growth rate is equal to 18%, slightly lower than Greece's average growth of nominal income in the 1980s, which was 20%. Thus, the estimates of money demand reported in Appendix 9.2, as well as other estimates of money demand in Greece, suggest that the government cannot hope to get more steady-state seigniorage by higher monetary growth. The option of public (and external) debt stabilization from their currently rising values through higher inflation simply does not exist.

5.1   Trade-offs between steady-state inflation rates and public deficits

Table 9.5 reports the trade-offs between inflation and the primary budget surplus that, according to the model, would ensure stabilization of the public debt to GDP ratio at its current ratio to GDP of approximately 100%. The estimates highlight that with budget deficits of the order that Greece has been experiencing in recent years, the government is clearly insolvent. In fact, if the government is insolvent, so is the country, as an unsustainable public debt accumulation process implies an unsustainable external debt accumulation process.

In the 2% 'gloomy' growth scenario, with world real interest rates of about 5% per annum, solvency requires that the government achieves a primary budget deficit of only 0.3% of GDP if inflation rates stay at their current level of about 20% per annum. If Greece were to contemplate joining the EMS, and eventually the EMU process, it would need to live with inflation rates of about 5% per annum or less. In that case, to be solvent, the public sector ought to be running a primary surplus of 0.6% of GDP. In the case of lower world interest rates, solvency could be achieved with higher budget deficits. For example, to stabilize the public debt to GDP ratio with world interest rates of 3% per annum, the government of Greece would need to reduce the primary budget deficit to 2.6% of GDP if inflation were to remain in the region of 20%. With the lower inflation rate that would be implied by membership of the exchange rate mechanism of the EMS, the primary budget deficit would have to fall to 1.7% of GDP.

If the growth rate rises to nearer the levels of the 1970s (say the 'rosy' scenario of 4% per annum), the deficit reduction requirements are that much looser. With 20% inflation, the primary deficits that would stop the debt to GDP ratios from rising are 2.6% with a real interest rate of 5% and 5.0% with a 3% real interest rate. If inflation falls to 5%, these targets fall to 2.1% and 4.5% respectively.

Note, however, that, as was suggested above, current forecasts of the OECD for GDP growth in Greece are nearer to the 'gloomy' growth scenario. The June 1990 *Economic Outlook* forecasts growth rates of 1.4% in 1990 and 2.1% in 1991 (p. 113). Its forecast for the primary deficit of the general government (i.e., excluding interest payments) is 6.5% of GDP in 1990 and 5.1% in 1991. This is a far cry from the 0.3% primary deficit that we calculate would be required to stabilize public and external debt ratios. The average gap that must be closed in the two years 1990 and 1991 is 5.5 percentage points of GDP per annum.[8]

5.2   Implications for the steady-state taxes and external debt

We next turn to the implications of the choice of different steady-state inflation rates (seigniorage) for taxes and external debt. Table 9.6 contains some calculations for the 'gloomy' (but realistic) scenario of 5% real interest rates and 2% growth rates. The differences in the share of taxes are very small for inflation rates between 5% and 25%. The ratio of taxes to GDP is of the order of 40%, to roughly maintain a zero primary deficit. However, different inflation rates have profound implications for external debt. If steady-state inflation is reduced from 15% to 5%, the external debt to GDP ratio associated with a stable 100% public debt to GDP ratio rises from 40% of GDP to 62% of GDP. The reason is that the reduction in steady-state inflation (and nominal interest rates) increases the demand for money, and private households dispose of external assets to maintain a constant ratio of their assets to income. The large reduction in foreign assets is a reflection on the high estimate of the interest rate semi-elasticity of money demand. With a rise in the average inflation rate to 25%, the external debt to GDP ratio would fall to 27%.

5.3   The dangers of a delayed stabilization, or why gradualism is not an option

It should be noted that the above analysis is based on the assumption that fiscal policy is immediately adjusted to ensure solvency. If action is delayed, public debt will continue to rise, and stabilization will require increasingly tougher measures. Equation (17) can be used to determine the upper bound on debt, beyond which a conventional stabilization is not feasible. After this is reached, the government will have to resort to debt repudiation or a surprise hyperinflation to wipe out part of its debt.

Table 9.6. *Trade-off among taxes, seigniorage, and external debt for public debt stabilization at 100% of GDP*
Scenario: $\gamma = 2\%$, $r = 5\%$, $g = 40\%$

Inflation %	Taxes % of GDP	External debt % of GDP
5	41	62
15	40	40
25	40	27

Notes: See notes to the previous table. The baseline of 40% external debt to GDP ratio at 15% inflation has been assumed to correspond with the actual experience of 1988.

Feasibility is ensured only when the primary surpluses implied by (17) do not exceed the maximum possible level, defined as

$$s_{max} = \tau_{max} - g_{min} \qquad (19)$$

where s_{max} refers to the maximum primary surplus, τ_{max} to maximum average taxes, and g_{min} to the minimum share of government expenditure, given institutional and social constraints.

Consider the following example: seigniorage is at its maximum possible level, i.e., roughly 2.6% of GDP, with inflation rates of 20%. Assume that fiscal toughness cannot go beyond achieving a primary surplus of 1% of GDP ($s_{max} = 0.01$). Then, a crisis will occur when public debt reaches 120% of GDP, under the low growth scenario ($\gamma = 2\%$), with real interest rates at 5% per annum. If no action was taken, and public sector deficits continued at the 1989 levels of about 20% of GDP, debt would have reached this crisis threshold in early 1991. With the deficit reduction package announced by the government in the interim 1990 budget, this may be delayed for a further 1–2 years. When and if the crisis point is reached, the only actions available will be a reduction in the debt stock, which could be achieved either by government fiat (say a repudiation of part of domestic debt) or a surprise hyperinflation.

One could, of course, reach different conclusions by making alternative assumptions about s_{max}. Needless to say, the above example should be taken, as indeed should all of the calculations, as indicative. A number of assumptions and forecasts are built into them, and they rely on the calibration of a rather simple model. However, it is also worth saying that these calculations are also quite robust, and similar to those reached by other experts (e.g., the OECD). Even if the exact numbers are wrong, we feel they are of the right order of magnitude, and that they show the order of the task of stabilizing the rising public and national indebtedness of Greece.

6   Conclusions

The conclusions of this paper can be summarized as follows: the rise in Greece's external indebtedness in the 1980s can be directly attributed to the rapid growth of government expenditure and the persistently high budget deficits. The rise in world real interest rates and the slowdown in economic growth have, of course, accentuated the rise in domestic and external debt.

We have shown that, if private households are forward-looking, public debt stabilization is a sufficient condition for external debt stabilization. However, the way in which public debt is stabilized has implications for the equilibrium level of external debt. Public debt stabilization through a reduction in government expenditure will result in a lower steady-state external debt to GDP ratio than any other option. The other two possible options are an increase in seigniorage revenue and an increase in taxes.

We showed that the average inflation rate in Greece is at a level that maximizes steady-state seigniorage. A further rise in the proportion of seigniorage revenue is not possible. A reduction in government expenditure and an increase in taxes are thus the only feasible alternatives.[9]

We have provided some calculations which show that the primary budget deficit must be reduced immediately to 0.3% of GDP for public and external debt to be stabilized. The OECD projection in the June 1990 *Economic outlook* is that the general government primary deficit is going to be 6.5% of GDP in 1990 and 5.1% in 1991. Thus, according to our calculations in Table 9.5, the average gap to be closed in 1990–1 is 5.5 percentage points of GDP per annum. Current plans would only lead to public and external debt stabilization if growth were to pick up to about 4% per annum, and world real interest rates were as low as 3% per annum. This is highly unlikely. Thus, the fiscal authorities in Greece have some way to go before public and external debt ratios are stabilized, and the danger of a crisis averted.

Our final word regards the possibility of drachma's entry to the exchange rate mechanism of the EMS, and Greece's eventual participation in EMU. This will lead to inflation rates of 5% or less, with associated losses in seigniorage revenue. Roughly, participation in the EMS will require an additional reduction of the primary deficit of about one percentage point of GDP in the low growth scenario, and half a percentage point in the high growth scenario. The reduction in inflation will also lead to higher external debt than otherwise. However, given the order of the overall task of deficit reductions required for stabilization, and the benefits the EMS seems to have brought to other countries anyway (see Giavazzi and Giovannini, 1989), these seem trivial. Provided adequate further fiscal stabilization measures are undertaken, there is no reason why Greece should not immediately enter the exchange rate mechanism of the EMS.

Appendix 9A   Stability analysis of the model

We consider here the system of equations (9a) to (9e). Given the identity (9e), stability of the system can be characterized by only studying the dynamics of consumption, total private wealth, and foreign assets. Domestic public debt is thus a residual and is stabilized whenever the other two stocks reach asymptotically stable ratios to GDP. (Note that the analysis in the text treats foreign assets as a residual.)

Writing the model in state space form, one can easily see that the characteristic polynominial is equal to

$$\phi(z) = (z - r + \gamma)\{z^2 - (2r - \gamma - \delta - \theta)z \\ + (r - \gamma)(r - \delta - \theta) - \xi\} \tag{A1}$$

where $\xi = \beta(\delta + \lambda)$, and $\gamma = \beta - \lambda + \theta$. γ is the growth rate of GDP.
With some manipulation we get

$$(r - \gamma)(r - \delta - \theta) - \xi = (r - \theta + \lambda)(r - \theta - \beta - \delta) \tag{A2}$$

so that the characteristic polynomial is written as

$$\phi(z) = (z - r + \gamma)\{z^2 - (2r - \gamma - \delta - \theta)z \\ + (r - \theta + \lambda)(r - \theta - \beta - \delta)\} \tag{A1'}$$

Saddlepath stability requires two stable (negative) and one unstable (positive) roots. We distinguish two cases:

Case 1: $r < \gamma$
In this case, saddlepath stability is guaranteed if the quadratic equation has one stable and one unstable root. The other is $z_3 = r - \gamma < 0$.
The condition for saddlepath stability then is that, $\theta - \lambda < r < \theta + \beta + \delta$. Since $\gamma = \beta - \lambda + \theta < \beta + \delta + \theta$, saddlepath stability obtains in the region

$$\theta - \lambda < r < \beta - \lambda + \theta \tag{A3}$$

In this case, stock to GDP ratios reach steady-state finite values and consumption is a jumping variable.

Under the additional assumption that households are net lenders in equilibrium, consumption is positive for $r > \delta + \theta$. Since $\delta + \theta > \theta - \lambda$, the last condition is modified to

$$\theta + \delta < r < \theta + (\beta - \lambda) \tag{A4}$$

This is possible only if $\delta < \beta - \lambda$, i.e., when the rate of pure time preference is lower than the population growth rate.

The upper-bound condition on the interest rate has the meaning that, although assets accumulate because of interest payments, they become a decreasing proportion of GDP. Positive private sector savings (and public sector deficits) are thus sustainable.

Case 2: $r > \gamma$

In this case, saddlepath stability would only obtain if the quadratic equation in (A1$'$) had two negative roots. A necessary condition for that is

$$2r < \gamma + \delta + \theta = \beta - \lambda + \delta + 2\theta \tag{A5}$$

Given that $r > \gamma$, this is only possible if $\delta > \beta - \lambda$, i.e., when the rate of pure time preference is higher than the rate of population growth.

For the product of the roots we must have that

$$(r - \theta + \lambda)(r - \theta - \beta - \delta) > 0 \tag{A6}$$

which is satisfied for either $r < \theta - \lambda$, or $r > \theta + \beta + \delta$. In combination with $r > \gamma$ the first requires $\beta < 0$ which is ruled out. The second contradicts (A5), since for (A5) to be satisfied it would require that $\beta + \lambda + \delta < 0$. Thus, $r > \gamma$ leads to instability. Note, however, that, as shown in the text, the sub-system of private sector assets and consumption is stable even in this case. What becomes unstable is the stock of foreign assets (and domestic bonds). The situation may be controlled by feedback fiscal policy rules to which we now turn.

Feedback fiscal policy rules

In the case when $r > \gamma$ feedback fiscal policy rules can remove one extra unstable root in (A1$'$). Restricting attention to simple rules, we consider two alternatives:

Feedback on the current account deficit (flow rule)

$$(\tau - g) = s_0 + s_1 \dot{f} \tag{R1}$$

Feedback on the stock of external debt (stock rule).

$$(\tau - g) = s_0 + s_1 f \tag{R2}$$

The flow rule suggests that the primary budget deficit falls as the current account deficit increases, while the second suggests that the primary budget deficit falls as external debt rises.

It is straightforward to show that flow rules of the type (R1) are not capable of stabilizing the process of external (and public) debt accumulation when the real interest rate exceeds the growth rate. The reason is that, when fiscal policy responds only to changes in assets, the explosive process that accumulates assets cannot be stopped, as even with zero net deficits assets keep accumulating. To stabilize the process of external and public debt accumulation in this case one should adopt stock-targeting rules, of the type (R2).

Appendix 9B   Estimates of money demand functions

The most important parameter for assessing the extent to which an increase in the rate of monetary growth increases seigniorage revenue, is the interest rate semi-elasticity of money demand. Since this parameter is so crucial for the question of seigniorage, we report here on the results of an investigation of money demand in Greece.

The estimates are based on a log-linear version of equation (13') in the text. Taking logarithms we get

$$\ln M_t = \ln P_t + \ln \Omega_t - \eta i_t + \ln k_t \tag{M1}$$

where i is the nominal interest rate.

A preliminary analysis suggests that one would not be able to reject the hypothesis that measures of money, prices, output, and the opportunity cost of money are non-stationary.

To test for stationarity we ran the following regressions on each of the variables.

$$\Delta x_t = \alpha + \beta x_{t-1} + \sum_{j=1}^{n} \gamma_j \Delta x_{t-j} \tag{M2}$$

where x is one of $\ln M$, $\ln P$, $\ln \Omega$, i. The Dickey and Fuller (1979) statistic is based on the 't-ratio' of the coefficient β, when all the γ_js are equal to zero, and the Augmented Dickey–Fuller statistic is based on the 't-ratio' of β, when at least some of the γ_js are allowed to be non-zero. When the 't-statistic' of β is lower than the critical values tabulated in Fuller (1976), one cannot reject the hypothesis that the relevant series is non-stationary

Table 9B.1. *Tests for unit roots of money demand variables*

	Annual data 1950–88		Quarterly data 1961 Q2–1989 Q2	
	DF	ADF	DF	ADF
ln M_t	− 1.19	− 0.23	—	1.45
ln P_t	—	1.29	—	1.34
ln Ω_t	− 3.82	− 3.09	—	− 3.25
i_t	—	− 0.87	− 0.30	− 0.39
Critical value	2.93	2.93	2.89	2.89

Notes: M is the narrow money supply M1. *P* is the GDP deflator (annual data) and the wholesale price index (quarterly data). *Ω* is GDP at 1970 prices (annual data) and the index of industrial production (quarterly data). *i* is the period average of the interest rate on savings deposits. DF is the Dickey–Fuller test, ADF is the Augmented Dickey–Fuller test and the critical value of the 5% value from Fuller (1976). The number of lags included in the ADF regression have been as proposed by Schwert (1987). Given our sample sizes these are one lag for annual data and four lags for quarterly data. The simple Dickey–Fuller test is not reported when the coefficients of lagged changes are statistically significant.

(has at least one unit root). The results for annual and quarterly data for Greece are tabulated in Table 9B.1.

The Dickey–Fuller and Augmented Dickey–Fuller statistics suggest that one cannot reject the hypothesis that money, prices, and the nominal interest have a unit root. Surprisingly, the unit root hypothesis seems to be rejected narrowly for GDP (annual data) and industrial production (quarterly data). However, when one allows for the change in the average growth rate of GDP and industrial production in the 1980s (by including a dummy variable that takes the value of one after 1980 and zero before), the unit root hypothesis cannot be rejected for GDP and industrial production either.

Given these results, the next question that arises is whether money, prices, income, and nominal interest rates are cointegrated (Engle and Granger, 1987). Cointegration tests are presented in Table 9B.2. The results for both annual and quarterly data suggest that these variables are not cointegrated. In terms of the money demand function (M1) lack of cointegration can be interpreted as a non-stationary money demand shock *k*.

Assuming that ln k_t is a random walk with drift ϵ, the money demand function (M1) can be written as

$$\Delta \ln M_t = \epsilon + \Delta \ln P_t + \Delta \ln \Omega_t - \eta \Delta i_t + v_t \qquad \text{(M3)}$$

where v_t is the white-noise process driving the random walk in ln k_t.

Table 9B.2. *Cointegration tests*

| | Annual data 1950–88 | | Quarterly data 1961 Q2–1989 Q2 | |
	DF	ADF	DF	ADF
	− 3.30	− 2.80	− 4.49	− 2.94
Critical value	4.35	3.98	4.22	4.02

Notes: The DF and ADF test are tests on the residuals of a regression of the log of the money supply on the log of income and prices, and the level of the nominal interest rate. The critical values are from Engle and Yoo (1987).

Estimates of (M3) are presented in Table 9B.3 for both annual and quarterly data. For each data set, the first column presents OLS estimates, and the second instrumental variables estimates, with the instruments being one lag of each regressor and the regressant.

The results suggest huge differences in the estimate of η between OLS and IV estimation. Since in the presence of simultaneity between money and interest rates the OLS estimates are inconsistent, we opt for the consistent IV estimates. The IV estimate of η for annual data is equal to 5.59 (ASE = 1.84), while for quarterly data it is equal to 9.89 (ASE = 3.95). Both estimates are statistically significant at conventional significance levels. Note that in OLS estimation there is a huge downward bias.

These estimates are not grossly at variance with the estimates of the interest rate semi-elasticity of money demand in previous studies. For example, Alogoskoufis (1985), using FIML in the context of a three equation macro-model for Greece, finds a long-run semi-elasticity of money demand equal to 8.24 (ASE = 2.87).

In the calibration of the model in the text we opt for the lower estimate of 5.6 from the regression with annual data. This is based on a longer time span (1952–88) and incorporates some of the interesting macroeconomic episodes of the 1950s, and is probably based on better quality data (e.g., GDP rather than industrial production as the income variable). In any case, the higher estimate in the quarterly regressions is not statistically different from 5.6, as it has a higher standard error as well.

NOTES

We have benefited from the comments of Paul Levine, and participants in the Athens conference. We also wish to thank Nikitas Pittis for excellent research

Table 9B.3. *Estimates of money demand functions*

	Dependent variable: $\Delta\ln(M/P\Omega)_t$			
	Annual data 1952–88		Quarterly data 1961 Q2–1989 Q2	
	OLS	IV	OLS	IV
Constant	0.03	0.03	0.01	0.01
	(0.01)	(0.01)	(0.01)	(0.01)
i_t	−1.99	−5.59	−0.71	−9.89
	(0.90)	(1.84)	(0.81)	(3.95)
s	0.057	0.069	0.048	0.070
DW	2.057	2.100	2.205	2.299

Notes: The quarterly estimates have been obtained with the addition of three quarterly dummies. The instruments used in IV estimation have been one lag of monetary growth, inflation, output growth, and the change in the nominal interest rate.

assistance. Alogoskoufis acknowledges with thanks financial assistance from the ESRC and the CEPR Research Programme in International Macroeconomics, supported by grants from the Ford Foundation (No. 890–0404) and the Alfred P. Sloan Foundation (No. 88–4–23).

1 Intertemporal models of private sector savings and investment have gone a long way towards replacing Keynesian *IS–LM* models in the open economy macroeconomics literature. The latter are not well suited to the consistent analysis of intertemporal aspects of fiscal policies. In the context of the explanation of current account and external debt behaviour one of the early papers in this mold was Sachs (1981). A large number of papers in the last ten years have utilized this approach, and the books by Bruno and Sachs (1985) and Frenkel and Razin (1987) have popularized it even further.

2 Note the difference between our model and Currie and Levine (1991). In their model, because the private sector is not modelled as choosing savings in an intemporally optimal way (this could be due to credit constraints and other imperfections), the external constraint is distinct from the government solvency constraint. Yet, even in their model, provided there is a sufficiently high wealth elasticity of aggregate demand, private assets can be stabilized.

3 Our focus here is entirely on the long run, and the dynamics of adjustment of consumption and debt. We abstract from problems of short-run adjustment on the supply side, such as wage, price, and employment dynamics. For a model that incorporates such features see Alogoskoufis (1989, 1990). See also Christodoulakis (1990), for an analysis of debt dynamics in a more traditional Keynesian open economy model, and Papademos (1990) for an analysis of issues relating to debt and wage-price dynamics in a model with a detailed financial sector.

4 Note, however, that our results indicate that the reduction in inflation brought about by EMS membership will, *ceteris paribus*, require a higher steady-state external debt to GDP ratio than otherwise. This could be higher by as much as 22 percentage points of GDP if the lost seigniorage revenue was replaced by a rise in other taxes (Table 9.6). This is an illustration of the public finance arguments put forward by Dornbusch (1988) in his advocacy of a two-tier EMS, with 'underdeveloped' countries like Greece following a crawling peg exchange rate rule, that would allow them to choose their inflation rate. We do not feel that a loss of seigniorage equal to 1% of GDP is sufficient reason for sticking with high inflation. After all, Greece was a successful member of the Bretton Woods system of fixed exchange rates for twenty years, and its inflation rate was as low as the OECD average, if not lower.

6 Alternative ways of stabilizing the public debt to GDP ratio, that rest on reaction functions of the primary deficit are sketched in Appendix 9.1. This also contains a fuller stability analysis of the model.

7 Note that the demand for money function is postulated rather than derived from the optimization problem of households. This is mainly for simplicity, but it also reflects the lack of consensus about the appropriate microfoundations of money demand.

8 The June 1990 issue of OECD's *Economic Outlook* contains calculations of indicators of the sustainability of fiscal policy in the OECD countries. These are similar to our sustainability indicator in that they measure the reduction of the primary deficit in percentage points of GDP, so that the public debt to GDP ratio is immediately stabilized. The OECD measure for Greece (by far the highest in the relevant table on page 18) is 7.7% of GDP on average for 1990 and 1991. Our own measure of this primary deficit gap is 5.5% (the average of 6.5 minus 0.3 and 5.1 minus 0.3). There must be slight differences in definitions and interest rate assumptions. However, what seems to fully account for the discrepancy is the treatment of seigniorage revenue. The OECD measure does not seem to take it into account. The advantage of our measure is that it does. In fact, we assume 20% inflation rates, which is the OECD forecast for Greek inflation. On the assumption of zero inflation, our measure of the primary deficit gap is 7.9%, which is very close to the OECD figure.

9 In a recent survey of structural problems of the Greek economy, Katseli (1990) briefly considers macroeconomic stabilization. Apart from espousing gradualism, she reaches a strong conclusion about taxes. She argues that, 'the brunt of the adjustment however has to be on the revenue side since total revenues cover only 60% of government expenditures in 1988, down from 87% in 1970 and 79% in 1980' (p. 303). This conclusion presupposes that the huge increases in government consumption and transfer payments that took place in the 1980s, and which were financed by borrowing, are socially desirable. It implies that the deferred taxes must now be levied with interest. We feel that such a conclusion is not warranted, and given the effects of higher taxes on external debt that are highlighted in our paper, as well as other disincentive effects, we would be extremely disinclined to endorse the view that the brunt of the adjustment has to be borne by taxation. The Greek tax system must be reformed for equity and efficiency reasons, but it is not at all clear that the average tax burden must rise.

REFERENCES

Alogoskoufis, G.S. (1985), 'Macroeconomic Policy and Aggregate Fluctuations in a Semi-Industrialized Open Economy: Greece 1951–80', *European Economic Review* **29**, 35–61.
  (1989), 'Macroeconomic Policy and the External Constraint in the Dependent Economy: the case of Greece', CEPR Discussion Paper no. 330, London.
  (1990), 'Competitiveness, Wage Adjustment and Macroeconomic Policy in the Dependent Economy: The Case of Greece', *Greek Economic Review* (forthcoming).
Alogoskoufis, G.S. and J. Nissim (1981), 'Consumption-Income Dynamics under Rational Expectations: Theory and Evidence', *Greek Economic Review* **3**, 128–47.
Blanchard, O.J. (1985), 'Debts, Deficits and Finite Horizons', *Journal of Political Economy* **93**, 223–47.
Bruno, M. and J.D. Sachs (1985), *The Economics of Worldwide Stagflation*, Oxford, Blackwells.
Buiter, W.H. (1988), 'Death, Birth, Productivity Growth and Debt Neutrality', *Economic Journal* **98**, 279–93.
Christodoulakis, N. (1990), 'Debt Dynamics in a Small Open Economy', mimeo, Athens School of Economics.
Currie, D. and P. Levine (1991), 'The Solvency Constraint and Fiscal Policy in an Open Economy', this volume.
Dickey, D.A. and W.A. Fuller (1979), 'Distribution of the Estimators for Autoregressive Time Series with a Unit Root', *Journal of the American Statistical Association* **74**, 427–31.
Dornbusch, R. (1988), 'The EMS, the Dollar and the Yen,' in F. Giavazzi, S. Micossi, and M. Miller (eds.), *The European Monetary System*, Cambridge University Press, STEP and CEPR.
Engle, R.F. and C.W.J. Granger (1987), 'Co-integration and Error Correction: Representation, Estimation and Testing', *Econometrica* **55**, 251–76.
Engle, R.F. and B.S. Yoo (1987), 'Forecasting and Testing in Co-integrated Systems', *Journal of Econometrics* **35**, 143–59.
Frenkel, J. and A. Razin (1987), *Fiscal Policy in the World Economy*, Cambridge, MA: MIT Press.
Fuller, W.A. (1976), *Introduction to Statistical Time Series*, New York: John Wiley.
Giavazzi, F. and A. Giovannini (1989), *Limiting Exchange Rate Flexibility: The European Monetary System* Cambridge, MA: MIT Press.
Giovannini, A. (1988), 'The Real Exchange Rate, the Capital Stock and Fiscal Policy', *European Economic Review* **32**, 1747–67.
Grilli, V. (1989), 'Seigniorage in Europe', in M. De Cecco and A. Giovannini (eds.), *A European Central Bank?*, Cambridge University Press.
Katseli, L.T. (1990), 'Structural Adjustment of the Greek Economy', in C. Bliss and J.B. de Macedo (eds.), *Unity with Diversity in the European Economy: The Community's Southern Frontier*, Cambridge University Press and CEPR.
Mankiw, N.G. (1987), 'The Optimal Collection of Seigniorage: Theory and Evidence', *Journal of Monetary Economics* **20**, 327–41.
Papademos, L. (1990), 'Greece and the EMS: Issues, Prospects and a Framework for Analysis', in P. De Grauwe and L. Papademos (eds.), *The European Monetary System in the 1990s*, London: Longman.

Sachs, J.D. (1981), 'The Current Account and Macroeconomic Adjustment in the 1970s', *Brookings Papers on Economic Activity* 1, 201–82.

Schwert, G.W. (1987), 'Effects of Model Mis-specification on Tests for Unit Roots in Macroeconomic Data', *Journal of Monetary Economics* 20, 73–103.

Yaari, M. (1965), 'Uncertain Lifetime, Life Insurance, and the Theory of the Consumer', *Review of Economic Studies* 32, 137–50.

Discussion

PAUL LEVINE

This is an extremely useful chapter both for its theoretical insights and its examination of policy options for Greece. At the theoretical level the chapter provides a synthesis of some recent contributions to the study of fiscal policy in open economies built upon solid micro-foundations with a more standard treatment of monetary policy and seigniorage. At the practical, policy-oriented level the results reported should concentrate the minds of policy-makers in Athens.

The main theoretical issue examined is the relationship between indebtedness and fiscal policy. In particular the question posed is whether the stabilization of the public debt to GDP ratio is sufficient for the stabilization of the external debt to GDP ratio. The answer provided by the chapter is that, if the private sector plans its consumption and savings in an intertemporally optimal fashion, then the stabilization of the public debt to GDP ratio is sufficient to stabilize the external debt to GDP ratio as well.

Another way of stating this result is that the household budget constraint and the government budget constraint (i.e., government solvency) together imply the foreign budget constraint or national solvency (see Newell and Symons, 1990). More generally any two of the household, government, and foreign budget constraints imply the third. This powerful result (in effect Walras' Law) only follows in a forward-looking context. If consumption decisions are modelled in a more traditional, non-intertemporal fashion then the foreign budget constraint does not automatically follow from government solvency. However, Currie and Levine (1991) in this volume provides analysis to suggest that, with quite modest wealth effects in consumption, external solvency *is* a consequence of government solvency even if consumption is not forward-looking. It is pleasing then to report a unifying theme running through a number of chapters in this volume.

Still at the theoretical level, the chapter goes on to examine the consequences for the external debt to GDP ratio of stabilizing the government debt to GDP ratio through higher taxation, higher seigniorage, or lower government expenditure. As they stand these results are less interesting, for it is not clear why an ultimately higher or lower foreign debt to GDP ratio actually matters. One possible reason is that an indebted nation faces an increasing risk premium component of its interest rate which will adversely effect capital accumulation – but this requires incorporating into the analysis. A more important constraint on policy than the external debt to GDP ratio is undoubtedly the concept of the maximum primary surplus (as a proportion of GDP) that the government can generate – but more on that presently.

Turning to the policy options for Greece, the authors' estimated demand for money function suggests that seigniorage as a proportion of GDP is now at its maximum with respect to inflation. In other words, to achieve government solvency the higher inflation option does not exist for Greece, irrespective of whether it is socially or politically desirable or indeed compatible with entry into the ERM. This fact, together with the results reported in Table 9.5, constitutes some very unpleasant arithmetic for policy-makers in Greece. The calculations reveal that stabilization of government debt at its current level requires that the primary deficit must fall from around 13% in 1989 to only 0.3% of GDP. This is on the assumption that the annual growth rate of GDP is 2% as forecast by the OECD. These figures, of course imply a quite spectacular drop in government spending and/or rise in taxation or other forms of revenue collection. It should be noted that these calculations do not draw upon the forward-looking consumption model of the chapter but are simply the consequence of the government budget constraint.

The Yaari–Blanchard household consumption model *is* used in Table 9.6, which calculates the external debt to GDP ratios outcome consistent with the previous table; but as commented before it is not clear why these are important. The government stabilization problem is to effect a downward adjustment of its primary deficit. On the realistic assumption of 2% growth and with an inflation objective of less than 5% this has to be transformed into a primary surplus. The longer the adjustment is delayed, the larger the eventual primary surplus must be. If, as suggested in the chapter, an upper bound for the primary surplus to GDP ratio exists, then this determines the maximum period of adjustment available to the government.

The concept of a maximum primary surplus to GDP ratio is central in this scenario. Let me finish by suggesting an alternative approach. The alternative is not to impose a long-run primary surplus to GDP ratio but instead to assume that adjustment costs, associated with changing the primary deficit, are high. This leads naturally to an intertemporal optimization approach to fiscal policy based upon the maximization of consumer welfare, possibly extended to include government services in the utility function. This alternative allows for an examination of policy options which focuses firmly on the welfare implications of the original Yaari–Blanchard consumption model – surely one of the great strengths of working from microfoundations. Either approach however can provide an excellent general framework for examining the problem of fiscal adjustment for other highly indebted governments.

REFERENCES

Currie, D. and P. Levine (1991), 'The solvency constraint and fiscal policy in an open economy', this volume.
Newell, A. and J. Symons (1990), 'The current account and incomes policy, mimeo.

10 Macroeconomic policy, external targets and constraints: the case of Spain

JUAN J. DOLADO and JOSÉ VIÑALS

1 Introduction

It is now generally accepted both in the literature and in policy discussions that the authorities should aim at achieving the internal macroeconomic target of non-inflationary high-employment growth. In reality, how high that growth rate is will critically depend on several structural constraints: the attitudes of employers and workers in the wage and price-setting process, the degree of labour mobility, and the size of the capital stock. It seems to be the case, however, that governments also care about the external accounts and that they often invoke the existence of external constraints when designing macroeconomic policies. In spite of this general practice, it is not always clearly understood why there should be external targets, and what is the correct notion of the external constraint.

The purpose of this chapter is twofold. On the one hand, to analyse to what extent and under what conditions the pursuit of external targets is justifiable from a conceptual point of view, and how these targets relate to the ultimate external constraint of the economy. On the other hand, to examine the macroeconomic performance and policy experience of the Spanish economy to find out: (i) how macroeconomic policies have been influenced in the past by the evolution of the external accounts, (ii) whether the economy is currently following a path consistent with meeting the external constraint, (iii) what current account and real exchange rate targets should the economy aim at in the future to continue to satisfy the external constraint, and finally (iv) what macro policies seem most appropriate for this purpose.

In order to address these issues, the chapter is organized as follows: Section 2 starts reviewing the recent performance of the Spanish economy by focusing on the specific episodes where balance-of-payments problems have led to significant changes in macro policies. Section 3 defines the

Table 10.1. *Spanish macroeconomic performance and policy, 1969–89*
(period averages unless stated to the contrary, in %)

	1969–73	1974–7	1978–9	1980–2	1983–5	1986–9
Macro-performance						
(a) External						
Current account[a]	0.6	− 3.1	0.9	− 2.6	0.4	− 0.7
Nominal exchange rate[b]	185.6	179.3	147.1	132.7	101.9	101.5
Real exchange rate[c]	90.2	102.1	112.0	111.0	98.0	113.3
Terms of trade[d]	116.6	105.5	114.5	94.1	90.0	109.3
Foreign reserves[e]	8.4	4.5	6.3	4.1	5.8	9.8
(net of gold)						
Net foreign debt[e]	− 2.6	8.0	3.7	12.0	11.5	− 1.1
(gross debt minus foreign reserves)						
(b) Internal						
Inflation (CPI)	7.4	18.4	18.0	15.1	10.5	6.5
Real growth (GDP)	6.7	3.0	0.6	0.7	2.0	4.7
Unemployment rate	1.6	4.2	8.3	12.8	20.1	18.5
Macro-policy						
Total liquid assets[f]	21.1	19.7	19.3	17.4	15.0	12.6
Budget balance[a]	0.4	− 0.2	− 1.7	− 4.0	− 5.8	− 3.6
Real unit labour costs[f]	0.0	0.8	0.3	− 0.5	− 3.0	− 1.3

Notes:
[a] As a percentage of GDP.
[b] Effective nominal exchange rate *vis-à-vis* developed countries (Index 1985 = 100).
[c] Real effective exchange rate *vis-à-vis* developed countries using CPIs (index 1985 = 100).
[d] Index.
[e] As a percentage of GDP. End of period.
[f] Growth rate.
Sources: Banco de España and European Commission.

external constraint and relates it to the concepts of solvency and deficit sustainability. Sections 4 and 5 test empirically if the Spanish economy is following a path consistent with the fulfilment of the external constraint. Section 6 provides policy guidelines to facilitate the task of ensuring that the future evolution of the Spanish balance of payments and the real exchange rate continue to satisfy both the internal and the external constraints. The final section summarizes the conclusions.

Table 10.2. *Components of the Spanish balance of payments, 1969–89 (period averages, % of GDP)*

	1969–73	1974–7	1978–9	1980–2	1983–5	1986–9
Exports	6.9	8.1	9.2	10.8	13.9	12.0
Imports	11.6	14.9	12.0	16.3	17.3	16.9
Trade balance	− 4.7	− 6.8	− 2.8	− 5.5	− 3.4	− 4.9
Services balance	3.6	2.5	2.5	2.1	3.0	3.3
Net transfers	1.7	1.2	1.0	0.8	0.8	1.0
Current account	0.6	− 3.1	0.9	− 2.6	0.4	− 0.6
Net long-term capital	1.5	2.4	1.8	2.2	0.8	2.5
Basic balance	2.1	− 0.7	2.7	− 0.4	1.2	1.9
Net short-term capital	0.1	0.5	0.2	0.1	0.2	0.6
Change in foreign exchange reserves	2.0	− 0.2	2.0	− 0.8	1.1	2.4

Source: Secretaría de Estado de Comercio.

2   Macroeconomic performance and policies in Spain

The purpose of this section is to highlight the most salient facts in the evolution of Spanish external accounts and to verify to what extent macroeconomic policy has been responsive to this evolution.[1] For this purpose, Table 10.1 contains a set of useful indicators of internal and external Spanish macroeconomic performance and macro policies during the last two decades, while Table 10.2 gives a more detailed breakdown of the balance of payments.

After having experienced a long period of rapid high-employment growth with a nearly balanced current account and a substantial accumulation of foreign reserves between 1959 and 1973, the economy entered into a stagflationary period following the first oil price shock. This shock coincided with the end of General Franco's regime and with the introduction of the political party system. Between 1974 and 1984, the country suffered a deep, long, and severe economic crisis. Three main reasons underlay this crisis: (i) the delayed response to the initial negative impact of the shock, so as to avoid political and social confrontations, augmented by a significant world recession, (ii) a substantial degree of real wage rigidity in the face of a severe terms of trade loss, and (iii) the existence of various other labour market inflexibilities which, in conjunction with the previous factors, contributed to a sharp decline in industrial employment by over 20% during the second half of the 1970s. Since 1985, however, the country has undergone a very strong recovery which has been fostered by adequate domestic policies, world recovery, and last – but not least –

by the opportunities and expectations created by Spain's accession to the European Economic Community.

Both tables further distinguish among subperiods based on the external performance of the economy. In this regard, it can be observed that after the foreign exchange reserves accumulation and satisfactory current account performance of the beginning of the seventies, the first oil shock led during 1974–7 to current account deficits, reserve losses, and nominal exchange rate depreciation pressures in the face of a real appreciation of the peseta. The substantial increase in net external debt by 10.6 percentage points of GDP between 1973 and 1977, and the danger of an unstoppable balance-of-payments crisis prompted the economic authorities of the newly elected Democratic Centre party government to implement a 15% devaluation of the peseta in July 1977 together with a series of monetary policy measures aimed at restraining demand growth, and a social agreement on wage moderation known as the Moncloa Pact. As a result, there was a significant improvement in the current account balance, a replenishment of foreign exchange reserves, and a drop in net external debt in 1978–9. On the internal side, although the tightening of monetary policy was not accompanied by a tightening of fiscal policy, there was nevertheless a significant reduction in the growth rate and a reversal of the accelerating inflation trend of the previous period.

However, the insufficient degree of wage and demand moderation combined with the persistence of many rigidities and distortions in labour markets produced, once the effect of the nominal devaluation disappeared, a new series of current account deficits, a drop in foreign exchange reserves, and a significant build-up of net external debt, which increased by 8.3 percentage points of GDP between 1979 and 1982. As a result, when the Socialist party took office by the end of 1982, there was again the danger of a balance-of-payments crisis. To avoid a crisis, the new economic authorities embarked on a 10% devaluation of the peseta in December 1982 and implemented a further tightening of monetary – but not fiscal – policy. These measures were accompanied by a set of structural supply-side reforms (industrial restructuring, energy savings, and labour market flexibility policies) designed to improve the production potential of the economy over the medium term.

Following this policy shift and helped also by a worldwide economic recovery, there was in 1983–5 a substantial improvement in the current account balance, a recovery of foreign exchange reserves and a slight reduction in net external debt. Moreover, the significant moderation of unit labour costs relative to previous periods allowed aggregate supply to expand, thus helping achieve a higher growth rate and a further reduction in inflation.

It was precisely towards the beginning of 1985 that the Spanish economy started the vigorous recovery which marked its entry to the EEC in the following year, and which has also led to a strong output growth rate and, until 1988, to a gradual disinflation process. However, coinciding with the entry of Spain to the EEC there has also been a marked shift towards a continuous widening of the current account deficit, which has gone from a surplus of 1.7% of GDP in 1985 to a deficit of 3.0% in 1989, and to an expected deficit of 3.5% in 1990.[2]

Nonetheless, there is an important difference between the recent episode and the other two discussed above, in spite of all of them being characterized by persistent current account deficits. While in the previous situations there was a loss of foreign reserves, a significant external debt build-up, and nominal depreciation pressures in the peseta market, in the latest situation there has been a major accumulation of foreign reserves, a switch from a net debtor to a net creditor position, and an appreciating peseta in both nominal and real terms. In other words, the recent widening current account deficit has been more than financed by capital flows and, specifically, by net foreign investment.

Moreover, while in the two previous episodes, which placed the economy near a balance-of-payments crisis situation, the current account deficit came from large reductions in total domestic saving in the presence of decreasing or stagnant investment, in the present episode the current account deficit is coming from an impressive increase in total domestic investment that cannot be fully financed by domestic saving. Indeed, as shown in Figure 10.1, in the first episode (1974–7) the saving and investment rates came down respectively by 3.8 and 5.7 percentage points of GDP. In the second period (1980–2), the savings rate came down by 2.1 points while the investment rate declined by 3.3 points. In contrast, in the third period (1986–9) the savings rate has gone up by 1.0 points while the investment rate has gone up by an impressive 5.6 points.

In spite of all the above, there is still a lot of uncertainty and disagreement in Spain nowadays regarding the extent to which the current external situation is sustainable or not. Specifically, if present trends continue will current account deficits become too large to be financed by stable direct investment flows, thus leading to an explosion of external debt in the absence of corrective policy measures? Or, on the contrary, could it be the case that the Spanish economy is not just solvent but dynamically inefficient, and therefore that it could run even larger current account deficits to take advantage of its present net creditor position? These issues will be addressed later in the chapter.

This section has provided some casual evidence in support of the hypothesis that the major policy changes which occurred in Spain during the

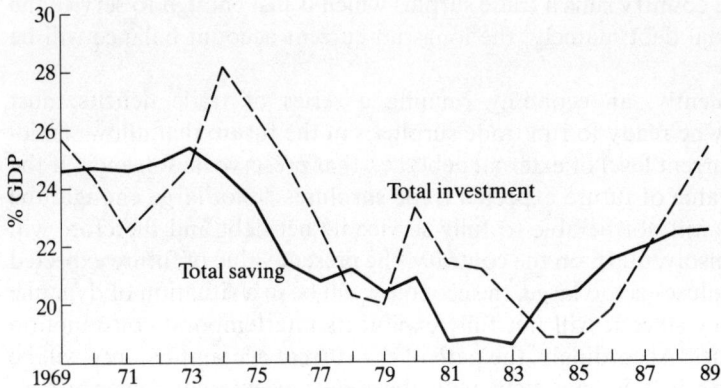

Figure 10.1   Total Spanish saving and investment, 1968–89. *Source:* National accounts.

last twenty years have been triggered by what was regarded as a highly unfavourable evolution of the external accounts. In the following section we try to ascertain the nature of the external constraint.

3   Solvency, sustainability, and the external constraint

3.1   The external constraint

As stated in the introduction, while there is a clear meaning attached to internal targets and constraints from a macroeconomic point of view, there is a lot more confusion and ambiguity in the popular definitions of what constitute external targets and constraints. For instance, standard macroeconomic textbooks have defined 'external balance' as a situation where the balance of payments is zero. At the same time, they have also emphasized that, while this balance can be automatically and continuously maintained under flexible exchange rates, it requires other policy instruments under fixed exchange rates.

It is now widely recognized, however, that a sensible interpretation of external balance should centre primarily around the current account balance, which is the determinant of the net asset accumulation process in the economy. Moreover, for a given current account balance, the role played by exchange rate policy is just left to influence the distribution of net asset accumulation between the private and the public sector.

Indeed, the external constraint of the economy should be understood in a long-run sense. Specifically, if a country runs a trade deficit in the present it will accumulate net external liabilities that will need to be paid for in the future. Thus, in the future there will be an equilibrium situation where the country runs a trade surplus which is just enough to service the net external debt; namely, the long-run current account balance will be zero.

Consequently, an economy running a series of trade deficits must inevitably be ready to run trade surpluses in the future that allow servicing the current level of external debt; i.e., that preserve its solvency. If the present value of future expected trade surpluses is not large enough, the economy will not be able to fully service its net debt and therefore will become insolvent. If, on the contrary, the present value of future expected trade surpluses is too large, the economy will be in a situation of dynamic inefficiency since it will not fully exploit its intertemporal consumption possibilities. Accordingly, the path of the current account balance will be sustainable if it is consistent with the long-run external solvency constraint.

Summarizing, in a long-run equilibrium situation the economy will satisfy the condition that the present value of its spending – on both domestic and foreign goods – plus the value of its net external debt be equal to the present value of domestic income. Furthermore, this constraint will apply regardless of the evolution of the overall balance of payments and of the specific exchange rate policy followed by the authorities.

It must be pointed out, however, that although the external constraint is a long-run one – i.e., the long-run current account must balance – there may be reasons why governments also worry about the shorter-run evolution of the current account. As explained in Viñals (1986), in a Walrasian world with fully flexible prices and wages, no distortions, no uncertainty, and perfect access to international financial markets, the long-run external constraint will be the only one facing the economy. In this case the paths of the current account and foreign debt levels would be socially and privately optimal and the policy-makers would not feel the need to express concern about them. Unfortunately this is not the world we live in. With markets ridden by imperfections and distortions, the authorities may have several reasons to be concerned about the short-run behaviour of the current account. Prominent among these reasons are the following: (i) sticky prices and wages, whereby a worsening of the current account is interpreted as a leakage in demand that boosts the foreign economy and slows down domestic growth, when output is demand determined; (ii) divergence between private and social costs of borrowing and lending abroad, which may motivate restrictions on capital inflows and outflows, reducing the mobility of capital and correspondingly elevating the current account as a policy goal (see Artis and Bayoumi, 1990); (iii) uncertainty about future flexibility to correct paths that, while satisfying long-run solvency, are excessively profligate today and will imply severe constraints in the future which it may be wise to avoid; (iv) influence of the current account on the attitude of financial markets, whereby a deterioration in the current account affects market sentiment, with corresponding speculative attacks against the domestic currency in a world of fixed exchange rates, and causes excessive short-run volatility of the nominal and real exchange rates when they are flexible; (v) influence of the current account and external debt paths on the cost of borrowing, whereby an externality is imposed on the country as a whole and on future borrowers by the marginal borrower; (vi) irreversibility arguments, by which once export markets are lost they are not easily regained; and finally (vii) protectionist threats, that may emerge from political pressures after an extended period of substantial current account deficits.

As a result, the authorities should always remain vigilant that the net external debt of the country does not grow beyond its ability to pay, while in the case of economies suffering from one or several of the imperfections and distortions just mentioned above, they may also want to set – generally upper – limits to the stock of the net external debt at any given point of time.

3.2 The arithmetic of the external constraint

To formalize these ideas, it is convenient to write the balance of payments of an open economy as

$$CA_t \equiv -CAP_t + \Delta R_t \tag{1}$$

where CA, CAP and ΔR are respectively the current and capital account balances, and the change in official foreign exchange reserves.

Each of these variables is defined in domestic currency as

$$CA_t \equiv p_t X_t - p^*_t e_t M_t + TR_t - i^*_{t-1} e_t B^*_{t-1} \tag{2}$$

$$(CAP_t - \Delta R_t) \equiv e_t(B^*_t - B^*_{t-1}) + IN_t \tag{3}$$

where p and p^* are respectively the domestic and foreign price levels, e the nominal exchange rate, M and X the import and export volumes of goods and services, IN net total foreign investment, TR transfers, B^* the end-of-period stock of net external debt valued in foreign currency and i^* the foreign interest rate.

Using identities (2) and (3), the balance-of-payments identity (1) can be rewritten as

$$p^*_t e_t M_t + i^*_{t-1} e_t B^*_{t-1} + e_t B^*_{t-1} \equiv p_t X_t + IN_t + e_t B^*_t + TR_t \qquad (4)$$

$$\underbrace{\qquad\qquad\qquad\qquad\qquad}_{\text{Outflows}} \qquad \underbrace{\qquad\qquad\qquad\qquad\qquad}_{\text{Inflows}}$$

According to (4), the economy obtains in each period a given amount of resources which are used to meet its external payments obligations. Specifically, in each period the economy needs to finance imports of goods and services, and interest payments and principal repayment on the net external debt with the revenues provided by exports of goods and services, transfers, net foreign investment and new external debt.

In this regard, we wish to emphasize that an important distinction might be made between those movements of net external liabilities associated with total investment (direct, portfolio, real estate) which do not necessarily have to be repaid in the event of a financial crisis, and movements which are proper debt assets or liabilities. Under this latter heading we prefer to include all assets or liabilities bearing an interest-payment obligation, which is the truly relevant definition of 'net external debt' in a country like Spain, where steady foreign investment plays a prominent role in the evolution of the external accounts (see Cooper and Sachs, 1985). We thus define the *'fundamental'* account balance of the economy (Z_t) as the sum of the primary current account balance and the net investment balance excluding the latter from the definition of debt

$$Z_t \equiv CA_t + i^*_{t-1} e_t B^*_{t-1} + IN_t \qquad (4')$$

or

$$Z_t \equiv (1 + i^*_{t-1}) e_t B^*_{t-1} - e_t B^*_t \qquad (4'')$$

Using an approximate version of (4''), linearized around a steady-state situation, where interest rate parity is fulfilled, and where the foreign interest rate, domestic real output growth and inflation are constant, the following standard debt accumulation equation can be obtained

$$b^*_t = (1 + \lambda) b^*_{t-1} - z_t; \qquad \lambda = (r^* - n)/(1 + n) \qquad (5)$$

where b^* and z are, respectively, the net external debt and the 'fundamental' account balance as a proportion of GDP, r^* the real foreign interest rate, and n the domestic trend GDP real growth rate.

As pointed out by Cohen (1985), when the real interest rate on the debt is smaller than the domestic growth rate $(\lambda < 0)$ any stable path of the 'fundamental' account balance is consistent with a stable external debt–GDP ratio, and a country is solvent no matter how large is its initial net external debt. In this case, when trying to integrate (5) forward it turns out that the present value of future 'fundamental' account surpluses is effectively infinity, no matter how small they are.

However, if the interest rate is higher than the rate of growth of the economy ($\lambda > 0$) expression (5) can be integrated forward, obtaining

$$b^*_t = \sum_{i=1}^{\infty} \rho^i E_t z_{t+i}; \qquad \rho = (1 + \lambda)^{-1} \qquad (6)$$

assuming that $\lim_{N \to \infty} \rho^N E_t b^*_{t+N} = 0$; i.e., the transversality condition holds. The requirement for this condition is obviously weaker than that whereby b^*_t should be stable, as will be seen subsequently.

Equation (6) represents the equilibrium intertemporal budget constraint of an open economy when $\lambda > 0$. It tells us that the present level of debt as a proportion of GDP must be equal to the present value of the 'fundamental' account surpluses. This situation is in contrast to that when $\lambda < 0$, where as we mentioned above a debtor country need only stabilize its ratio z_t without having to worry about obtaining future surpluses.

It is possible nevertheless to stabilize the level of net external debt in (6) around a chosen steady-state value (b^*) – both in cases where the interest rate is higher and lower than the growth rate ($\lambda \gtrless 0$) – by selecting a 'fundamental' balance target (z) so that

$$z = \frac{r^* - n}{1 + n} b^* \qquad (7)$$

Condition (7), which proves very strong, emphasizes that there is a close relationship between the economy's external indebtedness and the 'fundamental' balance that must be met on average in order to make the real resource transfer that is required to cope with the financial burden derived from such indebtedness. The level of z which satisfies this condition is generally termed the 'sustainable' level.

3.3 Popular misconceptions

The 'steady-state' version of the true intertemporal budget constraint of the economy in (7) is also useful to explain several popular misconceptions about the nature of the external constraint often used in policy discussions.

On the one hand, while it is true in a loose sense that the evolution of foreign variables – prices, output, and interest rates – influences domestic economic performance this is not really a constraint, although it does affect the external constraint. Namely, if we think of the 'fundamental' balance as being mainly determined, among other variables, by the evolution of domestic (n) and the foreign growth (n^*), and the real exchange rate (θ) ($z = z(n, n^*, \theta)$; $z_2 > 0$, z_1, $z_3 < 0$)[3] then a permanent drop in foreign growth tightens the constraint for a given net external

debt by lowering z, thus requiring a real depreciation to continue satisfying the external constraint, i.e., for z to remain the same. Similarly, a
permanent increase in the foreign real interest rate increases the fundamental balance surplus that a debtor country must run, on average, to
satisfy the external constraint. However, a neutral change in the foreign
price level will not affect the external constraint since the equilibrium real
exchange rate remains unchanged.

On the other hand, although it is clear that in a world of complete capital
immobility no deficit or surplus is sustainable, it is often claimed that the
influence of external constraints on the domestic economy becomes
greater as the country increases its degree of trade and financial openness
vis-à-vis the rest of the world. However, this is not necessarily so because,
while it is certainly the case that trade openness increases the elasticities of
the current account balance relative to output and competitiveness also
increases, it is also true that better financial integration allows deficit
countries to borrow internationally without exerting as much upward
pressure on domestic interest rates.

Finally, it is frequently heard that a credible commitment to follow a
stable exchange rate policy – like belonging to the European Monetary
System (EMS) – increases the weight of external constraints on the
domestic economy since the authorities are no longer able to accommodate domestic price increases through nominal exchange rate
depreciations, thus fostering policies oriented towards price stability. In
this regard, while it is certainly the case that – under certain conditions – a
credible commitment to exchange rate stability à la EMS will help achieve
price stability, this will be neutral in the sense of not affecting any of the
underlying real variables – output growth, the real exchange rate, the real
interest rate – which appear in (7) as the main determinants of the
long-run 'external constraint'.[4] Therefore, while EMS-type arrangements
constrain the steady-state behaviour of nominal variables, they do not
necessarily affect the steady-state intertemporal budget constraint of the
economy.

After this brief analysis of the nature of the external constraint of an
open economy, we test in the next two sections whether the external
performance of the Spanish economy is consistent with the solvency and
dynamic efficiency principles.

4   Testing for solvency and dynamic inefficiency

As shown in expression (6) of Section 3, which expresses the external
constraint in terms of the expected 'fundamental' account balance, an
economy is solvent if the transversality condition guaranteeing the

non-explosiveness of external debt to GDP ($\lim_{N \to \infty} \rho^{t+N} E_t b^*_{t+N} = 0$) is satisfied. In this section we describe alternative econometric tests for solvency and dynamic inefficiency which although originating in the government budget constraint literature can be readily adapted to the present context.

4.1 Hamilton and Flavin tests

These tests are derived from the methodology proposed by Hamilton and Flavin (1986) and Trehan and Walsh (1988). Assuming that the factor $\rho^{t+N} E_t b^*_{t+N}$ ($= a_0$) is non-stochastic and different from zero, which represents the alternative hypothesis to (6), the expression

$$b^*_t = \rho^N E_t b^*_{t+N} + \sum_{i=1}^{N} \rho^i E_t z_{t+i} \tag{8}$$

may be written as

$$b^*_t = a_0 (1 + \lambda)^t + \sum_{i=1}^{N} \rho^i E_t z_{t+i} \tag{9}$$

Thus the solvency constraint holds if $a_0 = 0$. To test whether $a_0 = 0$, Hamilton and Flavin propose two tests. First, assuming a univariate process for z_t, the stationarity of the discounted sum of future surpluses is tested (stationarity of the undiscounted surplus being sufficient for the stationarity of the sum of expected discounted surpluses if $\rho < 1$). Then, if this sum is stationary, b^*_t will be stationary if and only if $a_0 = 0$. The second test suggests estimating equation (9) directly, making different assumptions about the information set underlying the formation of expectations about future surpluses. If it is assumed that these expectations are based on past values of surpluses and debt, by taking an average value of λ, (9) can be replaced by

$$b^*_t = a_0(1 + \lambda)^t + c(L)z_t + d(L)b^*_{t-1} + \epsilon_t \tag{10}$$

where ϵ_t is an error term that includes the potential variability of interest rates and possible measurement errors. The test involves examining the statistical significance of a_0.

Several restrictive assumptions underlie the construction of these tests. First, it is assumed that factor λ, which is a real interest rate less the rate of growth of real GDP, is non-stochastic – a very strong assumption. Second, it is assumed that violations of the borrowing constraint are also non-stochastic, i.e., $a_0(1 + \lambda)^t$. Third, with regard to the first test described above, cointegration theory (see Engle and Granger, 1987) states that the non-stationarity of b^*_t and z_t in (9) is neither a necessary nor a sufficient condition for $a_0 = 0$. In other words, there is a possibility that z_t and b^*_t are cointegrated.[5] In such a case, the above test may lack power.

4.2   The Wickens test

In a recent paper Wickens (1989) suggests taking the possibility of cointegration into consideration by assuming that b^*_t and z_t are generated by the joint stochastic process

$$\Delta x_t = \mu + \theta x_{t-1} + u_t \tag{11}$$

where $x_t' = (b^*_t, z_t)$ and u_t is a stationary disturbance. Equation (11) is derived from the system of two equations formed by the debt accumulation equation (5) and

$$\Delta z_t = \eta + \beta z_{t-1} + \alpha b^*_{t-1} + e_t \tag{12}$$

where $e_t = \psi(L)\epsilon_t$, $\psi_0 = 1$, $\Sigma \psi_i^2 < \infty$.

Equation (12) may be interpreted as an automatic or discretional policy rule which includes possible attempts by the authorities to increase the surplus (reduce the deficit) when the proportion of debt in relation to GDP increases ($\alpha > 0$).[6] Therefore, (11) may be written as

$$\begin{pmatrix} \Delta b^*_t \\ \Delta z_t \end{pmatrix} = \begin{pmatrix} -\eta \\ \eta \end{pmatrix} + \begin{pmatrix} \lambda - \alpha & -(1+\beta) \\ \alpha & \beta \end{pmatrix} \begin{pmatrix} b^*_{t-1} \\ z_{t-1} \end{pmatrix} + \begin{pmatrix} -e_t \\ e_t \end{pmatrix} \tag{13}$$

Solving (13) backwards yields

$$\lim_{N \to \infty} E_t b^*_{t+N}$$
$$= \lim_{N \to \infty} e'_1 \rho^N \left[(I+\theta)^N x_t + \sum_{i=0}^{N-1} (I+\theta)^i \mu + \sum_{i=0}^{N-1} (I+\theta)^i E_t u_{t+N-i} \right] \tag{14}$$

where $e'_1 = (1, 0)$ and $e'_1 x_t = b^*_t$.

Note that (14) generalizes Hamilton and Flavin's test, allowing for the sum of the three components to be zero – even though some of them may not be null – provided they offset each other. Further, by establishing a stochastic process for u_t, the possibility that deviations with respect to the borrowing constraint are stochastic is allowed for.

For a straightforward analysis of the implications of (13), let us assume first that z_t is a non-stationary process, and, for illustration purposes, that it is governed by the following the IMA(1) process:

$$\Delta z_t = \eta + \epsilon_t - \psi_1 \epsilon_{t-1}; \quad -1 < \psi_1 < 1 \tag{15}$$

This implies that in (12), $\alpha = \beta = 0$. Generally, a sufficient condition for the existence of the first two terms of the right side of (14) is that the characteristic roots of the matrix $(I + \theta)$, η_i $(i = 1, 2)$ should be such that $|\eta_i| < \rho$. In the case at hand, these roots are $(1 + \lambda)$ and 1. Thus, diagonalizing $(I + \theta)$ yields

$$I + \theta = \begin{pmatrix} 1 + \lambda & -1 \\ 0 & 1 \end{pmatrix} = \begin{pmatrix} 1 & 1 \\ 0 & \lambda \end{pmatrix} \begin{pmatrix} 1 + \lambda & 0 \\ 0 & 1 \end{pmatrix} \begin{pmatrix} 1 & -1/\lambda \\ 0 & 1/\lambda \end{pmatrix} \quad (16)$$

Accordingly, assuming that $\lambda > 0$

$$\lim_{N \to \infty} e'_1 [\rho(I + \theta)]^N x_t = (\lambda b^*_t - z_t)/\lambda \quad (17)$$

$$\lim_{N \to \infty} e'_1 \rho^N \sum_{i=0}^{N-1} (I + \theta)^i \mu = -\eta(1 + 1/\lambda)/\lambda \quad (18)$$

$$\lim_{N \to \infty} e'_1 \rho^N \sum_{i=0}^{N-1} (I + \theta)^i E_t u_{t+N-i} = \psi_1 \epsilon_t/\lambda \quad (19)$$

Thereafter, substituting (17)–(19) into (14) gives the solvency condition

$$\lim_{N \to \infty} \rho^N E_t b^*_{t+N} = [\lambda b^*_t - z_t - \eta(1 + 1/\lambda) + \psi_1 \epsilon_t] = 0 \quad (20)$$

that is, either an initial 'fundamental' account surplus that offsets the payments for investment less the 'fundamental' account balance trend component is needed, or, if the initial position is that of a net creditor, the initial investment income should be sufficiently high to offset future 'fundamental' account deficits.

Likewise, on the basis of (5) the process governing b^*_t may be derived as

$$\Delta b^*_t = \eta/\lambda - \psi_1 \rho \epsilon_t \quad (21)$$

But since we already know from (5) that

$$\Delta b^*_t = \eta/\lambda - (1 - \rho^{-1} L)^{-1} (1 - \psi_1 L) \epsilon_t \quad (22)$$

comparison of (21) and (22) implies that $\psi = (1 + \lambda)$ or, in other words, that the MA(1) lag polynomial has a root at ρ.

The conclusion here is that, if z_t is I(1) with drift, then b^*_t will also have to be I(1) with drift. Further, if e_t is in general MA(m), $m > 0$, Δb^*_t will have a moving average of order $m - 1$ since the MA(m) lag polynomial must have a root at ρ. For example, in our case $m = 1$ and therefore the disturbance in (22) is white noise. Hence in this case z_t and b^*_t will be cointegrated but to verify the transversality condition, z_t must also satisfy the root condition. Notice that in the special case where $m = 0$, i.e., e_t is white noise, the previous condition can not hold and hence the transversality condition will not be satisfied (see Trehan and Walsh, 1988).

Similar implications can be drawn for other processes followed by the 'fundamental' balance, z_t. If, for instance, the process followed by z_t is stationary, and there is stabilization by the authorities, the process governing z_t will be

$$z_t = \eta + \alpha b^*_{t-1} + \epsilon_t - \psi_1 \epsilon_{t-1} \qquad (23)$$

In this case $\beta = -1$, and the roots of $(I + \theta)$ are $(1 + \lambda - \alpha)$ and 0. If $0 < \alpha < 2(1 + \lambda)$, the characteristic roots of $(I + \theta)$ are less than $(1 + \lambda)$ $(= \rho^{-1})$ and, therefore, the solvency constraint is automatically satisfied, i.e., the three terms of (14) tend to zero. However, when there has been no stabilization by the authorities, i.e., $\alpha = 0$, the characteristic roots of $(I + \theta)$ are $(1 + \lambda)$ and 0. In this case, by a similar argument to the one used above, it is easy to prove that the transversality condition holds provided that

$$b^*_t = \eta/\lambda - \psi_1 \rho \epsilon_t \qquad (24)$$

that is, b^*_t follows a similar process to (21) except that b^*_t, like z_t is I(0). Similarly, the root condition has to be satisfied by the MA lag polynomial of e_t.

Any of the previous conditions of the processes generating b^*_t and z_t are sufficient to ensure that the transversality condition holds. However, a necessary and sufficient condition that encompasses the previous ones can be obtained by noticing that both in (21) and (24) Δb^*_t is stationary. Thus, if, for example, in (13), it is assumed that $\lambda = \alpha$ and $\beta = -1$, it follows that

$$\Delta b^*_t = -(\eta + e_t) \qquad (25)$$

and

$$\Delta z_t = -\lambda \eta + e_t - (1 + \lambda) e_{t-1} \qquad (26)$$

so that the roots of $(I + \theta)$ are 0 and -1 which automatically satisfy the solvency constraint, while the MA(1) lag polynomial in (26) satisfies the root condition. Thus, testing for stationarity in Δb^*_t seems to provide the key test, complemented by the same degree of integration in z_t and b^*_t.

In spite of the generality of the analysis, as stated in the comments on the method proposed by Hamilton and Flavin, two problems are left unresolved by this procedure. First, factor λ is assumed to be positive since otherwise ρ^N would tend to infinity instead of to zero (see the derivation from (17)–(19)). Since λ represents approximately the difference between a real interest rate and the rate of growth of GDP in real terms, this assumption can be very restrictive. Second, it is once more assumed that λ is constant. One possible way of avoiding these difficulties has recently been proposed by Wilcox (1989), whose procedure is discussed in the following section.

4.3   The Wilcox test

The solution proposed by Wilcox consists of incorporating λ into the definition of the variables, working in terms of the present discounted value instead of the original propositions. Indeed, in the light of (5) we can define the real discount factor as

$$q_t = \prod_{j=0}^{t-1} \rho_j; \qquad q_0 = 1 \tag{27}$$

and multiplying both sides of (5) by q_t gives the discounted value of each variable back to period zero, i.e.,

$$q_t b^*_t = q_t(1 + \lambda_{t-1}) b^*_{t-1} - q_t z_t = q_{t-1} b^*_{t-1} - q_t z_t \tag{28}$$

where, by assuming that factor λ is variable, dating is suitable.

Representing by F_t the discounted value of b^*_t and by X_t the discounted value of z_t, (28) can be rewritten as

$$\Delta F_t = -X_t \tag{29}$$

Solving (29) forwards yields

$$F_t = F_{t+N} + \sum_{j=1}^{N} X_{t+j}$$

Therefore, the transversality condition, in discounted terms, is

$$\lim_{N \to \infty} E_t F_{t+N} = 0 \tag{30}$$

Assuming once more a process similar to (12), expression (11) in discounted terms is governed by the following joint process

$$\begin{pmatrix} \Delta F_t \\ \Delta X_t \end{pmatrix} = \begin{pmatrix} -\eta \\ \eta \end{pmatrix} + \begin{pmatrix} -\alpha & -(1+\beta) \\ \alpha & \beta \end{pmatrix} \begin{pmatrix} F_{t-1} \\ X_{t-1} \end{pmatrix} + \begin{pmatrix} -e_t \\ e_t \end{pmatrix} \tag{31}$$

Solving (31) backwards gives the condition equivalent to (14), with the exception that the term ρ^N is no longer included in that expression, i.e.,

$$\lim_{N \to \infty} E_t F_{t+N}$$

$$= \lim_{N \to \infty} e'_1 \left[(I + \theta)^N X_t + \sum_{i=0}^{N-1} (I + \theta)^i \mu + \sum_{i=0}^{N-1} (I + \theta)^i E_t u_{t+N-i} \right] \tag{32}$$

where now $X_t = (F_t, X_t)$.

Note that here a sufficient condition for the first two terms on the right

Table 10.3. *Solvency–dynamic efficiency tests*

	Hamilton–Flavin	Wickens	Wilcox
Null hypothesis	$a_0 = 0$ in (10) if $z_t \sim I(0)$	$\Delta b^*_t \sim I(0)$ with b^*_t and $z_t \sim I(d)$ $(d = 0, 1)$ and moving average satisfies root condition	$F_t \sim I(0)$ without drift in (29)

side of (32) to exist is that the characteristic roots of the matrix $(I + \theta)$, η_i ($i = 1, 2$), should satisfy $|\eta_i| < 1$, in which case (32) tends automatically to zero. Since, on the basis of (29), we know that F_t is an integrated process $I(d)$ when X_t is $I(d-1)$, a general condition for the solvency condition to hold is that $\eta = 0$ and X_t should be stationary with a unit root in its moving average; or, in other words, F_t should be a stationary process with mean zero. The usual unit root tests are the basis for this test, performed directly on F_t.

In short, we consider that the test using the discounted value of the variables is the best means of examining the solvency or transversality condition. However, for the sake of completeness, we will use all the versions proposed of the solvency tests in the empirical application to the case of the Spanish economy, as described in the following section. Table 10.3 summarizes the null hypotheses that will be tested.

5   How solvent and efficient is the Spanish economy?

Based on data only available since 1969, Table 10.4 contains the data for the evolution of the current-account balance (column 2), net investment (column 3) and net interest payments (column 4), all as percentages of GDP.[7] From these variables the 'fundamental' account balance (column 1) is constructed, as defined in section 3. Also included are net external debt (column 5) and the components of factor λ – the foreign real rate of interest (column 8) and the rate of real GDP growth (column 9).[8]

As can be observed from the sample averages in the lower part of the table, the average value of n during 1969–89 is 3.5% while the average value of r^* is 2.4%. As a result, $n > r^*$ and, therefore, $\lambda < 0$. Accordingly, one of the prerequisites of the tests proposed by Hamilton, Flavin, and Wickens would appear not to hold. In other words, the stability of debt seems assured for any stable path of the 'fundamental' balance. However,

Table 10.4. *Spanish net external debt and fundamental balance, 1969–89* (*as % of GDP*)

Year	z_t	ca_t	in_t	i^*eB^*/PY_t	b^*_t	i^*_t	π^*_t	r^*_t	n_t
1969	− 0.3	− 1.5	0.9	0.3	12.8	7.8	5.2	2.5	8.9
1970	1.7	0.6	0.8	0.3	10.9	8.5	6.2	2.2	4.1
1971	3.4	2.1	1.1	0.2	7.1	7.8	6.8	0.9	4.6
1972	2.5	1.2	1.2	0.1	4.2	7.6	5.9	1.6	8.0
1973	2.2	0.8	1.4	− 0.1	1.7	8.8	7.6	1.1	7.7
1974	− 3.2	− 3.2	0.7	− 0.3	4.8	11.0	11.1	− 0.1	5.3
1975	− 2.4	− 2.8	0.4	0.0	7.1	10.2	11.6	− 1.3	0.5
1976	− 3.2	− 3.6	0.1	0.3	10.2	10.0	8.6	1.3	3.3
1977	− 1.5	− 2.5	0.4	0.6	11.5	9.7	8.5	1.1	3.0
1978	2.2	0.9	0.6	0.7	9.3	9.6	8.1	1.4	1.4
1979	0.5	− 0.6	0.6	0.5	8.9	10.6	9.2	1.3	− 0.1
1980	− 1.8	− 3.0	0.6	0.6	10.7	12.7	11.0	1.5	1.2
1981	− 1.3	− 3.3	0.8	1.2	12.4	15.2	11.0	3.8	− 0.2
1982	− 1.5	− 3.2	0.6	1.2	14.4	13.7	8.6	4.7	1.2
1983	0.1	− 2.2	0.9	1.3	14.7	10.8	6.8	3.7	1.8
1984	3.0	0.7	1.0	1.3	12.2	10.6	5.6	4.7	1.8
1985	2.9	0.9	1.1	0.8	9.6	9.6	4.8	4.6	2.3
1986	4.6	2.2	1.8	0.5	5.1	8.5	4.2	4.1	3.3
1987	3.7	0.5	2.7	0.5	1.3	7.4	3.4	3.9	5.5
1988	1.9	− 0.9	2.4	0.4	− 0.6	6.8	3.6	3.1	5.0
1989	0.6	− 3.2	3.6	0.2	− 1.2	—	—	5.0	5.0
Averages									
1969–89	0.6	− 1.0	1.1	0.5	8.0	—	—	2.4	3.5
1969–73	1.9	0.6	1.1	0.2	7.3	—	—	1.7	6.7
1974–7	− 2.5	− 3.0	0.4	0.1	8.4	—	—	0.3	3.0
1978–9	1.4	0.2	0.6	0.6	9.1	—	—	1.3	0.7
1980–2	− 1.5	− 3.2	1.7	1.0	12.5	—	—	3.3	0.7
1983–5	2.0	− 0.2	1.0	1.2	12.2	—	—	4.3	2.0
1986–9	2.6	− 0.4	2.6	0.4	1.2	—	—	4.0	4.7

Notes:

z = 'Fundamental' account balance ($= ca + in + i^*eB^*/PY$).

ca = Current account balance.

in = Total net investment.

i^*eB = Net interest payments on the external debt. Interest paid – or received – net of interest for direct investment income, dividends and share subscription rights and property.

b^* = Net external assets − Net external liabilities. Net Assets and Liabilities are obtained by subtracting from total assets and liabilities the items relating to shares (including direct investment), other holdings and property, and leads and lags in payments and collections. The figures have been adjusted for valuation differences (taking 1988 as the initial condition for consistency with the balance-of-payments identity).

i^* = Average rate of interest on debt. Obtained as the ratio between interest payments and the average annual amount of the month-end stock of external debt.

π^* = G-7 rate of inflation (external debt-weighted).

$r^* = (1 + i^*)/(1 + \pi^*) - 1$.

n = Rate of growth of real GDP.

since λ is variable there are periods in which $\lambda > 0$ such as in 1978–85. This is why it is worthwhile examining the characteristics of the processes governing the evolution of external debt and the 'fundamental' account balance in accordance with the methodology summarized in Table 10.3. In this connection, we use the unit root tests developed by Dickey and Fuller (1981) in their extended version. The test involves estimating by OLS the regression model

$$\Delta y_t = \eta + \gamma y_{t-1} + \sum_{i=1}^{1} \phi_i \Delta y_{t-i} + \epsilon_t$$

to examine the null hypothesis $H_0: \gamma = 0$ against the alternative hypothesis $H_1: \gamma < 0$ in the behaviour of a generic variable y_t. If H_0 is rejected, the process is stationary; if not, the process is only stationary in first differences, i.e., I(1). In agreement with the discussion in the previous section the test is applied to z_t, b^*_t, and Δb^*_t.

The estimated parameters are the following (t-ratios in brackets)

$$\Delta b^*_t = 2.26 - 0.28 \, b^*_{t-1} + 0.86 \, \Delta b^*_{t-1} \tag{33}$$
$$(2.41) \quad (2.83) \qquad (5.02)$$

$$LM(4) = 2.8$$

$$\Delta z_t = 0.25 - 0.47 \, z_{t-1} + 0.32 \, \Delta z_{t-1} \tag{34}$$
$$(0.52) \quad (2.38) \qquad (2.50)$$

$$LM(4) = 3.2$$

$$\Delta^2 b^*_t = -0.17 \, \Delta b^*_{t-1} \tag{35}$$
$$(2.60)$$

$$LM(4) = 5.2$$

where $LM(4)$ is the LM-4th order autocorrelation statistic in the residuals, asymptotically distributed as a chi-squared with 4 d.f. The residuals do not appear to have serial correlation on the basis of this test. The critical values of the Dickey and Fuller tests for a sample size of twenty observations are 3.02 at 5% (2.65 at 10%) and 1.96 at 5% (1.63 at 10%) when there is or there is not a constant in the model (see McKinnon, 1990). In view of (33) and (34), this constant would appear to exist in the b^*_t process but not in the z_t process. When (34) is estimated without a constant, the t-ratio of the level is 2.85; consequently, on the basis of this test, the evidence is not clear on b^*_t being a I(0) or I(1)-with-drift process, while z_t is clearly I(0) without drift.[9] Similarly, the evidence is conclusive against Δb^* being I(1).

The possibility of b^*_t being I(1) would, however, appear to be confirmed when the regression of b^*_t on z_t is run

$$b^*_t = -0.26 - 1.02\, z_t + 1.02\, b^*_{t-1}$$
$$(1.46) \quad (2.59) \quad (32.39)$$

where it can be seen that the coefficient of b^*_{t-1} is very close to unity. Accordingly, the regression suggests that the appropriate specification is Δb^*_t on z_t, compatible with b^*_t being I(1) and z_t being I(0).

As discussed in the analysis of the Hamilton and Flavin procedure, summarized in the first column of Table 10.3, the non-stationarity of the non-discounted debt–GDP proportion is not a sufficient condition for the violation of the borrowing constraint. However, the stationarity of the fundamental balance–GDP proportion is indeed a sufficient condition for the violation of the borrowing constraint where the ratio debt–GDP is I(1) as would seem to happen in the case at hand. Thus, according to this test the transversality condition does not seem to hold.

We must ask how this evidence should be interpreted in a country which in 1989 had a net external debt–GDP ratio of -1.2%, i.e., was a net creditor rather than a debtor. Evidently, it is not a question of insolvency, but rather the contrary. If a country is initially in a creditor position and is not expected to generate deficits of a sufficiently offsetting size in the future, it will not satisfy the transversality condition either. This can be interpreted as a dynamic inefficiency situation (see Diamond, 1965) where the country's permanent income from its net external assets is greater than its planned spending. To resolve such inefficiency it could increase its present and future consumption.

To gather further evidence on this possibility, we perform the test described in (10) with $\lambda = 0.01$. Naturally, this test must be viewed with the greatest caution since the average sample value of λ is negative. The consequent regression is as follows

$$b^*_t = 2.68 - 3.28(1 + \lambda)^t - 1.05\, z_t + 0.19\, z_{t-1} + 1.21\, b^*_{t-1} - 0.18\, b^*_{t-2}$$
$$(2.20) \quad (2.17) \qquad (41.6) \qquad (0.63) \qquad (4.03) \qquad (0.60) \quad (36)$$

Once again a_0 is marginally significant and negative, in agreement with the dynamic inefficiency interpretation.

With regard to the Wickens test, the fact that Δb^*_t is I(0) seems to be the necessary and sufficient condition for satisfying the solvency constraint according to (25), though z_t being I(0) seems to contradict (26). A possible explanation is that with a small value of λ, it may be difficult to distinguish the I(1), process with drift in (26) from an I(0) process without drift.[10] However we reiterate that a necessary condition for this analysis is that $\lambda > 0$.

Table 10.5. *Discount factors and discounted debt–GDP ratios in Spain, 1969–89*

Year	q_t	F_t
1969	1.000	12.8
1970	1.062	11.6
1971	1.080	7.7
1972	1.118	4.7
1973	1.187	2.0
1974	1.263	6.1
1975	1.331	9.5
1976	1.357	13.8
1977	1.382	15.9
1978	1.406	13.1
1979	1.406	12.5
1980	1.406	14.8
1981	1.378	17.0
1982	1.320	19.0
1983	1.270	18.7
1984	1.243	15.2
1985	1.206	11.6
1986	1.178	6.8
1987	1.166	1.5
1988	1.182	− 0.7
1989	1.202	− 1.4

q_t: discount factor defined in expression (25) of the text.
F_t: discounted value of net external debt defined in expression (27) of the text.

Lastly, the results of the Wilcox test are given. This consists of examining the stationarity of the discounted value of external debt in proportion to GDP, in accordance with the analysis in (31). The first column of Table 10.5 includes the series of discount factors obtained from Table 10.4. The discount factor for 1969 is normalized to unity. The second column of Table 10.5 gives this discounted value, which is obtained by multiplying the values of b^* in Table 12.4 by the related factors in Table 10.5. As the values of λ are negative in most cases, the discounted values of the debt stands higher than the non-discounted value.

As shown in Figure 10.2, regardless of the measure chosen, a similar path is observable: a fall from 1969 to 1973; an explosive increase from 1974 to 1983 with a turning point in 1979 probably due to the effects of the 'devaluation cum stabilization' policy package of mid 1977; and an explosive decrease since 1983 as a result of the improvements in the current account balance up to 1986 and of the sharp increase of net

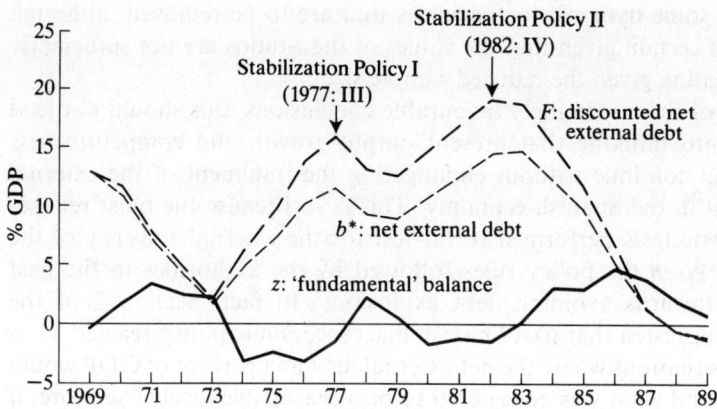

Figure 10.2 Spanish net external debt and fundamental balance, 1969–89 (% of GDP)

foreign investment after that year. It is this fall in the external net debt that the previous tests appear to be capturing.

The following regression provides formal evidence on the stationarity of F_t, in accordance with the third column of Table 10.3

$$\Delta F_t = 2.52 - 0.24 \ F_{t-1} + 0.86 \ \Delta F_{t-1} \qquad (37)$$
$$(2.14) \ (2.57) \qquad (4.78)$$

$$LM(4) = 2.0$$

In the light of (37), the evidence seems similar to that obtained in (33), i.e., the series is I(1) possibly with drift. However, as in the previous case, the small sample size available may hinder the distinction between this process and a I(0) process without drift. Thus the tentative conclusion is that no solvency problems exist in Spain but quite the contrary.

To examine the robustness of this conclusion to the assumption of relative PPP implicit in the construction of factor λ in (5), a new external debt and factors series based on (6) was computed without imposing the aforementioned assumption. The corresponding regression in discounted values is as follows

$$\Delta F_t = 2.79 - 0.30 \ F_{t-1} + 0.81 \ \Delta F_{t-1} \qquad (38)$$
$$(2.23) \ (2.70) \qquad (4.56)$$

$$LM(4) = 2.2$$

In the view of (38), the conclusions seem similar to those reached above: the Spanish economy is perfectly solvent now and it is not likely to have solvency problems in the future. Indeed, if anything, one could say that there are some dynamic inefficiencies that are to be removed, although this is not certain given that the values of the *t*-ratios are not sufficiently discriminating given the reduced sample size.

In spite of these seemingly favourable conclusions, this should not lead anyone into thinking that present output growth and competitiveness trends can continue without endangering the fulfilment of the external constraint in the Spanish economy. This is so because the most reliable econometric tests performed so far test for the external solvency of the economy *given* the policy rules followed by the authorities in the past directed towards avoiding debt explosions. In fact, Section 2 of the chapter suggested that past Spanish macroeconomic policy reacted so as to avoid situations where the net external debt as a percent of GDP would grow beyond what was considered to be a reasonable level. Therefore, if policy continues behaving this way there will be no future insolvency problems in the Spanish economy.

However, this is far from making the present situation an ideal one, given the evident overheating of an economy which has been growing at an average rate close to 5% since 1986, and whose international competitiveness has deteriorated by 24% since that year. It can be argued that Spain's present formal commitment to preserving exchange-rate stability inside the European Monetary System and its internationally high long- and short-term interest rates (shown in Figure 10.3) are attracting considerable capital flows, and therefore that drastic policy corrections like those in the past are no longer needed. Contrary to this, as stated in Viñals (1990a, b), this relaxed attitude may lead over time to a severe loss in competitiveness that, by substantially reducing the rate of return earned by foreign direct and portfolio investors, may cause a dry-up in net foreign investment at a time when the current account deficit gets larger.

If such a situation is allowed to happen then it would not be unthinkable

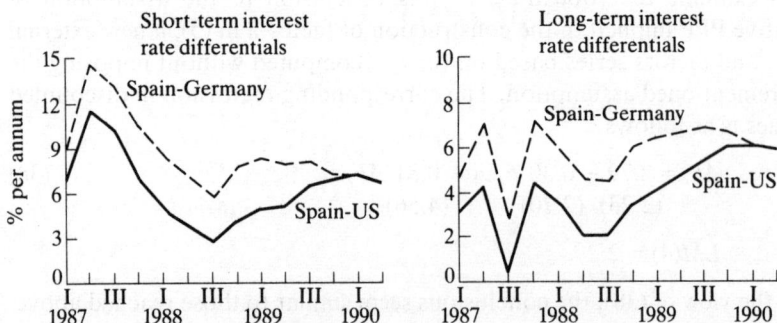

Figure 10.3   Interest rate differentials, Spain, Germany, and US, 1987–90. *Source:* OECD.

that the increased risk-premium on the Spanish economy will precipitate a massive outflow of short-run capital, thus forcing the authorities to take traumatic stabilization policy measures as in past episodes. If this is done as in the past, as our estimated reduced-form equations indicate, then the Spanish economy will not become insolvent. However, the net social and economic costs of acting just at the end rather than at the beginning of the process may be undesirably and unnecessarily large.

In sum, given the high sensitivity of financial and foreign exchange markets to the evolution of variables like competitiveness and the external accounts it is desirable that the government pursues the internal goal of non-inflationary growth, and at the same time ensures that this is not endangered now and in the future by unfavourable developments in the external accounts especially with regard to the role of foreign investment which has been so important in balancing the external accounts in the recent past. The next section explores what kind of policy guidelines can be established so that both internal and external equilibrium can be simultaneously achieved in Spain in the future.

6   External targets and economic policies

Based on the analysis of the former sections, a simple rule that a country could follow to satisfy the external constraint would be to run, on average, the 'fundamental' balance that is consistent with the chosen net external debt–GDP ratio (i.e., which is sustainable). Undoubtedly, what the appropriate size of such a balance should be in practice will depend on the net external debt–GDP ratio specifically chosen as well as on the future path of real interest and output growth rates.

Evidently, deciding what is the socially optimal debt level towards which the economy should converge in long-run equilibrium is not an easy task. However, there may be a simpler criterion based on the effect that external debt levels have on the ratings of the country in international financial markets and, consequently, on the country-risk premium charged when borrowing internationally.

Therefore we assume in what follows that the Spanish economy will approach a net external debt–GDP ratio which is consistent with the highest rating, and thus with the lowest cost of borrowing. Of course, this is a necessary but not a sufficient condition for the highest rating to be obtained since there are several other economic and non-economic criteria used in calculating ratings.

In practice, it turns out to be the case that the net external debt–GDP ratio consistent with the above cost-minimizing strategy ranges from values close to zero to negative values – that is, the country being a net creditor. Nevertheless, to simplify the calculations as much as possible, we assume that in the Spanish case this value can be taken to be zero. Consequently, our analysis should be viewed as an example rather than as a general case.[11]

Our assumption, while justifiable on practical grounds, also has the advantage of making the results not conditional upon the future – unknown – paths followed both by real interest rates and, to certain extent, by the growth rate of the economy. This is so because as indicated by expression (7)

$$z = \frac{r^* - n}{1 + n} b^*$$

when the specific value of external net debt (b^*) is zero, a specific average 'fundamental' balance (z) which is consistent with fulfilling the external constraint is also zero.[12]

Of course, the above simple rule for achieving external equilibrium is not the only one since, as indicated in Section 3, when the real growth rate of the economy exceeds the real interest rate on the external debt any stable path of the 'fundamental' balance (z) will stabilize the level of net external debt around the chosen steady-state value. Nevertheless, our policy rule has the virtues of simplicity and of few informational requirements.

In sum, a policy of maintaining an *average* balance for the 'fundamental' account approximately equal to zero during long periods of time is consistent both with the exploitation by the Spanish economy of the intertemporal and intergenerational trade opportunities that openness makes available while at the same time obeying the long-run external constraint. In other words, while the 'fundamental' balance can be different from zero in any given year, on average it must be zero over a period of many years.

Furthermore, when a country runs a series of 'fundamental' balance deficits, the authorities should recognize that a series of 'fundamental' balance surpluses must be run in the future. If there are no specific market mechanisms bringing about these surpluses then adequate policy actions should be implemented on a timely fashion to avoid last-minute traumatic policy changes.

In connection with the above, the evolution of net external debt and the 'fundamental' balance of the Spanish economy as shown in Figure 10.2 is very informative. As clearly seen in the Figure, major – and economically and socially costly – stabilization policies were implemented whenever there was a series of 'fundamental' account deficits leading to an excessive net external debt build-up. Besides, looking at the present evolution of the 'fundamental' balance it is also evident that, in spite of the impressive foreign investment boom of recent years, the continuous widening of the Spanish current account deficit has led to a gradual reduction in the 'fundamental' account surplus, which is now approaching zero.

It is our belief that this shrinking 'fundamental' surplus is the ultimate reason why the Spanish economic authorities are becoming increasingly worried nowadays about the evolution of the current account, and why the simple external equilibrium indicator based on a zero 'fundamental' balance presented in this section may be useful.[13]

However, if we wish the policy guidelines to be fully operational it is not enough to say that an average 'fundamental' account balance of zero should be obtained. It is also necessary to make sure that this external equilibrium situation is also fully consistent with internal balance – non-inflationary sustained growth – and, moreover, that the authorities can relate these goals to policy instruments.

For this reason, we estimate a very simple equation for the 'fundamental' account balance, using as explanatory variables those variables which could be considered as the main arguments of its different components; domestic and foreign GDP growth rates, an index of competitiveness, a real interest rate differential, and the degree of openness of the economy. The estimated equation is the following

$$\bar{z}_t = -0.28 - 0.62\,(y_t - \bar{y}_t) + 1.01\,(y^*_t - \bar{y}^*_t)$$
$$\quad (1.8)\quad (4.4)\qquad\qquad (7.5)$$
$$\quad - 15.18\,\theta_t + 0.12\,\omega_t + 0.10\,(r - r^*)$$
$$\quad (6.6)\qquad (2.1)\qquad (2.2) \tag{39}$$

S.E. $= 0.82\%$, $\bar{R}^2 = 0.88$, $DW = 2.43$

where $\bar{z}$ is the level of the 'fundamental' balance as proportion of trend GDP, $(y - \bar{y})$ is the difference between the logs of actual and trend domestic real GDP, $(y^* - \bar{y}^*)$ is the difference between the logs of actual and trend foreign real GDP,[14] θ is the real exchange rate, ω is an indicator of the degree of openness calculated as the sum of real imports and exports over trend real Spanish GDP, and $(r - r^*)$ is the differential domestic domestic and international *ex-post* long-term real interest rates.

As can be observed in equation (39), in spite of some signs of over-fitting with such a small sample size, all the coefficients are significant and their signs are in accordance with theory: excessive domestic growth leads to a worsening of the 'fundamental' balance while excessive foreign growth, and a real exchange rate depreciation (θ going down up) lead to an improvement. The long-term real interest rate differential also seems to point in the right direction, partially capturing the foreign investment boom. The estimated equation also indicates that as the Spanish economy

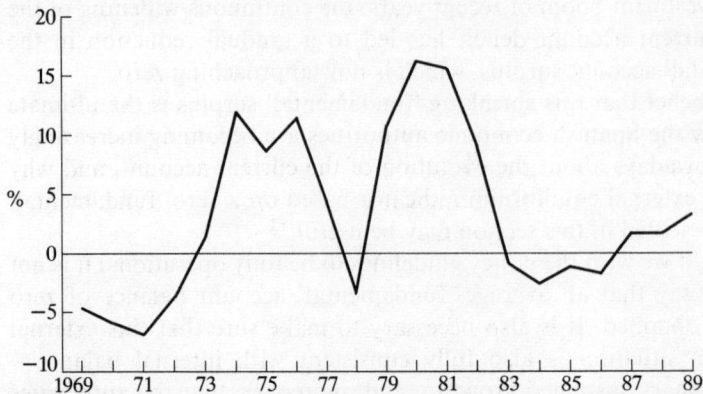

Figure 10.4   The Spanish real exchange rate gap, 1969–89. *Note:* Actual minus 'fundamental equilibrium' real exchange rate. Points above the zero line indicate an overvaluation of the real exchange rate; i.e., an insufficiently competitive economy.

has become increasingly more open over the years this has led to an improvement in the 'fundamental' account balance, therefore explicitly rejecting the fears of those who claim that the external liberalization of the economy necessarily generates external account problems.[15]

Equation (39) can be inverted to find out the differences between the actual path and the equilibrium path of the real exchange rate which would have been consistent over the period 1969–89 with the maintenance of a balanced fundamental account ($z = 0$) in a context of internal equilibrium – with output growing at their trend rates both in Spain and abroad – and equality of real interest rates.[16]

Figure 10.4 shows the evolution of the 'real exchange rate gap' in the Spanish economy, obtained according to the above-described procedure, during the 1969–89 period. Evidently, while it could be evidently claimed that the exercise violates Lucas' critique we want to argue that there are several reasons why it nevertheless remains useful.

First, Figure 10.5 shows that over the period there have been several episodes characterized by severe and long-lasting overvaluations of the peseta in real terms. Second, if we compare Figures 10.2 and 10.4 it so happens that in each of these episodes (1973–7 and 1979–82) there has been a marked deterioration of the 'fundamental' balance and a rapid build-up of net external debt. Third, it suggests that to a large extent the real appreciation of the peseta in recent years (see Figure 10.5) has been an equilibrium phenomenon, and that no clear devaluation is called for (even if such a measure were effective nowadays, which is highly doubtful given the high degree of *de facto* wage indexation in Spain). This

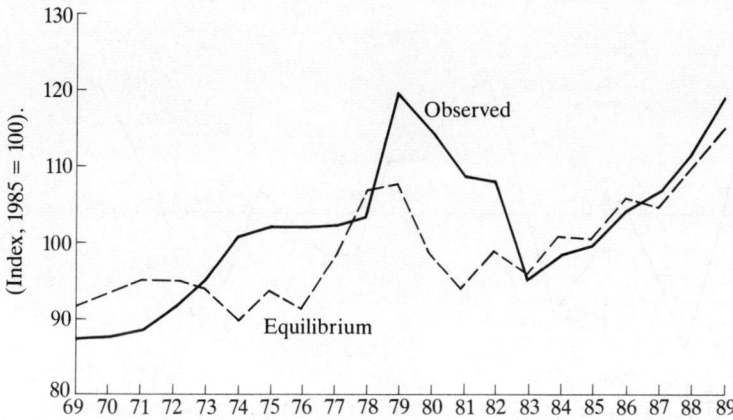

Figure 10.5 The Spanish real exchange rate, observed and equilibrium values, 1969–89. *Note:* Real effective exchange rate of the peseta *vis-à-vis* developed countries using CPIs. An upward movement indicates a real appreciation of the peseta.

evolution seems to suggest that the recent real appreciation of the peseta may have been driven by the large inflow of foreign capital, which, in a large proportion, went into financing direct investment in Spanish industry, implying strong gains in labour productivity in that sector. These large capital inflows have been attracted in part by real interest rate differentials, but when these differentials disappear, as in the simulation exercise, the equilibrium real appreciation of the peseta remains to a large extent, which can be interpreted in the sense that it was mainly the opening-up of the Spanish market to the rest of the EEC that triggered this equilibrium phenomenon. And fourth, it suggests that great attention should be paid to avoiding further real appreciations of the peseta – that is, further deteriorations in international competitiveness – that may jeopardize achieving non-inflationary sustained growth in the future because of external difficulties. As observed in Figure 10.4, in the last two years there are some signs of over-appreciation of the peseta in real terms which suggest that its strengthening may have gone too far and may need some adjustment of economic fundamentals in the future in order to avoid a significant loss of competitiveness of Spanish export industries.[17]

To complete the macroeconomic picture, Figure 10.6 represents the estimated evolution of the 'real output gap' in the Spanish economy, as measured by the percentage difference between actual and trend GDP (Figure 10.7). As can be seen, there are two periods of significant overheating of the economy in 1976–80 and 1987–9, which again broadly coincide with the periods when the Spanish authorities have voiced most

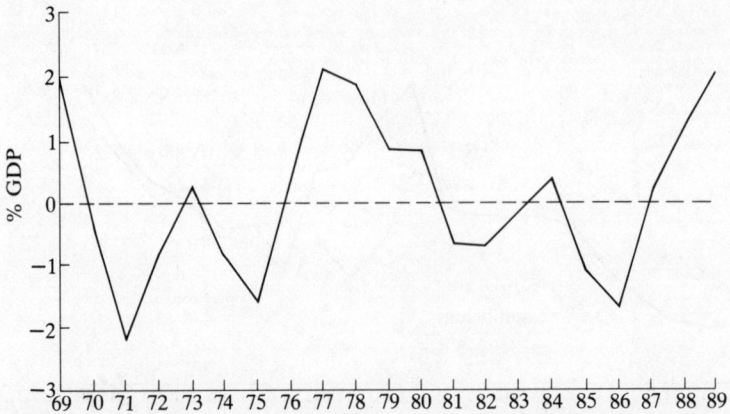

Figure 10.6   The Spanish real output gap, 1969–89. *Note:* **Actual minus potential GDP level. Points above the zero line indicate overheating of the economy.**

loudly their concern about getting into a messy situation characterized by both internal and external disequilibria. Furthermore, given that the real exchange rate of the peseta tends to appreciate '*ceteris paribus*' whenever there is excess domestic demand, this shows that internal and external disequilibria are nothing but the two sides of the same macroeconomic coin.

Consequently, if an excessive appreciation of the peseta is to be avoided in the future, it is necessary that the present 'real output gap' be eliminated in a permanent way by using demand policies designed to moderate demand growth, and structural supply policies designed to improve

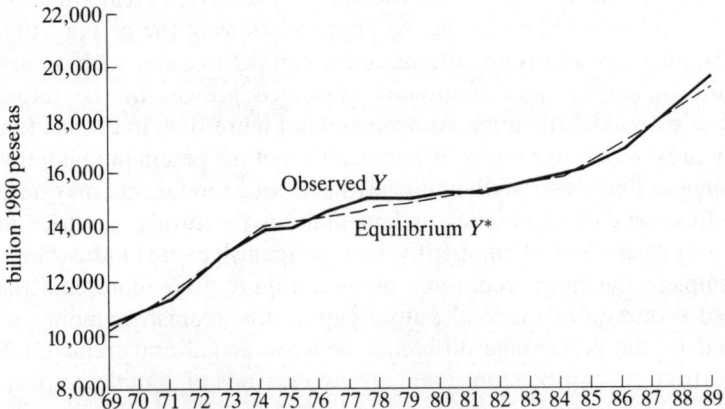

Figure 10.7   Spanish real output, observed, and equilibrium values, 1969–89

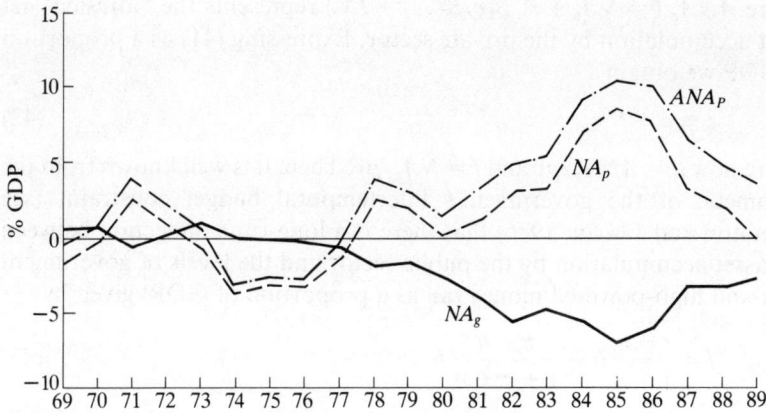

Figure 10.8 Spanish net asset accumulation by private and government sectors, 1969–89.
Notes: NA_p: net acquisition of financial assets by private sector.
ANA_p: adjusted NA_p.
NA_g: net asset accumulation by public sector.

potential output growth. Moreover, a more significant contribution of fiscal restraint is needed on the demand side since monetary policy will not be effective in permanently affecting real variables like real output, the 'fundamental' balance, or the real exchange rate. Monetary policy should rather be oriented towards guaranteeing price and nominal exchange rate stablity, specially given the expected timetable for the monetary integration process in the European Community.

Finally, a simple but illustrative exercise could be undertaken in terms of establishing a target level for net asset accumulation by the private sector (NA_p) which would be consistent with the desired levels of the corresponding net asset accumulation by the public sector (NA_g) and the fundamental current account balance chosen to stabilize the proportions of domestic and foreign debt in terms of GDP. Figure 10.8 shows the recent evolution of both borrowing requirements, together with an adjusted measure of NA_p which will be defined below.

To address this issue, use is made of the well-known open economy identity

$$CA \equiv NA_p + NA_g \tag{40}$$

which is converted into the 'fundamental' account balance by adding external debt interest payments and long-term net investment to CA and NA_p, as in (4'), giving rise to the transformed identity

$$Z \equiv ANA_p + NA_g \tag{41}$$

where ANA_p ($= NA_p + i^*_{t-1}e_t B^*_{t-1} + IN_t$) represents the 'adjusted' net asset accumulation by the private sector. Expressing (41) as a proportion of GDP we obtain

$$z \equiv a + f \tag{42}$$

where now $a = ANA_p/py$ and $f = NA_g/py$. Then, it is well known from the arithmetic of the government's intertemporal budget constraint (see Hamilton and Flavin, 1986) that there is a long-run connection between net asset accumulation by the public sector and the levels of government debt and high-powered money (all as a proportion of GDP) given by

$$f = \frac{r-n}{1+n} b - \frac{\pi+n}{1+\pi+n} h \tag{43}$$

where expression (43) indicates that, in the long run, a budget deficit ($f < 0$) is ultimately financed by the inflation tax collected by the government from the holders of its liabilities, namely debt (b) and high-powered money (h). Now, substituting (7) and (43) into (42), it is possible to obtain the long-run target level of the 'adjusted' net asset accumulation by the private sector, given by

$$a = z - f = \frac{r^*-n}{1+n} b^* - \frac{r-n}{1+n} b + \frac{\pi+n}{1+\pi+n} h \tag{44}$$

Table 10.6 contains some tentative calculations of values of a consistent with different values of b^*, including the previously used value $b^* = 0$. The 'golden rule' assumption $r = n$ has been made for simplicity as well as to avoid the always difficult task of measuring public sector debt. The value of h ($= 20.8\%$) corresponds to the end of 1989 money base–GDP proportion. The results in the table show that financial equilibrium in Spain requires, in the long run, average values of a ranging from 1% to 2.5% depending on the values taken by r^*, n, and π. Given that the unadjusted and adjusted values of a in 1989 are 0% and 3.8% respectively, the obtained target values seem to point out that the current decline suffered by the net asset accumulation by the private sector is still within the equilibrium bounds defined by the previous calculations, unless foreign investment suffers a severe dry-up. If, for instance, the sum of net foreign investment plus interest payments takes its sample value of 1.6%, this means that, in the worst possible situation in Table 10.6, the target value of a should be around 1%. Accordingly, given that the government borrowing requirement has fallen since 1987 and presumably will continue to fall in the future, the present worsening of the current account can be viewed as the outcome of the decision of the private sector which finds it appropriate to invest beyond its means in terms of saving

Table 10.6. *Targets for adjusted net acquisition of financial assets by the private sector*
(% of GDP)

		$r = n = 2$			$r = n = 4$		
		$\pi = 3$	$\pi = 6$	$\pi = 8$	$\pi = 3$	$\pi = 6$	$\pi = 8$
$b^* = 0$	$r^* = 2.0$	1.0	1.5	1.9	1.4	1.9	2.2
	$r^* = 6.0$	1.0	1.5	1.9	1.4	1.9	2.2
$b^* = 5$	$r^* = 2.0$	1.0	1.5	1.9	1.3	1.8	2.1
	$r^* = 6.0$	1.2	1.7	2.3	1.4	2.0	2.3
$b^* = 10$	$r^* = 2.0$	1.0	1.5	1.9	1.2	1.7	2.0
	$r^* = 6.0$	1.4	1.9	2.3	1.6	2.1	2.4

Note: See expression (44) in the text.

capacity. Thus, even if no radical measures seem necessary in the present situation, it may be sensible that emphasis should be placed on policy measures which promote private and public saving rather than on those restraining investment.

7   Conclusions

This paper has explored the conceptual nature of the external constraint and its practical relevance for the Spanish economy. The paper has shown that, while the true external constraint of the economy is a long-run one in the absence of distortions and market imperfections, it nevertheless may be rational for governments to monitor the shorter-run evolution of the external accounts for the purpose of avoiding future difficulties. Moreover, whenever such distortions and imperfections are important, governments may even be justified in setting specific short-run external targets.

Regarding the specific case of the Spanish economy, we have shown that its economic performance over the last twenty years offers clear and unambiguous examples of major policy changes being prompted by unfavourable external accounts developments. In particular, Spanish economic authorities of very different political persuasions have proceeded to adopt traumatic but nevertheless necessary macroeconomic policy measures in the past to avoid an explosion of the net external debt–GDP ratio.

The various cointegration tests carried out in the chapter suggest that the Spanish economy is at present far from facing any problems derived from the fulfilment of the external solvency constraint. Nevertheless, this does not mean that a relaxed or complacent attitude should be taken regarding the future evolution of international competitiveness, especially given the elimination of capital controls in Spain by 1993. Indeed, we advocate further fiscal restraint and supply-side structural policies.

To help establish a simple set of policy guidelines consistent with both internal and external equilibrium, we have proposed targeting the evolution of what we have defined as the 'fundamental' account balance to be zero on average over long periods of time. We have also provided tentative calculations of three variables: the 'real exchange rate gap' and 'real output gap' and a 'target' for the private sector's net acquisition of financial assets. These can be used by the authorities in the future as an approximate indicator of internal and external disequilibria, and as a useful tool for designing suitable macroeconomic policies.

NOTES

We are grateful to our discussant Yves Barroux, and to the participants at the Athens conference for their comments. We also wish to thank Samuel Bentolila and Diego González for their help at early stages of the project. The views expressed in the paper are those of the authors and do not necessarily represent those of the institutions to which they are affiliated.

1 Earlier detailed descriptions of the basic forces underlying the external performance of the Spanish economy can be found in De la Dehesa (1983) and Viñals (1983). A good overview of the current situation can be found in Fernández (1990).
2 For an analysis of the microeconomic and macroeconomic effects of Spain's entry to the EEC see Viñals et al. (1990). Fernández and Sebastián (1990) test if Spain's entrance into the EEC has had an impact on trade flows.
3 A rise in θ is interpreted as an appreciation.
4 We are abstracting from hysteresis-related effects.
5 Wilcox (1989) provides several examples of this possibility.
6 Although it is arguable that the authorities' reaction function responds to the 'fundamental' balance rather than the trade balance, the steady character of net foreign investment makes it easy to forecast, and therefore we believe that at least, in the case of the Spanish economy, this is a fairly reasonable assumption.
7 Cash-flow data have been used which are only available since 1969.
8 It should be borne in mind, however, that, if the interest rates for external assets and liabilities differ, changes in assets and liabilities that leave the level of net external debt unaltered may change the average cost of net external debt. Assets and liabilities are assumed to be homogeneous in the text.

9 It is important to test that there is no constant under the null hypothesis of the existence of a unit root. Were there to be such a constant, the appropriate critical values would be those of the standardized normal, e.g., 1.96% at 5% level (see Dolado *et al.*, 1990). In all cases studied, the constant was not significant under the null.

10 That is if $\lambda \simeq 0$, (26) would be similar to $z_t = e_t$ while Δb^*_t is still governed by (25).

11 The current Moody's rating of Spain's foreign debt position is AA minus, still three steps below the maximum rating of AAA. In this sense the assumption that b^* should be zero in the long run does not seem too restrictive.

12 However, from a historical perspective, the sustainability of deficits recorded in various subperiods could be roughly calculated using expression (7). Thus, for example, using the sample averages of the lower part of Table 12.2, if it had been wished to maintain in the 1974–7 period the average proportion of debt of the previous subperiod (7.3%), the designed fundamental balance would have been -0.20% of GDP. As the actual proportion was, on average, -2.5%, this indicates non-sustainability in that subperiod. On similar grounds, the 1980–2 subperiod does not satisfy the solvency constraint whereas the 1986–9 period does so comfortably.

13 For example, the sustainability of external deficits is often assessed in terms of alternative definitions of the basic balance. See Ortega *et al.* (1989) for an analysis of current account positions sustainability in the EEC using a definition of the basic balance which is identical to the 'fundamental' account balance used in the present paper.

14 Foreign GDP growth refers to G–7 countries and has been obtained using the same weights as to compute r^* earlier on. Trend GDP growth rates have been obtained through splices in 1974 and 1985.

15 For an analysis of the effects of openness on the Spanish economy after 1986 see Viñals *et al.* (1990).

16 Unlike in other analyses of fundamental equilibrium exchange rates, the structural component of foreign capital flows is not assumed but estimated. See, for example, Williamson (1985) and Barrel and Wren-Lewis (1989).

17 De Grauwe (1990) makes a similar point in trying to identify possible causes of the real appreciations in the currencies of the Southern countries in the EEC.

REFERENCES

Artis, M. and T. Bayoumi (1991), 'Saving, Investment, Financial Integration and the Balance of Payments', (this volume).

Barrel, R. and S. Wren-Lewis (1989), 'Fundamental Equilibrium Exchange Rates for the G-7', CEPR Discussion Paper No. 323.

Cohen, D. (1985), 'How to Evaluate the Solvency of an Indebted Nation', *Economic Policy* **1**, (1), 139–67.

Cooper, R. and J. Sachs (1985), 'Borrowing Abroad: The Debtor's Perspective', in G. Smith and J. Cuddington (eds.), *International Debt and the Developing Countries*, Washington D.C.: The World Bank.

De Grauwe, P. (1990), 'Convergence and Real Exchange Rates in the European Monetary System', mimeo, C.O.R.E., University of Louvain.

De la Dehesa, G. (1983), 'Ajuste externo y tipo de cambio', *Papeles de Economía Española* **15**, 282–304.

Diamond, P. (1965), 'National Debt in a Neoclassical Growth Model', *American Economic Review* **55**, 1126–50.

Dickey, D. and W. Fuller (1981), 'Likelihood Ratio Statistics for Autoregressive Time Series with a Unit Root', *Econometrica* **49**, 1057–72.

Dolado, J., T. Jenkinson and S. Sosvilla-Rivero (1990), 'Cointegration and Unit Roots: A Survey', *Journal of Economic Surveys* (forthcoming).

Engle, R. and C. Granger (1987), 'Cointegration and Error Correction: Representation, Estimation and Testing', *Econometrica* **55**, 251–76.

Fernández, I. and M. Sebastián (1990), 'El sector exterior y la incorporación de España a la CEE', *Moneda y Crédito* (forthcoming).

Fernández, V. (1990), 'La Insuficiencia de la Tasa de Ahorro Interno y el Futuro de la Balanza de Pagos en España', *Información Comercial Española* **611**, 127–46.

Hamilton, J. and M. Flavin (1986), 'On the Limitations of Government Borrowing: A Framework for Empirical Testing', *American Economic Review* **76**, 808–19.

McKinnon, J. (1990), 'Critical Values for Cointegration Tests', University of California, San Diego, Discussion Paper 90–4.

Ortega, E., J. Salaverría, and J. Viñals (1989), 'La Balanza de Pagos española en el contexto comunitario', *Boletín Económico*, Banco de España, November, 53–74.

Trehan, B. and C. Walsh (1988), 'Common Trends, the Government Budget Constraint and Revenue Smoothing', *Journal of Economic Dynamics and Control* **12**, 425–44.

Viñals, J. (1983), 'El desequilibrio exterior del sector exterior en España: una perspectiva macroeconómica', *Información Comercial Española* **604**, 23–28.

(1986), 'Fiscal policy and the current account', *Economic Policy* **1**, (3), 711–44.

(1990a), 'Los riesgos de la libre circulación de capitales', *Papeles de Economía Española* **43**, 74–83.

(1990b), 'The EMS, Spain and macroeconomic policy', CEPR Discussion Paper No. 389; forthcoming in P. de Grauwe and L. Papademos (eds.), *The European Monetary System in the 1990s*, London: Longman.

Viñals, J. et al. (1990), 'Spain and the "EC cum 1992" shock', in C. Bliss and J.B. de Macedo (eds.), *Unity with Diversity in the European Economy: the Community's Southern Frontier*, Cambridge University Press.

Wickens, M. (1989), 'Is the U.S. Insolvent?: A Test of the National Intertemporal Budget Constraint', mimeo, University of Southampton.

Wilcox, D. (1989), 'The Sustainability of Government Deficits: Implications of the Present-Value Borrowing Constraint', *Journal of Money, Credit and Banking* **21**, 291–306.

Williamson, J. (1985), *The Exchange Rate System*, Policy Analyses 5, Institute for International Economics, Washington D.C.

Discussion

YVES BARROUX

The chapter by Juan Dolado and José Viñals is very interesting and stimulating. The chapter addresses three different sets of questions:

First, it tells the story of macroeconomic policy in Spain for the last fifteen years and tries to give an idea of the importance of the external constraint over the period.

Second, it tries to give a more precise measurement of the external constraint by calculating the so-called 'fundamental account balance' and, with that instrument, it provides a wide range of econometric tests that lead to the conclusion that the Spanish economy is perfectly solvent, that it is not likely to have solvency problems in the future, and that it might even be deemed dynamically inefficient (which means simply that it could take more advantage of its solvency by running larger current account deficits).

Third, it tries to provide policy-makers with some guidelines that will help them to judge whether the recent evolutions of economic activity or the real exchange rate are likely to bring the fundamental account balance too far away from its targeted value.

As for the first part of the chapter, which provides us with a very interesting analysis of the balance-of-payments crises that Spain went through, I will just make a comment and a suggestion.

The comment is that I found it very appropriate to differentiate between the two (or three) crises by analysing their causes in terms of the saving–investment balance as the same gap on the three occasions (a shortage of saving of about 2.5% of GDP) was due either to a fall in the savings rate or to an increase in the investment rate.

The suggestion is that, in trying to undestand a balance-of-payments crisis, it might be interesting to analyse the financing of the current account deficit and, more specifically, to differentiate between net direct investment and net foreign debt. Unfortunately, this disaggregation of the 'net long-term capital' line is not provided in Table 10.2 and I suggest it should be added.

As for the second part of the paper, I will be very brief as I did not have enough time to come to grips with the econometric testing. However, as external con straints and solvency are often to be viewed as problems of credibility (and I will come back to that in a moment), the authors' reputation in econometrics is already well known to me. Obviously, I will leave it to the experts on the floor to confirm my opinion as I am not an expert on these matters.

The only thing I want to stress is that, in order to derive the concept of sustainable fundamental balance, you have to linearize relation (4″) of the chapter and, to do that, to assume that the real exchange rate is constant, interest-rate parity is fulfilled, and the foreign interest rate is constant. That leads me to a question about the approach itself: solvency, or sustainable fundamental balance, is viewed only as something related to the macroeconomic performance of the Spanish economy and there is a sort of linear relationship between those two sets of variables. In the real world, we all know that solvency is judged by the financial markets, in other words by the actual or potential lenders. In the chapter no attempt is made to endogenize the behaviour of the lenders, for example in the form of a non-linear reaction function that will link the rate of interest they will be asking to the macroeconomic performance of the country to which they are lending. The estimation of such a reaction function will of course be of great interest, as it is not sure that the lenders will come up with the same measure of the sustainable fundamental balance or will allow the actual fundamental balance to deviate so much from its sustainable value.

That leads me to the last part of the chapter. Before that, I should confess that, being a central banker, I was a bit worried about the conclusion that the Spanish authorities seemed to be too shy and should take advantage of the solvency of the economy in a more dynamic way by allowing it to run much larger deficits. But, in the last part of the chapter, I realized that it was a chapter written by central bank economists, as I noticed that the sustainable fundamental balance and the net foreign debt ratio they chose was zero.

They then estimate a function of the fundamental balance in terms of the rate of growth both at home and abroad, the real exchange rate, and the degree of openness of the economy. Inverting that function, they come up with indicators of the real output gap and the real exchange rate gap, that are designed to serve as guidelines and help policy-makers to reach their decisions. Obviously these indicators are very consistent with the story told about the Spanish economy in the first part of the chapter. However, what these indicators do not tell policy-makers is how big a deviation from the equilibrium level is acceptable both to the government and to the lenders, unless you accept the idea that former experiences leading to a turnaround of policies are to be judged as the upper limit of the acceptable band.

Looking at these two indicators and especially in the recent period, I would add two comments:

First, as for the real output growth gap, which, as can be seen from Figure 10.6, has been going up sharply and dangerously in the recent period, it seems to me that the appropriate indicator would be the differential between domestic and foreign output growth rather than the deviation of domestic real growth from its trend.

Second, as for the real exchange rate gap, the picture is less worrisome in the recent years, but I suspect that this has something to do with the strong appreciation of the peseta, which was triggered by the very high level of real interest rates in Spain. One may wonder whether, in spite of the apparently reassuring level of the indicator, it is going to be sustainable and would not lead to a large and unsustainable level of the current account deficit.

11 Macroeconomic policy and the external constraint: the Danish experience

SØREN BO NIELSEN and JØRGEN SØNDERGAARD

1 Introduction

Denmark has a long history of almost three decades of uninterrupted balance-of-payments deficits and ensuing accumulation of foreign debt. As a matter of fact, Denmark belongs to a small and exclusive group of heavily indebted OECD countries, the other members being Greece, Iceland, Portugal, Turkey, and Ireland, all with foreign debt amounting to about 40% of GDP or more. The Danish development is remarkable not only because of the size of the debt. The period of uninterrupted debt accumulation is rather long and embraces periods of very different external conditions, economic policies and internal economic developments. Over the years, as a full-fledged international capital market has emerged, the issue of financing the perpetual current account deficits has virtually disappeared and the country has never even been close to its solvency constraint. Yet, as evidenced by an abundance of citations from reports on economic policy, policy debates in Parliament, etc., in this entire period the external balance has indeed been of great concern to Danish policy-making. It seems to be beyond question that external considerations have limited the pool of feasible policies, but on the other hand history does indeed also highlight the 'softness' of this constraint.

This chapter briefly examines this development over the past three decades. We argue that foreign debt should be a matter of concern for policy-making even if the path of debt is sustainable and no immediate difficulties of financing are to be expected. In what way and to what extent the external balance should constrain domestic policies depends, however, on several factors including the causes that account for the deficits. Furthermore, it is not straightforward to identify why a country like Denmark, as opposed to its seemingly similar Northern European neighbours, has ended up having such a high foreign debt-to-GDP ratio.

Upon examining a variety of possible explanations we conclude that the

342

Danish external debt can be traced back to a mixture of equilibrium and disequilibrium phenomena. By equilibrium explanations we refer to long-run effects of, e.g., the tax and social security system that reduces private incentives to accumulate wealth, while negative supply shocks and attempts to use fiscal policies to accommodate such disturbances are examples of disequilibrium explanations of current account deterioration. The latter is obviously a matter of concern for stabilization policy, while it is less clear if and how foreign debt of an equilibrium nature should influence economic policy. Yet, we argue that this may be justified on several grounds. Governments may want to constrain foreign borrowing even if it is an equilibrium phenomenon due to, e.g., the vulnerability of the economy to interest rate 'shocks' and perhaps also uncertainty as to the long-run stability of international financial markets. Besides, equilibrium debt may be associated with distortions affecting private savings and investments. Thus, contries may rightly worry about the growth of external debt that follows from these distortions. Removal of such distortions of the allocation of resources would usually be a first-best policy while in the absence of such a policy, constraining foreign debt through macroeconomic stabilization measures may be a second-best choice.

The plan of this chapter is as follows. Section 2 gives a brief description of the Danish economy and its development since the early 1960s. In addition, it focuses on external disturbances and the main lines of stabilization policy. Section 3 examines equilibrium and disequilibrium causes of the particular Danish external debt position. Section 4 addresses the nature and the policy implications of the external constraint in the Danish case, before Section 5 concludes the chapter.

2   The Danish economy

2.1   The history of debt accumulation

Danish net foreign debt in per cent of GDP and the current account of the balance of payments, likewise relative to GDP, are shown in Figure 11.1 for the period 1960–89. Denmark's international indebtedness has been increasing steadily throughout the years. In 1960 net foreign debt amounted to a mere 2% of GDP; in 1989 the figure was 38%. Recently, however, foreign debt relative to GDP has fallen slightly.

As noted in the introduction, with a foreign debt of this size, Denmark is one of the most heavily indebted OECD countries. While Iceland, Portugal, Turkey, Ireland, and Greece are also 'up there', the two other Scandinavian countries and, e.g., the Netherlands, although in many respects similar to the Danish economy, have much smaller levels of

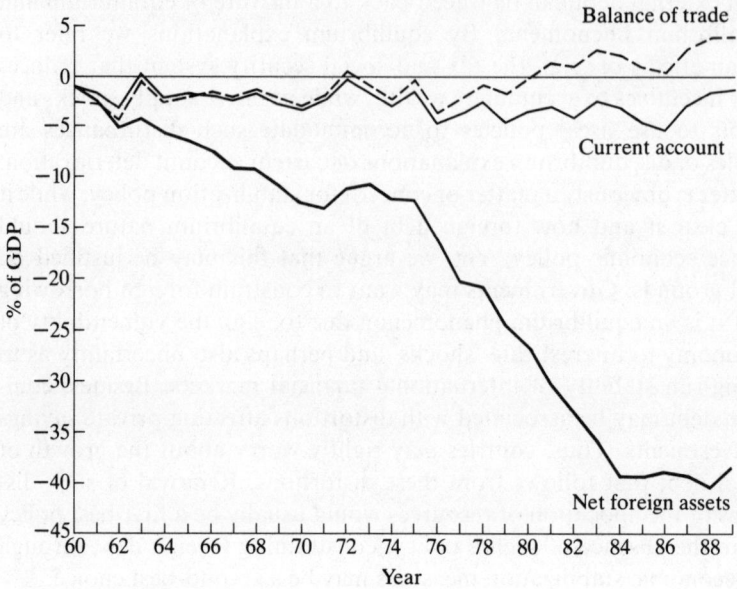

Figure 11.1   Danish foreign debt, current account, and balance of trade, 1960–89 (% of GDP). *Source:* Economic Council.

foreign indebtedness (actually the Netherlands can register a positive net foreign asset position).

Public debt relative to GDP in Denmark is currently close to the EEC average (see Figure 11.2). The history of public debt, however, diverges markedly from that of other countries, in that a long period with a positive public financial asset position throughout the 1960s was replaced by a period of rapid build-up of public debt until 1983 and a similarly notable stabilization thereof since then. It is also interesting that among the heavily (externally) indebted EEC countries Denmark has by far the lowest level of public debt.

The saving–investment balance shown in Figure 11.3 reveals a strong cyclical influence as well as a close negative correlation between public and private net savings.

One might wonder whether this close negative correlation is a sign of Ricardian equivalence in the Danish economy. As shown in Economic Council (1990), however, it might also reflect the economy's cyclical development initiated by recurrent shifts in the international business cycle.

While the debt accumulated by the public sector is not significantly larger than in other countries, the propensity to save among Danish

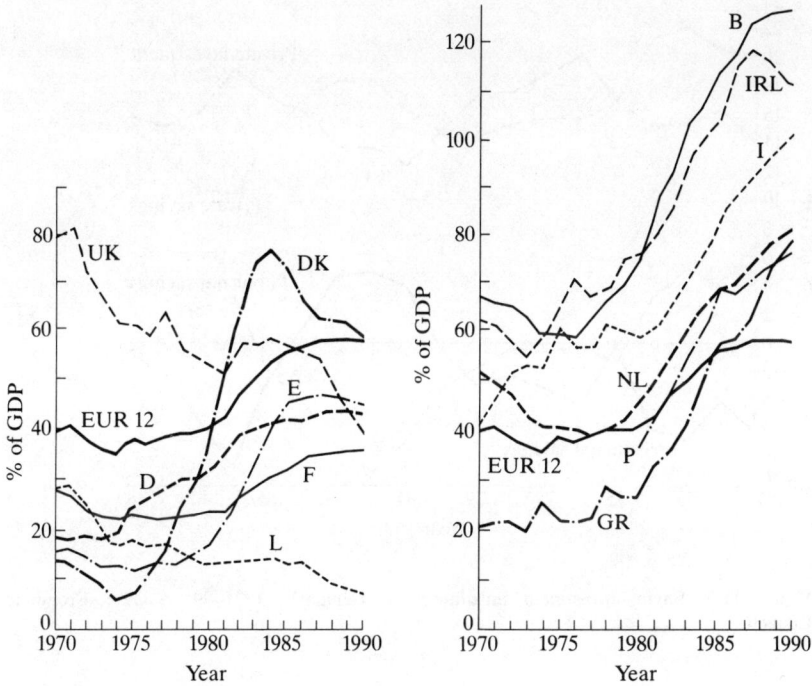

(a) Countries with public debt below or very close to the Community average in 1988

(b) Countries with high public debt in 1988

Figure 11.2   Gross public debt in EEC countries as % of GDP, 1970–89. *Source: European Economy*, **July 1989.**

households is very low. As shown in Table 11.1, the six-year average (1981–6) net saving rate for households was negative and significantly lower than in other Nordic countries, not to mention West Germany. Even if the latter part of this period displayed a consumption boom in Denmark and thus may represent an unusually low level of household saving it is nevertheless a striking feature of the Danish economy that household net saving is largely non-existent as a source of wealth accumulation.

2.2   Macroeconomic development since 1960

By the beginning of the 1960s, Denmark was still very much an agricultural–small manufacturing economy. Approximately 20% of the

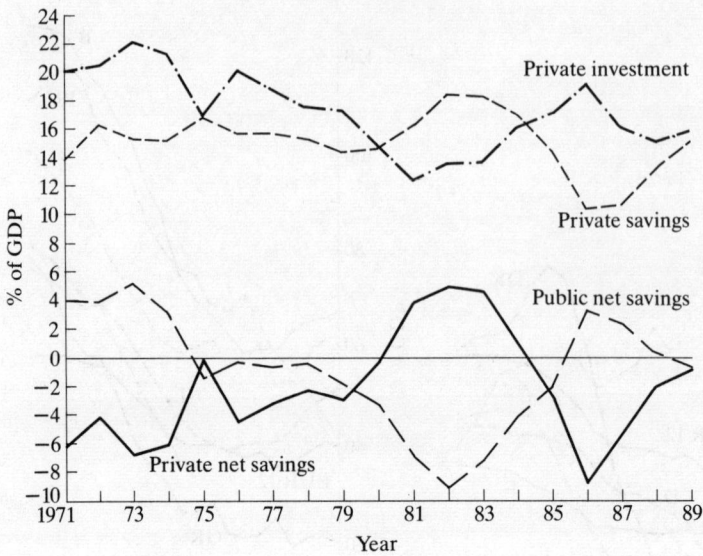

Figure 11.3 **Saving–investment imbalances in Denmark, 1971–89.** *Source:* Economic Council.

Table 11.1. *Net saving rates of households in the Nordic countries and West Germany, 1981–6*

	1981	1982	1983	1984	1985	1986	Average 1981–6
Denmark	2.3	6.0	− 0.1	− 2.0	− 6.5	− 12.0	− 2.1
Norway	4.5	3.9	4.3	5.1	− 2.7	− 7.2	1.3
Sweden	4.0	0.9	1.4	1.1	1.3	− 0.8	1.3
Finland	6.1	6.8	7.3	6.4	5.9	3.7	6.0
West Germany	13.3	12.8	10.9	11.2	11.2	12.1	11.9

Notes: Net saving as percentage of private consumption plus net saving.
Net saving equals gross saving less depreciation on the capital stock of households.
Source: Danmarks Statistik, *Statistiske Efterretninger*, 1990.

labour force was in agriculture, while 35% were employed in manufacture and construction, and 35% in private services. Public employment constituted 10% of the labour force. Unemployment was low, as was inflation. Ahead waited what were later to be termed 'the golden 1960s', a period of high growth and full employment, but also of permanent balance-of-payments deficits (the sole exception being the year of 1963).

With some eventual slowing down of growth, this process lasted until 1973, when the economy got into a severe crisis, inflicted partly by external shocks, but certainly also by domestic developments. Actually, since 1974 things have never been the same. The economy has not again experienced sustained growth for extended periods; unemployment rose easily and dramatically on two occasions (1973–5 and 1980–2) and has remained at or just below the two-digit level since then. Even in periods of deep recession, the current account of the balance of payments has remained in the red.

Table 11.2 summarizes macroeconomic developments: the real rate of growth of GDP, the rate of increase in the GDP deflator and in the consumer price level, the conventional measure of the rate of unemployment, the current account in per cent of GDP, and the rate of growth of domestic demand.

We shall not comment on Table 11.2 here, apart from noticing the rather abrupt changes in the cyclical position in Denmark around 1974, 1976, 1980, 1984, and lastly 1987. The contrast between booms and recessionary periods is remarkable, also, in an international context. Furthermore, when comparing it with the pattern of economic development in most other OECD countries since 1982 it is clearly seen that Denmark has been out of phase with the general pattern.

In a conventional unemployment–wage inflation diagram (Figure 11.4), outward shifts in the position of the economy can be discerned for the years 1973–5 and 1980–2. The employment situation obviously worsened seriously in the decade from 1973 to 1983. During the three years of domestic demand-led boom, 1984–6, the rate of unemployment fell somewhat without significantly higher wage increases until 1987 (it was a disinflationary period in the international economy), but when recession reappeared in 1987, unemployment started rising again without wage moderation until 1989.

It has been customary in the Danish economic policy debate to refer to the high unemployment rate and the continuous current account deficit as 'the double balance problem'. Again and again it has been claimed that neither monetary nor fiscal policy would be able to alleviate both problems at the same time; instead, a significant dose of improvement in competitiveness would be called for, either in the form of exchange rate

Table 11.2. *Macroeconomic development in Denmark, 1960–89 (%)*

	1960	1961	1962	1963	1964	1965	1966	1967	1968	1969
Growth in real GDP	6.1	5.6	5.5	-1.1	11.0	4.5	2.4	3.4	4.0	6.3
Growth of the GDP deflator	1.8	5.9	6.6	7.5	3.6	7.8	7.9	6.2	7.0	7.0
Growth of consumer prices	2.8	3.6	6.0	5.5	3.6	5.9	6.3	7.4	7.1	4.6
Unemployment rate	1.8	1.4	1.3	1.8	1.0	0.9	1.0	1.2	2.1	1.7
Current account in % of GDP	-1.0	-1.7	-3.3	0.3	-2.2	-1.7	-1.9	-2.4	-1.7	-2.9
Real growth in domestic demand	6.0	6.4	7.2	-2.7	13.1	4.4	3.2	3.6	3.0	8.4

	1970	1971	1972	1973	1974	1975	1976	1977	1978	1979
Growth in real GDP	2.0	2.7	5.3	3.6	-0.9	-0.7	6.5	1.6	1.5	3.5
Growth of the GDP deflator	8.3	7.7	9.2	10.7	13.1	12.4	9.1	9.4	9.9	7.6
Growth of consumer prices	6.6	8.3	8.2	11.7	15.0	9.9	9.9	10.6	9.2	10.4
Unemployment rate	1.3	1.6	1.6	1.0	2.3	5.3	5.3	6.4	7.3	6.2
Current account in % of GDP	-3.4	-2.4	-0.3	-1.6	-3.0	-1.5	-4.7	-3.8	-2.6	-4.6
Real growth in domestic demand	3.4	0.8	4.0	5.4	-3.1	-1.7	10.1	0.4	1.1	2.7

	1980	1981	1982	1983	1984	1985	1986	1987	1988	1989
Growth in real GDP	-0.4	-0.9	3.0	2.5	4.4	4.3	3.6	-0.6	-0.2	1.1
Growth of the GDP deflator	8.2	10.1	10.6	7.6	5.7	4.3	4.6	5.0	4.2	4.4
Growth of consumer prices	10.7	12.0	10.2	6.8	6.4	4.3	2.9	4.8	4.0	5.0
Unemployment rate	7.0	9.2	9.8	10.4	10.1	9.0	7.8	7.8	8.6	9.3
Current account in % of GDP	-3.6	-3.0	-4.1	-2.5	-3.1	-4.7	-5.4	-2.9	-1.6	-1.3
Real growth in domestic demand	-4.3	-4.1	3.5	1.4	5.1	5.4	6.1	-3.0	-2.2	0.6

Source: Economic Council.

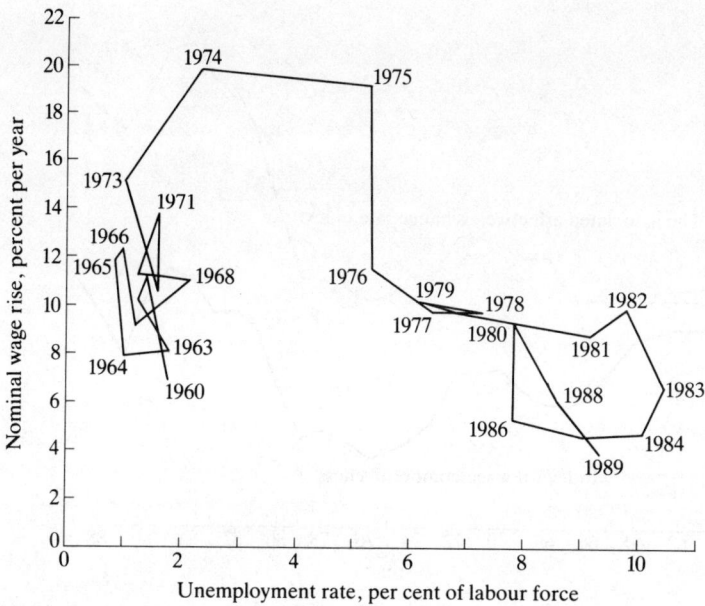

Figure 11.4   Nominal wage rise and unemployment rate in Denmark, 1960–89. *Source: Economic Council.*

adjustment or in the form of very low wage increases over a prolonged period. The development in one conventional competitiveness measure, relative hourly labour costs in common currency (abroad *vis-à-vis* in Denmark), is shown in Figure 11.5.

Figure 11.5 also shows the extent to which changes in the effective rate of the Danish Krone have affected competitiveness. It appears that competitiveness was slowly eroded during the 1960s and again more drastically in the mid 1970s, followed by improvements in the period 1979–82 on account of a series of devaluations of the Danish Krone and moderate wage increases.

Interest rate developments in 1960–89 are illustrated in Figure 11.6 which shows nominal long-term interest rates for Denmark and Germany. Quite low interest rates in the 1960s were followed by significant increases during the 1970s. Nominal interest rates peaked in 1981–2 when the public sector registered extensive budget deficits, boosting public debt very rapidly. The sustainability of public deficits – as well as the solvency of the public sector – was questioned in the mass media, and this as well as expectations of repeated devaluations and the downgrading of the Kingdom of Denmark by Standard and Poors may have

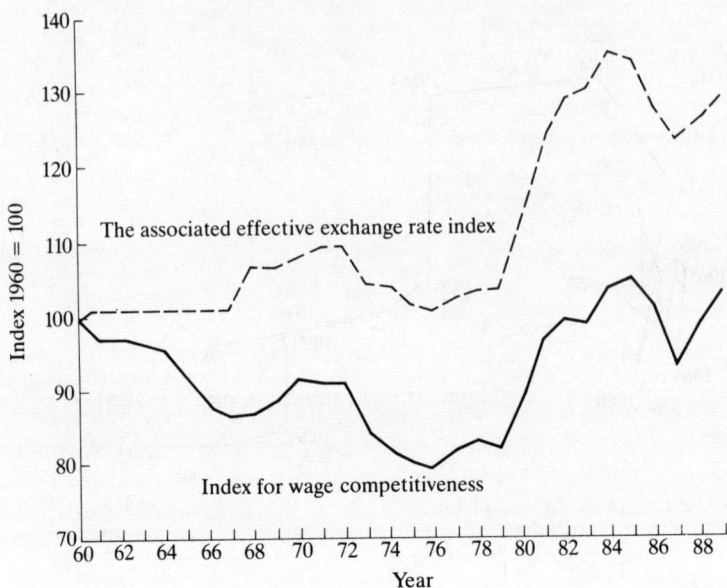

Figure 11.5   **Index for Danish wage competitiveness, 1960–89.** *Source:* **Swedish Employers' union and Economic Council.**

contributed to interest rates in excess of 20% per annum. A remarkable turnaround occurred after the declaration of the 'medium-term strategy' of the incoming conservative government in late 1982, a strategy which relied on significant public expenditure cuts and a fixed exchange rate policy.

2.3   External shocks

During the 1960s, the external environment of the Danish economy was largely very beneficial and conducive to economic growth. It was only at the end of this decade that growth began to slow and inflation to soar in trading partner countries. Then followed the pronounced boom in 1972–3, coupled with significant increases in food and materials prices, before the first round of oil price hikes and the ensuing international recession.

The oil price shock was more serious for Denmark than for most other industrial economies, since Denmark at that time completely lacked domestic energy resources. Later on, exploration and production in the Danish part of the North Sea oil and gas area was initiated, raising the economy's degree of self-sufficiency in oil and natural gas to almost 100%

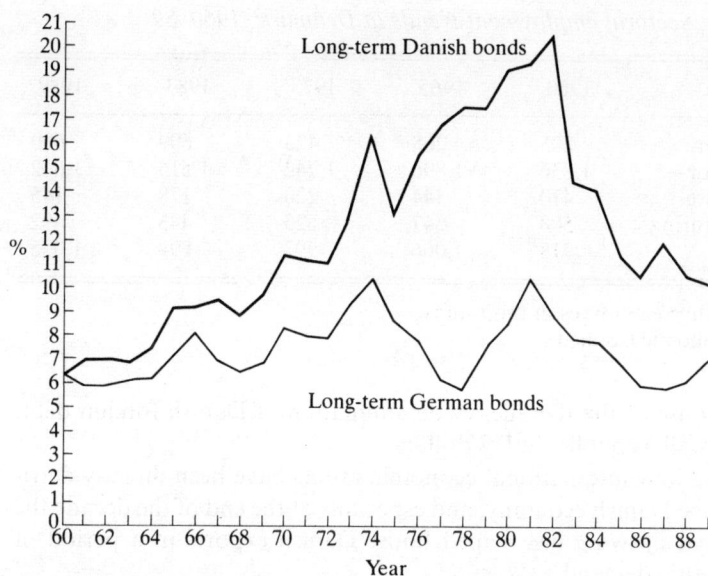

Figure 11.6 **Average nominal yield on Danish and German long-term bonds, 1960–89.**
Source: Economic Council.

at present. A rough measure of the pure terms of trade loss for Denmark associated with the first oil crisis is of the order of almost 4% of GDP. Add to this that the rest of Northern Europe and thereby Denmark's foremost trading partners was also rather severely hit, limiting the possibilities for Denmark to export herself out of the crisis.

Growth in the international economy resumed again towards 1976, and eventually the second oil crisis occurred, followed by a more shallow though also more long-lasting recession than after OPEC I. From 1980 onwards, significant changes in the external environment resulted from both the rise in international real rates of interest and in the dollar. As to the former, the resulting much higher interest payments on foreign debt accelerated debt accumulation and detracted from national income. It has been estimated that the *ex post* real interest rate applicable to foreign debt, inclusive of exchange rate gains or losses on the debt, changed dramatically from an average of about − 8% in 1967–76 to + 8% in 1977–87 (Economic Council, 1988).

It has been debated whether the appreciation of the dollar in 1980–5 was beneficial or deterimental to Europe, but the consensus in Denmark would have it that it above all contributed a significant stimulus to exports, although it certainly was not the 'best' way to devalue the Danish

Table 11.3. *Sectoral employment trends in Denmark, 1960–89*

	1960	1965	1973	1983	1989
Public sector	205	268	423	609	660
Private sector	1.836	1,896	1,742	1,515	1,662
Agriculture	410	344	220	178	145
Manufacturing	508	547	525	443	492
Other	918	1,006	997	894	1,025

Note: Full-time employees in thousands.
Source: Economic Council.

Krone because of the then heavy denomination of Danish foreign debt, private as well as public, in US dollars.

Since 1982, few international economic events have been directly detrimental to the Danish economy, and especially at the end of the decade the international upswing has helped boost Danish exports in a period of weak domestic demand.

2.4   Structural changes

Among the important structural changes that have occurred during this period one should count Danish membership of the EEC from 1973. It is beyond doubt that entering the Common Market gave rise to much optimism, especially concerning future incomes in agriculture and related sectors of the economy.

The swing in the composition of economic activity in Denmark, away from agriculture, fisheries, etc., and in periods also from manufacturing, towards private and public services constitutes another important development. This development, which is illustrated in Table 11.3, is, we acknowledge, to some extent influenced by policy, but unavoidable structural changes remain.

Finally, developments in the size and composition of the Danish labour force must to some extent be considered exogenous and outside the range of economic policy control. Table 11.4 compares the growth of the labour force in Denmark and in the OECD area. It is seen that the labour force has grown relatively fast due to a pronounced increase in the participation rate of women, resulting in a stronger adjustment pressure on the Danish labour market. As also displayed in the table, employment has on average shown a faster increase in Denmark so that present unemployment is close to the European average or even slightly lower. Meanwhile, wage inflation was almost at the European average for the period as a whole,

Table 11.4. *Wage, labour force, and employment trends in Denmark and OECD Europe, 1960–89*

	1960–73	1973–82	1982–8	1960–88
Average annual growth rates				
Labour force				
Europe	0.4	0.8	0.8	0.6
Denmark	1.2	1.2	0.9	1.2
Employment				
Europe	0.4	0.1	0.7	0.4
Denmark	1.3	0.2	1.8	1.0
GDP per capita				
Europe	3.8	1.4	2.1	2.6
Denmark	3.6	1.2	2.0	2.5
Hourly wage costs in manufacturing				
Europe	10.4	14.1	6.6	10.7
Denmark	11.8	12.4	5.4	10.6
Average levels				
Unemployment rate (%)				
Europe	3.1	5.8[a]	10.2[b]	5.4
Denmark	1.3	6.5[a]	9.0[b]	4.5
Current account – GDP ratio (%)				
Europe	0.3	– 0.5[a]	0.7[b]	0.1
Denmark	– 1.9	– 3.5[a]	– 3.4[b]	– 2.7

Notes: Europe is a weighted average of 11 European OECD countries.
[a] 1974–82
[b] 1983–8
Source: Economic Council.

somewhat higher in the 1960s, but somewhat lower in the 1970s and 1980s.

2.5   Stabilization policy

During the last three decades, Danish macroeconomic policy has been altered in a number of important respects, partly but not exclusively related to the impact of external shocks. Notably the monetary regime moved from a 'fixed exchange rate-capital control system' in the 1960s through a transitional period from 1972 to 1982 of 'variable exchange rate pegging-capital control' to the present regime of 'fixed exchange rate within the EMS-free capital mobility'. The scope for autonomous monetary policy for stabilization purposes has narrowed accordingly.

Monetary policy

During most of the 1960s, monetary policy was generally aimed at stabilizing nominal interest rates and was hence quite expansionary since interest rates were relatively low. Real interest rates were around 3%.

However, starting in the mid 1960s a number of quantitative regulations of credit were introduced. Whether these instruments aiming at distributing cheap financial capital to production while restraining consumer credit were at all effective is questionable, and in the late 1970s when the role of monetary policy had become oriented towards curtailing domestic demand, leading to high real interest rates, these measures were almost completely abolished.

In fact, the orientation of monetary policy was first changed in 1969 when a serious speculative attack on the Danish Krone occurred, and stabilization of foreign exchange reserves has been a primary concern for monetary policy since then. At time, though, restraining domestic demand and the continuing deterioration of the current account motivated even tighter policy stances. Thus for two decades now monetary policy has been heavily oriented towards one or the other aspect of the external constraint.

Exchange rate policy

During the 1970s, exchange rate policies varied significantly. After the breakdown of the Bretton Woods system the Danish Krone joined the 'snake' in 1972, so the Krone was never freely floating. Despite depreciations *vis-à-vis* the German mark the Krone appreciated by some 10% in effective terms from 1972 to 1976. In 1979, however, when Denmark joined the EMS, Danish exchange rate policy for a short period became an active devaluation policy which together with the appreciation of the dollar established an effective devaluation of the Krone by more than 20% from 1979 to 1981. In 1982 a fixed exchange rate policy (*vis-à-vis* the EMS-basket) was announced and it has been followed since then. The dismantling of exchange controls which came about gradually, but accelerated after 1982, may have reinforced the credibility of the switch of exchange rate policy. At least partly due to this new monetary regime, interest rates decreased rather sharply, and since 1983 Danish interest rates have been in the range of approximately 3%–4% above the German level, as shown in Figure 11.6.

Fiscal policy

Evidence on the fiscal policy stance in the past is mixed. During the 1960s and early 1970s the public sector accumulated a modest net wealth. Yet, it is generally claimed that the rapid expansion of public expenditures in this

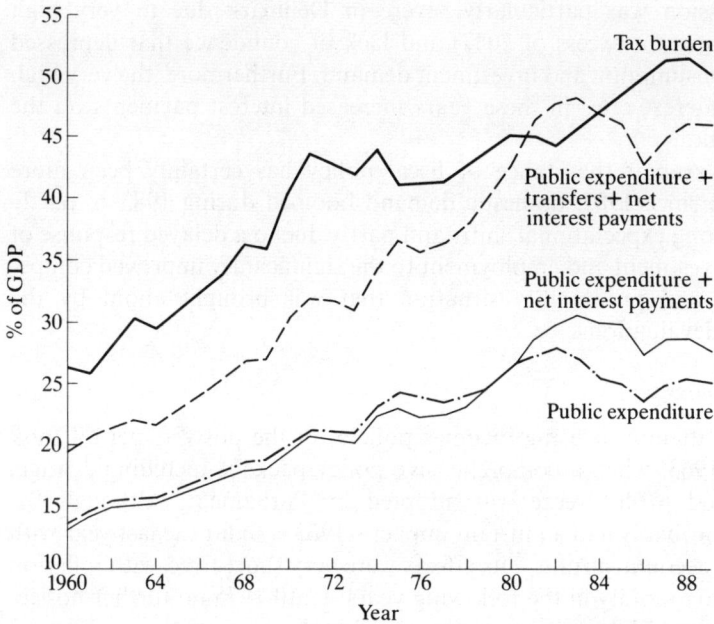

Figure 11.7 **Tax burden and public expenditure in Denmark as % of GDP, 1960–89.** *Source:*
Economic Council.
Note: **Public expenditure does not include investment.**

period, see Figure 11.7, gave a stimulus to domestic demand even if taxes
were increased simultaneously. At times fiscal policy was also quite
accommodating, something that was even more pronounced after 1973.
After the oil price shock fiscal policy was greatly expansionary until 1976,
the budget turning into a deficit of 1.5% of GDP in 1975. As it became
evident that the recovery would be weaker than expected and the current
account deteriorated rather dramatically, fiscal policy became less expansionary in terms of its effects on aggregate demand. However, as part of
this policy change an attempt was made to shift domestic demand in the
direction of public services which are on average more labour-intensive
and less import-intensive than private consumption.

From 1979 fiscal policy became restrictive while expenditure shifting
continued. Nevertheless, fiscal deficits increased dramatically from less
than 2% of GDP in 1979 to more than 9% in 1982. How can this be
explained? First of all the large public sector is tantamount to very
effective automatic stabilizers that give a strong cyclical element in the
budget. The marginal improvement of public sector finances following an
exogenous GDP rise is of the magnitude of 2/3 of the increase in GDP.

The recession was particularly severe in Denmark due to very high interest rates (in excess of 20%) and lack of confidence that depressed private consumption and investment demand. Furthermore, the very high level of interest rates in these years increased interest payments on the public debt.

Finally, even if the stance of fiscal policy has certainly been more restrictive since 1982, domestic demand boomed during 1983–6, partly due to strong expectational shifts and partly due to a delayed response of private investment and employment to the significantly improved competitiveness and profitability situation that was brought about by the effective devaluations.

Incomes policy

The first attempt at using incomes policies in the postwar period took place in 1963, when a comprehensive policy package including a wage, salary, and profit freeze was adopted by Parliament. Although the package probably had an instant impact – 1963 is so far the last year with a current account surplus – its effects were very short-lived with inflation accelerating rapidly in the following years. Until 1975 no further noticeable incomes policy measures were introduced.

In the ten-year period from 1975 to 1985, however, incomes policies played a major role in Danish macroeconomic policy, most notably by gradually reducing the importance of wage indexation which was finally completely abolished by 1983, and by having most of the wage rounds settled by Parliamentary intervention. It may be argued, though, that even in this rather strict form such measures are not very successful and that wage inflation against the background of high and increasing unemployment would have been moderated in any case. Danish aggregate wage equations (see, for instance, Economic Council, 1990 and OECD, 1990) as well as the fact that wage 'drift' – the decentralized component of the rise in wages – accounts for a significant part of total wage increases are often seen as supportive to this view. Recently, the perception of incomes policy seems to have changed in the sense that general labour market conditions and the wage incentives from labour market institutions have attracted more attention at the expense of direct intervention in the wage setting (Pedersen and Søndergaard, 1989).

3   Foreign debt: how did we get there?

It is very important to attempt to provide an explanation for the rise in external debt, since the balance of payments has for such a long period stood out as a key factor in Danish economic policy formation. And never has this central position been well argued for. If foreign debt is a 'natural' consequence of non-distorted savings and investment decisions of domestic citizens, forward-looking and well-endowed with information, the current account position becomes less interesting for policy-making than if it results from myopic, erratic or distorted behaviour on the part of Danish citizens or from mismanagement in economic policy.

In the light of this, we shall dwell on equilibrium aspects as opposed to disequilibrium aspects of foreign debt, and a rough classification of factors which may account for debt accumulation will be presented. A general observation at the beginning must be that the literature has been surprisingly unconcerned with these issues, hence the somewhat speculative character of the remarks to follow.

3.1   Equilibrium explanations

At face value, current account positions different from zero could be taken to be a reflection of a country's making use of the options of intertemporal trade. Just as the international trading system allows the exchange of goods and services at a given point in time or within a period (*intra*-temporal trade), it also allows some trade across points in time, *inter*temporal trade. With reference to standard trade theory, a balance-of-payments surplus would then be taken to mean net exports of present goods and services – in exchange for future net imports of goods and services. A country running a surplus on its trade balance would hence be interpreted as having a comparative advantage in present (as opposed to future) production of goods – or as being populated with especially patient citizens with a comparative preference for consumption of goods in the future as opposed to the present. Buiter (1981) shows how a low rate of time preference will lead to a balance-of-payments surplus in a two-country, free trade and (financial) capital mobility context.

These first remarks indicate an obvious, though nevertheless crucial point: current account deficits (surpluses) and foreign debt (net foreign assets) represent and derive from *asymmetries* between the economy under consideration and its environment. The economy could differ with respect to production possibilities or with respect to time preferences, or it could differ in a number of other ways of relevance for its foreign asset position. Some of these will be mentioned briefly in the following.

Since foreign assets by definition represent the excess of cumulated savings over cumulated investment (as long as revaluation of assets is duly taken into account), the factors affecting a nation's savings and investments in long-run equilibrium come to the forefront.

An issue of prime importance for savings decisions in developed economies is the social security system, broadly defined. A major line is drawn between 'funded' and 'pay as you go' versions of social security systems (especially concerning pensions). It has been demonstrated within theoretical life-cycle models of overlapping generations that a pay as you go system depresses saving (Kotlikoff, 1989), although effects working to the contrary have also been identified (Feldstein's 'induced retirement effect' for pensions, see Feldstein, 1974). The empirical evidence, however, does not lend unambiguous support to the hypothesis, see, e.g., the survey by Atkinson (1987).

The 'precautionary' motives for saving should also be closely related to the social security system, broadly defined. An economy in which people rely heavily on the ability of the welfare system to assist in case of unemployment, loss of ability to work, death of family head, serious illness, need for further education, etc. should display a low savings propensity, *ceteris paribus*.

The Danish public pension scheme is tax-financed and thus may be taken to be a 'pay as you go' system in the sense that no funding rules exist at all. By providing also extensive services to the elderly largely free of charge the public sector greatly reduces the individual life-cycle motive to save for retirement. Sickness pay, disability pensions, and health services free of charge are elements in a comparatively generous, largely tax-financed social security system which modifies precautionary motives for individuals to save. It is important to emphasize the comprehensive access to pensions, services, and social security. Dependence on family income is generally weak and often absent and all social groups are covered by the public schemes.

While it is beyond question that the social security system provides stronger disincentives to private saving in Denmark relative to her average trading partner, these disincentives are not unambiguously stronger than in other Scandinavian countries. It may be the case, though, that the impact on foreign borrowing has been stronger in Denmark, since the private sector has had earlier and more extensive access to international financial markets.

The life-cycle hypothesis of consumption has led us to presume that individuals offset the effects of a hump-shaped income profile by saving primarily mid-way through the life cycle. In international comparisons of savings rates of the private sector such as Horioka (1987) and Koskela and Viren (1989), it is argued that the demographic composition of the population should be important for the aggregate savings rate of the economy. It is frequently found that countries which have a high share of elderly people (say with ages sixty-five and over) feature a low savings propensity. Similarly, the savings ratio can be related to labour force participation of aged people. Balance-of-payments deficits can in this way result as a simple consequence of a country's demography differing from that of the rest of the world. In empirical analyses of cross-country savings patterns like the ones just mentioned, saving is also often found to be positively related to the country's growth rate. This effect which relies on a particular life-cycle pattern of savings, has however been questioned (see Koskela and Viren, 1989).

It may be the case that a fraction of the Danish foreign debt should be seen as a consequence of its divergent demography, the share of elderly being somewhat higher than the OECD average. Yet, a very low level of household savings is found among all age groups, implying a rather weak life-cycle effect in aggregate savings. This of course is consistent with the savings disincentives from the social security system just mentioned.

A low rate of return to savings could be another reason for low savings. Thus, the system of capital income taxation could potentially be important. It is well known, though, that there have been great problems in determining empirically the reaction of savings to changes in real (after-tax) interest rates.

In a theoretical model Nielsen and Sørensen (1990) demonstrate how various instruments for taxing elements of capital income affect a small, open economy's net foreign asset position. While a uniform capital income tax in that model induces the accumulation of foreign debt, some isolated tax instruments like the corporate income tax will work in the opposite direction.

On the investment side, subsidies of various types obviously affect investment activity and thereby the balance of payments and foreign indebtedness. Investment tax credits and generous depreciation allowances for business investment as well as the implicit subsidies in the housing sector can be mentioned in this regard. A country which offers especially high subsidization of investment should count on incurring foreign debt, at least in the short to medium run. The long-term effect on a country's net foreign asset position of investment tax credits is not unambiguous, however, and will hinge on the specific financing of the investment subsidy (see Nielsen and Sørensen, 1990).

The Danish tax system relies heavily on the personal income tax which includes nominal interest income in its base. As is well known from the tax literature, taxing nominal interest income implies an increasing tax burden on real interest income (an increasing subsidy on real interest expenditures), the higher the rate of inflation in the economy.

In the Danish case with high average marginal nominal tax rates this has led to negative after-tax real interest rates throughout the 1970s and well into the 1980s. As shown in Figure 11.8, this margin between the

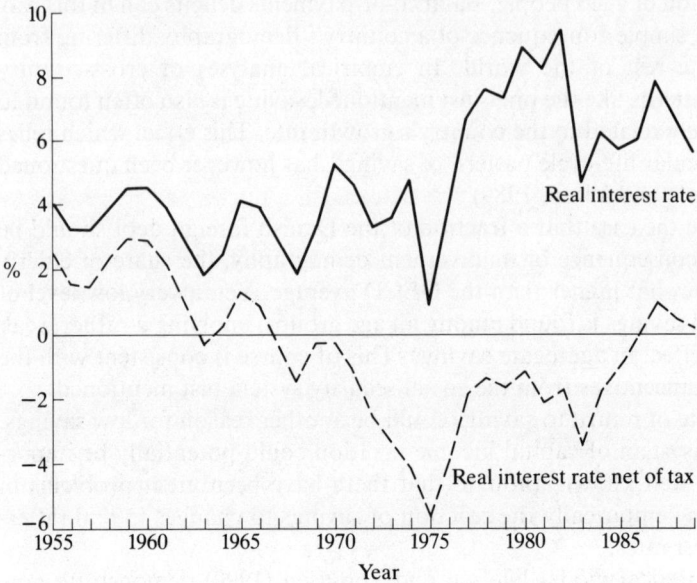

Figure 11.8   Real interest rates on Danish long-term bonds, 1955–89. *Source:* Economic Council.
Note: Real interest rates were calculated using a three-year moving average of consumer price changes. The net of tax rates were calculated using a weighted average of marginal income tax rates.

consumers' marginal rate of intertemporal substitution and (one plus) the real interest rate was steadily increasing during the 1960s and early 1970s. The very significant margin reached in the mid 1970s was maintained for some ten years while there has been a slight narrowing in recent years due to lower inflation as well as a tax reform, which has reduced the average marginal tax rate on capital income from around 0.57 in 1987 to around 0.53 in 1989.

For owner-occupied housing the tax system has, despite the inclusion in the tax base of imputed rents, produced significant indirect subsidization, because the imputed rent since the early 1960s has been much lower than real interest rates, while nominal interest payments on mortgages have been fully deductible. Hence the real return that a house owner would need in order to make his house investment profitable has been well below the real interest rate. Through capitalization of the expected future stream of subsidies house prices tend to overstate the real estate component of national wealth; subsidizing owner-occupied housing may therefore also tend to encourage private consumption.

The high marginal tax rate on a nominal tax base applies not only to households but also to firms, although the corporate tax rate for most of the period under consideration has been slightly below personal tax rates. The counterpart of the high marginal tax rates, however, has been rather generous depreciation allowances introduced back in the late 1950s. These investment incentives may have been supportive of the rapid transformation from agriculture to manufacture during the 1960s, but in particular after the mid 1970s a wide margin has existed between the user cost of capital and interest rates on foreign debt. It seems that there have therefore been incentives at the margin to undertake private investments that would reduce national wealth.

The relation between the general level of public sector activity and foreign indebtedness is often brought forward – and too often overly simplified views can be heard which stress a direct casual connection between budget and current account deficits. Matters are, however, a bit more complicated than this. What it is safe to say is that bringing forward public expenditure or postponing taxation should lead to the accumulation of foreign debt – the latter at least in an overlapping generations context in which individuals are effectively 'disconnected' (to use Weil's, 1987, term). For the proof that the lowering of taxes for a single generation will lead to current account deficits and foreign indebtedness see Persson (1985).

Perhaps even more interesting in this context is the observation that a balanced-budget expansion of public sector activity in a small, open, and growing economy with generational overlap will (under reasonable assumptions) lead to balance-of-payments deficits and foreign indebtedness. From this we infer that economies with a relatively large public sector should tend to have foreign debt and deficits on the current account, *ceteris paribus*. Recalling the very rapid expansion of the public sector during the 1960s and 1970s, Denmark should be expected to be a debtor country on this account. In fact, among OECD countries at present only Sweden has (slightly) higher public expenditures relative to GDP.

3.2 Disequilibrium explanations

Contrary to the above, a series of 'disequilibrium' aspects of foreign debt might be suggested. External shocks, rigidity in wage formation, unwarranted extravagance of fiscal policy, imperfections in credit markets due to, say, asymmetric information and limited liability, short-sightedness of economic agents or policy-makers, heavy uncertainty, etc. could potentially be responsible for a nation's incurring debt. But again, only to the extent that the economy differs from the rest of the world in these respects.

The very notion of a country experiencing foreign shocks points to an asymmetry between that country and the rest of the world. One would of course expect that a country's balance of payments and net foreign asset position would be affected by such external shocks. Yet, as the literature on the Harberger–Laursen–Metzler effect (see, e.g., Sen and Turnovsky, 1989) has shown, it is not always obvious how the economy's external balance will react to a negative foreign shock.

Having said this, it seems quite clear that in the short run the two oil shocks deteriorated the current account of those countries like Denmark that relied completely on imported energy. However, if policy had not been changed both abroad and in Denmark, these immediate effects on the current account of the supply shocks might have been fairly modest. But the way Denmark attempted to accommodate the first oil price shock turned out very expensive in terms of foreign debt. By having traditional Keynesian fiscal stimuli in significant doses accompany an appreciation of the currency while most trading partners followed a more restrictive course, a dramatic deterioration of the current account as well as of competitiveness occurred from 1973 to 1976. In the following years interest payments on the foreign debt became increasingly important and in fact account for a very large share of the rise in foreign debt after 1976 (see Figure 11.1).

During the 1960s Danish fiscal policy was also quite lax and accommodating, but due to, e.g., low interest rates and favourable supply conditions its costs in terms of foreign debt were fairly moderate. Simulations with a macroeconometric model indicate, however, that accommodative fiscal policy in order to stabilize employment in case of negative supply shocks can be extremely costly in terms of foreign debt, in particular if real interest rates are high (Economic Council, 1990).

Inflexibility in the labour market may be another source of foreign debt, yet, it is worth noticing that the relation between, e.g., high and rigid wages and the current account is by no means unequivocal. As shown in Nielsen (1990) wages that become stuck during a certain period at too high a level to secure full employment may be associated with either a current account deficit or a surplus, depending on the length of the 'contract period' and the sensitivity of investment to variations in profitability. If wages stay too high for an extended period and investment reacts strongly to reductions in profitability, the current account could well go into surplus in the short run. But of course, if such an internal negative supply shock is accommodated by fiscal measures the effects on the current account could indeed be detrimental.

Looking at the inflation–unemployment trade-off in Figure 11.4 one might get the impression that the labour market in Denmark is suffering from serious rigidities. Upon closer examination this becomes less clear, however, because the north-east move from the early 1970s to the early 1980s was heavily affected by the large net inflow into the labour force. In fact, when evaluated on the basis of estimated wage equations, the Danish labour market comes close to the European average in terms of the elasticity of wages with respect to unemployment (see, e.g., Andersen, 1989 and OECD, 1990). It was probably the case, however, that the accelerating growth of the labour force during the 1970s and the associated very rapid increase in unemployment drew fiscal policies towards a more expansionary stance.

As to possible imperfections in credit and capital markets, it is well documented that economic agents encounter vast difficulties in borrowing against future income. To the extent that such borrowing constraints are effective, saving of young generations is higher than warranted, and national wealth similarly higher than desired (see Hubbard and Judd, 1986). From this one is led to conclude that economies characterized by relatively insignificant credit constraints may incur foreign debt and – in a growth context – balance-of-payments deficits. Such an effect is revealed in the empirical analysis in Koskela and Viren (1989); see also the interesting analyses of the effects of liberalizing credit markets on consumption by Bayoumi and Koujianou (1989) and Lehmussaari (1990).

As mentioned above, the timing of liberalization of credit markets and the removal of exchange controls constitutes one of the few differences between Denmark and the two other Scandinavian countries that may help explain the particular Danish foreign debt position.

3.3   Evaluation

Drawing on the above, how does one explain the present Danish foreign debt position of about 40% of GDP? Equilibrium explanations probably account for a significant part of the debt. The general notion is that the welfare and social security system is relatively well-developed in Denmark (for comparisons with other European countries see Economic Council, 1989). Precautionary motives for saving could accordingly be quite weak. Saving for the old age is probably also small, although the degree of pay as you go financing of pensions is perhaps not significantly larger than in neighbouring countries.

Moreover, there is a relatively high proportion of elderly people in Denmark as compared to the OECD average, and the growth rate of per capita real income net of tax has been below the average of the OECD area during the last three decades. Both facts point to balance-of-payments deficits in Denmark. As to the reward on saving it is well-established that marginal tax rates on most parts of capital income have been very high in an international context in Denmark and the opportunities for deducting interest payments similarly pronounced. While the consequences hereof for aggregate savings are disputed, it is less unclear that the comparatively favourable tax treatment of business investment in Denmark and high implicit subsidies in the housing sector work in the direction of high investment and thus balance-of-payments deficits.

The size of the public sector in Denmark is now very large in an international context, although the relative magnitude of public debt is not as overwhelming, see Figure 11.1. Hence the rapid expansion of the public sector during the 1960s and 1970s may also be part of the reason for foreign debt and current account deficits. And comparatively well-functioning financial markets, not the least in respect of the financing of housing (where people apparently do not have to provide as much money 'up front' as in many other countries) may be further reasons for low saving, balance-of-payments deficits and foreign debt.

On the more speculative side one may wonder whether the bequest motive for saving which seems to be surprisingly important for wealth formation (see Kotlikoff, 1989) perhaps could be relatively weak in Denmark. In an economy with effective mechanisms for equalizing income and living conditions, the incentives to leave bequests could be less strong, in part because it would be more difficult to 'target' these bequests (bequests could be partly taxed away or could give rise to smaller transfers and services from the public sector, etc.). Moreover, the distribution of wealth is less unequal than in most other countries. This may further reduce the importance of bequests, which are normally found to be particularly important among the very rich.

One might also speculate about the importance of corporate savings as a determinant of national wealth. It is generally assumed that corporate saving is only partly counterbalanced by the saving behaviour of households (see, e.g., Smith, 1990), at least in the short run. Corporate saving in Denmark was possibly quite low during the 1960s and 1970s. The non-availability of corporate savings statistics prior to 1981 makes it impossible, however, to substantiate this conjecture. The argument would be that the structural change from agriculture and small trade and industry to manufacturing and services occurred during this period. Small and immature firms with high investment and possibly low saving therefore dominated the corporate sector.

During the 1980s corporate saving has been increasing and the present level seems close to that of trading partners.

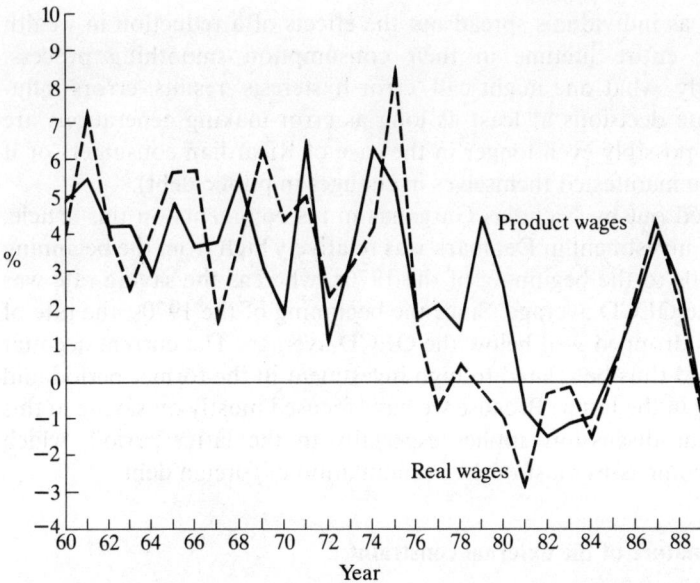

Figure 11.9   Annual changes in real wages and product wages in Denmark, 1960–89. *Source:* Economic Council.

All this said it must be added that another part of the present foreign debt probably *is* the result of mistaken consumption-saving and investment decisions on the part of individuals and firms and mistaken policies. These errors have resulted from errors in expectations as to future income and price trends or lack of understanding of the contemporaneous cyclical position of the economy. A good example is the adjustment (the word is almost being misused in this connection) of the Danish economy to the first oil price shock. In the labour market, real and product wages rose by about 12% over the two years 1973–5, clearly at odds with future employment opportunities (see Figure 11.9). On the policy side, experiments like the temporary lowering of VAT rates in 1975–6, the real appreciation of the Danish Krone in the mid 1970s, and the general fiscal policy accommodation of supply shocks (including growth of the labour force) all proved expensive with regard to foreign indebtedness. The same can be said about the underestimation of the expectational effects associated with movements in employment and the public budget after the adoption of the medium-term strategy in late 1982.

Such errors on the part of private agents and policy-makers have resulted in semi-permanent increases in foreign debt. When consumption and/or investment have been 'too high' (when judged with hindsight) for a certain period, the consequences of this may remain in the system for a long time, as individuals spread out the effects of a reduction in wealth over their entire lifetime in their consumption smoothing process. Accordingly, what one might call 'error hysteresis' results: errors influence private decisions at least as long as error-making generations are alive (and possibly even longer in the case of Ricardian consumers or if errors have manifested themselves in changes in public debt).

As pointed out by Nicholas Garganas in his comments on this article, the rate of investment in Denmark was relatively high from the beginning of the 1960s to the beginning of the 1970s, whereas the saving rate was close to the OECD average. Since the beginning of the 1970s, the rate of saving has dropped well below the OECD average. The current account deficit could thus be related to high investment in the former period and low saving in the latter. Because we have focused mostly on saving in this section, our discussion applies especially to the latter period, which indeed encompasses most of the accumulation of foreign debt.

4   The nature of the external constraint

In this section we attempt to address the nature of the external constraint in the case of the Danish economy. The discussion here will in part continue along the lines of the previous section, stressing the relation between foreign debt and the characteristics of the economy.

In the inconvertible currency period under the European Payments Union in the 1950s, the external constraint was easy to identify. Also later in the Bretton Woods period with limited exchange reserves, economic policy was not supposed to act in a way which threatened these reserves. As touched upon in Section 2, there have been regular stints of massive capital outflows from Denmark, the most remarkable ones being in 1969, 1972 (in connection with the Norwegian and Danish referenda on EEC membership), 1976, 1982 (associated with the change of government), and in 1986. Only the first of these events came close to an exchange crisis, though. At present when Denmark in principle has access to vast short-term financing in the EMS system in case of private capital outflows, reserve considerations act as a much softer constraint on economic policy. At the same time it must be added that international capital mobility has increased substantially during the last three decades.

It is fairly obvious then that the external constraint no longer assumes the form of a borrowing constraint. It rather looks more like an ordinary intertemporal budget constraint. This, of course, raises the question whether the economy is following a path consistent with its solvency constraint.

In line with the contribution by Dolado and Viñals in this volume, we have investigated the sustainability of current account and budget deficits in the Danish economy, using the approach by Wilcox (1989). (The reader is referred to Nielsen *et al.*, 1990, available upon request from the Economic Council.) We found, using data for the period 1963 to 1989 that neither discounted foreign debt nor discounted public debt seem to be stationary. Instead, both series are integrated of at least order 1. This evidence could be interpreted as implying problems with the solvency of the public sector and the economy as a whole in the long run.

Such a conclusion we would, however, consider premature on at least three grounds. First, it ignores the rather drastic changes in the economic policy regime that have taken place several times in the last three decades, especially in 1982 with the launching of the conservative government's medium-term strategy. Second, a more satisfactory statistical analysis would allow for possible cointegration between, e.g., foreign debt relative to GDP and other non-stationary stochastic processes (which might be subject to control by policy-makers or could turn stationary later on). Third, a foreign debt which rises over time may reflect adjustment to increasing opportunities to finance a (warranted) savings deficit externally.

In addition, foreign debt relative to GDP has levelled off during the last four years, while public debt relative to GDP has fallen significantly since 1985, as we saw in Figures 11.1 and 11.2.

Under the circumstances of stabilized foreign indebtedness and no borrowing constraints, should foreign debt be of any concern to policy-making? A number of arguments may be put forward that would suggest an answer in the affirmative.

The interest rates which Danish firms or the Danish government have to pay on foreign loans may vary with the size of total foreign debt – or the current account position – of the Danish economy. Yet, the rise in foreign debt in the past seemingly did not much affect the conditions for financing current account deficits. Neither domestic private firms nor the public sector have encountered appreciable interest rate premia in foreign financial markets. Admittedly, the Kingdom of Denmark has experienced occasional down-grading of its creditworthiness, but the consequences in the form of interest rate premia on loans denominated in foreign currencies have been close to negligible.

A more awkward way in which the foreign debt/current account position manifests itself has to do with domestic interest rate formation. Domestic interest rates are somewhat geared to news about the trade and current accounts and bounce about following good or bad news about the balance of payments. Moreover, short and long rates still seem to include some kind of exchange rate adjustment premium. Agents in domestic financial markets (as well as foreign buyers of Danish government bonds) apparently do not exclude the possibility of a future adjustment in the value of the Danish Krone, even though the government has kept close to its explicitly announced fixed exchange rate policy throughout the last eight years. In the beginning of this period there was some uncertainty about what a fixed exchange rate would imply but time sorted this out: the Krone is meant to be tied to the 'middle' of the EMS rather than the Deutschmark alone. Accordingly, the interest rate differential *vis-à-vis* Germany (see Figure 11.6) might reflect some expectations of a revaluation of the Mark although this does not seem sufficient to explain a differential of 3%–4% per annum.

There are other more subtle ways in which the balance of payments and foreign debt may act as a concern for policy. Variations in the international real rate of interest will markedly affect national income in a high-debt economy. The economy thus makes itself vulnerable to an additional category of external shocks. This could be welfare-reducing to the extent that the induced swings in income cannot be offset by changes in the economy's international borrowing. Especially in long periods of unexpectedly high real interest rates abroad, such problems may be encountered. An asymmetry may furthermore aggravate the effects of varying international real interest rates. Domestic firms that have borrowed extensively abroad may be forced to lay off workers (or close down) in periods of high real interest rates, whereas periods of low interest rates may entail smaller employment effects and perhaps add to inflation instead.

Looking at the history of international financial markets and exchange rate regimes suggests that their stability cannot be taken for granted. We would not argue that the present system must prove unstable, but governments may rightly take into account even very small probabilities of financial instability. Since there is no international legal system comparable to national laws regulating the relation between creditor and debtor, the foreign asset position will be important to the effects of financial instability for a particular country.

In Section 3 we argued that a significant part of foreign debt may be the result of identified structural asymmetries between the Danish economy and its environment. To the extent that foreign indebtedness is caused by a different age structure of the population, by a well-functioning welfare state or by well-functioning credit markets, this should in itself be a cause of concern only in as far as the intergenerational distribution is considered. However, to the extent that indebtedness is due to, e.g., tax and subsidy distortions affecting national saving and investment it should be a matter of concern also from an efficiency point of view. The first-best policy would be to remove such distortions, but if this is not possible (for, e.g., distributional reasons) curtailing the current account by way of fiscal policy may be a second-best policy.

As also argued above, part of foreign debt might be related to expectational errors on the part of private agents or policy-makers. Such errors may end up affecting future generations in the economy, either because domestic citizens end up leaving smaller bequests to their heirs, or because a higher amount of public debt is carried on in the system. Intergenerational concerns may thus also motivate that the consequences of such errors be redressed by, e.g., contractionary fiscal policy 'before error-making generations leave the system'.

5   Conclusions

In this chapter we have reviewed economic development, shocks, and policy in the Danish economy throughout the last three decades in order, among other things, to address the question of the nature of the external constraint which has operated on macroeconomic policy formation. We furthermore enquired about the reasons why Denmark has attained a level of foreign debt of about 40% of GDP.

While the 1960s contained a period of quite successful economic development, the economy from 1973 and on encountered severe difficulties with respect to unemployment and inflation, for which neither the private sector nor policy-makers were well prepared. Unemployment quickly rose and has remained high ever since, even though fiscal policy was in periods quite accommodative. All along, foreign debt continued to rise. While it seems possible to relate part of indebtedness to various characteristics of the economy and to policy with respect to the size of the public sector, the tax system and the social security system in a broad sense, another part is related to private and public sector errors and a generally accommodative fiscal policy.

We identified four reasons why the external position should be of concern to policy-making even though no borrowing constraint occurs and the development of the economy satisfies the solvency constraint:

Interest rates seem to depend to some extent on the external position and furthermore foreign debt makes the economy vulnerable to international interest rate 'shocks'.

National governments may attach non-zero probabilities to future instability of international financial markets.

Foreign debt may mirror internal distortions of private saving and investment.

Indirectly, foreign debt may be associated with redistribution between generations.

Looking ahead, it appears as if a new dimension may be added to the external constraint. An economic and monetary union would tie down national monetary policy even further due to the completely fixed parities while fiscal policy could be further conditioned by central guidelines as to, e.g., public sector budget deficits. Moreover, voluntary as well as forced harmonization of tax rates will likewise condition fiscal policy.

In fact, one can argue that we shall in short have gone through a full cycle here. The Danish economy started out in the 1950s with an easily identifiable external constraint related to the scarcity of foreign exchange, then went into an intermediate period in the 1960s to 1980s with an altogether softer and less identifiable external constraint which manifested itself in several different ways, and is now about to enter a phase with again more easily identifiable and simple external constraints associated with a monetary union. However, for the reasons just mentioned foreign debt will remain a matter of concern for national economic policy.

NOTE

We are grateful to Nicholas Garganas and Peder J. Pedersen for comments on a previous draft. The usual disclaimer applies. Any views expressed are those of the authors and in no way should be construed as representing the views of the Danish Economic Council.

REFERENCES

Andersen, P.S. (1989), 'Inflation and Output: A Review of the Wage-Price Mechanism', BIS Economic Papers, No. 24.
Atkinson, A.B. (1987), 'Income Maintenance and Social Insurance', in A. Auerbach and M. Feldstein (eds.), *Handbook of Public Economics*, vol. 2, Amsterdam: North Holland.
Bayoumi, T. and P. Koujianou (1989), 'The Effects of Financial Deregulation on Consumption', unpublished manuscript, IMF.
Buiter, W.H. (1981), 'Time Preference and International Lending and Borrowing in an Overlapping Generations Model', *Journal of Political Economy* 89, 769–97.
Economic Council (1988), *Danish Economy*, December.
   (1989), 'Tax Burden and Public Expenditure in Denmark, Germany and the Netherlands', Working Paper.
   (1990), 'SMEC: Modeldokumentation og beregnede virkninger af økonomisk politik (Documentation of the macroeconometric model SMEC and simulated effects of economic policy)'.
Feldstein, M. (1974), 'Social Security, Induced Retirement and Aggregate Capital Accumulation, *Journal of Political Economy* 82, 905–26.
Horioka, C.Y. (1987), 'Why is Japan's Private Saving Rate So High?', in R. Sato

and T. Negishi (eds.), *Japanese Economic Research*, Tokyo: Academic Press/Harcourt, Brace Jovanovich Inc.

Hubbard, R.G. and K.L. Judd (1986), 'Liquidity Constraints, Fiscal Policy, and Consumption', *Brookings Papers on Economic Activity* 1, 1–50.

Koskela, E. and M. Viren (1989), 'Taxes, Credit Market "Imperfections" and Inter-Country Differences in the Household Saving Ratio', Bank of Finland Discussion Paper No. 21/89.

Kotlikoff, L. (1989), *What Determines Savings?*, Cambridge, MA: The MIT Press.

Lehmussaari, O.P. (1990), 'Deregulation and Consumption: Saving Dynamics in the Nordic Countries', *IMF Staff Papers* 37, 71–93.

Nielsen, S.B. (1990), 'Current Account Effects of a Devaluation in an Optimizing Model with Capital Accumulation', *Journal of Economic Dynamics and Control* (forthcoming).

Nielsen, S.B. and P.B. Sørensen (1990), 'Capital Income Taxation in a Growing Open Economy', *European Economic Review* (forthcoming).

Nielsen, S.B. *et al.* (1990), 'On the Sustainability of Foreign and Public Debt in Denmark', mimeo, Economic Council.

OECD (1990), *Economic Survey of Denmark*.

Pedersen, P.J. and J. Søndergaard (1989), 'Det inflationaere danske arbejdsmarked (The inflationary Danish labour market)', *Nationaløkonomisk Tidsskrift* 127, 1–20.

Persson, T. (1985), 'Deficits and Intergenerational Welfare in Open Economies', *Journal of International Economics* 19, 67–84.

Sen, P. and S.J. Turnovsky (1989), 'Deterioration of the Terms of Trade: A Reexamination of the Laursen-Metzler Effect', *Journal of International Economics* 26, 227–50.

Smith, R.S. (1990), 'Factors Affecting Saving, Policy Tools and Tax Reform: A Review', *IMF Staff Papers* 37, 1–70.

Weil, P. (1987), 'Permanent Budget Deficits and Inflation', *Journal of Monetary Economics* 20, 393–410.

Wilcox, D.W. (1989), 'The Sustainability of Government Deficits: Implications of the Present-Value Borrowing Constraint', *Journal of Money, Credit and Banking* 21, 291–306.

Discussion

NICHOLAS C. GARGANAS

I first have to say that I found this chapter analytically very interesting and highly relevant to policy issues currently facing some other indebted small open economies, although Denmark's experience in the 1980s was in some respects rather peculiar, particularly since fiscal retrenchment was associated with an expansion of domestic demand and activity and (until 1986) a worsening rather than an improvement of the current external balance.

The chapter by Nielsen and Søndergaard addresses the question of the persistent current account deficit and the accumulation of foreign debt in Denmark taking a thirty-year perspective, going back to the beginning of the 1960s.

In Section 2 the authors present a brief account of economic developments and performance over these past thirty years. They also give a description of major shocks and structural changes that have affected the Danish economy and examine the orientation of economic policies during this thirty-year period.

One can broadly accept their account of the Danish experience since the beginning of the 1960s. However, I would have liked to see a more precise analysis and documentation of the Danish policy approach in terms of specific objectives, the analytical foundations of policies and results for the various sub-periods, since the role of policy seems very relevant for explaining the current external imbalances which have built up during these three decades.

Though their precise impact is difficult to gauge, the historical record suggests that macroeconomic policies were, on the whole, too expansionary for most of the last three decades. So it would seem that, basically, the persistent current account deficit reflected stronger growth of Danish domestic demand compared to that in partner countries, and – perhaps related to that – an inadequate level of international competitiveness (see Figure 11.5). However, it may well be argued that the fact that the current account has been deteriorating for so many years would suggest that the underlying forces perhaps are of a more structural nature.

The authors argue that ever since the early 1960s the main emphasis of policy has been placed on efforts to deal with the external imbalance. I would not agree with this view. My reading of the historical evidence is that during the 1960s the fundamental aim of policy was to maintain high rates of economic growth and sustain full employment. The pursuit of strongly expansionary fiscal policies gave stimulus to domestic demand, whilst a monetary policy aiming at maintaining low nominal interest rates also contributed to an expansion of investment.

Expansionary demand management policies continued into the 1970s. In particular, the so-called 'expenditure-twist' policy (the rationale of which was to improve imbalances by exploiting the different import and employment propensities in private and public sector demand), which also aimed at cushioning the adverse demand effects of the first oil price shock, led to rising public-sector deficits, whilst after-tax real interest rates continued to be negative.

Only when two decades of almost uninterrupted expansion led to an unsustainable balance-of-payments position in the late 1970s was policy finally reorientated towards restriction, aiming at reducing the current external deficit. Between 1979 and 1982 the krone was devalued on several occasions in the context of EMS realignments, in order to establish a strong competitive position. However, the external balance deteriorated as a result of the second oil price shock and the associated international recession.

In late 1982 the authorities adopted a strategy of fiscal retrenchment and a firm incomes policy combined with an exchange rate strictly fixed within the EMS. But conditions on Danish financial markets (where the adoption of a firm exchange rate policy and a scrapping of most currency regulations led to a sharp fall in interest rates), in combination with weaknesses in the tax system, particularly the full tax deductibility of interest payments, generated a strong expansion of domestic demand. Thus, following an initial improvement in 1983, helped by a strengthened competitive position and falling world interest rates, the current account deficit worsened again for three consecutive years, reaching $5\frac{1}{2}$% of GDP in 1986.

The tight fiscal policy orientation was maintained and strengthened until 1986, but the main impact of deflationary policy was felt only after the introduction of a policy package aimed at damping credit-financed consumption in October 1986. As a result, domestic demand declined and the current account deficit gradually shrank (partly helped by international recovery), falling to only about $1\frac{1}{2}$% of GDP in 1989.

In the remainder of the chapter the persistent current account deficit is looked at from the savings-investment side, and the nature of the problem is discussed in terms of the factors that affect the domestic pattern of saving and investment, concentrating in particular on the behaviour of saving. The authors adopt a taxonomic approach, listing all the factors that could possibly explain the low rate of national saving. There is, probably, an element of truth in every explanation suggested in this rather general catalogue of related factors, but one would have liked to see a more rigorous and consistent analysis within a more explicit structural model. One would have liked to see also some empirical evidence that would substantiate the role of these factors.

While the chapter looks at the disparity between national saving and investment rates, which has been reflected in persisting current account deficits and the accumulation of Denmark's foreign debt, it focuses mainly on the causes that have been associated with the underlying behaviour of national saving. The authors note that Denmark's saving rate has generally been lower than that of other countries over the past three decades and then proceed to examine a number of factors that may explain this disparity in saving rates. The factors identified in the chapter as potential explanations of the lower rate of saving in Denmark include Denmark's well-developed welfare and social security system, the larger proportion of elderly people in Denmark as compared to the OECD average, higher taxation of capital income and more generous provisions for tax deductibility of interest payments, more developed financial markets, and greater access by households to credit, especially to loans for house purchase, and a relatively weaker motive to save for bequests because of the existence of mechanisms that lead to more equal distribution of incomes and standards of living. Other factors that are cited in the paper as possible reasons for the relatively low rate of national saving in Denmark are the lower rate of economic growth in Denmark as compared to the OECD average during the last two decades, the expansion of the public sector, and the lower rate of corporate saving, reflecting the small size of firms. The authors also argue that the low saving rate in Denmark may be in part a reflection of erroneous consumption-saving decisions on the part of individuals which may 'have resulted from errors in expectations as to future income and price trends . . .'

It would have been interesting and useful to be able to see if all these potential explanations of the deficiency of Denmark's national saving rate are supported by empirical evidence.

As noted earlier, in attempting to account for the imbalance between national saving and investment within Denmark, the authors have focused attention on the decline in the rate of saving since the early 1960s. Yet, data from the OECD (see, for example, the recent study by Dean *et al.* (1990), Chart A and Table 1) reveal that until the early 1970s the Danish current account deficits were largely a reflection of abnormally high rates of investment rather than low rates of saving. The tendency of the saving (and the investment) rate to decline emerged after the first oil price shock in 1973, the magnitude of decline generally being greater than that of other countries. Thus, if one compares Denmark's saving rate with that of the OECD area as a whole for the past three decades one will observe that the gross national saving rate was close to the OECD average until the early 1970s. In fact, the net saving rate was higher in Denmark, depreciation having been less important than in other OECD countries. But there has been a dramatic fall in the national saving rate in Denmark relative to the OECD average since then; for 1981–8 the Danish gross national saving rate was lower by about five percentage points than the OECD average. Hence, the search for empirical evidence on the role of the factors that are stressed in the paper as potential causes for the relatively low level of national saving in Denmark must focus mainly on the period after 1973.

Although one has to acknowledge that no single model can capture all the potential motivations for an individual's saving behaviour, let alone the saving behaviour of the household sector as a whole, one can nevertheless develop an acceptable model which takes into account some of the factors that seem most relevant for explaining household consumption and savings behaviour in the Danish case. One should then try to determine whether the decline in private saving in Denmark can be adequately explained through variations in the factors entering the consumption function, or whether the decline in the saving rate has been caused by some more fundamental structural changes in the economy, as the authors seem to suggest.

In a recent International Monetary Fund study Lehmussaari (1990), using a modified consumption function, similar in general specification to that developed originally for the United Kingdom by Hendry and von Ungern-Sternberg (1981), finds that household saving behaviour in Denmark can be adequately explained without having to resort to the effects of factors other than those included in this model. He argues that the deregulation of financial markets in Denmark and the wealth effect associated with higher prices of financial and real assets were perhaps the most important factors that have contributed to the decline in private saving in Denmark in the 1980s. There is thus some suggestion in these results that many of the factors that have been stressed in the paper by Nielsen and Søndergaard as possible reasons for the relatively low rate of household savings in Denmark may have played only a minor role, if any, in explaining the developments in household saving in the 1970s and the 1980s. One may argue, for example, that the system of social security was already more or less fully developed in the early 1970s, which would suggest that the social security system may not have been an important reason for the fall in the household saving ratio in the period in which we are interested.

One important issue that is overlooked by Nielsen and Søndergaard is the net effect of changes in public sector saving on overall national saving. Figure 11.3 in the paper shows the values since 1971 of the ratio of the net public sector saving (and investment) to GDP and the ratio of private saving (and investment) to GDP. A comparison of the two saving ratios reveals that changes in public saving were, to a large extent, offset by opposite changes in private saving. While the evidence of important offsets between variations in public and private saving rates may partly reflect common cyclical influences on both variables which make it difficult to sort out the causation in these variations, it would nevertheless be consistent with 'Ricardian equivalence' (Barro, 1989). Testing Ricardian equivalence in the Danish case would therefore seem an issue of substantial significance. I would not expect that the empirical results would support strict Ricardian equivalence in the sense of concluding that fiscal policy is unable to influence the current account of the balance of payments. But an expanded empirical model that would incorporate factors that may contribute to Ricardian equivalence would provide a useful framework for assessing the efficiency of fiscal policy in influencing the current account of the balance of payments.

With these remarks I do not mean to belittle the considerable effort of the authors, but merely to suggest that some of their propositions deserve further consideration and that for this reason it is perhaps worthwhile to make a further effort in this extremely interesting area of research.

REFERENCES

Barro, R.J. (1989), 'The Ricardian Approach to Budget Deficits', *The Journal of Economic Perspectives* **3**, 37–54.
Dean, A., M. Durand, J. Fallon, and P. Hoeller (1990), 'Saving Trends and Behaviour in OECD Countries', *OECD Economic Studies* **14**, 7–58.
Hendry, D.F. and T. von Ungern-Sternberg (1981), 'Liquidity and Inflation Effects on Consumers' Expenditure', in A. Deaton (ed.), *Essays in the Theory and Measurement of Consumer Behaviour*, Cambridge University Press.
Lehmussaari, Olli-Pekka (1990), 'Deregulation and Consumption: Saving Dynamics in the Nordic Countries', *IMF Staff Papers* **37**, 71–93.

Index